DISUNION

A Study of the Weatherhead East Asian Institute

DISUNION

Anticommunist Nationalism and the Making of the Republic of Vietnam

Nu-Anh Tran

University of Hawai'i Press
HONOLULU

© 2022 University of Hawai'i Press
All rights reserved
Paperback edition 2022

Printed in the United States of America

Library of Congress Cataloging-in-Publication Data

Names: Tran, Nu-Anh, author.
Title: Disunion : anticommunist nationalism and the making of the Republic
of Vietnam / Nu-Anh Tran.
Other titles: Studies of the Weatherhead East Asian Institute, Columbia
University.
Description: Honolulu : University of Hawai'i Press, [2022] | Series:
Studies of the Weatherhead East Asian Institute, Columbia University |
Includes bibliographical references and index.
Identifiers: LCCN 2021056676 | ISBN 9780824887865 (hardback) | ISBN
9780824891633 (pdf) | ISBN 9780824891640 (epub) | ISBN 9780824891657
(kindle edition)
Subjects: LCSH: Nationalists—Vietnam (Republic) | Vietnam
(Republic)—Politics and government.
Classification: LCC DS556.9 .T725 2022 | DDC 959.704—dc23/eng/20220107
LC record available at https://lccn.loc.gov/2021056676

ISBN 9780824891626 (paperback)

Studies of the Weatherhead East Asian Institute, Columbia University

The Studies of the Weatherhead East Asian Institute of Columbia University were
inaugurated in 1962 to bring to a wider public the results of significant new research
on modern and contemporary East Asia.

Cover art: Ngô Đình Diệm casting his ballot in the presidential elections of 1961
(Everett Collection) *Cover design:* Aaron Lee

University of Hawai'i Press books are printed on acid-free paper and meet the guidelines for
permanence and durability of the Council on Library Resources.

In memory of my mother

Contents

Acknowledgments   ix

Abbreviations   xiii

INTRODUCTION
Rethinking the Republic of Vietnam
1

CHAPTER ONE
Birth of Anticommunist Nationalism, 1920s–1954
12

CHAPTER TWO
Quest for National Unity, 1954–1955
45

CHAPTER THREE
Debate on Democracy, 1955–1956
76

CHAPTER FOUR
Diversity and Fragmentation, 1956–1959
106

viii   Contents

CHAPTER FIVE
Rupture or Reconciliation? 1960–1962
134

CONCLUSION
The Revolution of 1963 and the Legacy of Diệm's Republic
163

APPENDIXES
Ngô Đình Diệm's Cabinet, 1954–1955
A1 Government of July 7, 1954   171
A2 Coalition Government of September 24, 1954   173
A3 Government of May 10, 1955   174

Notes   175

Bibliography   217

Index   231

Acknowledgments

It was a meandering path that led me to write this book, and I have incurred countless debts along the way.

My first foray into serious research began in the graduate program at the University of California, Berkeley. Peter Zinoman guided me with his savvy advice and critical feedback. Penny Edwards and Kerwin Klein nudged me along with their patient encouragement. The late Jeffrey Hadler deepened my understanding of Southeast Asia, and Nguyễn Nguyệt Cầm introduced me to Vietnamese literature on the Vietnam War. I also benefited from the mentorship of Christine Trost, Deborah Lustig, and David Minkus during my year as a graduate fellow at the Institute for the Study of Societal Issues.

The warm friendship and intellectual camaraderie of Chi Ha and Siti Keo sustained me throughout my sojourn in Berkeley. Many other friends and colleagues in the United States and Asia also stimulated my development as a historian and reminded me that there was life outside of research, among them Claudine Ang, Michitake Aso, Trang Cao, Wen-Chin Chang, Jessica Chapman, Haydon Cherry, Rebekah Collins, Va Cun, Sean Fear, Cheong Soon Gan, Caroline Herbelin, Tuan Hoang, Alec Holcombe, Kevin Li, Ian Loman, Trinh Luu, Van Ly, Kelley and Allen McCarthy, Shawn McHale, Hoang Ngo, Marguerite Nguyen, Martina Nguyen, Phi Van Nguyen, Van Nguyen-Marshall, John Duong Phan, Jason Picard, Joe Pittayaporn, Brett Reilly, Arjun Subrahmanyan, Meghan Simpson, Ivan Small, Maria Stalford, Geoffrey Stewart, Allen Tran, Rick Tran, Chuong Dai Vo, Eileen Vo, and Vũ Đường Luân.

I began research on this book while on tenure track and had limited time to collect sources. Fortunately, several colleagues generously shared their materials with me. Chi Ha gave me a trove of documents about the Ministry of

x   Acknowledgments

Information and the press in the Republic of Vietnam. She and Jason Picard provided numerous articles from historical newspapers. Kevin Li and Brett Reilly passed along French and Vietnamese archival documents, and Brett gave me a copy of Hồ Hữu Tường's memoir. François Guillemot sent me copies of archival sources from France. Additionally, Sean Fear, Siti Keo, Kevin, Shawn McHale, Ryan Nelson, Martina Nguyen, Phi Van Nguyen, Jason, Brett, and Peter Zinoman let me read their unpublished research. I also thank François Guillemot, Janet Hoskins, Kevin, Phi Van, and Jason for answering my questions about various religious and political groups.

Historical research would be impossible without libraries and archives, and I express deep gratitude to the librarians and archivists who facilitated my work: David Langbart at the National Archives and Records Administration; the friendly staff of the Cornell University Library; Nguyễn Thị Như Trang, Tô Thị Chí Trung, Bùi Thị Bích Thủy, Bùi Thị Hảo, Lâm Thị Ngọc Thư, and Nguyễn Thị Lệ Ninh at the General Sciences Library, Vietnam; and Cù Thị Dung, Đặng Thị Vân, Nguyễn Thị Luyến, and Trần Thị Thùy Linh at the National Archives Center II, also in Vietnam. Đặng Thị Cẩm Tú and Đỗ Kiên facilitated my research access in Vietnam, and several research assistants helped me collect and catalog materials, including Sarah Hodge, Marika Lohmus, Frances Martin, Ngô Hạnh, Nguyễn Ngân, Marc Reyes, Megan Streit, Võ Anh Tuấn, Hoang Vu, Yang Zheng, and Max Zimmerman.

Funding for my research came from the Fulbright-Hays, Mellon-CLIR, and University of Connecticut. I revised the manuscript while on a fellowship at the University of Connecticut Humanities Institute, and the Felberbaum Family Faculty Fund and other funds from the university covered the miscellaneous costs of manuscript preparation.

I have often felt lost during this journey and am thankful for the mentors who helped me find my bearings again and again. Edward Miller has mentored me informally since I was a graduate student. He answered endless questions about archival research, sent relevant primary sources my way, and shared his knowledge of American foreign relations and Ngô Đình Diệm's rule. Lien-Hang Thi Nguyen expressed interest in the book before I had even written a word and later encouraged me to submit the manuscript to the Weatherhead series. Tuong Vu heroically read a raw, unfinished draft and was unstinting in his encouragement and advice. At the University of Connecticut, Jason Chang, Sylvia Schafer, and Cathy Schlund-Vials showed me the ropes of departmental life and provided many suggestions on the manuscript.

The careful work and kindness of many individuals helped turn the manuscript into a book. Masako Ikeda at the University of Hawai'i Press helped me throughout the publication process, and two anonymous reviewers offered invaluable feedback. Grace Wen oversaw the production of the book, Helen Glenn

Court copyedited the manuscript, and Vicki Low prepared the index. Hồ Thị Bảo Tiên and Jacob Raterman proofread Vietnamese- and French-language terms, respectively. Erin Greb prepared a superb set of maps, and Phan Quang Tuệ, Trần Văn Tòng, and the Cornell University Library generously provided images of historical figures.

I was only a teenager when I first peered down the long road of graduate training, and I thank my high school history teacher Chris McQueen for taking me aside and suggesting I consider an academic career. It was a brief conversation that changed the course of my life. At Seattle University, Theresa Earenfight, Hazel Hahn, and William Kangas introduced me to the joys of research and advised me on my applications to graduate school. Outside the classroom, the support of my dear friends Kevin Grove, Rebecca Khalil, Jasmine Marwaha, Meg Matthews, Evan Pham, and Aaron Van Dyke strengthened my resolve to pursue graduate studies. The warmth of the Sanoner family made me feel at home during my first stint studying abroad and assured me that I had what it took to live overseas.

Although doing so is somewhat unconventional, I would like to mention people and institutions that rarely receive formal recognition in the acknowledgments of academic books. I came to the United States as a refugee, and I am grateful to the social workers, volunteers, charities, social service organizations, and government agencies that eased my family's resettlement in the United States. I feel similar gratitude toward the teachers and librarians who contributed to my education from Head Start through high school. As an adult, I often employed domestic workers to clean my home during my residence abroad and, more recently, in the United States. I am all too aware that their physical labor made my intellectual labor possible.

Ultimately, my journey can be traced back to my family and relatives, and it is to them that I owe my greatest debt. I thank my husband Peter Lavelle for his unwavering love and support. He shared my excitement when I made new discoveries, comforted me when I faced setbacks, and suggested revisions when I struggled with my writing. I could not ask for a better partner in life or in research. I am grateful to my brother and his family and my husband's family for offering much needed refuge away from academic work. In Vietnam, my cousin was my confidant and best friend, always ready with friendly advice or a funny story. Most of all, I thank my parents for teaching me Vietnamese and supporting my decision to become a historian. They came of age in Saigon in the 1960s and 1970s and their tales of the life they left behind piqued my research interest in the Republic of Vietnam.

My mother deserves special recognition as my first teacher of Vietnamese history. Throughout my childhood, she taught Vietnamese-language classes on top of her full time job and, despite having no pedagogical training, designed her

xii   Acknowledgments

own curriculum on the literature, history, and geography of Vietnam. After I began graduate school, she assiduously collected overseas Vietnamese memoirs and history books to aid me in my research. Although my mother did not live to see the completion of this book, it is in so many ways a testament to her hard work. I dedicate this book in her memory.

Abbreviations

ARV	Association for the Restoration of Vietnam
ARVN	Army of the Republic of Vietnam
AS	Ministry of Foreign Affairs Archives, Academia Sinica
CBVNCH	*Công báo Việt Nam Cộng Hòa*
CDF	Central Decimal Files
CĐCN	*Con đường chính nghĩa*
CIA	Central Intelligence Agency
CGR	Classified General Records
CMQG	*Cách mạng quốc gia*
CPC	Committee for Peaceful Coexistence
CR	Citizens' Rally
CREST	Central Intelligence Agency Record Search Tool
DB	Democratic Bloc
DRV	Democratic Republic of Vietnam
ĐICH	Office of the President Collection, First Republic
FEC	French Expeditionary Corps
FEV	Bureau of Far Eastern Affairs, Vietnam Subject Files
FD	Front for Democratization
FPB	Freedom and Progress Bloc
FRUS	*Foreign Relations of the United States*
HĐQNCM	Revolutionary Military Council Collection
ICP	Indochinese Communist Party
MPF	Movement to Preserve Freedom
MSN	Movement to Safeguard the Nation
MUP	Movement for Unity and Peace

xiv   Abbreviations

NARA	National Archives and Records Administration
NLF	National Liberation Front
NRF	National Resistance Front
NRM	National Revolutionary Movement
NYT	*New York Times*
PThTVNCH	Office of the Prime Minister Collection
QC	*Quần chúng*
QG	*Quốc gia*
RC	Revolutionary Council
RG	Record Group
RMC	Revolutionary Military Council
RVN	Republic of Vietnam
SDP	Social Democratic Party
SHAT	Service Historique de l'Armée de Terre
SNF	Subject-Numeric Files
SVN	State of Vietnam
TC	*Tiếng chuông*
TD	*Tự do*
TĐBCHNP	Office of the Regional Delegate for Southern Vietnam Collections
TL	*Thời luận*
TTLTQGII	National Archives Center II
UC	Unity Committee
US	United States
USDDO	United States Declassified Documents Online
VNA	Vietnamese National Army
VNP	Vietnamese Nationalist Party
VRL	Vietnamese Revolutionary League
VTX	Việt Nam Thông Tấn Xã (news agency)
VTX	*Việt Nam Thông Tấn Xã* (report published by news agency)
VVA	Virtual Vietnam Archive
WWII	World War II

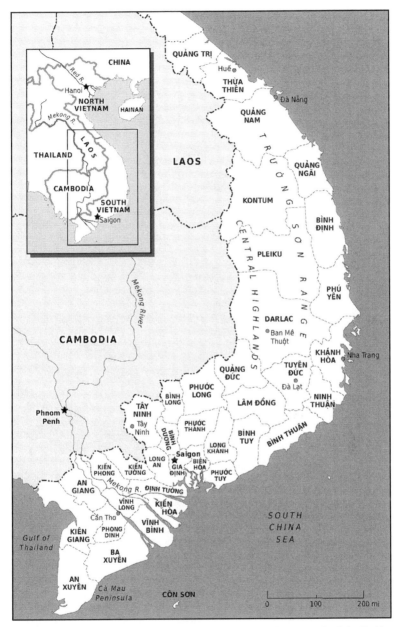

Map 1. Province map of the Republic of Vietnam, circa 1960 (map by Erin Greb)

INTRODUCTION

Rethinking the Republic of Vietnam

Rufus Philipps knew little about Vietnam when the Central Intelligence Agency sent him to Saigon in August 1954. The sprawling city was the capital of the State of Vietnam (SVN), and he arrived at a time of momentous change for the regime. Philipps was aware that the new prime minister, Ngô Đình Diệm, had taken up the reins of government just a month earlier. The young intelligence agent also knew that the Geneva Accords had just divided Vietnam into two zones, assigning the southern half to the Saigon-based government and stripping the regime of its territories farther north. But Philipps had no familiarity with the country beyond those generalities even though he was there to join a covert mission to "save South Vietnam," the moniker for the regime after the Geneva Accords. Although he had passable French, he did not know a word of Vietnamese, and he found the Vietnamese people to be polite but distant. Most important for his mission, he could hardly make sense of local politics. Street demonstrations were held during his early weeks in country, but he could not understand the speeches or the slogans splayed across the banners the demonstrators carried. Nor could he and the other American operatives determine who the demonstrators were or which groups they represented. In a memoir written decades later, Philipps recalled,

> The demonstrations, we soon learned, were against the Geneva Accords, particularly against dividing the country in two, but we still had no idea if they were led by nationalists unwilling to lose the North or communist sympathizers who felt the same about the South. There we were, working for the Agency, and we couldn't decipher a street demonstration.[1]

2   Introduction

Phillips' initial confusion was typical of Westerners who tried to understand Vietnamese politics during Ngô Đình Diệm's tenure (1954–1963). Like Philipps, the vast majority of American policymakers, diplomats, journalists, and scholars involved with Vietnam in the 1950s and early 1960s did not know the Vietnamese language. They struggled to distinguish between the country's numerous political groups and tease out the relations among them. In the spring of 1955, when a street battle broke out between Diệm's government and a crime syndicate known as the Bình Xuyên, the *New York Times* found the conflict so odd that the paper described it as "Struggle Weird in South Vietnam." Even President Dwight D. Eisenhower admitted that he found the battle "strange and inexplicable."[2] Foreign observers had an equally hard time comprehending the ideas of the different politicians and parties, including those who headed the government. The American journalist Robert Shaplen recounted in his memoir that Diệm's brother and adviser Ngô Đình Nhu baffled foreigners with overly abstract explanations of personalism, the regime's political philosophy. "A number of Americans, including some visiting scholars, spent considerable time trying to understand and explain personalism, but they usually gave up because it seemed such a hodge-podge, and because whatever it was, it was only a theory, while in practice it was what Nhu wanted it to be," Shaplen remembered.[3]

In actuality, the politics of the State of Vietnam (1949–1955), later renamed the Republic of Vietnam (RVN, 1955–1975), was never as inscrutable or bizarre as some Westerners believed. Had the Americans taken the time to study Vietnamese history, they might have realized that the politics of the Saigon-based state grew out of a strand of revolutionary nationalism that had originated decades earlier. I call this "anticommunist nationalism." Anticommunist nationalism first emerged within the revolutionary movement of the late colonial period. The anticommunists were adherents of republicanism and sought to liberate their homeland from foreign domination and establish an independent Vietnamese republic.[4] They clashed with the communists over the most suitable ideology for the country and the type of government that should rule Vietnam after independence. The disagreement created a deep rift between the two sides, and the anticommunists eventually resolved to build a separate state from the one the communists had founded. When the Geneva Accords ended the war of independence against France in 1954, the anticommunists seized the moment, hoping to realize their vision for the future of the country with the establishment of the Republic of Vietnam.

What happened next has been overshadowed by the more familiar story about the RVN's role in the American war against communism. The Saigon-based regime allied with the United States and emerged as a key participant in the Vietnam War (1954–1975). Washington sent an increasing number of diplomats, military advisers, and soldiers to serve in Vietnam, and the allies fought

Introduction   3

against the communist Democratic Republic of Vietnam (DRV) and the communist-led National Liberation Front (NLF). Throughout the conflict, the RVN seemed plagued by political factionalism and instability without any seeming cause. But behind this conventional portrait was a more complex history about the contradictory legacies of the revolutionary movement and the heterogeneity of Vietnamese society. On the one hand, the intense rivalries of the revolutionary movement lingered and festered in the southern republic, undermining all efforts at political cooperation during the regime's formative decade following the Geneva Accords. On the other, the rich diversity of the movement survived and flourished and gave rise, in the latter half of the 1960s and early 1970s, to the most politically pluralistic society in Vietnamese history.

THE RVN IN ACADEMIC SCHOLARSHIP

Philipps' inability to make sense of Vietnamese politics during his early days in Saigon foreshadowed much of the scholarship on the southern republic. The earliest Western scholars to write about the Saigon-based state were political scientists who visited Vietnam during Diệm's tenure but lacked training in Vietnamese language and history. Although they found the local political scene intriguing, they could comprehend neither public debates nor newspapers in the local language and evaluated the RVN simply by judging it against Western democratic norms. For these reasons, early scholars showed only a superficial grasp of the political groups that populated the southern republic and rarely managed to explain the platform of any group other than Diệm's faction. Still, the political scientists produced vivid eyewitness accounts and conducted rare interviews with historical figures that remain valuable to researchers to this day.[5]

The expansion of the Vietnam War in the mid-1960s ushered in a second wave of scholarship that largely ignored the RVN. The Vietnam scholars who dominated this wave did have language training, and their research laid the foundation for the modern field of Vietnam studies. But because the Vietnam scholars sought to explain the success of the DRV and NLF in the war, they chose to study the communists rather than the anticommunist republic.[6] Researchers argued that the main trend in modern Vietnamese history was the struggle for national liberation, beginning with anticolonial resistance in the nineteenth century, continuing to the revolutionary movement and the creation of the DRV, and culminating in the communist victory at the end of the Vietnam War.[7] This communist-centered narrative implicitly dismissed the RVN as an exception to the historical struggle for Vietnamese self-determination. But in focusing on the communists to the exclusion of other groups, scholars of the second wave conflated Vietnamese communism with Vietnamese nationalism and

4   Introduction

failed to consider that the Saigon-based state may have represented an alternative form of nationalism. They also relied on communist Vietnamese sources rather than materials produced in the RVN, the very sources that would shed light on the regime's origins and political character. Although other Vietnam scholars later challenged the conventional narrative by highlighting the contributions of noncommunist groups to the development of Vietnamese nationalism, few researchers chose to make the RVN the focus of their work.[8]

Starting in the 1980s, as the Vietnam War receded into the past, American diplomatic historians began studying the Saigon-based regime through the lens of US foreign relations and produced a third wave of scholarship on the RVN. The diplomatic historians depicted the southern republic as little more than an instrument of American imperialism that was devoid of indigenous roots. This portrayal reinforced existing assumptions about the RVN as an aberration in the history of Vietnamese nationalism. Like the early political scientists, the diplomatic historians did not know Vietnamese and consulted only Western-language sources, which were inadequate for understanding Vietnamese ideas and experiences. Moreover, their focus on American diplomacy obscured the importance of domestic Vietnamese politics.[9] In sum, academic knowledge about the RVN stagnated because researchers neglected the southern regime and failed to appreciate its connection to Vietnamese history.

The rise of the "new Vietnam War scholarship" at the beginning of the twenty-first century made the politics of the RVN the object of serious study once again. The change began when a young generation of US diplomatic historians spearheaded a multi-archival approach to exploring the Vietnam War. Equipped with the requisite language training, they conducted research at American archives and previously inaccessible Vietnamese institutions. Scholars of the fourth wave analyzed Diệm's regime as a distinct partner in an unequal alliance with the United States rather than simply a tool of American foreign policy. They argued that anticommunist leaders pursued their own ideas and agendas rather than followed American plans. They found that local conflicts in Vietnam had profound consequences for international relations. Yet this group of scholars left much unexplored. Because their studies typically had a dual focus that toggled between Saigon and Washington, they devoted only limited attention to exploring the relations between anticommunist groups within the RVN. In addition, most of the young diplomatic historians either treated Diệm's faction as the sole representative of the southern republic or wrote about other anticommunists without examining their ideas. Consequently, the new Vietnam War scholarship had the effect of oversimplifying the RVN's complex political landscape and casting factional disputes as struggles for power rather than disagreements about the future of the country.[10]

Only recently has a fifth wave of research finally made domestic developments within the RVN the primary focus of scholarly inquiry. Building on the new Vietnam War scholarship, historians specializing in Vietnam have analyzed a wider range of Vietnamese-language materials and examined a greater array of historical actors to create a Vietnam-centered approach to the study of the RVN. This fifth wave of scholarship is itself part of a larger "Vietnam studies" turn in research about the southern half of the country between 1945 and 1975, and Vietnam historians are on the cusp of creating a more inclusive historical narrative about the region.[11] Brett Reilly has argued that the State of Vietnam was an amalgamation of previous state projects and various militarized religious groups and political parties.[12] Sean Fear, Olga Dror, Van Nguyen-Marshall, Phi Van Nguyen, Jason Picard, and Sophie Quinn-Judge have all in their research contributed to a more sophisticated understanding of the social and political diversity of the RVN.[13] Additionally, Stan Tan's study of the central highlands and David Biggs's work on the Mekong delta and the region of Huế have highlighted the geographically varied experiences of the RVN's politics.[14] As these many contributions make clear, pluralism and internal division were defining features of the RVN that merit further scholarly analysis.

ANTICOMMUNIST NATIONALISM AND THE MAKING OF DIỆM'S REPUBLIC

This book contributes to the fifth wave of scholarship by reinterpreting the domestic politics of the southern republic under Diệm's rule. The RVN was home to a wide range of political groups whose endemic factionalism threatened to tear the regime apart. To make sense of this discord, historians must trace the politics of the Saigon-based state back to the revolutionary movement of the 1920s to the 1950s. As a whole, revolutionaries tried to violently topple the French colonial regime and form an independent Vietnamese state, but the movement included an array of parties and organizations from across the political spectrum. Such diversity led to sharp disagreements among the revolutionaries, and the movement gradually diverged into two distinct branches: communism and anticommunist nationalism. The communists argued that Vietnam's future government should be based only on the Vietnamese working class and peasantry. In contrast, the anticommunists insisted that the ideal state was a democratic republic that incorporated all ethnic Vietnamese. The fissure between the two sides widened during the Anti-French Resistance (Kháng Chiến Chống Pháp, 1945–1954), a decade-long struggle for independence. At the start of the Resistance, the communists declared the independence of the newly formed Democratic Republic of Vietnam, and revolutionaries of all persuasions allied to

6   Introduction

defend the fledgling state from French invasion. But the communists and anti-communists could not set aside their differences, and their alliances ruptured amid violent clashes. As a result, the division between the two branches hardened into an irreconcilable schism.

My characterization of the anticommunists as revolutionaries challenges the conventional assumption that only the communists deserved such a label. Since the latter half of the 1960s, scholars have mostly depicted the communists as the main torchbearers of revolutionary change in Vietnam. Yet Vietnamese anticommunists, like their communist counterparts, were subversive in organizing illegal, underground networks dedicated to toppling French rule and forming a sovereign government. The colonial authorities considered these conspiracies to be seditious regardless of whether the revolutionaries espoused communism. The anticommunists were also revolutionary insofar as they intentionally set themselves apart from the reformers and refused to cooperate with French authorities as a long-term strategy. Reformers were politicians who wanted to work with the colonial government to modernize Vietnam. During the decades between the two world wars, these men hoped to implement republican reforms in anticipation of a distant future when Vietnam would be free of French rule. Reformers abhorred the violence of the revolutionary movement, rejected class struggle, and did not actively fight for independence during the Resistance. Thus they shared the republicanism and anticommunism of the anticommunist nationalists but were not revolutionary, and the anticommunists often reviled reformers as collaborators who served colonial interests. Vietnamese nationalists of all kinds sometimes switched between revolutionary and reformist activism or defected from anticommunist organizations to join the communist party. Therefore, the terms "reformers," "communists," and "anticommunists" do not refer to static groups with unchanging membership but to evolving categories of historical actors who adopted specific political stances at key historical junctures.

In the wake of the schism with the communists, the anticommunists emerged as a coherent bloc with a distinct agenda, though they never united to form a single organization. Their goal was to establish an alternative Vietnamese state. But before they could make much headway, the French sponsored a nominally independent government—the State of Vietnam—in 1949, and the anticommunists temporarily split over whether to serve in it. Those who supported the SVN quickly grew disillusioned because France flagrantly violated the regime's sovereignty. In 1953, the anticommunists came together to articulate a shared vision of a fully autonomous Vietnamese republic that would break away from France completely, unite all anticommunist nationalists, and enable them to participate freely in a democratic system. The ideals of independence, unity, and democracy remained a guiding light for the anticommunists in the years ahead.

After 1954, anticommunist nationalists expanded as a political category to include many groups and individuals whose politics aligned with the ideals of

1953 but who had not participated in the revolutionary movement or fought in the Resistance. Old and new anticommunists alike opposed the DRV and favored the existence of a sovereign, democratic Vietnamese government. The growth of anticommunist nationalism was intimately entwined with the rise of Ngô Đình Diệm. Diệm ascended to the premiership of the State of Vietnam in 1954, founded the Republic of Vietnam the following year, and declared himself the regime's first president. Under his leadership, anticommunist nationalism became the political orthodoxy in the RVN. Diệm and other anticommunists tried to secure independence by pushing for the withdrawal of French troops from Vietnamese soil. Many hoped to achieve national unity and called for cooperation among the various anticommunist groups. Most important, they tried to realize democracy and made plans for a constitution and a national assembly.

But the anticommunists also had to grapple with the heterogeneity and discord that had long shaped their history. They held very different interpretations of democracy and unity, and their clashing ideas drove a continuous factional struggle throughout Diệm's rule. Politicians and activists debated how democratic Vietnam should be and which groups could legitimately participate in political life. Diệm's faction, whose members I call Diemists, was the most illiberal participant in the debate. The Diemists favored severe limitations on civil liberties, insisted on controlling the government, and pressured other groups to join the president's faction in the name of national unity. Most anticommunists, however, refused. They demanded that the government allow greater freedom and political pluralism and contended that Diệm should share power with his rivals to achieve true unity.

The disagreements grew so acrimonious that they provoked a rupture between the anticommunist factions in the RVN reminiscent of the earlier split between the communists and anticommunists within the revolutionary movement. Diệm and his partisans sidelined their rivals and established an authoritarian government that had the trappings of democracy. In response, every major anticommunist group broke with Diệm in the latter half of the 1950s. His rivals organized a movement of political opposition and pushed the regime to liberalize. The conflict peaked in 1960 when some oppositionists spontaneously joined an abortive coup led by disaffected military officers. The outraged Diệm launched a brutal crackdown and arrested numerous opposition figures, further alienating his rivals. This second schism henceforth remained a permanent division within anticommunist nationalism.

NEW APPROACHES TO STUDYING THE POLITICS OF THE RVN

In addressing factional conflicts in the RVN, this book builds on the fifth wave of scholarship. First, analysis of a broad field of organizations and individuals

8   Introduction

reveals that a wide variety of anticommunists, not just the Diemists, shaped the evolution of the southern republic. This comprehensive approach makes clear that the RVN remained politically heterogeneous despite Diệm's attempt to suppress differences. Although the regime's political landscape also included neutralists and underground communists, the history of those activists is beyond the scope of this study because it was largely after Diệm's downfall that neutralism and covert communism became major currents in the politics of the RVN. The one exception was the distinctly anticommunist form of neutralism championed by the Cao Đài religious leader Phạm Công Tắc. As explained in chapter 4, Tắc understood neutralism to mean eliminating communist and American influences from Vietnamese politics, unlike later neutralists who advocated for negotiating or even sharing power with the communists.

Second, the book takes ideas seriously by analyzing the competing programs of the various anticommunists. I argue that politicians and activists had substantive disagreements about the meaning of democracy and national unity, and many groups proposed forward-looking programs for political, economic, and social reform. It was this struggle over ideas that made Vietnamese politics so contentious rather than just a competition for power.

Third, the book argues that the partisan rivalries of the RVN had a complex political geography that historians have largely ignored. Although I focus on the national politics that took place in the capital, the analysis also explores the relationship between changes in Saigon and other regions and locales. The partition of Vietnam in 1954 marginalized northern-based anticommunist groups throughout Diệm's rule, and his early consolidation of power in central Vietnam exacerbated his problems with his sectarian rivals in the south. Later, Diệm's decision to invade sectarian territories in provincial Vietnam forced many opposition leaders to seek refuge elsewhere, and Saigon emerged as the center of political opposition to the president along with Paris and Phnom Penh.

One further benefit of studying Vietnamese political diversity is the possibility of seeing American foreign policy in a new light. Although the United States could have chosen from a range of allies to advance its crusade against communism, the Americans decided to back the most authoritarian faction at the expense of more liberal but equally anticommunist elements. During the debates on democracy and the constitution in 1955 and 1956, the Americans favored Diệm over less authoritarian parties and leaders, though it is unclear whether US policymakers fully understood the differences between the various anticommunists. By the early 1960s, when Diệm's rivals renewed the call for liberalization, the American embassy in Saigon clearly realized that the oppositionists were more liberal than Diệm was. Yet the ambassador and embassy officers defended the incumbent administration on the grounds that Vietnam was not ready for democracy. It was never the case that the Americans tolerated the dictatorial

Diệm because no other partners in the struggle against Vietnamese communism were available. In fact, US foreign policy favored him in part because his authoritarianism aligned with American perceptions of Vietnam, to the detriment of more liberal anticommunists.

The study is presented in five chapters. Chapter 1 traces the rise of anticommunist nationalism within the revolutionary movement during the late colonial period and the Anti-French Resistance. The schism between communists and anticommunists convinced the latter that they needed to form a government of their own, and in 1953 the activists articulated a shared set of ideals that would remain a touchstone for anticommunists in the RVN. Chapter 2 analyzes disagreements between Diệm and his rivals over the meaning of national unity. Most anticommunists favored political pluralism and a national union government, but Diệm preferred a narrow administration and insisted that it was his prerogative to impose a unitary system of government on South Vietnam. The arguments provoked a series of confrontations from July 1954 to April 1955 that marked the beginning of the schism among the anticommunists. The transformation of the State of Vietnam into the Republic of Vietnam, the constitutional transition, and the debate on the democracy in 1955 to 1956 are subjects of chapter 3. The anticommunists proved unable to come to an agreement on how to organize the new republic. Diệm subsequently crushed his rivals and promulgated a constitution reflecting only his faction's political ideas.

Chapter 4 explores the fragmentation of anticommunist nationalism between 1956 and 1959. The Diemists and the main opposition groups continued to subscribe to the shared ideals but developed competing programs to realize them. The schism between the anticommunists widened at the turn of the decade. Diệm's rivals publicly demanded that he liberalize the government. He retaliated by cracking down on the opposition following a failed coup, as seen in chapter 5. Attempts by some Diemists and oppositionists to forge a compromise between the two camps failed. The conclusion briefly considers the fall of Diệm in 1963 and his political legacy. The anticommunists played a very limited role in the unrest that roiled the RVN that year, yet their ideas had become so mainstream that other activists and the military government that succeeded Diệm invoked the principles of unity and democracy in an attempt to establish political legitimacy. Thus the anticommunists' ideas lived on even as internal conflicts and political turbulence made it impossible for the activists to realize their aspirations.

A NOTE ON SOURCES AND TERMINOLOGY

This study combines the multi-archival research used by scholars of the fourth wave with a more comprehensive examination of Vietnamese materials favored by historians of the fifth wave. The archives of the RVN, housed in Ho Chi Minh

10   Introduction

City (Saigon), provide valuable insight into Ngô Đình Diệm's political program, the inner workings of his administration, and the activities of the opposition. A contrasting perspective is offered by the archives of the US State Department, housed at the National Archives and Record Administration in College Park, Maryland. In particular, missives from the American embassy in Saigon to the State Department include candid conversations with anticommunist leaders and detailed descriptions of elections, coups, political meetings, legislation, and national assembly debates. The opposing viewpoints of these archival sources allow researchers to compare Vietnamese ideas and actions with American perceptions of Vietnam.

Additionally, the book makes use of a larger volume and wider range of Vietnamese-language materials than other monographs about the politics of the RVN. Three bodies of sources feature especially prominently. The first includes historical newspapers and journals published in the RVN. These periodicals reflect the ideas of a wide array of anticommunists ranging from the Diemists to their bitterest opponents and open a window onto the vigorous political debates that most scholars have ignored. Second are compilations of religious documents and political tracts produced by Diệm's opponents, including the Cao Đài religious group and the Hòa Hảo Buddhists. These collections include key documents missing from the archives. The last group of sources is a mixture of monographs by nonprofessional Vietnamese scholars (working outside the university setting), memoirs by former politicians or their confidantes, and hybrid accounts that intersperse research with personal experience. Many of these authors were historical figures in their own right, and their writings offer insider accounts of Vietnamese politics and the often tortuous relations between the anticommunists. Researchers have barely scratched the surface of this rich body of work though they have relied heavily on American memoirs. Together, these varied archival and published sources yield a richer and more complex picture of the internal politics of the RVN than any yet available.

Some readers may be confused by the ways in which Vietnam has been divided geographically. The Vietnamese traditionally separated their country into three cultural and geographical regions. The tripartite division originated as administrative units in the nineteenth century before the French conquest, and the colonial government and the State of Vietnam continued to employ a similar system of administrative organization. The book refers to these regions in lower case: the north, the central region, and the south. The Geneva Accords of 1954 partitioned Vietnam at the seventeenth parallel into two zones. I refer to the areas above and below the demarcation line in upper case, North Vietnam and South Vietnam, respectively. The Republic of Vietnam specifically refers to the Saigon-based state, not to South Vietnam as a whole, because the government did not fully control the entire territory below the seventeenth parallel.

Personal names are another potential source of confusion. In Vietnamese, the family name precedes the given name, and in the first half of the twentieth century, respected members of the scholarly class were known by their family names. The practice later faded in favor of given names. Following these conventions, I refer to early figures such as Phan Bội Châu, Phan Châu Trinh, Hồ Chí Minh, Nguyễn Thế Truyền, and Hồ Nhựt Tân by their family names but use given names for all other historical figures. When multiple individuals have the same given name, I use the full name of less important persons to avoid confusion.

CHAPTER ONE

Birth of Anticommunist Nationalism, 1920s–1954

In 1925, Vietnam's most famous nationalist reformer, Phan Châu Trinh, delivered a public speech on democracy and monarchy to a packed audience in Saigon.[1] Phan had spent most of his life thinking about the plight of his homeland under colonial rule and his audience received his words with rapt attention. In his world, two models of government dominated: the democratic, republican government of France and the traditional Vietnamese monarchy. Phan praised democracy (*dân chủ* or *dân trị*) and criticized monarchy (*quân trị*) with equal fervor and lamented that his compatriots still favored the latter but knew nothing about the former.[2] He declared indignantly that a monarchy reflected the whims of the king and ignored the popular will; democracy, he contended, was superior because the people themselves established the government. "In a democracy the people create their own constitution and select officials, who will act according to the will of the people to look after their nation's business," Phan explained. Citing the example of the French political system, he emphasized that constitutions prevented democracies from backsliding into autocracy:

> The power of the government is also stipulated in the constitution, and therefore there is little room for negligence and autocracy. In addition, if there is a violation of the constitution, everyone will be treated according to the same law—from the president to a common person in the countryside.[3]

His speech left no doubt that he believed the future of Vietnam lay in democracy.

Three decades later, Phan's vision of a democratic republic seemed to be on the cusp of realization in the newly established Republic of Vietnam (RVN), an independent government based in Saigon. The regime was in the midst of a

Birth of Anticommunist Nationalism 13

constitutional transition. A recent plebiscite had deposed the last monarch, and the government was busy preparing for the election of an assembly to review the constitution. The transition, though, was full of rancor and debate. Many politicians objected that the constitutional process was not democratic. A "study group" led by the opposition politician Phan Quang Đán called on the government to make changes to the process. The activists argued that a democratically elected assembly should be invested with the power not merely to review the constitution but to write it. In their words, such an assembly "will have the standing to draft a constitution suitable to the nation. It will be a forum for the people to express their aspirations and [through which the government can] consult their opinions on matters relating to the national economy and the people's livelihood."[4] The concept of democracy had become so mainstream, in the activists' view, that they assumed their compatriots fully understood democracy and even clamored for it. "In recent history, the Vietnamese people have always struggled for a democratic national assembly," the group declared.[5]

Although the RVN did not live up to Phan Châu Trinh's lofty ideals, the affinities between early nationalists like him and activists in the southern republic reveal a historical connection that scholars have been slow to analyze. For decades, researchers have hesitated to trace the origins of the RVN to the republican nationalism and revolutionary fervor of the late colonial period.[6] Instead, they have portrayed the Saigon-based regime as a creature of foreign design, first as a product of French colonialism and later as a client of the United States.[7] But the RVN had deep roots in the Vietnamese past. A close examination reveals that the politics of the republic developed from a strand of revolutionary nationalism that long predated French efforts to sponsor a nominally independent Vietnamese regime.

In fact, many leading politicians and political groups in the RVN had participated in the modern revolutionary nationalist movement of the 1920s to the 1950s. Outraged at the oppressive character of colonial rule, the revolutionaries aimed to overthrow the French in an armed uprising and form an independent republic with democratic institutions. Yet this shared goal masked remarkable diversity among the revolutionaries. The movement reflected Vietnam's heterogeneous society and encompassed a profusion of groups with starkly different social and regional backgrounds. The revolutionaries produced a rich variety of ideas and political programs, and many individuals switched their allegiance between groups with relative ease. Yet diversity also created challenges for the revolutionaries. Groups and individuals disagreed vehemently on strategy and objectives. The various organizations tended to conflate their interests with those of the nation, and many refused to cooperate with each other on an equal basis. Perhaps most crucially, despite the revolutionaries' professed commitment to

14   Chapter 1

democracy, none ever established a political system in which all groups would be allowed to participate.

Diversity and discord were already apparent within the movement by the 1920s, when communism and anticommunist nationalism emerged as two distinct branches of the movement. Early revolutionaries advocated for a democratic republic, but some later rejected republicanism in favor of communism. The communists considered the peasantry and the working class to be the ultimate source of political legitimacy and described the nation as including only these social elements to the exclusion of other classes. Moreover, the communists regarded the liberation of Vietnam as a step toward their ultimate objective of a world socialist revolution.[8] In contrast, anticommunists remained faithful to the early vision of a democratic republic. They championed the legitimacy of the nation based on the shared bonds of Vietnamese ethnicity and opposed communism because they rejected class warfare and single-party rule.

Divisions within the revolutionary movement hardened during the Anti-French Resistance. The revolutionaries competed for power, and their violent conflicts produced an irrevocable schism. Whereas before the schism the communists and anticommunists sometimes cooperated and engaged in dialogue, afterward neither would accept a government that included the other. The anticommunists eventually came together in 1953 to present a political vision that was inspired by republican nationalism and shaped by the recent schism. The appointment of the noted anticommunist nationalist Ngô Đình Diệm to the premiership of the State of Vietnam (SVN), the predecessor to the RVN, raised the hopes of many activists, and they expected him to carry out their shared vision. Much to their dismay, however, the RVN also inherited the factionalism of the revolutionary movement and its reluctance to fully embrace democracy.

DIFFERENT PATHS TO INDEPENDENCE

The revolutionary movement of the mid-twentieth century originated in early Vietnamese nationalism. The first wave of nationalists came of age during the French colonial conquest of the 1860s to the 1880s. They watched as the colonizers stripped the Nguyễn dynasty of its sovereignty, divided the kingdom into three regions with distinct legal status, and combined them with Cambodia and Laos to form French Indochina. From then on, Vietnamese nationalists dreamed of the day that their homeland would be liberated from colonial domination, but they understood that independence could not mean a return to the traditional kingdom of the past. Instead, they had to build a new Vietnam in keeping with the changes that had reshaped their world.

Early nationalists looked to other countries in East Asia for examples of political change. Many admired Japan because the island empire had maintained its independence despite the surging tide of Western imperialism. Beginning in the mid-nineteenth century, Japan adopted Western-style technology, education, and military organization and remade the government into a constitutional monarchy with a partially elected legislature. These changes transformed the previously vulnerable state into a modern government that could compete militarily against Western powers. The Xinhai Revolution in China presented the Vietnamese with a more radical path of political transformation. In 1911, Chinese revolutionaries and soldiers overthrew the Qing dynasty and established a republican government. The revolution took inspiration from the ideas of Sun Yat-sen, who defined the Chinese nation (Chin. *minzu*, Viet. *dân tộc*) as a historically and racially defined entity that had suffered at the hands of Western imperialists and the Manchu emperors of the Qing dynasty.[9] Sun sought to bring about a national renewal and favored a strong, centralized, and democratically elected republic that ensured the collective liberty of the nation.[10]

Vietnamese nationalists also turned to France for inspiration and were deeply impressed by the republicanism of the Third Republic. Like Sun, French republicans opposed monarchism and championed the primacy of the nation, but they were more liberal in valorizing the universal rights of man, civil liberties, expanded suffrage, and mass education.[11] The French colonial state promised to teach republican values to the Vietnamese people and to restore Vietnam's sovereignty when the country reached France's level of political maturity.[12] Yet colonial policy blatantly contradicted republican principles.[13] The authorities preserved the Vietnamese monarchy as a ceremonial institution, never conferred citizenship and civic rights on the masses, and refused to form genuinely representative assemblies.[14] Even so, French republicanism fired the imagination of Vietnamese nationalists, who argued that their nation should be governed under democratic institutions too.

Although the early nationalists agreed on the need for independence and democracy, they pursued different strategies for realizing these goals. Some wanted to violently overthrow the French and swiftly achieve independence; others preferred to prepare for eventual self-rule by implementing moderate reforms within the colonial system. The classically trained scholar Phan Bội Châu exemplified the first impulse. Phan preached revolutionary resistance against the French and initially favored establishing a constitutional monarchy similar to that in Japan, whose military and political strength he admired. He was the first Vietnamese thinker to associate the nation with the people rather than a monarch. Referring to the land of Vietnam, Phan asked rhetorically, "If my people did not exist, this place would be no more than a vast forest on a plain or an immense deserted wilderness. . . . How could a nation exist there? Where would Vietnam be?"[15] He argued that the nation was the basis for political legitimacy

16   Chapter 1

and praised the Japanese emperor for tending to his people's needs and sharing power with a representative assembly.[16]

Phan chose Prince Cường Đế, an anticolonial descendant of the Nguyễn dynasty, to be Vietnam's future constitutional monarch, and, beginning in 1905, arranged for young Vietnamese activists to study in Japan in hopes that they would go on to lead the revolutionary struggle. The venture ended in failure when Tokyo expelled the students, however, leaving Phan deeply disappointed in Japan. A few years later, the Xinhai Revolution revived his hopes and inspired him to espouse Chinese-style republicanism. Phan relocated to southern China and formed a revolutionary organization that advocated for the formation of a democratic republic. Living in exile meant that Phan and his followers could organize in relative safety beyond the watchful eyes of the colonial police.[17]

His contemporary Phan Châu Trinh championed an alternative, reformist path to independence. He believed that political sovereignty was meaningless without modernizing the country, and cooperation with France was the best way to achieve this goal. An admirer of French republicanism as well as Japanese-style modernization, he helped found a school that taught Western studies to Vietnamese students and urged the colonial government to make good on its promise to inculcate republicanism among his compatriots. Phan expected France to remake his country into a colonial republic by expanding public education in Vietnam, abolishing the monarchy, and introducing representative government. The authorities exiled him to France for his dissidence, but he continued to agitate there alongside liberal French politicians and other Vietnamese activists.[18] Back in Vietnam, some reformers followed Phan Châu Trinh's advice to collaborate with the colonial government. The reformers were especially active in southern Vietnam. In the 1920s, they joined the regional colonial assembly and lobbied the French to enact liberal reforms, such as expanding suffrage and protecting the freedom of association and of press.[19]

MODERN REVOLUTIONARY NATIONALISM AND THE ORIGINS OF THE SCHISM

The early nationalists inspired a rising generation of Vietnamese to embrace political activism in the 1920s and 1930s. These activists were mostly middle-class students educated in colonial schools and too young to remember the time before French rule. They followed their elders in championing republican nationalism but grew impatient with unfulfilled promises of liberal reform and resolved to carry out a violent revolution and form an independent republic themselves. They organized underground parties with tighter discipline than any of the groups that Phan Bội Châu ever formed. They were also more cosmopolitan, and their openness to new ideas, including communism and fascism, encouraged greater political diversity as well as fiercer disagreements. As a result, the modern revolutionary nationalist movement gradually split into groups and individuals who favored communism and those who ardently opposed it.

The first modern revolutionary party was the Vietnamese Nationalist Party (Việt Nam Quốc Dân Đảng, or VNP) (see table 1.1). A student named Nguyễn Thái Học and his friends organized the party in Hanoi in 1927 and adopted aspects of both French and Chinese republicanism. Like the French, the VNP favored constitutional rule, universal suffrage, and freedom of press. Emulating the Chinese, the activists named their party after the Chinese Nationalist Party (Chin. Guomindang, Viet. Quốc Dân Đảng) and adopted much of Sun Yat-sen's political philosophy and strategy. The VNP planned to overthrow the colonial regime and establish a military government controlled by the party. The military government would teach the population about democracy and oversee the country's transition to become a democratic republic.[20] The VNP was not ideologically anticommunist, though it followed Sun in rejecting class struggle as a basis for politics.[21] Party membership drew mostly from northern Vietnam and initially consisted of students and schoolteachers before expanding to include clerks, journalists, women, workers, and soldiers in the colonial military.[22]

Table 1.1 Main Revolutionary Groups, Mid-1920s to Mid-1950s

Name	*Notable Leaders*
Anticommunist nationalism	
Vietnamese Nationalist Party	Nguyễn Thái Học, Nguyễn Tường Tam
Đại Việt Nationalist Party	Trương Tử Anh, Nguyễn Tôn Hoàn, Phan Huy Quát, Đặng Văn Sung, Hà Thúc Ký
Cao Đài (Tây Ninh branch)	Phạm Công Tắc, Trần Quang Vinh, Trình Minh Thế, Nguyễn Thành Phương
Hòa Hảo	Huỳnh Phú Sổ, Trần Văn Soái, Nguyễn Bảo Toàn, Lâm Thành Nguyên, Nguyễn Giác Ngộ, Lê Quang Vinh
Bình Xuyên	Lê Văn Viễn
Northern Catholics	Lê Hữu Từ, Phạm Ngọc Chi
Ngô Đình Diệm faction	Ngô Đình Diệm, Ngô Đình Thục, Ngô Đình Nhu, Ngô Đình Cẩn, Ngô Đình Luyện
Communism	
Indochinese Communist Party (later, Vietnamese Labor Party)	Hồ Chí Minh
Việt Minh (front organization)	Hồ Chí Minh, Trần Văn Giàu
Trotskyists	Tạ Thu Thâu

Source: Author's tabulation.

18   Chapter 1

Although the idea of a democratic republic excited Học and his friends, the young Hồ Chí Minh abandoned republicanism and gravitated toward communism. Hồ was one of several activists who had gathered around Phan Châu Trinh during the latter's exile in France. Hồ grew tired of waiting for France to implement republican reforms and set out on a more radical path. In the early 1920s, he participated in the founding of the French Communist Party, traveled to the Soviet Union, and joined the Comintern, the Soviet agency for spreading communism around the world. He made his way to southern China in 1924 and recruited Phan Bội Châu's followers into a communist-inspired revolutionary organization.[23] Hồ's attempt to displace Phan must have irritated the older revolutionary, and relations between Hồ's and Phan's organizations were often tense.[24]

The decline of the VNP in 1930 provided an opening for Hồ and his followers. In February of that year, Nguyễn Thái Học's party launched an abortive insurrection in Yên Bái province, northwestern Vietnam, provoking a brutal French crackdown. The authorities executed Học and nearly destroyed the VNP. Only a handful of leaders escaped to southern China. They struggled to rebuild the party in exile and joined the remnants of Phan Bội Châu's network, which was now under the leadership of Phan's associate Nguyễn Hải Thần.[25] The near destruction of the VNP opened the way for the communists. That fall, Hồ Chí Minh met with several Vietnamese communist groups in Hong Kong and united them to form the Indochinese Communist Party (Đông Dương Cộng Sản Đảng, or ICP). The ICP broke with other revolutionaries in favoring a struggle that pit social classes against one another. The party called for a two-stage revolution. The "bourgeois democratic phase" would topple French colonialism and native landlords, and the "proletarian phase" would eliminate private property and achieve socialism.[26] The membership of the ICP was almost exclusively Vietnamese, but the party aimed to liberate all of French Indochina in accordance with the Comintern's directives.[27] The ICP established its headquarters in southern China and expanded into all three regions of Vietnam. More so than the VNP, the communist party prioritized the recruitment of peasants and workers.

The divergence between the communists and the other revolutionaries grew steadily. The VNP and ICP competed for recruits among Vietnamese exiles in southern China, clashed in colonial prisons in Vietnam, and tried to lure away each other's members. Large numbers of partisans defected from the VNP to join the communists in the decade and a half leading up to World War II.[28] As a consequence, the VNP turned firmly against communism. External factors also contributed to the bad blood. In China, a polarizing civil war between the Chinese Nationalist Party and the Chinese Communist Party affected politics throughout the region and drove the Vietnamese parties further apart.[29] Discord soon spread among Vietnamese nationalists worldwide. In France, the

Vietnamese exile community largely sided with the VNP. Activists unconnected to the party accused the ICP of colluding with the French in the repression of the VNP and argued that nationalism was more suitable for the Vietnamese people than communism.[30] In response, the communists insisted that their doctrine was superior to nationalism and scoffed at the idea of national union (*union nationale*).[31] Mainstream political discourse reinforced the division. The most prominent intellectuals of the 1930s aligned themselves with republican nationalism and criticized the communists. Figures such as the poet and journalist Phan Khôi, the novelist Vũ Trọng Phụng, the literary critic Trương Tửu, and influential writers of the Self-Reliant Literary Group (Tự Lực Văn Đoàn) complained that the communists were factional, ruthless, and hypocritical. Many also attacked the ICP for its obedience to the Comintern and railed against the totalitarianism of the Soviet Union.[32]

The rift deepened with the establishment of the Đại Việt Nationalist Party (Đại Việt Quốc Dân Đảng) in 1938.[33] A law student named Trương Tử Anh formed the party in Hanoi, and most early members were his classmates. Theirs was the largest of several revolutionary parties named for the premodern Vietnamese kingdom of Đại Việt. Anh developed a political doctrine called the Survival of the People (Dân Tộc Sinh Tồn) that brought together Sun Yat-sen's nationalism, Social Darwinist anxieties about survival and extinction, and the authoritarianism and racialist thinking of Japanese and German fascism.[34] Anh and other party theorists argued that the most basic natural law was the struggle for survival. In their view, the primary purpose of the nation was the perpetuation of the Vietnamese race, and the struggle for independence was a life and death struggle between nations, though Anh never advocated for biological racism.[35] Throughout the 1940s, the party championed an authoritarian regime secretly controlled by party elites and favored robust social welfare and state intervention in the economy.[36] Some of Anh's disciples later modified his political vision and proposed a temporary period of dictatorship to unite the nation, followed by the introduction of democratic elections.[37] The Đại Việt party opposed communism ideologically because leaders feared that class warfare would divide the nation.[38] Such a stance made conflict with the ICP all but inevitable.

IN THE SHADOW OF THE JAPANESE EMPIRE

The nationalist movement expanded during World War II when the Japanese occupied French Indochina. The island empire invaded the colony in 1940 and made vague promises to help Vietnam secure independence. But the Japanese allowed the French to continue administering Indochina and did little to prevent the colonial authorities from violently suppressing the revolutionaries. For the country as a whole, the anticipation of independence fanned the flames of

20   Chapter 1

Vietnamese nationalism, and the revolutionary movement attracted the support of previously apolitical organizations. These groups did not necessarily conceive of themselves as political parties, and some never developed a distinct political program, but they actively fought for self-rule. At the regional level, the war was a time of great uncertainty as the balance of power shifted between the communists and other revolutionaries. The movement seemed poised to finally achieve independence at the end of the war but was too divided to mount a unified struggle.

In southern China and northern Vietnam, the ICP enjoyed considerable growth relative to the anticommunists during the war years. In 1935, the Comintern had responded to the rise of fascism in Europe by instructing communists around the world to temporarily set aside class struggle as their primary organizing principle and form anti-fascist alliances with a wide range of social groups.[39] The change in the Comintern's policy prompted the ICP to establish a national front in 1941 known as the Vietnamese Independence League (Việt Minh Độc Lập Đồng Minh Hội, or Việt Minh) under the leadership of Hồ Chí Minh. While exercising control over key leadership positions, the communists encouraged noncommunists from all social classes to join the lower ranks of the Việt Minh.[40] The new strategy enabled the ICP to channel popular support for the cause of independence yet maintain the party's tight structure. Party leaders calculated that if they led the struggle for national liberation, they could steer all of Indochina toward a socialist revolution afterward.[41] Hồ Chí Minh had the foresight to situate the headquarters of the front in the far north of Vietnam. This gave the communists greater access to the Vietnamese population than the China-based VNP and enabled them to organize among the local people.[42] One of the Việt Minh's finest moments came during the winter of 1944–1945, when a famine ravaged northern and north-central Vietnam. The Việt Minh was the only group capable of delivering effective relief and won the loyalty of countless peasants.

Its success exacerbated the rivalry between the communists and the anticommunist parties. At the time, the Việt Minh front and the VNP competed in southwestern China for the patronage of the Chinese Nationalist Party. The Chinese general who oversaw the region hoped to use the émigré parties in a possible future invasion of Vietnam, and he pressured them to form a single coalition that would receive Chinese aid. The result was the Vietnamese Revolutionary League (Việt Nam Cách Mệnh Đồng Minh Hội, or VRL) headed by Phan Bội Châu's old comrade Nguyễn Hải Thần. The VRL included the Việt Minh, the VNP, and several smaller groups.[43] But the Chinese could not persuade the members of the league to trust each other. The émigré groups refused to coordinate their strategies and persisted in maintaining separate armies.[44] The Đại Việt Nationalist Party felt alarmed by the rise of the Việt Minh and joined with the VNP to form an alliance against their shared rival in the spring of 1945.[45] The partnership was the first of many anticommunist alliances.

Meanwhile, in southern Vietnam, the revolutionary movement gained the support of new organizations during the war but fractured into two camps over the question of collaboration with the Japanese. The anti-Japanese camp consisted of the ICP and the Trotskyists, both of which regarded the occupiers as imperialists. Vietnamese Trotskyism had emerged in the late 1920s when southern Vietnamese leftists in France adopted the ideology of the Soviet Union's ousted leader.[46] The radicals returned to Saigon around 1930 and organized a handful of loosely knit Trotskyist groups.[47] The Trotskyists and the southern ICP harbored deep suspicions of each other given the rupture of their previous alliance in the mid-1930s.[48] These internal differences mattered little to the wartime colonial regime, which treated all Vietnamese communists as similarly subversive. After the southern ICP launched a failed uprising in 1940, the French arrested large numbers of mainstream communists as well as Trotskyists. Consequently, both branches of southern Vietnamese communism emerged from World War II badly battered and numerically weak.

Other Vietnamese, however, cooperated with the Japanese because they hoped the occupiers would provide protection from the French and liberate Vietnam. In 1939, Phan Bội Châu's former associate Prince Cường Để founded the League for the Restoration of Vietnam (Việt Nam Phục Quốc Đồng Minh Hội) with Japanese sponsorship.[49] The party aimed to overthrow French colonialism with Japanese military assistance, restore the prince to the throne, and establish a constitutional monarchy. Afterward, the league planned to form a national assembly that would unite all Vietnamese nationalists and organize elections.[50] Cường Để's partisans formed a branch in Saigon and successfully recruited two religious mass movements to join the party.[51]

The older and larger of these mass movements was the Cao Đài religion, founded in 1926 by a coterie of colonial civil servants in Tây Ninh province. The founders claimed to combine Buddhism, Confucianism, Daoism, Christianity, and local spiritual traditions into a single syncretic faith.[52] Cao Đài dignitaries organized their ecclesiastical hierarchy based on the model of the Catholic church and acted as spirit mediums to receive messages from the divine. One of the earliest such messages prophesied that the faith was destined to become the national religion (*quốc đạo*). The dignitaries drew on this message in their attempt to unite the nation under the Cao Đài banner. For them, the Cao Đài faith was the only indigenous Vietnamese religion and therefore uniquely capable of liberating the country from its dependence on foreign faiths. The religion would provide a spiritual foundation in the struggle to recover national sovereignty, the dignitaries believed.[53]

22   Chapter 1

The Cao Đài religion spread rapidly throughout southern and south-central Vietnam and boasted between half a million and a million adepts by the end of World War II.[54] Division went hand in hand with growth, and the faith splintered into multiple autonomous sects, each with its own Holy See. The Tây Ninh branch was the largest and most politically active. Its head spirit medium Phạm Công Tắc rose into the leadership of the Holy See in 1935 and led his followers to support Prince Cường Để. Tắc was a lifelong nationalist who had once planned to study in Japan under Phan Bội Châu's mentorship. Now, Tắc and other dignitaries hoped to serve in the prince's future court and use their position to propagate their faith throughout the country.[55] But Tắc's activism aroused French suspicion. In 1942, the colonial authorities raided the Holy See and sent him to prison in Madagascar.[56] Such heavy-handed measures on the part of the French provided a political opportunity for the Japanese, and the latter sought out Tắc's interim successor Trần Quang Vinh and convinced Vinh to join Cường Để's party.[57]

The second religious group to cooperate with the Japanese was the Hòa Hảo Buddhists. A charismatic young peasant named Huỳnh Phú Sổ had established the reformed Buddhist sect in his native village of Hòa Hảo, Châu Đốc province, in the Mekong delta in 1939. Sổ astonished his family and neighbors one day when he claimed to be a messenger of the Buddha and offered an impromptu religious lecture.[58] The young prophet developed a simplified version of Mahayana Buddhism that was based on a local millenarian tradition. Within a few years, the faith attracted hundreds of thousands of adepts in the upper delta and became politicized.[59] One of the core concepts of Hòa Hảo Buddhism was the Four Gratitudes (Tứ Ân), including gratitude to one's compatriots.[60] Sổ elaborated on the idea of compatriots to argue that the Vietnamese people were an ethnically defined nation with a collective responsibility for the fate of the country.[61] The prophet's popularity alarmed colonial officials, and they placed him under detention for fear that the religious movement might turn seditious.[62] In 1942, Sổ's associates conspired with the Japanese to kidnap him from the French, and he eventually agreed to support Cường Để.[63]

For a time, the prince's party and the religious groups benefited from their collaboration with the occupiers. The Japanese provided these nationalists with a certain degree of protection, which shielded them from the full brunt of French repression and enabled them to increase their size and form their own armies. The Cao Đài and Hòa Hảo also raised funds for the prince's party in anticipation of his assumption of national leadership.[64] But an unexpected turn of events prompted the pro-Japanese nationalists to question their support for the wartime occupation. On March 9, 1945, the Japanese overthrew the French in a lightning military coup. Much to the dismay of the Cao Đài and Hòa Hảo, the occupiers refused to grant Vietnam genuine independence and instead set up a client state called the Empire of Vietnam. The Japanese shunted aside Cường Để and chose the reigning, French-appointed King Bảo Đại to be the emperor.

Yet the revolutionaries felt that independence was within their grasp. They realized that Japan would lose the war and that a brief power vacuum would fill the interval between the surrender of Tokyo and the arrival of the Allies. The revolutionaries hoped to take advantage of this window to finally liberate Vietnam from foreign rule. The prospect of independence intensified the competition between the revolutionaries, and they vied against each other to assert their place in Vietnam's future political order. The Việt Minh was the strongest contender because it was more organized and operated on a national scale. In comparison, the Đại Việt party was just starting to expand beyond the north, the VNP was strong only in southern China, and the influence of the religious groups and the Trotskyists was confined mainly to the south.[65] Yet the Cao Đài and Hòa Hảo dwarfed all other groups in size and were serious contenders in the political landscape of southern Vietnam.

A REVOLUTION IN AUGUST

When Japan surrendered on August 15, 1945, the revolutionaries scrambled to seize power. The Việt Minh was the swiftest to act. The communist-led front captured Hanoi on August 19 as the VNP and the Đại Việt party floundered due to weak discipline and internal disagreements.[66] In the south, several groups—including the Cao Đài, the Hòa Hảo, a Japanese-sponsored youth group, and possibly some Trotskyist elements—formed a coalition under the aegis of the Empire of Vietnam.[67] The coalition organized a popular demonstration in Saigon in favor of independence and prepared to coordinate an armed struggle.[68] But the Việt Minh chose a more aggressive approach. Trần Văn Giàu, the leader of the southern Việt Minh, fractured the coalition by engineering the defection of the youth group, and the front captured Saigon on August 25.[69] The Việt Minh now controlled both northern and southern Vietnam and was poised to form a national government. The ascent of the front raised questions that the incipient state and every subsequent Vietnamese regime faced: How should the dominant party manage the political diversity of the revolutionary movement? Should the government incorporate rivals to represent the heterogeneity of Vietnamese society or sideline them to prevent dissension? Communist leaders clearly preferred the latter option. On establishing control over Saigon, Trần Văn Giàu announced a provisional regional government composed exclusively of members of the ICP and communist sympathizers.[70] On September 2, Hồ Chí Minh formally declared the independence of the Democratic Republic of Vietnam (DRV) to much fanfare in Hanoi. He introduced a cabinet that excluded the anticommunist parties entirely, though he did give some portfolios to individual noncommunists.

24   Chapter 1

The August Revolution, as the front's seizure of power became known, inspired a groundswell of popular support for the Việt Minh. Thousands of Vietnamese joined the front out of patriotic fervor. Few people knew or cared that the leaders of the Việt Minh were communist. The new adherents came from many segments of society, including peasants, rural elites, middle-class intellectuals, colonial soldiers, and government officials. Among the groups that threw their support behind the Việt Minh was the Bình Xuyên. The Bình Xuyên was an umbrella name for an array of criminal bands that emerged in the 1930s and 1940s on the southern and southwestern margins of Saigon. In 1945, Trần Văn Giàu recruited hundreds of the outlaws to join the Việt Minh, and they chose the name of a local village as their moniker. The criminals organized themselves into a loose confederation and fought for the communist-led front after the August Revolution.[71] Another large group that supported the Việt Minh was made up of Catholics in the dioceses of Bùi Chú and Phát Diệm, located in northern Vietnam in the lower Red River delta near the coast. Almost half of the country's Catholic minority resided in the twin dioceses. Vietnamese Catholic nationalism had grown out of a popular desire to establish a national church led by a native clergy, and this impulse translated into support for an independent national state.[72] After the August Revolution, Vietnamese bishops expressed support for the DRV in a series of open letters to the pope and Christians around the world, and the Việt Minh appointed Bishop Lê Hữu Từ of Phát Diệm to be the supreme counselor of the new government.[73]

If popular patriotism represented one face of the revolution, then internecine violence was the other. In mid-August, the Việt Minh murdered Tạ Thu Thâu, a gifted Trotskyist orator and labor leader, as he traveled through Quảng Ngãi province in central Vietnam on his way home to the south.[74] In early September, the DRV outlawed the Đại Việt party and arrested large numbers of partisans belonging to the Đại Việt, the VNP, and several smaller anticommunist parties.[75] The conflict was especially intense in the south. Trần Văn Giàu outraged the Hòa Hảo Buddhists when he shut them out from the provisional regional government, and his followers often excluded Hòa Hảo elements from the DRV's local administration in the Mekong delta. The religious adepts demanded that the Việt Minh share power, and skirmishes erupted between the two groups in several delta provinces. The bloodiest confrontation took place in the city of Cần Thơ, where more than fifteen thousand Hòa Hảo adepts demonstrated against the communist-dominated local government. Việt Minh forces opened fire on the crowd and later executed three captured leaders from the demonstration. Back in Saigon, Giàu's agents almost succeeded in arresting Huỳnh Phú Sổ.[76] But the religious group refused to accept defeat, and several Hòa Hảo commanders retaliated by massacring Việt Minh supporters.[77] The front also continued to target the Trotskyists. The Việt Minh stormed Trotskyist meetings in Saigon, arrested

Birth of Anticommunist Nationalism 25

suspected Trotskyists, and assassinated selected leaders, possibly because some Trotskyists had participated in the Hòa Hảo uprising.[78] The campaign eliminated the Trotskyists as a political force, and Vietnamese communism was thereafter synonymous with the ICP and its successor, the Vietnamese Labor Party.

The incident in Cần Thơ alarmed the leaders of the DRV in Hanoi, who hastily instructed Giàu to incorporate the religious groups into the regional government for fear that the fledgling state would crumble in the south. Giàu dutifully formed a regional coalition government on September 10 consisting of the Tây Ninh branch of the Cao Đài, the Hòa Hảo, and the Việt Minh, but the suspicious allies insisted on maintaining their own armies.

"WE MUST RID OURSELVES OF PARTISANSHIP": THE SCHISM IN THE NORTH

For Vietnamese who lived through the tumultuous decades of the mid-twentieth century, the August Revolution ushered in a distinct period known as the Anti-French Resistance. Western scholars call the same conflict the First Indochina War (1946–1954) to refer to the war between the DRV and France, but the Vietnamese term is more expansive in depicting the Resistance as a coherent period that began with the declaration of independence in September 1945, more than a year before the formal outbreak of war. The revolutionaries engaged in two simultaneous struggles during the Resistance: the fight for independence and the contest to prevail against political rivals. The revolutionaries initially prioritized the first struggle and formed broad coalitions to combat the French. But violence soon shattered these coalitions. The Việt Minh's rivals all turned anticommunist, and the rift that first emerged in the 1920s and 1930s turned into a permanent schism, the ICP and the Việt Minh on one side and the remaining revolutionaries on the other. For the rest of the Resistance, the mutually hostile camps faced a two-front conflict against each other as well as the French.

The timing of the schism differed between the north and the south in part because of the decision to divide Vietnam into two occupation zones at the end of World War II. The Allies made the Chinese Nationalists responsible for disarming the Japanese north of the sixteenth parallel. In September 1945, Chinese troops streamed into northern Vietnam, accompanied by the VNP and the Vietnamese Revolutionary League. The anticommunist parties hoped that the Chinese would overthrow Hồ Chí Minh's government and place the returning exiles at the helm of the DRV. The VNP and the VRL installed their troops at strategic locations en route to Hanoi and swept aside the local Việt Minh administration. But the Chinese merely forced Hồ to incorporate the anticommunists into the existing government, and a fragile coalition cabinet emerged in early 1946 with Hồ as president, Nguyễn Hải Thần of the VRL as vice president, and Nguyễn

26   Chapter 1

Tường Tam of the VNP as foreign minister.[79] Tam, better known by his pen name Nhất Linh, was a celebrated novelist who had founded the Self-Reliant Literary Group in the 1930s. He later formed a revolutionary party and merged it with the VNP. The communists dominated the government for the time being, but Hồ still worried about the anticommunist orientation of the Chinese Nationalists and ordered the ICP to publicly announce its self-dissolution to assuage Chinese concerns.[80] In actuality, the party continued to operate clandestinely behind the façade of the Việt Minh.

Meanwhile, the Chinese Nationalists prepared to withdraw their troops. The occupiers feared that the move would precipitate a war between the DRV and France and forced the two sides to accede to a peace agreement. The Preliminary Convention of March 6, 1946, allowed French troops to replace the Chinese and mandated that Paris recognize the DRV as a "free state" within the Indochinese Federation.[81] Although the agreement did not fully explain the last point, French policy envisioned the Indochinese Federation as a modified form of colonial rule. The federation would include the three Vietnamese regions, Cambodia, and Laos as five distinct entities, and each subsidiary state would have a local parliament and army. The federation would join other former French colonies in adhering to the French Union, a new framework to replace the French Empire, and Paris would dictate the federation's diplomacy, defense, and commerce.[82]

The Việt Minh disliked the proposed federation and did not expect the convention to ensure peace. The communists anticipated that they would soon have to fight the French and the anticommunists simultaneously. The leaders of the ICP decided to avoid such a prospect by preemptively attacking their Vietnamese rivals. As the Chinese troops departed in the spring and summer of 1946, the communists launched a campaign to annihilate the other parties. The military of the DRV overran anticommunist bases in the countryside, and Việt Minh agents arrested and assassinated their political enemies. The campaign decimated the anticommunist parties and led to the murder of Đại Việt founder Trương Tử Anh. Several thousand anticommunist partisans perished in northern Vietnam between 1945 and 1947.[83] The fighting tore apart the coalition government and quickened the DRV's transformation into a single-party state.[84]

The beleaguered anticommunists decried the persecution and accused their opponents of divisiveness, a charge that drew on critiques of the ICP dating back to the previous decade. The newspaper of the VNP bemoaned the internecine violence: "How can people of the same blood and ancestry hate each other like that? Can it be that fraternal love and the love of compatriots fade next to faith in an ideology or the interests of one's own organization?" The journal called for national unity (đoàn kết) and argued that different parties should work together for the good of the country: "If we want unity, then we must rid ourselves of partisanship and place the nation above all else."[85] Such pleas failed to stop the

Việt Minh's campaign of violence. The anticommunist partisans who survived the persecution fled to southern China or to the Catholic-dominated area of the Red River delta.[86]

As the coalition government collapsed, friction grew between the Việt Minh and the northern Catholics. The communists tried to recruit the faithful into joining government-sponsored Catholic associations, but Bishop Lê Hữu Từ was wary of any attempt to interfere in religious life.[87] He tried to carve out an independent Catholic zone that could resist Việt Minh influence and arranged for the dioceses of Bùi Chu and Phát Diệm to raise their own troops, similar to the militarization of the Cao Đài and the Hòa Hảo in the south. The weakness of the DRV's authority in the Catholic zone made the area a haven for anticommunist partisans; their presence would later become a source of conflict between the bishop and the DRV.[88]

"A DISGUISED DICTATORSHIP": THE SCHISM IN THE SOUTH

The schism developed very differently in the south. The Allies instructed the British to disarm the Japanese below the sixteenth parallel, and the British arrived in Saigon in mid-September 1945. But unlike the situation farther north, the occupiers of the southern zone refused to recognize the DRV as a legitimate government. Moreover, the British liberated French troops that had been imprisoned by the Japanese and allowed the French to seize Saigon from Trần Văn Giàu's coalition government. The French assault on September 23, 1945, forced the revolutionaries to retreat to the surrounding countryside and sparked an undeclared war between the southern DRV and France. The newly formed French Expeditionary Corps (FEC) arrived a few weeks later. Working closely with the British, the corps retook urban areas and communication routes by early February 1946 and assumed authority over the entire southern zone the following month when the British departed.[89] The sudden onset of war laid bare the latent disagreements within the southern coalition government. Whereas the Việt Minh considered itself the rightful leader of the nationalist resistance and demanded that other groups submit to its authority, the Cao Đài and Hòa Hảo were determined to preserve their military and political autonomy and insisted that the coalition was one between equals. As the disputes intensified, the religious groups realized that they were too weak to defend against both the Việt Minh and the French simultaneously.

Among the many issues that brought the Việt Minh and the Cao Đài into conflict was the question of military centralization. Trần Văn Giàu wanted to unify the south's disparate armed forces and demanded that the Cao Đài troops be integrated into the Việt Minh's. But when the Cao Đài refused, Giàu

28   Chapter 1

summarily arrested the interim religious leader Trần Quang Vinh.[90] Meanwhile, the French experimented with a strategy of encouraging defections, and Giàu's controversial attempt at centralization played into French hands. The colonial police nabbed the entire leadership of the Tây Ninh branch in May 1946, including Trần Quang Vinh, who had escaped from the Việt Minh just a few months before. The head of the police made Vinh an offer: the prisoners could go free if the Cao Đài agreed to ally with the French and fight the communists.[91] Vinh's successive arrests had taught him the danger of a two-front conflict; he reluctantly agreed.[92] The Tây Ninh sect subsequently withdrew from the DRV to enter into a formal military alliance with the French. By the spring of 1947, the tense conflict between the Việt Minh and the Cao Đài had erupted into open warfare.[93]

The escalating violence turned the Cao Đài into fervent anticommunists. The French repatriated the exiled religious leader Phạm Công Tắc as part of the agreement. That fall, Tắc warned his followers in a somewhat melodramatic sermon: "We have in front of us an enemy, an antagonist that has the ability to destroy us: [they are] the communists of the Third International, who have debilitated and destroyed human psychology."[94] In 1947, the Cao Đài formed the Association for the Restoration of Vietnam (Việt Nam Phục Quốc Hội, or ARV) with the express purpose of attracting nationalists of all religious persuasions and siphoning resistance fighters away from the DRV. The ARV appears to have taken inspiration from Cường Để's old party, bearing a similar name to the defunct group and aiming to unite all nationalists, though the ARV never gained a serious following outside the Tây Ninh branch of the faith. The party championed independence, equality between social classes, and democratic freedoms and rights.[95]

The Hòa Hảo was the next major group to leave the DRV over the question of centralization. The reformed Buddhists wanted to maintain some degree of autonomy and authority within the framework of Việt Minh leadership. They demanded control over their own armed units and the inclusion of Hòa Hảo elements in the DRV's administration in the Mekong delta.[96] Local autonomy, though, ran counter to the communists' insistence on a unified resistance. Hanoi recalled Trần Văn Giàu that winter and appointed Nguyễn Bình as commander of the DRV's armed forces in the south. Bình's mission was to bring the different revolutionary forces under his command. In April 1946, he worked with various organizations to establish a coalition that included the Hòa Hảo and the Việt Minh, with Huỳnh Phú Sổ as the chair.[97] But Bình dissolved the group several months later because he feared losing control of the coalition to the Hòa Hảo.[98] Sổ then tried to unify the southern resistance without Bình. In September 1946, the prophet convened a meeting of the noncommunist intellectuals who had participated in the defunct coalition and organized them into the Vietnamese Social Democratic Party (Việt Nam Dân Chủ Xã Hội Đảng, or SDP).[99] The formation of the SDP signaled the determination of the Hòa Hảo to pursue an independent political strategy while remaining within the DRV. Sổ brought to the party a mass following of devoted religious adepts, and the intellectuals provided him with a modern political platform.

The SDP was arguably the most progressive anticommunist party of its time. The Mekong delta had a highly stratified plantation society of wealthy landlords and indigent tenant farmers, and the party adapted European visions of social democracy to address the specific needs of the southern Vietnamese peasantry. The SDP championed a multiparty democracy, a mixed economy with private and state-owned sectors, robust social services for the poor, and labor reforms for peasants and workers.[100] To distinguish the party from the communists, the SDP explicitly rejected class warfare and emphasized the party's adherence to republicanism. Party leaders associated democracy (*dân chủ*) with popular sovereignty and pluralism and obliquely attacked the Việt Minh's attempt to monopolize power. The official newspaper of the SDP, *The Masses* (*Quần chúng*), contended that "It's either the politics of the entire people based on the principle of democracy, or it's single-party politics [*nhứt đảng chánh trị*] which is a disguised dictatorship, but those two policies cannot go together."[101] Like the VNP, the Hòa Hảo-affiliated party defined unity as cooperation between groups and criticized the DRV's coercive centralization. As the newspaper declared, "Unity means preserving all of the existing forces and organizing them into ranks under a single command. . . . Unity does not mean the elimination of individuality. Nor does it mean telling other people to passively follow a single organization."[102]

Huỳnh Phú Sổ tried to patch up relations with the Việt Minh but remained determined to assert Hòa Hảo autonomy. The SDP and the Việt Minh issued a joint statement in February 1947 calling for cooperation, and Sổ traveled to the delta to settle local clashes between the two sides.[103] But at the same time, the SDP sent a delegation headed by Nguyễn Bảo Toàn to China to negotiate with the exiled anticommunists who had fled Việt Minh violence in northern Vietnam.[104] According to French intelligence records, Sổ also discussed the possibility of forming an anticommunist movement with the Bình Xuyên and the Cao Đài and asked the French for weapons to defend the Hòa Hảo from the Việt Minh.[105] The Việt Minh grew suspicious and abruptly arrested and executed Sổ in April.[106] The execution unleashed a surge of violence on all sides. The Hòa Hảo army murdered Việt Minh followers, the latter responded in kind, and casualties quickly climbed into the thousands.[107] Sổ's death turned his followers into diehard anticommunists, and from then on, the reformed Buddhists prioritized defending the faith against the Việt Minh rather than the French. In May 1947,

30   Chapter 1

Hòa Hảo army commander Trần Văn Soái entered into a military alliance with the French, just as the Cao Đài had done a few months earlier.[108]

As the schism provoked violence in the south, tensions escalated between the DRV and France in the north. Paris and Hanoi tried to avoid war by opening talks in the spring of 1946, but successive conferences failed to produce an agreement. Then, on December 19, 1946, the DRV launched a surprise assault on French positions in Hanoi. The attack marked the formal start of war between the two countries. The French Expeditionary Corps counterattacked and recaptured Hanoi, and the DRV's forces withdrew to the countryside, relying on guerilla tactics to fight back. The war spread throughout northern Vietnam, and by 1948, the two sides settled into a stalemate, the French occupying the cities and the DRV controlling rural areas.

ANTICOMMUNIST NATIONALISM AND THE STATE OF VIETNAM

Anticommunist nationalism coalesced into a distinct bloc in the wake of the broken coalitions. Anticommunists across Vietnam increasingly believed that cooperation with the Việt Minh was impossible and worked together to form alliances that excluded the communists. The activists' ultimate objective was to create an alternative Vietnamese state, and many turned to former emperor Bảo Đại to serve as its leader.

In February 1947, leaders of the VRL and VNP who had fled to southern China spearheaded another political front from their temporary base in Nanjing. They invited several southern groups to join the coalition, most notably the Social Democratic Party, and the leadership of the Nanjing front included Nguyễn Hải Thần of the moribund VRL, Nguyễn Tường Tam of the VNP, and Nguyễn Bảo Toàn of the SDP.[109] The front was the first anticommunist alliance to include northern and southern organizations. The multipartisan character of the leadership highlighted a fundamental contrast between the communists and the anticommunists. Whereas the former wanted to subsume differences under the exclusive leadership of the communist party, the latter preferred to incorporate differences into broad alliances in which each member remained autonomous.

In March, the Nanjing front announced plans to form a new Vietnamese government that would rival the DRV and take the form of either a constitutional monarchy or a republic.[110] The declaration made clear that the anticommunists no longer believed in reconciliation with the communists. The Nanjing front appealed to Bảo Đại to head the coalition and sent delegates to Hong Kong, where the former emperor now resided. Bảo Đại had abdicated the throne in support of the Việt Minh during the August Revolution but later grew disillusioned with Hồ Chí Minh's regime. For the anticommunists, the former emperor was a symbol of

Birth of Anticommunist Nationalism   31

Vietnamese unity that transcended political rivalries and a link to the independent Vietnamese kingdom of the precolonial past.

Just as the anticommunists settled on Bảo Đại as their choice for head of state, the French devised a scheme to turn him into a figurehead of the Indochinese Federation. In the spring of 1946, High Commissioner Georges Thierry d'Argenlieu announced the creation of an autonomous republic in southern Vietnam as a first step in creating a federal structure.[111] His successor Émile Bollaert advocated using Bảo Đại as a figurehead to rally Vietnamese support for the French project. In September 1947, Bollaert offered to open negotiations with the former emperor on the question of Vietnamese sovereignty and the anticipated federation.[112] Bảo Đại wanted the advice of his supporters before responding and therefore convened a conference of nationalists in Hong Kong that included the Nanjing front, the VNP, the Đại Việt party, the Cao Đài, the Hòa Hảo, representatives of the autonomous southern republic, and other groups and individuals. The conference split between those who categorically rejected any cooperation with the French and others who favored a negotiated independence.[113] The disagreement eventually led to the collapse of the Nanjing front.[114]

Bảo Đại understood that he and the anticommunists occupied a position of weakness relative to both the DRV and France but he resolved to make the best of a bad situation. He entered negotiations with Bollaert and tried repeatedly to push for full independence only to find that the French would not budge. Long months of frustrating talks culminated in the Élysée Accords of March 8, 1949, which Bảo Đại and French President Vincent Auriol signed. The accords reflected the French vision of modified colonialism rather than the nationalists' dream of independence. The agreement established the State of Vietnam as an associated state within the Indochinese Federation alongside Cambodia and Laos and gave Paris control over the foreign policy, defense, and economic affairs of the associated states. Actual independence would come gradually as the French High Commission transferred public agencies to the SVN based on a timetable yet to be negotiated.[115] Even the nominally independent Vietnamese National Army that formed in 1951 remained under the command of the French Expeditionary Corps. Despite these limitations on sovereignty, Bảo Đại did exercise some meaningful autonomy. He served as chief of state with the authority to appoint the prime minister and expressed public support for the reforms that Vietnamese nationalists had long demanded. On assuming power, he declared that sovereignty belonged to the people and promised to hold elections for a constitutional assembly as soon as conditions permitted.[116] In 1953, the SVN initiated a series of indirect elections for a national assembly, though the government carried out only two of the three scheduled elections and never actually convened an assembly.[117]

32   Chapter 1

MASS DEFECTIONS AND THE RADICALIZATION OF THE DRV

As the anticommunists adopted an increasingly hard-line stance against Hồ Chí Minh's government, changes within the DRV hardened the schism from the communist side. In the late 1940s and early 1950s, a surge of defectors broke away from the communist state in response to internal rivalry and increasingly radical policies. The defectors rejected communism and threw their lot in with the anticommunist nationalists. This peeling away of supporters left behind a dedicated communist core, with the result that Vietnamese communism became politically narrower and more ideologically cohesive. The communists were no more interested in reconciliation than the anticommunists, and intransigence on both sides rendered the schism a permanent division within the revolutionary movement.

Infighting within the Việt Minh led to the defection of the Bình Xuyên in the spring of 1948. Lê Văn Viễn, the Bình Xuyên chief, and Nguyễn Bình, the regional commander of the armed forces, vied for the control of the DRV's underground security apparatus in Saigon and military command in southeastern Vietnam. The jealous Bình attacked the headquarters of the Bình Xuyên in the Sát Jungle, near the mouth of the Saigon River, and assassinated Viễn's closest associates.[118] The gang leader fled to Saigon. Afterward, the embittered Viễn entered into an alliance with the French and rallied to the provisional Vietnamese administration that would become the SVN. He publicly denounced "Nguyễn Bình's dictatorial communist band" and directed his partisans to clear Saigon of underground Việt Minh agents.[119]

Farther north, the Catholics broke away from the DRV over the issue of local autonomy. A long-standing point of contention was the presence of the anticommunist parties in the Catholic zone. Anticommunist partisans had fled to the area a few years earlier to escape Việt Minh repression and had by the late 1940s gradually reconstituted their parties. The parties recruited local Catholics and directed the new members to assassinate Việt Minh agents that dared to wander into the zone. Bishop Lê Hữu Từ proved unable to curb the violence. The DRV responded by arresting thousands of suspected anticommunists over the bishop's objections, an act that directly threatened Catholic autonomy. At the same time, the war between France and the DRV intensified in the lower Red River delta and made it harder for the bishop to shelter his flock. In 1949, he appealed to Bảo Đại for military assistance and reluctantly accepted weapons that French troops delivered in response.[120] As attacks by the DRV made it increasingly difficult to maintain the autonomy of the zone, the bishop gravitated toward the SVN and sided with the anticommunists.

Birth of Anticommunist Nationalism 33

Meanwhile, the DRV was undergoing a process of radicalization that triggered an even larger wave of defections. During the early years of the Resistance, the communists had downplayed their leadership of the government as well as the Việt Minh and had concealed the party's social revolutionary agenda. The communists allowed members of all social classes to join the front and to serve in the state apparatus of the DRV. But, starting in the late 1940s, the party emphasized the importance of class struggle and began preparations for the transition to a socialist state.[121] The change accelerated after October 1949, when the Chinese Communist Party announced the establishment of the People's Republic of China and chased the Chinese Nationalists from the mainland. Hồ Chí Minh now had a friendly government on the DRV's northern border, and the Chinese communists sent a steady stream of advisers, weapons, equipment, and food to the DRV.[122] Strengthened by the assistance, the Vietnamese communist party openly asserted its dominance in 1951. The party reemerged as the Vietnamese Labor Party (Đảng Lao Động Việt Nam) and arranged for the Việt Minh to be absorbed into a different political front. The DRV subsequently launched a Chinese-style rectification campaign (Chin. *zhengfeng,* Viet. *chỉnh huấn*) to indoctrinate party members, soldiers, and government personnel in communist ideology. During the campaign, lower-class individuals received promotions and middle- and upper-class individuals faced demotion, dismissal, or arrest.[123] Perhaps the most radical policy of all was the land reform program, inaugurated in 1953 to redistribute land to poor peasants. The program staged show trials in which communist cadres encouraged peasants to publicly denounce accused landlords, and thousands of convicted landlords lost their land, their freedom, and their lives.[124]

This radicalization provoked widespread disillusionment among wealthier social groups, and thus numerous intellectuals, civil servants, teachers, administrators, and landlords fled to areas controlled by the French and the SVN. The defections took place on such a massive scale that the Vietnamese coined a specific term, *dinh tê,* to describe the action of leaving the resistance areas and entering enemy territory.[125] Some defectors chose to serve the SVN, others joined existing anticommunist groups, and still others supported anticommunist nationalism in principle but withheld their support from any political entity.

The schism within the Vietnamese revolutionary movement coincided with the polarization of global politics. The establishment of the SVN transformed the internecine conflict between the communists and anticommunists from a collection of local conflagrations to a civil war between competing Vietnamese states. Revolutionaries were now fighting for both Hồ Chí Minh's and Bảo Đại's governments. At the same time, the Vietnamese struggle for national liberation took on greater international significance as the Cold War spread to Asia. In 1950, the

34   Chapter 1

superpowers began arranging themselves on either side of the Vietnamese war. The People's Republic of China and the Soviet Union extended diplomatic recognition to the DRV, and the United States and Great Britain recognized the SVN. Equally important, Washington provided military aid to France and, within a few years, was funding more than 80 percent of the French war effort.

ACCOMMODATION AND THE BIG FIVE

The success of the SVN in gaining international recognition could not remedy the regime's domestic shortcomings. Indeed, many anticommunists expressed disappointment that Bảo Đại had failed to obtain genuine independence for Vietnam. For his part, the chief of state was upset to find that the French had no intention of granting the SVN any real autonomy. They merely wanted to use him as a ceremonial figurehead to attract peasant support for the French-sponsored regime. The disillusioned Bảo Đại opted for passive resistance. He refused to play the role of a French puppet and retreated to the resort city of Đà Lạt, where he pursued a lavish lifestyle filled with sport hunting and women. To the disgusted anticommunists, this behavior looked more like dissipation than resistance.[126]

Many activists also saw little to like in the Francophile premiers Bảo Đại appointed. Trần Văn Hữu, the prime minister from 1950 to 1952, reputedly spoke French better than Vietnamese, and his successor Nguyễn Văn Tâm was a French citizen and famously loyal to France.[127] Yet these politicians had their own agendas and were not collaborationist lackeys, as some anticommunists insinuated. The premiers resembled earlier reformers in believing that working with France would facilitate reforms. For example, Tâm favored social and agrarian reforms and organized the indirect elections for a national assembly mentioned earlier.[128] What set men like Tâm and Hữu apart from the anticommunists was that the highest leaders of the SVN had never participated in the armed struggle against France and, in some cases, had helped suppress anticolonial resistance. For this reason, the anticommunists questioned the politicians' commitment to Vietnamese nationalism. Rumors of corruption further undermined the reputation of the SVN's leaders. Tâm was especially notorious for allowing his mistress to use his political connections to further her business interests. When fires erupted in Saigon in the early 1950s, residents gossiped that her henchmen had committed arson to increase the sales of construction materials.[129]

The anticommunists temporarily split over the question of whether to serve the government of the SVN. The most powerful groups favored accommodation with Bảo Đại's state because they wanted to continue the struggle for independence, support France's war against the DRV, and strengthen their own position. The accommodationists included the Cao Đài, the Hòa Hảo, the Bình Xuyên, the northern Catholics, and the northern Đại Việt party. The Western press referred

Birth of Anticommunist Nationalism   35

to them collectively as the Big Five (*cinq grands*), and French officials described the three southern groups as the sects, even though the Bình Xuyên had no religious affiliation. Accommodation came with military advantages that the Big Five deftly exploited. The French Expeditionary Corps recognized the armies of the sects and the northern Catholics as supplementary forces (with independent commands, in some cases), awarding military titles to leaders of the Big Five and offering regular subsidies to defray the cost of fighting the DRV. These funds came out of the substantial military aid that the United States provided France. The subsidies enabled the sects to reach the height of their strength in the first half of the 1950s. Military might in turn gave them political power, and every administration of the SVN had to obtain their loyalty by offering cabinet seats or by consulting them on high-level appointments.

Despite the accommodationists' willingness to work with the SVN, they had an ambivalent relationship with the central government. The sects and the northern Catholics resisted integration into Bảo Đại's regime, just as they had defended their autonomy from the central authority of the DRV. They formed autonomous zones that operated like states-within-a-state, or fiefs, as the French derisively described the zones.[130] These groups taxed the population, recruited young men into the supplementary forces, maintained public order, and administered justice. The Cao Đài and Hòa Hảo zones proved especially successful as miniature states, in part because the religious groups had assumed many public functions even before the August Revolution. Sect leaders encouraged farming and small-scale manufacturing, invested in transportation and infrastructure, established markets and agricultural collectives, built schools and hospitals, and organized charities.[131] Although Cao Đài and Hòa Hảo rule was undemocratic, their zones emerged as oases of peace and prosperity amid the chaos of war. Refugees flocked to the zones and willingly converted to the local faith in exchange for security and employment. By contrast, other groups focused less on community welfare. The Bình Xuyên operated its own zone in western Saigon. Lê Văn Viễn, appointed a general by the FEC, oversaw a vast empire of shipping enterprises, bordellos, opium distilleries, and casinos but funded very few social services for local residents.[132]

Accommodation came with costs as well as benefits. It rendered the Big Five vulnerable to charges of serving French interests and provoked internal dissension. In the case of the Đại Việt party, the group sought political appointments in the government of the SVN rather than military subsidies. A Đại Việt leader twice served as the governor of northern Vietnam, and the party virtually controlled the entire regional administration during both terms.[133] But the decision of northern party leaders to participate in Bảo Đại's government upset other members of the party, and the Đại Việt fragmented into separate regional branches.[134] Similarly, Trần Văn Soái's military agreement with the French in

36   Chapter 1

1947 outraged some Hòa Hảo leaders. The Social Democratic Party severed its ties with him, and several of his subordinates broke away and continued fighting the French.[135] By 1948, at least four armed Hòa Hảo factions were operating in the Mekong delta. These dissident armies eventually submitted to the SVN but never reunified.[136] Cao Đài support for Bảo Đại's government proved similarly divisive, and a splinter group returned to the maquis in 1951, as will be discussed.

ATTENTISME AND THE EMERGENCE OF THE NGÔ ĐÌNH DIỆM FACTION

In contrast to the Big Five, other anticommunists denounced the SVN as a puppet regime and refused to work with the government. The French dismissed such individuals as *attentistes* (fence-sitters); their Vietnamese detractors mocked them as *trùm chăn* (covered with a blanket). The implication was that the *attentistes* were playing a game of wait-and-see before casting their lot with either the SVN or the DRV. Yet *attentisme* was more than just noncooperation with the two governments, and some leaders proposed a different path to independence that steered clear of both communism and collaboration.

The most prominent *attentiste* was the Catholic nationalist Ngô Đình Diệm (figure 1). Diệm was the scion of a mandarin family from central Vietnam and had a reputation for rigid, uncompromising politics. He had served in the imperial bureaucracy in the 1920s and early 1930s but resigned in protest after the French refused to implement reforms. In early 1946, he spurned Hồ Chí Minh's offer of a cabinet post because the Việt Minh had murdered members of the Ngô family. Diệm attended the conference in Hong Kong and supported Bảo Đại in 1947 but distanced himself from the former emperor after the Élysée Accords of 1949 failed to deliver genuine national sovereignty.[137]

That same year, Diệm issued a public declaration explaining his refusal to collaborate with the SVN. He pointed out that the regime's nominal independence fell short of the dominion status that Great Britain granted its former colonies in South Asia and argued that the relationship between France and Vietnam had to be based on equality. He then sketched an alternative vision of an independent Vietnamese state: resistance fighters should lead the country, democratic procedures should be respected, a social revolution was necessary to improve the lives of peasants and workers, and all political leaders should put aside their differences to work for the common good of the nation. Diệm's declaration contained few new ideas, but it was significant for being the clearest public articulation of *attentisme*.[138]

In 1950, Diệm abruptly left Vietnam to avoid assassination by the communists. Although he did not know it at the time, his travels would have profound consequences for his political fortunes. He was accompanied by his elder brother

Birth of Anticommunist Nationalism 37

Figure 1. Ngô Đình Diệm casting his ballot in the presidential elections of 1961 (Everett Collection)

Ngô Đình Thục, an influential bishop in Vĩnh Long province, southern Vietnam. Thục had joined other bishops in signing the open letter in support of the DRV but later turned to *attentisme*. The brothers spent an extended sojourn in the United States, during which Diệm met prominent religious leaders, government officials, and academics, aided in part by Thục's Catholic connections. *Attentisme* made Diệm attractive to American officials because it coincided with the latter's idea of a "third force," that is, nationalist movements that rejected both colonialism and communism during the global wave of decolonization following World War II. Moreover, Diệm presented himself as a progressive reformer who would stimulate economic development in Vietnam and use American aid judiciously. The aspiring leader managed to impress powerful figures such as Supreme Court Justice William Douglas and Senators Mike Mansfield and John F. Kennedy.[139]

Meanwhile, Diệm's second brother Ngô Đình Nhu remained in Vietnam and built a political movement for Diệm (figure 2). Nhu believed that the anticommunist nationalists needed a robust ideology to counter communism; he chose the Catholic philosophy of personalism based on the writing of the French thinker Emmanuel Mounier as the ideological basis for Diệm's movement. Nhu

Figure 2.   Ngô Đình Nhu (AP Images)

and other personalists argued that political systems should be based on communities to nurture the development of the human person within a web of social relationships. Adherents of personalism framed it as a middle way between communism and capitalism. Whereas communism allowed the collective to oppress the individual, and capitalism led to rampant individualism and the atomization of society, personalism fostered the fulfilment of the person within the community. Diệm and the rest of the Ngô clan adopted personalism at Nhu's urging.[140]

The younger Ngô brother organized an anticommunist nationalist group known colloquially as the Ngô Đình Diệm faction (*phe* Ngô Đình Diệm) or the Ngô Đình Diệm group (*nhóm* Ngô Đình Diệm). Its defining characteristic was support for Diệm as the future leader of Vietnam. The Diemist faction originated as an amalgamation of Catholic socialist organizations, labor unions, and study groups that the Ngô brothers and their associates had formed between the 1930s and the early 1950s.[141] In 1953, Nhu assembled the leaders of these groups into the clandestine Revolutionary Personalist Labor Party (Cần Lao Nhân Vị Cách Mạng Đảng, better known as the Cần Lao). The party called for the establishment of an independent state based on both personalism and democracy and favored political pluralism, religious and civil liberties, popular participation in the government, and economic and social welfare programs.[142] Observers have correctly noted that Diệm's closest associates tended to be his relatives and fellow Catholics, due in large part to the penchant of the Ngô clan for using social and familial connections as the basis for political organizing. At no time, though, were Vietnamese Catholics synonymous with the Diemists. The faction was distinct from Bishop Từ's Catholic zone, and several leading Diemists did not share the Ngô family's faith. The Ngô Đình Diệm faction was a small but significant contender in anticommunist politics by the mid-1950s.

Another prominent figure who embodied the *attentiste* quest for a new political path was the Cao Đài general Trình Minh Thế, even though the term *attentisme* usually referred to politicians rather military leaders. General Thế is best known to Western readers as the bandit leader in Graham Greene's novel *The Quiet American,* but the historical figure had a political agenda that his fictional counterpart lacked. Thế was an adept from Tây Ninh province who had joined the sect-affiliated army during World War II and had risen to become an officer.[143] In 1951, he abandoned the Cao Đài army and secretly led his men into the jungle. Thế announced that his dissidence would pave the way for a popular uprising against the communists and the SVN.[144] The rogue general established his own resistance zone in Tây Ninh province along the Vietnamese-Cambodian border and carried out a two-front war against the DRV and the French. His exploits won him considerable admiration from the urban middle class in the south, and he achieved international notoriety in the early 1950s when he masterminded a series of terrorist bombings in Saigon.[145] Neither he nor Diệm managed to inspire a popular movement, but their words and actions presented an alternative to accommodation that would attract more attention in the coming years.

"ALL NATIONALIST POLITICAL PERSUASIONS WILL BE FREE TO FLOURISH": THE IDEALS OF 1953

The year 1953 marked the beginning of a new chapter in the history of anticommunist nationalism. Accommodationists and *attentistes* came together once again, articulating a shared set of ideals and forming another coalition. The impetus for the endeavor was France's unilateral decision in May to lower the official exchange rate between the franc and the Indochinese piaster. The piaster was overvalued during the Resistance, and many French and Vietnamese speculators enriched themselves by trafficking in francs, dollars, and piasters.[146] But the French high commissioner failed to confer with the SVN in violation of its legal right to consultations on economic affairs.[147] The devaluation came as an economic and political shock: it doubled the price of food and commodities, forced the Vietnamese government to reduce expenditures, and gave the lie to French claims of respecting Vietnamese national autonomy.[148] The crisis was a

40   Chapter 1

lightning rod for political frustrations with the SVN. Bishop Lê Hữu Từ demanded the abrogation of the Élysée Accords and urged Bảo Đại to grant Vietnam a constitution. The Cao Đài religious leader Phạm Công Tắc pushed for a new treaty with France that would ensure complete independence and called for elections to form a national assembly.[149] French Prime Minister Joseph Laniel tried to mollify the anticommunists by announcing that France would transfer the remaining government agencies to the SVN, and Chief of State Bảo Đại declared that he would soon travel to Paris to discuss the matter.[150] The anticommunists realized that the negotiations in Paris could finally grant the SVN full independence, but in the wake of the devaluation, the activists had little confidence in Laniel's and Bảo Đại's promises.

The anticommunists seized the opportunity to push for political reform and immediate independence. In July, several groups met in Saigon and resolved to hold a political conference to prepare for a national assembly and the formation of a national coalition government.[151] They planned to call for ending corruption, drafting a constitutional charter, and granting freedom of the press and of association.[152] The organizing committee included both accommodationists and *attentistes* and publicly declared that the meeting would unite all anticommunists in order to achieve independence.[153] The much awaited Unity Congress (Đại Hội Đoàn Kết) opened on September 6, 1953, at the headquarters of the Bình Xuyên. The attendees included the Big Five, the VNP, the Diemists, various branches of the Đại Việt party, and numerous unaffiliated individuals. Even the guerilla general Trình Minh Thế sent a representative.[154] On the eve of the meeting, the organizers issued an Appeal to the People that decried the absence of democracy in the SVN: "Even today, in Southeast Asia, when all countries enjoy independence under the direction of leaders elected by their people, Vietnam remains the only country in which compatriots continue to be oppressed and in which the people still await direct participation in the management of national affairs."[155]

Despite the professed unity, the meeting quickly split between the *attentistes* and the accommodationists, and the accommodationist Lê Văn Viễn evicted the conference from his headquarters when the *attentistes* gained the upper hand. The participants hastily regrouped at a nearby facility belonging to the Cao Đài political party.[156] Over the course of the deliberations, the congress repeatedly affirmed the necessity of uniting all nationalists in order to achieve independence, and the meeting concluded with the formation of the Movement for Unity and Peace (Phong Trào Đại Đoàn Kết và Hòa Bình, or MUP).[157] Nhu emerged as a leader of the coalition, and his journal *Society (Xã hội)* defined the objectives of the MUP as the union of all anticommunist nationalists within a pluralistic democracy. The journal explained the goal in terms that resembled the agenda of the Cần Lao party: "To come together with the determination to construct a

Birth of Anticommunist Nationalism   41

[political] system for the homeland, [a system] in which all nationalist political persuasions will be free to flourish and the entire people will directly participate in national affairs." *Society* then specified that the preferred system would be a democracy capable of protecting national interests. The journal insisted that the anticommunists refrain from political violence among themselves. "All those who have accepted the program and the objective of the Movement for Unity must jettison private views and interests and purge partisan tendencies [such as] attacking each other or using one's power to oppress fellow nationalists who have different inclinations," the journal admonished.[158] The MUP eventually included the Cao Đài, the Diemists, the Đại Việt party, and possibly a minor Hòa Hảo faction, but the Bình Xuyên and General Trần Văn Soái's faction of the Hòa Hảo opposed the coalition.[159]

The liberal demands of the Unity Congress alarmed Bảo Đại, and he hastily organized the National Congress (Đại Hội Toàn Quốc) to neutralize the *attentistes*.[160] The Big Five and representatives of the SVN's municipal and rural administration dominated this second meeting; *attentiste* participation was not significant.[161] Yet this meeting proved similarly liberal. It called for full independence, argued that the SVN should not remain in the French Union in its present form, and insisted on the abrogation of the Élysée Accords and all previous treaties with France. Echoing the MUP's call for democracy, the final resolution demanded that all future treaties had to be ratified by a national assembly chosen through popular elections.[162]

The successive congresses revealed that the anticommunists had the same basic vision for the political future of Vietnam despite their factional struggles. The vision drew on ideas from republican nationalism and spoke to the last decade of failure and disappointment. The many broken alliances with the Việt Minh in the mid-1940s convinced the anticommunists of the danger of single-party rule. The activists therefore affirmed the importance of unity and defined it as coalition-building or a coalition government based on cooperation between groups. The dependency of the SVN on France throughout the early 1950s demonstrated the ineffectualness of reformism, and the accommodationists joined with the *attentistes* in insisting on immediate and total independence. Moreover, the regime never made good on Bảo Đại's promise to form a national assembly and remained an unpopular, authoritarian government that failed to guarantee even basic freedoms. For the anticommunists, the answer to these manifold problems was a democratic system that would incorporate diverse groups and reflect the national will. These ideals—unity, independence, and democracy—dated to the early twentieth century, but it was recent experiences that gave the vision particular urgency.

Still, the congresses left many questions unresolved. They did not explain how the SVN could achieve lasting independence given its military dependence

42 Chapter 1

on France. The Vietnamese National Army was not yet capable of taking over the war effort, and the regime remained vulnerable to attacks by the DRV. Another issue was whether a government based on the principle of national unity would incorporate the communists. Large sectors of the population still supported the communists, and any genuinely representative government would have to include them in some way. Last, the anticommunists offered few specific details regarding what type of democratic system they preferred or how they planned to transition to a democracy. These issues would trouble the SVN in the future.

AN ANTICOMMUNIST NATIONALIST FOR THE PREMIERSHIP

The anticommunists launched a vigorous campaign of political opposition following the congresses. In November 1953, the MUP urged Bảo Đại to purge collaborators from the administration. The group also pushed the chief of state to establish a unity government (*gouvernement d'union*) composed of anticommunist nationalists and form a provisional national assembly.[163] In response, the chief of state dismissed Nguyễn Văn Tâm later that year and appointed a royal relative, Prince Bửu Lộc, to the premiership for the duration of the independence negotiations in Paris.[164] But when Bửu Lộc failed to convene the unity government the MUP desired, the group pressed the prince to grant cabinet posts to coalition members and sent a brief to Paris complaining that he did not represent the Vietnamese people.[165] At this juncture, France announced that it intended to negotiate a peace settlement with the DRV at an upcoming international conference in Geneva. France, the United States, Great Britain, and the Soviet Union—the so-called Four Powers that had emerged victorious at the end of World War II—would host the conference. Bảo Đại now needed the anticommunists' support for peace talks in Geneva and independence negotiations in Paris. The overwhelmed chief of state assented to a national assembly on condition that he could appoint one-third of the seats.[166] He then left for Paris in April 1954 to participate in the negotiations.[167]

Bảo Đại regarded Bửu Lộc's cabinet as a caretaker government and began contemplating a successor. The chief of state understood that the next prime minister had to command the loyalty of the anticommunists or risk their continued opposition. The top contender for the position was Ngô Đình Diệm, who was now living in Europe. The MUP had catapulted Diệm and Nhu to the forefront of anticommunist politics and demonstrated that the Ngô brothers could secure the cooperation of fellow activists. Other leading candidates included Nguyễn Tôn Hoàn, the southern Đại Việt chief, and Phan Huy Quát, the longest-serving defense minister of the SVN and a leader of the northern Đại Việt party.

Birth of Anticommunist Nationalism   43

A series of diplomatic and military developments boosted Diệm's candidacy in Bảo Đại's eyes. At the time, the chief of state and the anticommunists harbored deep suspicions about French intentions at Geneva.[168] Rumors spread that France would partition Vietnam as the basis for a ceasefire, and false reports circulated that Paris was secretly negotiating with the DRV.[169] On April 25, the day before the Geneva Conference opened, an indignant Bảo Đại flatly refused to sign the treaties on independence. He denounced the partition of his country, asserted that the negotiations with the DRV would be a violation of Vietnamese sovereignty, and insisted that his government needed full assurances of its independence and territorial unity before finalizing the treaties.[170] Back in Vietnam, the SVN and anticommunist groups organized large demonstrations in cities and towns across the country to protest the anticipated partition.[171]

Meanwhile, other events convinced Bảo Đại that the SVN should look to the United States rather than France as a patron. In mid-March, the final battle between the DRV and France commenced at the remote garrison of Điện Biên Phủ in the mountainous northwestern corner of Vietnam. French troops endured weeks of relentless bombardment by the DRV until finally surrendering in early May. The defeat must have raised serious doubts in Bảo Đại's mind as to whether France was even capable of defending the SVN. The proceedings at the Geneva Conference confirmed his worst suspicions. On May 12, the delegation of the SVN presented a peace plan in which the United Nations would oversee elections for a democratic government under Bảo Đại and the DRV's troops would integrate into the army of the SVN.[172] The proposal was utterly unrealistic given the military superiority of Hồ Chí Minh's government relative to Bảo Đại's regime. Nevertheless, the chief of state could not help but notice that the United States was alone among the Western powers to endorse his government's position. The moment was a painful realization. "We could no longer count on France. At Geneva, the Americans remained our only allies," Bảo Đại later recalled ruefully.[173]

This pivot toward the United States likely prompted Bảo Đại to select Ngô Đình Diệm rather than alternative candidates for the premiership. Although Diệm did not command a mass following, he met several important criteria. The chief of state believed that Diệm enjoyed strong support from the anticommunists and that Diệm's *attentisme* appealed to the population. Moreover, Diệm was one of the few nationalists who had lived in the United States and could boast connections to prominent Americans, and Bảo Đại felt that the selection of Diệm would enhance the likelihood of US support. Last, a personal connection may have facilitated the former emperor's decision. Bảo Đại had a long history of friendship with Diệm's youngest brother, Ngô Đình Luyện, and asked Luyện to be the personal representative of the chief of state at the Geneva Conference.[174] Luyện undoubtedly took advantage of the position to promote Diệm's candidacy.

44   Chapter 1

In mid-May 1954, Bảo Đại offered Diệm the premiership and granted the incoming premier "full powers" (*toàn quyền*) over the SVN, including authority over government agencies that would not be transferred from French custodianship until a year later. The following month, outgoing Prime Minister Bửu Lộc agreed to the long-awaited treaty on independence, Diệm returned to Vietnam to take up his new position, and Bảo Đại stayed in Cannes to enjoy the creature comforts of the French Riviera.[175]

The appointment was a victory for the Diemist faction and, to a certain extent, the anticommunists more generally. One of their own had finally ascended to the highest executive office of the SVN, and Diệm's tenure promised to be a sharp break with the Francophile governments that had preceded him. The anticommunists had reason to feel cautiously optimistic despite the ongoing military crisis in northern Vietnam and the impending partition of the country. Many shared the Ngô brothers' political ideals as the MUP enunciated them, and the power of the premiership meant that Diệm was far better positioned to form an enduring coalition than those who had tried before. Some activists even welcomed the opportunity to work with the uncompromising *attentiste*.[176] It remained to be seen whether Diệm's administration would finally satisfy their dream of a united, pluralistic, and democratic republic.

CHAPTER TWO

Quest for National Unity, 1954–1955

The sound of gunfire punctured the stillness of the noonday siesta on April 28, 1955. Residents of the Chợlớn neighborhood of Saigon looked out their windows to see shells raining down near the Y-Shaped Bridge, close to the headquarters of General Lê Văn Viễn's Bình Xuyên gang. Soon afterward, another round of shells originating from the vicinity of the bridge flew through the air toward the official residence of Premier Ngô Đình Diệm. For weeks, tensions had escalated between the Bình Xuyên and Diệm's government. Now these volleys became sparks in the tinderbox of Vietnamese politics, setting off conflagrations that were not easily extinguishable. Pitched fighting erupted near the Y-Shaped Bridge and along Trần Hưng Đạo Boulevard that afternoon. The Bình Xuyên attacked the headquarters of the police and army in Chợlớn and pressed eastward toward downtown Saigon. Diệm called in paratroopers to defend strategic locations and to block the gang from entering the heart of the city. Outmatched, the gang seized the campus of a local secondary school and fired at any military vehicle that approached.[1]

The outbreak of the Battle of Saigon seemed to reveal the hollowness of the promises that both the Ngô Đình Diệm faction and the Bình Xuyên had made to respect national unity just two years earlier. Indeed, anticommunists of all stripes had repeatedly affirmed their commitment to cooperation and unity. Yet, paradoxically, the idea of unity lay at the root of the long simmering conflict that led to the bloody battle. Although the anticommunists still embraced the ideals put forth during the congresses of 1953, leaders interpreted unity in starkly different ways and debated the range of groups and individuals that should participate in the government. Most groups understood unity to mean political pluralism and a national union government. Diệm and his faction championed a populist

45

46   Chapter 2

understanding of unity and preferred an administration composed of loyal followers. The anticommunists also struggled with the difficult process of political and military centralization. Diệm and his rivals agreed that Vietnam needed a unitary system of government and a unified military. He expected them to give up their armies and territories but turned a deaf ear to their demands for compromise.

The failure to reach an agreement on these issues provoked a succession of crises. First, the southern sects conspired against the premier and pressured him into forming a coalition government in the fall of 1954. Then the central regional branches of the Đại Việt party and the Vietnamese Nationalist Party (VNP) seceded from the State of Vietnam (SVN) that winter, and Diệm's government went to war against the Bình Xuyên the following spring. Although the premier triumphed over his many challengers, the victory destroyed any possibility of achieving a genuine national union. These conflicts triggered a new political schism that gradually split the anticommunists into supporters and opponents of the government.

The premier's early struggles against his rivals is well-trodden territory in the historiography of the Vietnam War, but a reluctance to take those rivals seriously has precluded a deeper understanding of what they aimed to achieve. Most historians have depicted the premier's sectarian challengers as opportunists who hankered for power rather than as shrewd actors with distinct political objectives. Moreover, academic accounts have typically focused on southern Vietnam and ignored the Diemists' rivals in the central region.[2] But as this chapter makes clear, the anticommunists were serious leaders who disagreed on issues such as the composition of the government, military integration, and political centralization, and the events in central Vietnam were integral to the larger rupture within anticommunist nationalism.

CAST OF CHARACTERS

The seven major anticommunist nationalist groups in the SVN at the twilight of the Anti-French Resistance were the Ngô Đình Diệm faction, the three southern sects, the northern Catholics, the Đại Việt Nationalist Party, and the Vietnamese Nationalist Party (see table 1.1).

The Diemists

The small and weak Diemist faction was on the ascent thanks to Diệm's appointment to the premiership. The group's most important leaders were the brothers of the premier designate, especially Ngô Đình Nhu and Ngô Đình Cẩn, who served as Diệm's political advisers. Nhu was the faction's main ideologue as well as the leader of the southern wing of the secret Diemist party, the

Cần Lao. At the time, Nhu's branch of the party included two subgroups.[3] The first was the Spirit Group, a cluster of anticommunist intellectuals and professionals associated with the journal *Spirit* (*Tinh thần*). Nhu met the group in the late 1940s through his wife's uncle, Trần Văn Đỗ, the *attentiste* political director of the journal. Đỗ and his colleagues appeared to have joined the Cần Lao because they were attracted to personalism as a humanistic and political philosophy.[4] The other subgroup consisted of labor leaders, most notably Trần Quốc Bửu, the chief of Vietnam's largest union, the Vietnamese Confederation of Christian Laborers (Tổng Liên Đoàn Lao Công Việt Nam). Bửu likely joined the Cần Lao party because his commitment to trade unionism dovetailed with Nhu's interest in French syndicalism. The labor chief was an anticommunist nationalist from south-central Vietnam who had fought in the Cao Đài army during the early years of the Resistance. He never converted to the faith and later left the maquis. Bửu founded a labor union in 1948 in partnership with a French customs officer, and the group affiliated with the Christian International, a Catholic labor federation based in Europe, though Bửu and most of the rank-and-file were not Catholic.[5] By the mid-1950s, the union had expanded into urban areas throughout the country and counted as many as forty-five thousand members.[6]

Diệm's fourth brother, Ngô Đình Cẩn, led a separate branch of the Diemist faction in central Vietnam. Cẩn had dabbled in political organizing as early as the 1930s but remained in his native village near Huế to care for his elderly mother when the other brothers left home. He and his partisans emerged as a regional locus of Catholic and anticommunist nationalism following the radicalization of the Democratic Republic of Vietnam (DRV). Many of his followers were Catholic activists and Việt Minh defectors from the surrounding provinces who had fled to Huế and other regional cities to escape arrest by Hồ Chí Minh's government.[7] Cẩn also drew on the Ngô family's ties with regional elites and the rural gentry. Fed by these many sources, he built an autonomous wing of the Cần Lao party that was larger, better organized, and more unswervingly loyal than Nhu's.[8] One of Diệm's first administrative acts was to name Cẩn's partisan Nguyễn Đôn Duyến to be the government's regional delegate (*đại biểu chính phủ*) in central Vietnam, a supervisory role that replaced the previously powerful position of regional governor. Duyến happily served as a façade for his patron, and Cẩn reportedly grew so strong during Diệm's tenure that no government official could serve in the region without his approval.[9]

A small, northern branch of the Cần Lao party rounded out the Diemist faction. A Catholic lawyer named Trần Trung Dung led the Hanoi-based group. Dung had joined the Đại Việt party after the August Revolution and participated briefly in the National Assembly of Hồ Chí Minh's coalition government in 1946. The lawyer later left his party to become one of Diệm's earliest devotees. Dung

48   Chapter 2

spent the next decade organizing Catholic socialist groups in northern Vietnam and popularizing Diệm's ideas in newspapers.[10]

The Sects

The Diemists could not yet match the size and military might of the southern sects. The Cao Đài, Hòa Hảo, and Bình Xuyên collectively commanded tens of thousands of troops, and as many as a million Vietnamese lived under their control (see map 2).[11] The sects had formed political parties and enjoyed the advice of educated intellectuals from nonsectarian backgrounds. The largest and strongest of the sect factions was the Tây Ninh branch of the Cao Đài faith, though the branch was divided between two centers of power: the religious hierarchy led by Phạm Công Tắc and the politico-military wing headed by General Nguyễn Thành Phương. Tắc enjoyed unparalleled moral authority within the faith, and thousands of adepts revered the sexagenarian as a holy man. Phương had an alternate power base in the sect's army and political party. The middle-aged soldier was a native of Cần Thơ province and had served in the Cao Đài army since its inception. He rose through the ranks to become the commander of the army in 1953 and had some ten thousand men at his disposal (up to thirty thousand, according to some estimates). He also harbored political aspirations. He took over the main Cao Đài political party, the Association for the Restoration of Vietnam (ARV), in 1952 and helped organize the Movement for Unity and Peace (MUP) the following year.[12] By 1954, the platform of the party had expanded to favor land reform and anti-vice policies, and the ARV opposed what it considered the twin evils of communism and corruption.[13] The party claimed to have as many six hundred thousand followers.[14]

The Cao Đài splinter group led by General Trình Minh Thế was much smaller than the main branch. The brash, young Thế ruled over a resistance zone headquartered on Bà Đen Mountain (known to the Americans as Black Virgin Mountain), about ten kilometers from the provincial capital of Tây Ninh. His guerilla band of a few thousand men was grandiosely styled the National Alliance Army (Quân Đội Quốc Gia Liên Minh). In 1951, Thế founded a political party called the National Resistance Front (Mặt Trận Quốc Gia Kháng Chiến, or NRF), though little is known about its politics. The party championed democratization, the improvement of living standards, and the creation of a more egalitarian society. It also rejected monarchism and opposed French colonialism, communism, and Bảo Đại.[15] Thế remained in the maquis in the summer of 1954, though he was rumored to be in contact with the main Cao Đài army.

The Hòa Hảo Buddhists were the second largest sect and the most internally divided. The father of the deceased prophet Huỳnh Phú Sổ was the widely recognized religious leader, but the sect was fragmented militarily and politically. The Hòa Hảo armed forces had split into four autonomous armies, totaling between

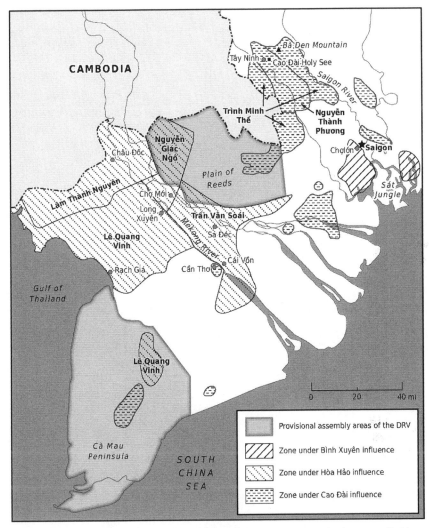

Map 2. Southern Vietnam, circa 1955, showing the approximate territories controlled by the sects and the provisional assembly areas of the DRV as mandated by the Geneva Accords (map by Erin Greb)

eight thousand and 12,500 soldiers.[16] A different general commanded each army, and former members of the nearly defunct Social Democratic Party (SDP) advised the competing military leaders. The original commander General Trần Văn Soái continued to lead its main branch. Soái was an aging, illiterate man better known by his nickname of Fiery Five (Năm Lửa). The number five likely

50   Chapter 2

referred to Soái's birth order within his natal family, in accordance with southern Vietnamese naming customs. Soái's forces were based in Cái Vồn, just across the river from city of Cần Thơ, and he presided over a large and prosperous autonomous zone in the central Mekong delta.

The remaining Hòa Hảo generals had started out as Soái's officers but abandoned him after he rallied to the French. Soái's former lieutenant Lâm Thành Nguyên commanded the second largest armed faction and controlled a stretch of land that extended westward from the mountains of Châu Đốc near the Cambodian border.[17] Soái's one-time political commissar, Nguyễn Giác Ngộ (real name, Nguyễn Văn Ngượt), led another armed group based in Ngộ's native district of Chợ Mới, Long Xuyên province, which doubled as the seat of his autonomous zone.[18] Ngộ was a former warrant officer who renamed himself Nguyễn the Enlightened on converting to Hòa Hảo Buddhism.[19] He had given up the soldier's life after the death of Huỳnh Phú Sổ, but the prophet's father pleaded with Ngộ to form a new Hòa Hảo army after the original one splintered.[20] The young tenant farmer Lê Quang Vinh led the smallest faction, and his men were scattered in the western delta. Vinh was better known as Stumpy Three (Ba Cụt) because he had allegedly chopped off one of his fingers to demonstrate his courage.[21] All four Hòa Hảo armies had agreed to become supplementary forces for the French Expeditionary Corps, but Vinh defected and rallied several times during the late years of the war, ostensibly because he found each administration of the SVN to be insufficiently nationalist. His latest rally to the regime was in early 1954.[22]

The Bình Xuyên led by General Lê Văn Viễn was the smallest and wealthiest of the sects. By the end of the war, Viễn was better known for his decadence and ruthlessness than his exploits in the Resistance. He controlled the lucrative vice trade in Saigon, and his most prized possession was the Grand Monde, a huge casino in the Chinese neighborhood of Chợlớn and reputedly the largest gambling house in Asia. The Grand Monde was a concession that belonged to the SVN, and in 1950, Bảo Đại granted the right to operate the Grand Monde to Viễn in exchange for a handsome payment.[23] Viễn's wealth enabled him to maintain an army of some two thousand men largely at his own expense. Unlike the Hòa Hảo and Cao Đài generals, he received a small subsidy from the government and none from the French.[24] The Bình Xuyên occupied strategic locations close to the seat of power in Saigon, including Chợlớn, the river route between the Saigon and the sea, and a handful of smaller outposts. The gang was less politically developed than the other sects and did not form a political arm until Viễn took over the obscure government-sponsored Popular Front (Mặt Trận Bình Dân) in 1953.[25] Yet Viễn did exercise political influence by offering his support and paying bribes to government officials. In the spring of 1954, the gang leader persuaded Bảo Đại to appoint Viễn's adviser Lại Văn Sang to become the director of the National Police and Security Service in a secret financial arrangement.[26] The security service (Fr. *sûreté,* Viet. *công an*) was the successor to the colonial security service and operated as both a political police and an investigative unit. Viễn and Sang subsequently purged officers disloyal to the Bình Xuyên and filled the vacancies with the gang's shock police, set apart by their distinctive green berets.[27] Although other sect leaders were open to working with Diệm's faction, relations between Viễn and the incoming premier were bad from the start. Viễn's extreme accommodationist stance clashed with the Ngô brothers' *attentisme,* and Nhu had championed the MUP while the kingpin opposed it. Politics aside, Diệm reviled the vice operations of the crime syndicate.[28]

Northern Catholics and Secular Political Parties

In the north, the most powerful anticommunist nationalists were the Catholics. The aging Bishop Lê Hữu Từ in Phát Diệm and his rising protégé, Bishop Phạm Ngọc Chi of Bùi Chu, served as the spiritual and temporal leaders of the Catholic zone. No estimates are available for the population living under their control, but well over a million souls resided within the borders of the twin dioceses, of which more than three hundred thousand were believers.[29] The Catholics had formed their own army during the Resistance, though the force integrated into the Vietnamese National Army in 1951.[30] The northern Catholics had no political party of their own and did not always support Diệm, as observers sometimes assumed. The *attentisme* of the Ngô family was initially at odds with the accommodationist stance of the church leaders.[31] Bishop Từ did not support Diệm until after the Unity Congress, and even then, the cleric continued to pursue a separate political path from the Diemists.[32]

The Đại Việt Nationalist Party exercised significant power too. The once unified party had split into three regional branches. The northern branch was largely autonomous, but the other two continued to coordinate with each other. The northern Đại Việt party was under the leadership of Phan Huy Quát, who had twice served as the defense minister of the SVN, and Quát's brother-in-law Đặng Văn Sung. Their branch of the party was strong in the greater Hanoi area, the coastal zone around Hải Phòng, and the lower Red River delta. The head of the southern wing was Nguyễn Tôn Hoàn, a Catholic from Tây Ninh province.[33] His followers numbered two or three thousand in the south and were strongest in Saigon, Ninh Thuận province, and pockets of the Mekong delta. Hà Thúc Ký, a forestry engineer from Huế, was the chief of the central Vietnamese branch.[34] Many of his partisans had defected to join the Diemists, and he subsequently commanded as few as fifty followers. His zone of influence included Huế and parts of Quảng Nam, Quảng Trị, and Quảng Bình (just north of Quảng Trị) provinces.[35] The weakest anticommunist group was the Vietnamese Nationalist Party. Although it still enjoyed an illustrious reputation, the party had fractured into multiple factions over the decision of a party leader to sign the Preliminary

52   Chapter 2

Convention of March 6, 1946. The later split between accommodationists and *attentistes* deepened the fissure. By 1954, the VNP was little more than a shell of its former self, counting only a few hundred members in northern and central Vietnam.[36]

Other Friends and Foes

The anticommunists had to contend not only with each other but also with the French, the Vietnamese National Army, and the Americans—all of whom served to remind the nationalists that their country had still not achieved genuine independence. General Paul Ély wielded considerable military and political power as both the commander of the French Expeditionary Corps (FEC) and the French high commissioner. Ély's soldiers had ballooned to 271,000, and the FEC continued to exercise military authority throughout the regime's territory.[37] Ély also controlled several government agencies that would transfer to the SVN within the next year, including the justice system, the central bank, and the office of foreign exchange. He even occupied Norodom Palace, the former residence of the governor-general of French Indochina and a potent symbol of colonial dependency.

The Vietnamese National Army (VNA) was yet another reminder of the regime's colony-like status. The army of some 170,000 regulars relied entirely on the FEC for training, logistics, and supplies.[38] General Nguyễn Văn Hinh was its commander and the son of former premier Nguyễn Văn Tâm. The VNA had a reputation for collaborationism, given that Hinh and most of his officers had fought in the French military or the colonial army, including in campaigns against Vietnamese revolutionaries during the Resistance.[39] Yet the army had come under the influence of revolutionary nationalism. Many young officers were eager to achieve full independence, and the VNP, the Đại Việt party, and the Cần Lao had all formed secret cells within the officer corps. The political divisions within the army would later emerge as a factor in General Hinh's downfall.

The anticommunists found a potential ally in the United States, the wealthiest and most powerful patron of the SVN. The Americans had provided aid to the regime since 1950, though channeled through the French. The activists realized that they had little hope of resisting the DRV without American support, and many lobbied Ambassador Donald Heath to provide direct assistance. But Heath thought poorly of them, and the northern Đại Việt was perhaps the only group that embassy and consular officials considered competent.[40] The recently arrived Edward Lansdale proved more sympathetic. The flamboyant US Central Intelligence Agency (CIA) agent was an astute political operative whose success in shoring up Magsaysay's government in the Philippines had earned him the reputation of a kingmaker in Asia. In Vietnam, the affable Lansdale was the chief of the Saigon Military Mission, an independent CIA station focused on psychological warfare and paramilitary operations, and he deliberately befriended Vietnamese personalities of all political persuasions.[41]

PLURALISM, POPULISM, AND NATIONAL UNION

The anticommunists waited with bated breath in the weeks following the announcement of Diệm's appointment to the premiership. They expected him to form a broad, diverse government, and many secretly hoped that he would invite them to join the cabinet. Previous premiers had made it a point to allocate portfolios to the Big Five and recruit officials from different religious and regional backgrounds. More recently, the congresses of 1953 had enshrined national unity as a shared ideal, and Nhu had advocated for political cooperation in his capacity as a leader of the Movement for Unity and Peace. But Diệm defied expectations. When the premier formally assumed office on July 7, 1954, he unveiled a cabinet drawn almost entirely from the Diemist faction and his extended family. This loyalist cabinet had an upper tier of ministers and a lower tier of secretaries. Prime Minister Diệm insisted on serving as interior and defense minister concurrently. Trần Văn Đỗ of the Spirit Group was the foreign minister, and three other members of the group received cabinet seats as well. Diệm named his brother-in-law the economic secretary and made Trần Văn Chương, who was Đỗ's brother and Nhu's father-in-law, a minister of state without a portfolio. In contrast, the premier offered only two seats to rival anticommunist groups. The defense secretary belonged to the VNP, and the information secretary had ties to the northern Catholics. Not a single seat went to the Đại Việt party or the sects (see A1). The narrowness of the cabinet made most anticommunist leaders indignant, and they lamented that Diệm had betrayed national unity.

Their disappointment revealed a fundamental disagreement in how they and the Diemists conceived of unity. Influenced by the congresses of the previous fall, most anticommunists associated national unity with broad coalitions, cooperation between different groups, and a national union government (Fr. *gouvernement d'union nationale,* Viet. *chính phủ liên hiệp quốc gia*) incorporating all of the major political organizations. The leaders of the MUP had favored an all-encompassing alliance of anticommunists that would give rise to a unity government of diverse nationalists. These ideas lived on after the organization dissolved in the spring of 1954. In May, Bishop Lê Hữu Từ, the Bình Xuyên chief Lê Văn Viễn, the Cao Đài cleric Phạm Công Tắc, and the Hòa Hảo general Trần Văn Soái formed an alternative coalition. The group used rhetoric similar to the MUP's and called on all anticommunists to unite against the partition and in the struggle for independence.[42] Influenced by the anticommunists, Bảo Đại too had expected Diệm to include every political group in the administration.[43] This

54   Chapter 2

conception of national unity reflected a pluralistic vision of politics. The anticommunists understood that no group was strong enough to defeat the communists singlehandedly and believed that a coalition was necessary for survival. Underpinning the many appeals to national unity was the principle that all groups should refrain from internecine violence, just as Nhu's journal *Society* had insisted after the Unity Congress. Yet the anticommunists' vision of national union was limited. They largely believed that the communists should play no role in Vietnamese politics, as will be seen in chapter 3, and many sought to block specific rivals from the government.

In contrast, Diệm and his followers rejected coalition-building and a national union government. They realized that virtually all anticommunist groups had tried but failed to form an enduring alliance, and the premier and his associates had little interest in pursuing an unsuccessful strategy. Nhu appears not to have participated in any collective endeavor after the MUP collapsed, and the youngest brother Ngô Đình Luyện disdainfully rebuffed a proposal for coalition-building from a northern Đại Việt cadre in Geneva.[44] Later that fall, when several sect leaders pressured Diệm into broadening the government, he ridiculed his own cabinet as a "patchwork coalition" that was unable to govern effectively.[45] In the eyes of the premier, coalitions were ineffectual, motley collections of discrete interest groups.

Although few sources address the Diemist vision of national unity, the existing evidence suggests that the premier and his followers championed a populist vision of unity in which Diệm directly led the Vietnamese people. In a conversation with J. Lawton Collins, Eisenhower's envoy to the SVN in the winter of 1955, the premier claimed that his legitimacy came from his broad appeal to the common people rather than any one party.[46] Accordingly, he never joined any of the Diemist organizations and presented himself as a leader who inspired others to spontaneously organize on his behalf. For Diệm, the main cooperative relationship was between the government and the population rather than between political groups. In a speech near Huế soon after his return to Vietnam, he declared that he expected the people to voluntarily assist his government in carrying out its programs: "I believe that my compatriots will unite [*đoàn kết*] and struggle vigorously to achieve the total revolution advocated by the government[,] [a revolution] that will bring freedom and happiness to the people and independence and unity to the fatherland."[47] During his inaugural address on July 7, Diệm promised that his administration would realize the universal will of the people. "An important task of the government is to quickly realize the shared and deeply held aspirations of all Vietnamese people, including warriors in the ranks of the Việt Minh," he proclaimed.[48] Diệm's notion of shared aspirations assumed an underlying unity that bound all Vietnamese people despite the profusion of parties and groups.

Set against the longer history of the revolutionary movement, the premier's conception of unity resembled communist attempts to assert leadership over rival groups. Diệm aimed to transcend differences rather than incorporate them, and his highest ideal was a populist consensus rather than pluralism. He fervently urged his rivals to offer their unconditional support even as he excluded them from the government. He concluded his inauguration speech with a special appeal to other nationalists: "I fervently call on all patriots, without distinction to party or religion or class, to actively assist the government in saving the people from oppression, inequality, divisive strategies, and all forms of enslavement."[49] "Divisive strategies" was an allusion to the partition, and "enslavement" was an epithet for colonialism and communism. Diệm's message to other anticommunists was clear: if they wanted to achieve national unity, the onus was on them to comply with his demands.

THE GENEVA ACCORDS AND THE MIGRATION OF NORTHERNERS

News from the peace conference in Switzerland temporarily distracted the anticommunists from the question of a national union government. The Geneva Accords of July 20, 1954, announced the cessation of hostilities between France and the DRV and the partition of Vietnam into two regroupment zones. The DRV's army was to withdraw north of the seventeenth parallel, and the FEC and the VNA would regroup to the southern half of the country. The accords specified that Vietnam would be reunified through a national election after two years. In the interim, civilians could relocate to the zone of their choice during a three-hundred-day period of free movement.

The Geneva Accords transformed the SVN geographically and politically. First, the partition redrew the contours of the regime. The anticommunist state resembled a collection of territories scattered across the country, and the partition raised the possibility that the regime could achieve a consolidated, contiguous territory throughout the southern regroupment zone, now called South Vietnam. The agreement required the SVN to relinquish strongholds in the north, including Hanoi and the Catholic zone. In exchange, the regime would finally be able to penetrate communist territories that the accords forced the DRV to abandon, especially the Cà Mau peninsula and south-central Vietnam. Second, the regroupment inadvertently created winners and losers among anticommunist nationalists. Many northern anticommunist groups moved south during the period of free movement, and the migration severely weakened their organizations. Conversely, the partition strengthened the position of groups already in South Vietnam, and the sects emerged as the anticommunist nationalists most capable of challenging Diệm in the immediate future. Last, the withdrawal of the DRV

56   Chapter 2

left a vacuum of power in former communist territories, and an intense competition erupted between different anticommunists over which group would occupy those areas.

After the announcement of the Geneva Accords, the Bình Xuyên, the Cao Đài, and the Diemists all encouraged northerners to flee to South Vietnam to escape communism. Lê Văn Viễn claimed that he could settle fifty thousand people in the Bình Xuyên zone.[50] The religious leader Phạm Công Tắc welcomed northerners to Tây Ninh and asked adepts to give up a meal to donate to the resettlement effort.[51] Sect leaders were undoubtedly sincere in these endeavors, but their highly publicized efforts were also a bid to court the allegiance of the migrants.

Perhaps no one was as anxious to promote migration as Diệm. The northern Catholics were the premier's most important ally among the main anticommunist groups, and a recent political convergence had brought him and Bishop Lê Hữu Từ especially close. After the French defeat at Điện Biên Phủ, the bishop proposed that the twin dioceses be recognized as a neutral zone not under the authority of either the French or the DRV. The Catholics hoped to maintain their autonomy in the face of growing communist power, and Diệm endorsed the plan because he wanted to retain a foothold in the north.[52] The Geneva Accords rendered the plan moot, but the premier resolved to hold on to the support of the northern Catholics and made the migration his highest priority. In late July, he announced the government's program for evacuation and resettlement and obtained French assistance for the project. Diệm personally traveled to Hanoi to persuade northerners to come south and instructed his information secretary to promote the migration.[53] In August, the premier convinced the Americans to provide additional transportation and formed a special government agency devoted to evacuation and resettlement.[54] Lansdale's team of intelligence operatives carried out a secret campaign of psychological warfare to encourage migration too, though recent research suggests that the project had little effect on the actual migration.[55]

The migration of 1954 to 1955 quickly overwhelmed all those who sought to take advantage of it. More than eight hundred thousand Vietnamese moved southward in what was undoubtedly the largest mass migration in Vietnamese history. The movement represented a shift of 4 percent of the country's total population and an increase of 9 percent in the number of people living in South Vietnam.[56] Most migrants were civilians, though a substantial minority were soldiers serving in the national army and their families. The southern population called the migrants northern émigrés (*Bắc di cư*), and anticommunists hailed the new arrivals as refugees (*ty nạn*). In contrast, only 140,000 southerners moved in the opposite direction, and most were DRV military and political personnel.[57] Anticommunists pointed to the discrepancy as proof of communist illegitimacy, but a better explanation was that the FEC and the US navy transported more migrants than the communist allies of the DRV did.

The tide of northerners brought new types of anticommunists to South Vietnam. The largest category of politicized émigrés were Catholic nationalists. About three-quarters of civilian migrants were Catholic, though this figure is misleading because not all Catholic émigrés were politically engaged. Instead, it is more instructive to consider that large sectors of Bishop Từ's autonomous zone moved south and preserved their social and political cohesion. More than 70 percent of parishioners in Bùi Chu and Phát Diệm and an even higher proportion of priests relocated, including the two bishops.[58] These émigrés migrated as intact communities, then resettled in separate villages or neighborhoods. Consequently, Catholic migrants remained a distinct political constituency from their southern coreligionists. Additionally, the migration included members of the northern Đại Việt party and the VNP as well as Việt Minh partisans who had defected during the radicalization. Although no estimates are available on their numbers, these émigrés would go on to play an important role in shaping the politics of their new home.

Diệm and his followers reaped enormous political benefit from the migration. It boosted the premier's standing in the international community, and many Western observers claimed that the émigrés "voted with their feet" in favor of Diệm and against communism. Within Vietnam, the government's resettlement project overshadowed the efforts of the sects, and the Catholic émigrés helped Diệm weather challenges from other rivals.[59] Bishops Từ and Chi were allies of the premier, and Catholic émigrés staunchly supported Diệm because they believed they would enjoy religious freedom under his government. In turn, the Diemists perceived northern Catholics to be reliable followers, and the government appointed an increasing number of Catholics and northern émigrés to prominent posts.[60] Such practices gave rise to the widespread perception that Diệm favored his coreligionists, though only a small proportion of Catholic migrants ever received government employment through his preferential treatment. More important, the premier and his followers expected émigrés to serve the Diemist agenda, and Diệm did not hesitate to rein in Catholic activism when it did not suit his needs.

ENTANGLED PLOTS AND THE HINH CRISIS

As the shock of the Geneva Accords abated, the sects took up the cause of a national union government in earnest. They demanded that Diệm broaden his cabinet and offered their support in exchange for specific ministries and other posts. The sects took advantage of a different conflict between Diệm and General Nguyễn Văn Hinh of the VNA and alternatively conspired with and against Hinh

58   Chapter 2

to put pressure on Diệm. Sect leaders aimed not only to secure a place in the government but also to form a broader administration.

The sects asked Diệm to grant them appointments to the interior, defense, and economic ministries and justified the bold request on the grounds that the sects had made exemplary contributions to the anticommunist struggle.[61] *Combat (Chiến đấu),* the official journal of General Soái's army, stressed that that Hòa Hảo soldiers had sacrificed their lives fighting the communist enemy: "We, the religious parties who have engaged in a 'nationalist revolution' from the start, did not cease to fight the Việt Minh communists with our blood and bones until the very last days [of life]." The journal acknowledged the armed resistance of the other members of the Big Five but criticized the *attentistes* as "passive and inactive." The implication was that the Hòa Hảo and other groups had a greater claim to legitimacy than the *attentiste* Ngô clan.[62] Religious leader Phạm Công Tắc insisted that only a national union government with sectarian participation would enjoy genuine legitimacy. He publicly declared, "During a time of crisis, only a presidium nominated by a united national front that includes all religious groups and all political organizations would have sufficient prestige to direct the fate of the country and implement a policy of political as well as economic restoration for Vietnam."[63] Diệm flatly rejected the sects' demand. He regarded his rivals as selfish collaborators who were unfit for political leadership. In a conversation with Ambassador Heath, the premier asserted that the sects had fought for the French and were little more than profit-seeking mercenaries.[64]

The growing friction between Diệm and the sects intersected with the premier's clash with General Hinh. Diệm privately ridiculed Hinh as a "factitious Frenchman" and had made plans to dismiss the general even before returning to Vietnam.[65] Hinh criticized the anti-French stance of the Ngô brothers and repeatedly threatened to overthrow Diệm in a military coup.[66] This civil-military conflict, known as the Hinh crisis, would grip Saigon and some parts of the country throughout the late summer and fall. Opposition to Diệm pushed Hinh and the sects into a temporary coalition in early August. Several sect leaders, Bishop Tử, and General Hinh banded together to pressure the premier into accepting their demand for a broadened government, but the subsequent negotiations quickly deadlocked.[67] Frustrated, Generals Trần Văn Soái, Nguyễn Thành Phương, and Lê Văn Viễn began plotting with Hinh to remove the premier, though the bishop apparently declined to join the plot. The conspirators knew that their combined forces could easily overthrow the government, and they planned to form a ruling directorate composed of various anticommunist groups.[68] The plan suggests that the sect generals were borrowing Hinh's hand to achieve a national union government or at least a broad coalition government. The only question was whether they could obtain American aid.

Growing French opposition to Diệm heartened the conspirators. In mid-August, the French diplomat Jacques Raphael-Leygues arrived in Vietnam with the official mission of strengthening the government of the SVN, but his actual task was to advocate for Diệm's removal.[69] Leygues hosted a cocktail party that doubled as a meeting of the conspirators, and when Ambassador Heath arrived, the Cao Đài political adviser Phạm Xuân Thái brazenly asked, "Is it all right to go ahead and change the government?"[70] Thái was disappointed to find that Heath and the United States adamantly opposed a coup. Over the next few days, the ambassador repeatedly warned the conspirators that the forcible overthrow of Diệm would produce an "unfavorable impression" in America. The United States would only provide aid to an "honest, progressive, popular government," Heath threatened.[71] Diệm deftly manipulated his opponents. The premier bluntly told Hinh that the Americans would withhold aid if the general staged a coup and asked Heath to deliver the same message to the sects.[72] The plot promptly collapsed.

Hinh turned to conspiring with senior army officers to carry out a different coup, and Diệm countered by resuming negotiations with the sects to isolate Hinh.[73] Just as the premier and the sects began to parley, General Viễn left for Europe to lobby Bảo Đại to dismiss Diệm. The renewed opposition was a boon to Generals Phương and Soái, who used Hinh's and Viễn's machinations to pressure Diệm to make concessions. In early September, Phương and Soái presented the premier with a plan to enlarge the government. They proposed that Diệm retain five incumbent members of the cabinet, add several new portfolios, and reserve the remaining posts for the sects, the southern Đại Việt party, the VNP, and Hinh. Soái, Viễn, Phạm Công Tắc, and Bishop Từ would serve on an advisory council.[74] The proposed administration encompassed all of the main anticommunist groups, though not every faction of each group, and favored the sects while excluding the northern Đại Việt. Nevertheless, the plan reflected an enduring commitment to pluralism and coalition-building.

Meanwhile, the conflict between Hinh and Diệm escalated. On September 8, the premier placed two of Hinh's officers under house arrest for conspiring against the government, and the incident sparked a heated argument between Diệm and the general. The premier angrily relieved Hinh of his duties and ordered the general on a six-month study mission in France.[75] Hinh refused to leave Vietnam and instructed the army radio station to attack Diệm on the airwaves.[76] The premier responded with an olive branch and offered the post of defense secretary to Hinh's associate, the retired General Nguyễn Văn Xuân, who had been a figurehead of Thierry d'Argenlieu's autonomous southern republic back in 1947.[77] Hinh continued to flout Diệm's orders and publicly appealed to Bảo Đại to resolve the standoff.[78] The crisis worsened when Lê Văn Viễn

60   Chapter 2

returned from France and announced that he had received authorization from Bảo Đại to consult with other groups regarding Diệm's possible resignation.[79] Xuân then resigned and declared that he was Bảo Đại's choice to form a new government.[80]

The next Diemist maneuver was to mobilize northern émigrés in support of the premier. On September 21, Ngô Đình Nhu's wife Trần Lệ Xuân, better known as Madame Nhu, staged a rally in Saigon in support of Diệm. Glamorous and educated, Madame Nhu boasted an illustrious lineage with ties to the royal family and the planter class of the Mekong delta. Her familial and social connections had long facilitated her husband's activism, and Diệm's ascent to the premiership and the growing stature of her menfolk whetted her interest in politics.[81] The premier did not authorize her to act, and little is known about how she organized the event. Madame Nhu apparently arranged for trucks to transport émigrés from nearby reception centers to Saigon, and rumors circulated that the émigrés received payment for their participation. Some four thousand protesters marched through downtown Saigon chanting support for Diệm and holding banners reading, "Put Down the Saboteurs of National Independence," an obvious reference to General Hinh.[82] The émigrés gathered in front of Norodom Palace and passed a motion affirming their confidence in Diệm.[83] The French High Commission had transferred the building to the SVN weeks earlier, and the premier had made it his official residence and renamed it the Independence Palace.

SHIFTING ALLIANCES AND THE COALITION GOVERNMENT OF 1954

The turn of events strengthened Phương and Soái's hand, and they forced Diệm to cave to their demands.[84] The three men surprised their rivals on September 24 by announcing a new administration composed of the Diemists and the main Cao Đài and Hòa Hảo factions. Phương, Soái, and their partisans collectively controlled a third of the cabinet. The Spirit Group held four posts, and several other Diemists stayed on from the previous government. The Bình Xuyên, the Đại Việt party, and the VNP received no portfolios (see table A2). The arrangement eased tensions among Diệm, Phương, and Soái and temporarily neutralized the threat posed by Hinh.

However, the premier lost one of his oldest allies amid the negotiations for reasons that remain unclear. The southern Đại Việt leader Nguyễn Tôn Hoàn had worked with Diệm in a short-lived coalition back in 1947 and later with Nhu and Cẩn in the Movement for Unity and Peace.[85] Hoàn apparently served as a liaison between the Hòa Hảo and the Ngô family and likely advised Diệm to cooperate with the sects during the Hinh crisis.[86] But the Đại Việt chief abruptly broke with his former friend and went abroad that fall. Hoàn would henceforth engage in opposition against the premier, and both the Diemists and the southern Đại Việt felt betrayed by their erstwhile ally.[87]

Bảo Đại inadvertently reignited the Hinh crisis in early October. From his villa on the French Riviera, the chief of state ordered Diệm to incorporate Generals Hinh, Viễn, and Xuân into the cabinet.[88] "Thus will be realized that great national union which you yourself certainly always hoped to establish around [the] Chief of State," the former emperor admonished, reminding Diệm that the latter had once advocated for a national union government.[89] Bảo Đại also telegrammed the premier's opponents and instructed them to accept Diệm's invitation to join the cabinet.[90] Hinh needed no other encouragement. The general demanded that Diệm follow Bảo Đại's orders and threatened to stage a coup if the premier refused.[91] That night, a pair of army vehicles circled the Independence Palace, and rumors swirled that the Bình Xuyên and the VNA would overthrow Diệm the next day.[92] The premier had little choice but to negotiate with the trio, but he stalled for time by repeatedly proffering and retracting cabinet posts over the next several weeks.[93] Meanwhile, the negotiations dismayed the Americans and other sect leaders. Ambassador Heath rushed to France to convince Bảo Đại to refrain from any action that might encourage Hinh, and the chastened chief of state bid Hinh, Viễn, and Xuân to cooperate with the premier.[94] A few weeks later, Eisenhower's special envoy J. Lawton Collins arrived to replace Heath and immediately proclaimed to the press, "I have come to Vietnam to bring every possible aid to the Government of Diem and to his Government only."[95] Diệm received yet another boost when President Eisenhower sent the premier a personal letter announcing that Washington would start providing aid directly to the SVN.[96] The successive Americans actions signaled to Diệm's opponents that he alone enjoyed American support.

Meanwhile, the Diemists worked behind the scenes to strengthen the premier's position. A small cabal of Cần Lao cadres in south-central Vietnam plotted to undercut Hinh's authority within the VNA.[97] The area had emerged as a hotspot of the crisis, and antagonism ran high between Diemist officers and government officials, on the one hand, and local military officers who were still loyal to Hinh, on the other.[98] In mid-November, the Diemist military commanders in Ninh Thuận and Bình Thuận provinces publicly repudiated Hinh's authority and declared their loyalty to the premier. One commander even led his men into the highlands to form a loyalist resistance zone.[99] Although the mutiny involved only a minority of officers, the incident revealed that Diemist influence over the army was growing at Hinh's expense. Ngô Đình Luyện played the decisive role in resolving the crisis. Diệm had dispatched Luyện to France in late October to personally plead the premier's case with Bảo Đại, and the emissary persuaded the chief of state to summon Hinh to France for a study mission.[100] Hinh left Vietnam on November 19 but brashly announced to the press on his

62   Chapter 2

arrival in France that he would return to Vietnam regardless of Bảo Đại's instructions.[101] The indignant chief of state relieved the general of his command, thus ending the Hinh crisis.[102]

Hinh's departure did not bring concord to Vietnamese politics, however. The alliance forged by Diệm and Generals Phương and Soái was a marriage of convenience, and the friction between them prevented the coalition government from ever cohering into an effective administration.[103] The premier disliked working with the sects, and multiple cabinet members complained that he would not discuss important matters with anyone outside his inner circle.[104] As a result, the administration achieved little during its half year in existence. Yet the dysfunction was by no means inevitable, and common ground on which Diệm and the sect ministers could have built a cooperative relationship was considerable.

In the premier's speech introducing the cabinet on September 24, he offered an overview of a program of reforms that he dubbed the "national revolution" (*cách mạng quốc gia*). Diệm envisioned a gradual process of democratization that began with the convocation of an advisory council of leaders from different organizations. Then, a provisional national assembly that included all political persuasions and the representatives of various occupational groups would be established. The premier promised a number of reforms, including land for sharecroppers, expanded rural health care, new educational institutions, improvements to the country's infrastructure, and an end to corruption. He offered no timeline for implementing his program.[105]

The following month, the Cao Đài and Hòa Hảo ministers circulated a "minimum program" within the cabinet that echoed many of Diệm's ideas. They agreed with the premier's plan for a provisional assembly and proposed a slew of changes in addition to those that Diệm suggested. The minimum program called for the establishment of farmers' cooperatives, the construction of rural markets, agricultural banks offering zero-interest loans, subsidized housing, the recognition of squatters' rights, labor reform, and poor relief. Other measures included the replacement of regressive tolls with sumptuary and luxury taxes, the conversion of the VNA into a volunteer army, a propaganda campaign to inculcate nationalism and anticommunism among the people, and a ban on prostitution, gambling, and opium. The sects insisted, to quickly win over the loyalty of the population, that the plan be implemented immediately for three months.[106]

The similarities between the programs revealed a basic agreement within the coalition government and suggests that the administration could have introduced reforms had the Diemists and the sects worked together. Equally important, the minimum program demonstrated that the Cao Đài and Hòa Hảo had serious policy proposals and were not merely interested in protecting their privileges, as the premier so often claimed. The joint proposal drew directly from the platforms of the sect-affiliated parties and built on the economic and social projects that had

Quest for National Unity   63

flourished in the sectarian autonomous zones during the Resistance. Indeed, the minimum program was far more developed than Diệm's vague description of his vision and arguably the most socially progressive program by a major anticommunist group during Diệm's premiership. Yet the coalition government never implemented either program and instead devolved into infighting.

CENTRALIZATION AND THE CONTEST FOR THE CÀ MAU PENINSULA

The main points of contention within the administration and between Diệm and the sects more generally was military and political centralization. During the Anti-French Resistance, the SVN's military force included an array of armed groups, including the national army, the sect armies, and various regional and provincial militias. The regime itself was a decentralized state that combined a weak central government and a collection of autonomous zones. Diệm's ambition was to establish a unitary military and a unitary state—that is, one in which the central government enjoys absolute supremacy over regional and local authorities, unlike a federation or a confederation. The premier planned to integrate the sect armies into the VNA, to place all armed forces under a single command, and to send the national army to reoccupy areas evacuated by the DRV. He then aimed to dismantle the autonomous zones and extend the administrative apparatus of the central government throughout South Vietnam. Although the sects had earlier resisted assimilation into Bảo Đại's government, many sect leaders now expressed support for the premier's plan but insisted that he negotiate and compromise rather than act unilaterally. Some Hòa Hảo generals also contested Diệm's claim to former communist territories in the Mekong delta.

Diệm, Phương, and Soái agreed on the need for military centralization, and the premier issued two ordinances that fall integrating three thousand soldiers from the Cao Đài and Hòa Hảo armies into the VNA.[107] But, like so many other promised reforms, no integration took place. It is unclear whether the premier and the sects ever discussed political centralization, but all sides understood that dissolving the sect armies meant giving up the autonomous zones because the sects would be unable to defend their territory. The unrealized integration formed the backdrop to the Quát affair. The northern Đại Việt chief, Phan Huy Quát, had lobbied for a cabinet appointment for months, and the arrival of J. Lawton Collins in November invigorated Quát's candidacy. Collins and other Americans pushed Diệm to name Quát as defense secretary, a post left vacant by Nguyễn Văn Xuân's resignation.[108] The Quát affair proved far more contentious than Collins expected. Although the premier seriously considered the suggestion, Phương and Soái balked. Quát had earned the enmity of the sects during his

64   Chapter 2

earlier stint as defense minister when he tried to draft sect soldiers directly into the national army.[109] Because the details of integration were not yet determined, Phương and Soái likely feared that Quát would impose unfavorable terms on the sect armies. An irritated Soái threatened to withdraw from the cabinet, and Phương protested that the Đại Việt leader would put a squeeze on the Cao Đài army.[110] The generals' protest revealed that their vision of national union never included all anticommunists. Diệm put the matter to rest in mid-December by offering the position to Assistant Minister of Defense Hồ Thông Minh, who was a member of the Spirit Group.[111]

Meanwhile, the negotiations on military integration went poorly. The dispute centered on the level of subventions and the number of troops to be integrated. The SVN and the FEC had paid the sects for the maintenance of their troops during the war. By the end of 1954, Generals Phương, Soái, Nguyễn Giác Ngộ, and Lâm Thành Nguyên received a combined total of 18.6 million piasters per month from the government. Phương and Ngộ received another 3.6 million each to provide for village defense forces.[112] General Lê Quang Vinh had retreated into the maquis to protest the Geneva Accords and currently received no funds. Diệm angered the generals when he tried to lower their subsidies substantially.[113] The sects grew even more alarmed after the FEC announced the cessation of its subventions in December. Confronted with a financial time bomb, Phương suggested that his forces convert into light companies and join the national army.[114] That, though, was no longer possible because Diệm had to reduce the VNA by half in response to a drop in French and American aid.[115] There was simply not enough space to retain all of the soldiers in the various armies.[116]

The sect generals were adamant that their soldiers deserved priority over the VNA. Phương contended that his men were idealistic volunteers relative to the apathetic draftees of the national army and demanded that Cao Đài soldiers constitute 10 percent of the reduced army, that is, more than three times the allotment of three thousand soldiers.[117] Ngộ claimed that his forces had fought for the SVN before the VNA had been established, which implied that Hòa Hảo soldiers deserved to be retained out of respect for their seniority.[118] Soái grumbled that the premier had promised to accept three thousand men from his army but now gave some of those spots to other Hòa Hảo factions.[119] But Diệm refused to increase the quota, and the generals found themselves competing for a dwindling number of spots.

Diệm's next gambit was to sow disunity among the sects and thereby undermine Phương's and Soái's positions in the negotiations. Although the premier continued to authorize monthly subsidies, he lured away subordinates and smaller factions with financial inducements and promises of integration.[120] The funds came from the regular CIA station in Saigon, though Diệm appears to have controlled the payments.[121] In mid-January 1955, the premier convinced

Soái's chief of staff to defect to the government with three thousand soldiers.[122] On February 22, General Ngô announced at a press conference that he was bringing eight thousand soldiers over to the regime. The rally was part of a larger effort to transform his faction from an army into a political organization. Standing by the general's side at the press conference was Nguyễn Bảo Toàn, the leader of the reconstituted Social Democratic Party.[123] Ngô may have asked the government to grant the party legal recognition as part of the terms of the rally, and the SDP would become one of the most important parties in the SVN in the months ahead.[124] More immediately, the successive rallies depleted Soái's forces and undercut his bargaining position.

Then Diệm dropped a bombshell: the rogue General Trình Minh Thế was rallying to the government with his troops.[125] The unexpected alliance reflected both practical calculations and political affinities. Diệm needed another ally to counter the other sect generals, and General Thế longed to return to legality, fearing that the French and the communists might simultaneously attack his army now that his enemies were no longer at war with each other.[126] Moreover, Thế's politics had long aligned with the Ngô brothers' *attentisme*. Money played a role as well. Nhu had secretly contacted Thế as early as the previous summer and later traveled to Bà Đen Mountain to continue the negotiations and provide funds. Lansdale helped initiate the talks, and the premier completed them during a visit to Tây Ninh.[127] Thế would henceforth displace Phương as the preeminent Cao Đài military leader in the SVN.

Diệm followed his announcement regarding General Thế with a long speech about the necessity of forming a unitary state. In a formal address celebrating the dedication of the Cao Đài basilica in Tây Ninh, the premier claimed that it was the will of the people for all nationalists to rally to the regime: "All compatriots as well as the government and I fervently desire that every class, every tendency, and every religion assemble around the government and form a single bloc."[128] The vision of a unitary state was the logical extension of his populist conception of national unity, and Diệm's ideal government was a highly centralized state built on consensus. "Every modern state, unlike countries in the feudal past, must be built on a firm, unified foundation and under [the direction of] a strong central government, in which the interests of different groups as well as the individual give way to the supreme interests of the nation," he declared.[129]

Cao Đài military leaders embraced aspects of Diệm's vision but not his methods. During a ceremony in Saigon celebrating the rally of General Thế, the guerilla chief delivered a long speech affirming his willingness to set aside group interests, just as Diệm urged. "We have come here to cooperate with you to demonstrate the principle of 'broad nationalism,' without narrow partisanship or individual egotism," the general declared. But Thế gently criticized Diệm's expectation of immediate compliance. "Because the different perspectives have

66 Chapter 2

not been completely reconciled, one is forced to wait for [the passage of] time to gradually erase the differences," Thế admonished.[130] General Phương also indicated that he endorsed military and political centralization even if he rejected Diệm's terms. Phương's political party held a congress in early February, and he oversaw the passing of a resolution calling for the unification of the armies and the establishment of the government's administrative apparatus at the village and district level.[131] The statement hinted that he would accept the penetration of the central government into the Cao Đài autonomous zone.

As the negotiations stalled, a different disagreement broke out between the premier and some Hòa Hảo factions over who would control the Mekong delta. The conflict was the outgrowth of larger military changes. According to the Geneva Accords, the DRV's troops would regroup to a few provisional assembly areas in South Vietnam before withdrawing to the north, and the FEC would take over the territory relinquished by the communists (see map 2).[132] A separate agreement between France and the SVN specified that the FEC would transfer military authority over South Vietnam to the VNA and would leave the country by that spring. The deal apparently made no mention of the sect armies.[133]

In February, the DRV began evacuating the provisional assembly area on the Cà Mau peninsula, a delta-shaped swath of land that formed the southernmost tip of the delta. The peninsula had been the communists' largest contiguous territory in the south. Soái's and Lê Quang Vinh's autonomous zones lay just to the north, and both planned to occupy the former communist stronghold. Given the recent agreement with France, however, Diệm considered the territory to be the exclusive prerogative of the VNA and instructed the national army to retake Cà Mau. Without consulting the sect generals, he apparently authorized the VNA to move through the Hòa Hảo autonomous zones. Several clashes erupted between the VNA and the sect armies in mid-December.[134] On February 8, 1955, war nearly broke out in the delta when the national army launched Operation Liberty (Chiến Dịch Tự Do) to pacify the peninsula.[135]

Hòa Hảo leaders rightly suspected that Diệm intended to undermine their authority over the autonomous zones. The government began appointing province chiefs in sect-dominated provinces in January without consulting the local Hòa Hảo leadership.[136] During Operation Liberty, the VNA surrounded Soái's headquarters, pressured his troops to withdraw from territory recently evacuated by the communists, and even attacked posts that the Hòa Hảo had held since the late 1940s.[137] Soái again threatened to leave the government unless the premier withdrew the national army.[138] But Diệm coldly maintained that Hòa Hảo troops were not authorized to occupy many of the areas that the VNA retook.[139] The disagreement between the premier, Soái, and Phương grew so bitter that the coalition government was on the brink of dissolution by the end of February.

THE STRUGGLE FOR CENTRAL VIETNAM

The rise and decline of the coalition government in Saigon found a parallel in the developments in central Vietnam. There, the leading anticommunist groups were the Diemist faction under Ngô Đình Cẩn and the regional branches of the Đại Việt party and the VNP. The three groups had worked together in the Movement for Unity and Peace, and after Diệm's rise to power, Cẩn decided to continue the alliance on terms that favored the Diemists. The most pressing task facing the younger Ngô brother was to expand the administration of the SVN into the areas abandoned by the departing communists. Cẩn packed the highest echelons of the regional government with his trusted followers but had too few partisans to fill the rest of the administration. He therefore allowed the Đại Việt party to run the provincial government in Quảng Trị province, the VNP to do the same in Quảng Nam and Quảng Ngãi provinces, and both parties to staff the lower levels in other provinces. Meanwhile, Cẩn worked to expand the Diemist faction.[140] But relations grew strained between the allies, possibly in part because of the break between the premier and the southern Đại Việt leader Nguyễn Tôn Hoàn, and the regional alliance violently ruptured in the winter and spring of 1955.

The first and largest conflict was in Quảng Trị, the northernmost province of the SVN (see map 3). The province chief Trần Điền was a dynamic administrator and a Catholic Diemist, and his brother-in-law Hà Thúc Ký led the central regional branch of the Đại Việt party. Ký's partisans had a strong presence in the administration and the provincial militia and even included the latter's commanding officer. That fall, at the behest of the province chief, the militia began expanding into former communist areas, and the successful endeavor earned Trần Điền high praise from Diệm.[141] Next, Điền and his Đại Việt partners aimed to pacify the mountainous hinterland of Quảng Trị and planned an operation for February. But for reasons that remain unclear, the regional government controlled by Cẩn's partisans abruptly canceled the operation just as the militia was about to depart. The surprised province chief allowed the troops to proceed. The attempted cancellation alarmed Đại Việt officers who commanded military units stationed nearby, and the officers hastily led their troops to join the operation in the mountains. On February 11, the officers declared the secession of the Ba Lòng Resistance Zone from the SVN. The zone was named for a local mountain valley. The rebellion infuriated the Diemists. The government ordered the VNA to crush the resistance zone, dismissed the province chief, removed all local officials suspected of involvement in the affair, and jailed dozens of party members.[142] Even party cadres with no connection to the incident faced scrutiny and arrest.[143]

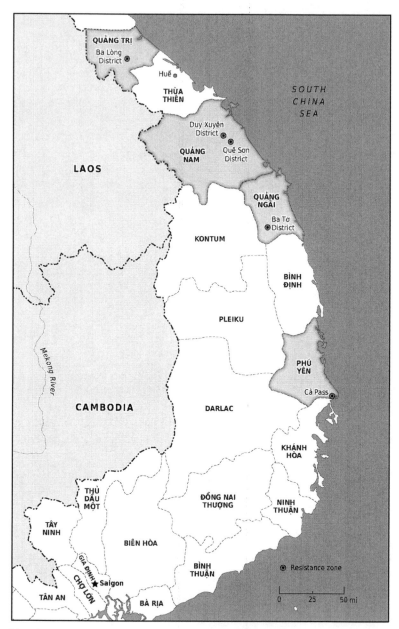

Map 3. Rebellions in central Vietnam, winter-spring 1955, indicating the location of the resistance zones established by the Vietnamese Nationalist Party and the Đại Việt Nationalist Party and the provinces (shaded) affected by the rebellions (map by Erin Greb)

The unrest spread to the coastal province of Phú Yên, the birthplace of the party's deceased founder, Trương Tử Anh. The Diemist province chief collaborated with the local Đại Việt chapter headed by the founder's brother and father, Trương Tử An and Trương Bội Hoàng, respectively. The province chief appointed An the commander of the provincial militia and the director of its military school and even entrusted him to organize a political front to rally popular support for the administration. But the rebellion in Quảng Trị and An's growing power aroused Diemist suspicions. In a sudden about-face, the authorities put An under surveillance, ordered the VNA to guard his school, and dissolved a company under the command of one of his partisans. The indignant An organized large demonstrations against Diệm and led several militia units to form a secessionist resistance zone near the treacherous Cả Pass in April. The VNA attacked the rebels the following month, and the government arrested all party members in the local administration.[144]

A different dynamic animated the rebellion of the VNP. The party was strong in the four contiguous provinces of Quảng Nam, Quảng Ngãi, Kontum, and Bình Định and had successfully maintained skeleton organizations in communist-controlled areas during the Resistance.[145] The VNP enjoyed good relations with the Diemists and supported the premier during the Hinh crisis.[146] But a disagreement erupted over the party's handling of suspected communists. The VNP and local officials carried out an assassination campaign against communist cadres without the approval of the Diemist regional government, and the latter was determined to bring its subordinates in line.[147] In February and March, the province chief of Quảng Ngãi arrested party cadres, broke up the party organization, and removed suspected party members from the administration. The crackdown reportedly spread to Quảng Nam. The chiefs of both provinces were members of the VNP, and it is unclear whether they participated in the suppression of the party.[148] Whatever the case, the VNP laid the blame at the feet of the Diemists.[149] Party members withdrew into the foothills of Quảng Nam and Quảng Ngãi and formed a string of short-lived resistance zones in Quế Sơn, Duy Xuyên, and Ba Tơ districts (see map 3). The national army overran most of the zones in April as part of Operation Liberation (Chiến Dịch Giải Phóng), the campaign to occupy former communist areas in south-central Vietnam, and the VNP's last remaining outpost surrendered the following month.[150]

The unifying thread that connected the rebellions in central Vietnam was Cẩn's consolidation of power. The available evidence suggests that the Diemists regarded their allies as competitors and resented the latter for flouting Diemist orders. The security agency of the national army reported that Trương Tử An used the political front in Phú Yên to recruit new members into his party, and newspaper accounts claimed that he secretly formed a private army.[151] The chief of Quảng Ngãi province implied the same when he complained that some

70   Chapter 2

members of the VNP worked for their organization rather than for the Vietnamese people.[152] Yet Cần Lao partisans took advantage of their positions in the military and the government to enlarge the ranks of the Diemist party and faced no punishment for doing so. More to the point, the Diemists used the mutinies as a justification for eliminating political rivals. The mass arrests, purges, and deliberate destruction of party networks went beyond punishing specific offenders to a blanket suppression and cleared the way for the recently enlarged Diemist faction to the fill the lower levels of the administration.

The rebellions irrevocably split the Diemists and the southern and central branches of the Đại Việt party. Both branches went underground and conspired against Diệm throughout the latter half of the 1950s, as described in chapter 4. The rebellions also damaged Diệm's relations with the VNP, though the latter group was so fragmented that the effect is difficult to assess. More broadly, the attacks on the rebel bases violated the recognized taboo against armed violence between anticommunist nationalists. Minor clashes between the anticommunists had broken out before, but the campaigns in central Vietnam were the first military operations that aimed to systematically annihilate a rival group. The VNP alluded to the taboo in a propaganda tract recounting events in Quảng Nam and Quảng Ngãi. Referencing the party's martyred founder, the handbill opined,

> It is so ironic and cruel that the blood of the spiritual heirs of the national hero Nguyễn Thái Học has been senselessly spilled, not by the guns and bullets of the colonialists or the Vietnamese communists but by the guns and bullets of a government that often touts itself as a "national revolution."[153]

After such violence, a politics of national union including both the Diemists and the rebellious branches of the Đại Việt and the VNP was no longer possible.

Historians have largely ignored the mutinies in central Vietnam to focus on Diệm's conflict with the sects in the south, but both were part of the same process of political rupture within anticommunist nationalism. In fact, rumors about Cẩn's consolidation of power helped fuel the struggle in the south. General Phương heard that Diệm was organizing a Catholic militia in central Vietnam and pondered whether to retain the Cao Đài army for self-defense.[154] General Lê Quang Vinh contributed to the gossip with an endless stream of propaganda. One handbill accused Cẩn of forming Catholic assassination squads to murder members of the VNP, the Bình Xuyên, and other anticommunist groups.[155]

As the handbill hinted, a different conflict between Diệm and the Bình Xuyên emerged at the same time as the central Vietnamese rebellions. The gang's vice operations had long disgusted the prudish premier, and Diệm refused to renew the contract for the Grand Monde casino in January, thus depriving the gang of a major source of revenue. Lê Văn Viễn dutifully shut down the operation but remained determined to retaliate.[156] The growing mistrust between Diệm and the Cao Đài and Hòa Hảo sects provided Viễn with an opening, and a full-blown crisis exploded in Saigon that spring.[157]

THE SECT CRISIS AND THE QUESTION OF UNCONDITIONAL INTEGRATION

The underlying disagreement between Diệm and the sects remained unresolved after months of wrangling. The sects refused to give up their armies and autonomous zones until the premier broadened the government, but he expected them to do so unconditionally. Exasperated with Diệm's intransigence, several Cao Đài and Hòa Hảo elements chose to intrigue with Viễn. On March 4, 1955, Phạm Công Tắc announced a new coalition called the United Front of Nationalist Forces (Mặt Trận Thống Nhứt Toàn Lực Quốc Gia) at a press conference, and Viễn's political adviser read aloud the group's manifesto. Without mentioning Diệm by name, the document decried the "dictatorship and sectarian policy which would provoke fratricidal war and cause [the] collapse of [the] nationalist cause."[158] The front promised that its members would integrate their armies into the VNA but made it clear that in return Diệm had to introduce democratic reforms and incorporate all anticommunist groups into a national union government. The coalition would "unify their armed forces and join the national army on condition that there is a healthy, democratic coalition government," the manifesto explained.[159] The term "healthy" referred to a regime that was free of corruption. Tắc signed the document in his capacity as chair of the front, and Generals Viễn, Soái, Vinh, and Nguyên all added their signatures.[160] Cao Đài Generals Phương and Thế secretly assented but asked that their participation be kept secret.[161] Nguyễn Tôn Hoàn's southern Đại Việt party appears to have joined the front later, as did several prominent southern intellectuals with ties to the Bình Xuyên.[162] Only the Hòa Hảo General Nguyễn Giác Ngộ categorically refused to lend his name.[163] The front's announcement marked the start of the sect crisis of 1955.

Diệm did not think that the sects had any standing to make demands. In a statement released later that month, he openly denounced the sect armies as mercenaries and accused sect leaders of pursuing partisan interests:

With the official purpose of relieving the burden on the French and Vietnamese armies [the FEC and the VNA], a tribal policy was instituted in [our] country modeled after a policy implemented in North Africa, that is, granting authority and many privileges to a certain number of people so that they would recruit small armies of partisans.

72   Chapter 2

Given the end of the war, he continued, it was necessary to unify the various armies and suppress the autonomous zones before the central government could implement major reforms. "There are people who care too much for their personal interests and want to keep their privileges, so they try to create obstacles to the government's policy of unity," Diệm complained.[164] Contrary to his statement, the sect armies actually emerged before the outbreak of war with France and the establishment of the VNA.

The statement outraged the sect leaders. On March 21, Tắc fired off a scorching counterattack. First, the Cao Đài religious leader blasted Diệm for likening the sectarian struggle for Vietnamese independence to "a tribal struggle like that of the savage African tribes." The premier's description cheapened the sacrifices of the war dead who belonged to the Hòa Hảo, Cao Đài, Đại Việt party, VNP, and Catholic groups, Tắc fumed. The cleric actually exaggerated the meaning of Diệm's original phrasing. Second, the chair of the front enumerated the premier's shortcomings: Diệm had failed to carry out any reforms during his nine months in office, showed blatant favoritism toward the northern émigrés, provoked mass defections in central Vietnam, filled the administration with his partisans, and refused to cooperate with sect groups that offered to integrate their forces. With this detailed list, Tắc demonstrated that the front cared about leadership, policies, and fairness, not just profit and military privileges. He warned that Diệm's wrongheaded policies would cause the country to fall to communism. The statement ended with an ultimatum giving Diệm five days to assemble a new cabinet that met with the approval of the United Front. The goal was to "build a healthy and democratic government of national union," the ultimatum explained. This time, Generals Thế and Phương joined the earlier signatories in signing the document.[165] The incensed Diệm replied that he served the nation's interests and offered to prove it by forming a nonpartisan cabinet free of his associates.[166] Soái and Tắc called Diệm's bluff and ordered the sect ministers to resign immediately.[167] The premier never followed through on the offer.

Although the United Front appeared strong, Generals Phương and Thế were playing a double game. On the same day that Diệm offered to form an impartial government, Thế announced his withdrawal from the front and explained that he had joined to help reconcile Diệm with the opposition. Thế considered the task accomplished now that the premier had promised to form a nonpartisan administration.[168] But the statement masked ulterior motives. Thế had asked Diệm to provide additional financial assistance to the general's guerilla army and to allow Thế's political party to operate legally, and the general signed the ultimatum to bolster his bargaining position.[169] No records showing whether Diệm provided the subsidy are available, but the Ministry of the Interior quickly granted legal recognition to the party just days afterward.[170] Phương was also engaged in discreet negotiations with the Ngô brothers. The commander of the largest sect army had spent weeks pushing the premier to provide larger subsidies and to integrate a greater number of Cao Đài troops; joining the United Front was an effective ploy to extract concessions.

Diệm felt confident that the front was on the verge of cracking and shifted his attention back to the Bình Xuyên. The gang's control of the police and security service had long been a thorn in the premier's side, and he planned to sack the Bình Xuyên police chief, Lại Văn Sang. On March 29, Diệm informed his subordinates of his intentions and ordered the army to forcibly seize the headquarters of the National Security Service. Secretary of Defense Hồ Thông Minh objected that such action would provoke violence and resigned in protest. General Lê Văn Ty, the new chief of staff of the VNA, also resisted the order. It finally fell to General Ély and other French generals to convince Diệm to cancel the plan, but the provocation had its intended effect.[171] Late that night, the Bình Xuyên shelled the Independence Palace and attacked the headquarters of the police and the national army on Trần Hưng Đạo Boulevard.[172] The French hastily mediated a truce the following day.[173]

Another rally bolstered the premier's position. On the night of the clash, Phương visited Diệm at the Independence Palace to finalize their negotiations, and the premier reluctantly agreed to integrate eight thousand troops from the main Cao Đài army into the VNA.[174] The two men probably discussed payments too, though the total amount that Diệm provided is not known.[175] For a second time, Phương had exploited a crisis to secure a major concession; he announced his withdrawal from the United Front.[176] The successive rallies decisively altered the balance of power between Diệm and the front. The defections not only undermined the coalition's political position, they also gutted two-fifths of the front's military capacity.[177]

Meanwhile, thousands of miles away in southern France, Chief of State Bảo Đại followed the crisis with growing alarm. The former emperor worried that the situation in his homeland was approaching a "civil war with religious overtones," American embassy officials in Paris reported.[178] Bảo Đại sternly ordered Diệm and the United Front to extend the truce and to peacefully resolve their differences.[179] But another skirmish erupted on April 19 between the Bình Xuyên and the VNA, and Bảo Đại decided that Diệm had to go.[180] The chief of state blamed the premier for mishandling the crisis and suggested to the Americans that Diệm be replaced with the northern Đại Việt chief Phan Huy Quát. Bảo Đại intended to summon both men to France, then offer the appointment to Quát while providing Diệm with a face-saving measure.[181] It is unclear whether the chief of state developed the plan independently or was influenced by the French, but he appears to have selected Quát to please the United States.[182] The American envoy Collins enthusiastically embraced the proposal. Ever since the clash in late March, he had concluded that Diệm's government was near collapse and had recommended

74   Chapter 2

that Washington confer with France regarding possible successors to the premier.[183] Collins was in Washington for consultations when he learned of Bảo Đại's intentions and, along with officials at the State Department, developed a tentative plan to resolve the sect crisis by restricting Diệm and the sects to advisory roles.[184] But Bảo Đại wanted to act quickly, and he sent a flurry of telegrams instructing Diệm and other political and military leaders to come to France immediately.[185]

THE BATTLE OF SAIGON AND THE DEATH OF NATION UNION

Back in Saigon, Diệm decided it was time to act. On April 26, he dismissed the Bình Xuyên police chief and declared the dissolution of the gang's shock police.[186] The police chief refused to vacate his post, however, and the Battle of Saigon broke out three days later. It was the largest military confrontation yet between the anticommunists. Although observers doubted that the VNA would remain loyal to Diệm, many young officers were eager to the fight the Bình Xuyên, and the national army forced the gang out of Saigon within a couple of days.[187] Major operations ended on May 5 when the Bình Xuyên retreated to the Sát Jungle, which had been the gang's base since the late 1940s.[188] The battle inflicted immense human suffering despite the short duration. The most intense fighting took place in the densely populated neighborhood of Chợ Lớn, and the indiscriminate shelling by both sides set entire city blocks ablaze. With houses in flames and gunfire in the streets, trapped residents had nowhere to flee. Many jumped in the nearby canal; others escaped by hacking holes in the walls of their burning homes to avoid the dangerous streets.[189] Hundreds of people died, thousands were wounded, and tens of thousands found themselves homeless.[190] One historian has suggested that Saigon suffered almost as much destruction as during the Tet Offensive.[191]

The battle decisively ended the sect crisis. The Hòa Hảo members of the United Front offered little assistance to the Bình Xuyên during the fighting, and the coalition subsequently disintegrated.[192] In contrast, the battle raised Diệm's prestige as the defender of the country against violent gangsters and tightened the bonds between the premier and the rallied sect generals. Phương's and Thế's armies fought alongside the VNA, though Ngô's troops were too far from the city to join the battle.[193] Perhaps most important, Diệm's victory convinced the State Department to scrap Bảo Đại and Collins' plan. Collins returned to Saigon in late May and received a surprising message from Secretary of State John Foster Dulles. "In the US and the world at large Diem rightly or wrongly is becoming [a] symbol of Vietnamese nationalism struggling against French colonialism and corrupt backward elements," Dulles explained.[194] The premier had indeed triumphed on all fronts.

The Battle of Saigon and the suppression of the rebellions in central Vietnam were watersheds in the history of anticommunist nationalism. Ever since the Unity Congress, the underlying assumption behind the calls for unity was that no group would try to exterminate a rival anticommunist organization, but the Diemists broke that taboo in the winter and spring of 1955. The violence destroyed the possibility of national union and provoked a new political schism that pitted Diệm's supporters against his opponents. The Diemists and the rallied sect factions continued to champion the premier's leadership. Meanwhile, the Bình Xuyên, most Hòa Hảo groups, and some elements of the Đại Việt party and the VNP engaged in opposition. In between these extremes were the northern Đại Việt and the Catholic émigrés, neither of whom staked a public position on Diệm's government. The premier had also alienated some former loyalists, most notably the Spirit Group, which objected to his decision to use force against the Bình Xuyên.[195]

More specifically, the Battle of Saigon split the various sect groups and raised the question of why some factions opposed Diệm and others rallied to him. Many commentators have assumed that bribery won over the ralliers, but that explanation fails to consider the sects' broader objectives.[196] Sect generals worried about their financial ability to maintain their troops and feared that Diệm might violently suppress the sect armies. Many factions also aspired to participate in regional and national politics and aimed to reshape the country according to their distinctive vision. Financial inducements addressed only a few of these concerns. A better explanation is that Diệm's opponents perceived the premier's centralization as detrimental to their interests and the ralliers did not. The dissident Hòa Hảo generals wielded power through their armies, Viễn's strength rested on the Bình Xuyên economic empire, and Phạm Công Tắc's authority was based in Tây Ninh. These men stood to lose if they gave up their armies and autonomous zones. In contrast, Generals Phương, Thế, and Ngộ boasted organized political parties. Defecting to Diệm and integrating their armies resolved their financial problems, and the ralliers anticipated that they could secure a place in the government, especially in a future national assembly. That is, they gambled that they could give up their armies and continue to exercise political power. Future developments would tell whether their gamble would pay off.

CHAPTER THREE

Debate on Democracy, 1955–1956

The atmosphere was tense as the anticommunists filed into the Independence Palace on April 29, 1955, in the middle of the Battle of Saigon.[1] The Bình Xuyên and the national army were fighting just a few miles away, and the windows of the palace rattled every time a mortar fell close to the building. Premier Diệm arrived soon after and explained that he had received instructions from Bảo Đại to go to France for consultations. The chief of state had also summoned General Lê Văn Ty, the commander of the national army, and specified that Ty should transfer his command to General Nguyễn Văn Vỹ, a known opponent of Diệm. The news was staggering. Diệm's guests immediately grasped that the chief of state wanted to dismiss the premier but did not know that American policymakers in Washington had put Bảo Đại's plan on hold.[2] Diệm asked his guests to advise him on whether to obey the order and left the room for them to deliberate in private. The premier had invited only groups that supported him, especially the Diemist organizations and the rallied sect elements, and he was confident that his guests would urge him to disregard the summons.[3] But the unthinkable happened. Rather than confining themselves to the issue at hand, the conference announced the immediate overthrow of Bảo Đại and the complete dissolution of the incumbent government. When the attendees proudly presented Diệm with their decision, the premier reportedly blanched and asked, "Do you want me to make a *revolution?*"[4]

The premier could not have imagined that a mere advisory meeting would prove so historic. Republican reformers like Phan Châu Trinh had popularized the concept of democracy during the late colonial period, and the congresses of 1953 had affirmed it as a shared ideal among the anticommunists. Now, the conference at the Independence Palace launched a constitutional transition to realize

76

the long held aspiration. Yet the anticommunists' commitment to republicanism was tempered by their fear of communism, and their broad objective was to create a democracy that could withstand the communist threat. They believed that a representative republic was more legitimate than a dictatorship but worried that unfettered liberty and free elections would leave the state vulnerable to communist subversion. As Vietnamese leaders well knew, thousands of underground communists remained in South Vietnam and might infiltrate the government or incite dissatisfaction against the regime. Many anticommunists believed that the solution to the conundrum was to implement partial democracy, but this consensus concealed significant differences. The Diemists championed an abstract, philosophical understanding of democracy and envisioned an authoritarian, single-party government concealed behind a façade of representative institutions. In contrast, the rallied sect groups and their allies defined democracy in institutional terms. These anticommunists insisted on a more pluralistic state but stopped short of endorsing a full-fledged liberal democracy. Thus the disagreement was over the degree of democracy and authoritarianism suitable for Vietnam rather than a binary choice between opposing forms of government. The debate also reflected the political competition among the anticommunists, and arguments on all sides were shaped by partisan interests as well as political principles. In the end, the Diemists defeated their rivals and carried out a decidedly undemocratic constitutional transition. Although the other anticommunists lost, their arguments preserved more liberal strains of Vietnamese political thought that later activists would use to challenge authoritarian rule.

The debate unfolded in three phases with a changing cast of interlocutors. First, the Diemists and the rallied sect groups forged an alliance during the meeting at the palace. Both sides wanted to remove Bảo Đại and to establish a representative government but sparred over what type of democratic system to adopt and how to start the transition. The next phase centered on the constitutional process. The Diemists insisted on writing the constitution and selecting the assembly that would ratify it. The sects balked and joined with other anticommunists to form a political opposition, only to be brutally attacked by the regime. The last phase focused on the constitution itself. Diệm and his followers wanted the document to reflect their unique interpretation of democracy and to adopt certain authoritarian features, and both domestic and foreign critics objected to no avail. In October 1956, Diệm promulgated a constitution that paid lip service to democracy while enshrining authoritarian power in the highest law of the republic.

The chapter departs from the existing scholarship in arguing that the constitutional transition was both a battle of ideas and a struggle for power. Most accounts of this period have focused only on the political and military contest between Diệm and the sects, ignoring the ideas that drove either camp.[5] A few

78   Chapter 3

studies have analyzed the Diemist vision, but none have considered the sects' political aims.[6] By failing to study the political arguments of the different sides, researchers have missed what was at stake in the struggle. It was a question not only of which group would prevail but also of whose ideas would shape the government, and Diệm's consolidation of power was a triumph for authoritarianism as much as for himself and his partisans.

AN AMBIVALENT ALLIANCE

The conference at the Independence Palace translated the abstract ideals of democracy (*dân chủ*) and independence (*độc lập*) into specific, timely demands. The attendees deliberated for hours before passing three motions that summed up the goals of the invited groups.[7] The first motion blamed the Battle of Saigon on the Bình Xuyên and the French Expeditionary Corps (FEC). Rumors of French assistance for the gang during the preceding weeks had inflamed Vietnamese public sentiment against the FEC.[8] The second and most important motion called for a total reorganization of the political system. The attendees denounced Bảo Đại as a puppet of French colonialism, called for his removal, and demanded the dissolution of Diệm's administration because it was established on the authority of the chief of state. The motion empowered Diệm to form a provisional government that would secure Vietnamese independence by requesting the departure of the FEC. The provisional government would also "swiftly organize a national assembly that is elected by the people so as to return sovereignty to the people."[9] The motion implied that Vietnam could not be considered independent or democratic until the FEC departed, Bảo Đại disappeared from the political scene, and the government introduced representative institutions. The French had already begun a gradual military withdrawal, but the anticommunists apparently wanted the FEC to leave more quickly. The motion stopped short of setting a date for the elections and did not mention a constitution, though later events made clear that the attendees had plans for one. The last motion praised the Vietnamese National Army (VNA) and the rallied sect generals.

The attendees resolved to establish the People's Revolutionary Council (Hội Đồng Nhân Dân Cách Mạng, or RC) to ensure the implementation of the motions.[10] The council presented itself as a broad coalition with a unified agenda, but the RC actually broke down into two blocs with quite different motives. The first bloc represented the rallied sect groups, which favored the establishment of an assembly because they hoped to exercise influence over it. The second reflected the interests of the Diemists and their faithful followers. These council members nominated the premier to form a new government because they wanted to strengthen his personal power. The establishment of the RC marked the start of an alliance between the Diemists and the rallied sects, and the ambivalent

Debate on Democracy   79

Table 3.1   Sectarian Armed Factions and Parties, 1955–1956

Sect	Military Leader	Affiliated Party	Notable Party Leaders	Affiliated Newspapers
Hòa Hảo	Trần Văn Soái			
	Lâm Thành Nguyên			
	Nguyễn Giác Ngộ	Social Democratic Party	Nguyễn Bảo Toàn	The Masses
	Lê Quang Vinh			
Cao Đài	Trình Minh Thế	National Resistance Front	Nhị Lang	The Nation
	Nguyễn Thành Phương	Association for the Restoration of Vietnam	Hồ Hán Sơn	Vietnamese Politics, Epoch

Source: Author's tabulation.

relations within the council closely mirrored those between the allies more generally. The two sides agreed as much as they disagreed, and their tumultuous relationship would shape the first half of the constitutional transition.

The sectarian bloc was initially stronger than the Diemist bloc and dominated the council. The former controlled the top positions in the RC's permanent committee and likely spearheaded the effort to pass the three motions.[11] The bloc comprised representatives from the political parties that were affiliated with the rallied sect groups, namely, the Social Democratic Party (SDP) with ties to General Nguyễn Giác Ngộ's Hòa Hảo army, the National Resistance Front (NRF) linked to General Trình Minh Thế's Cao Đài guerilla band, and the Association for the Restoration of Vietnam (ARV) affiliated with General Nguyễn Thành Phương's Cao Đài army (see table 3.1). The power of the parties rested on the military and economic strength of the sect generals. At the time, the generals collectively controlled some nineteen thousand troops and continued to receive subsidies due to the slow pace of military integration.[12] Sect leaders also collected taxes from the local population because the central government had yet to penetrate the autonomous zones, and the generals channeled a portion of their funds into the affiliated parties.

Nguyễn Bảo Toàn (real name, Nguyễn Hoàn Bích) was the chair of the RC and the general secretary of the SDP. A Catholic from southern Vietnam and one of the founding members of the party, Toàn had served as the SDP's emissary to southern China in 1947 and had helped establish the Nanjing Front. He subsequently spent several years in exile, not returning to Vietnam until early 1955, when he reorganized the SDP and affiliated with General Ngộ.[13] Toàn was

80   Chapter 3

arguably the most prominent politician to participate in the conference at the Independence Palace, and his reconstituted party had a large Hòa Hảo following in the general's autonomous zone in Long Xuyên province.

Second to Toàn within the RC was the impulsive and daring Nhị Lang (real name, Thái Lân), the general secretary of the council and the preeminent cadre of the NRF. Nhị Lang was a journalist from central Vietnam who had started his revolutionary career in the Vietnamese Nationalist Party. He survived imprisonment at the hands of the Việt Minh and married the daughter of his party chief. But Nhị Lang later abandoned his wife to join General Thế in the maquis.[14] The vice chair of the RC was Colonel Hồ Hán Sơn (real name, Hồ Mậu Đề), who represented the ARV. Sơn was a young firebrand from north-central Vietnam and had formerly fought for the Việt Minh. He later defected, joined an anticommunist Catholic militia, and eventually became an officer in the main Cao Đài army. He was now a rising star in sectarian circles thanks to his charisma and military prowess.[15] The power base of the Cao Đài parties consisted mostly of faithful adepts in Tây Ninh province.

The Diemist bloc was the weaker partner within the council and held only a few seats on the permanent committee. The bloc consisted of obscure figures representing four parties. The most important were the Diemist parties, that is, the semi-secret Cần Lao and an emerging mass party called the National Revolutionary Movement (Phong Trào Cách Mạng Quốc Gia, or NRM) that served as a front for the Cần Lao. Both parties were strong in central Vietnam but weak in the south. Ngô Đình Cẩn had turned the Cần Lao into a robust organization in his region of influence and had established the NRM soon after the Hinh crisis.[16] In contrast, Ngô Đình Nhu had been too distracted by the successive crises in Saigon to devote much attention to party building.[17] Additionally, the bloc included two minor parties that had formed under the aegis of the Ngô clan but were not entirely under Diemist control. The Movement to Preserve Freedom (Phong Trào Tranh Thủ Tự Do, or MPF) consisted of a few dozen Saigon professionals led by Minister of Justice Bùi Văn Thinh, and the Citizens' Rally (Tập Đoàn Công Dân, or CR) was a predominantly Catholic group headed by the southern regional delegate Trần Văn Lắm.[18]

Although the balance of power within the RC favored the sectarian bloc, the Diemists dominated the government and the political fortunes of the sect parties remained uncertain. Their star rose in early May after the Cao Đài generals and Nhị Lang thwarted a coup attempt by General Nguyễn Văn Vỹ, whom Bảo Đại had chosen to take over the VNA.[19] But General Thế died fighting the Bình Xuyên a few days later.[20] His reputation had lent the sectarian bloc much of its prestige, and the death made it easier for Diệm to sideline the sect parties. On May 10, 1955, the premier announced a new cabinet made up of Diemists and members of the minor pro-Diệm parties but that excluded sectarian politicians

Debate on Democracy   81

(see table A3). The leading figures in this government were Minister of Information Trần Chánh Thành and Nguyễn Hữu Châu, whose unwieldy title was minister of state at the premier's office (later minister at the presidency). Both men were professional lawyers Nhu had taken under his wing. Trần Chánh Thành was a Việt Minh defector from south-central Vietnam who had served in the Ministry of Justice of the Democratic Republic of Vietnam. He later switched to the Diemist faction and became a founding member of the Cần Lao party.[21] Nguyễn Hữu Châu was the son of a wealthy southern landowner and had spent the wars years comfortably working for the Saigon Court of Appeals. His marriage to Madame Nhu's sister gave him an entrée into the Diemist inner circle, and he subsequently became influential as an assistant to Diệm.[22] Together, Nhu, Thành, and Châu formed a powerful clique of palace insiders that helped Diệm direct the constitutional transition.[23]

BETWEEN DEMOCRACY AND AUTHORITARIANISM

A vigorous debate erupted between the Diemists and the sect parties that summer, clarifying differences between the allies and revealing fundamental similarities. The two sides disagreed on the meaning of democracy, the suitability of a presidential or parliamentary system for Vietnam, and the best way to start the constitutional transition. Yet the Diemists and the sect parties also had much in common. Both sides rejected liberal democracy and instead favored what political scientists call a hybrid regime, one that mixes democratic and authoritarian features. The allies argued that Vietnam should become a constitutional republic with representative institutions but also severe limitations on civil liberties. Given these similarities, the differences between the Diemists and the slightly more liberal sect parties were of degree rather than of kind.

The political views of the sect parties are somewhat elusive. The main source for understanding the parties are their newspapers, and the material is too thin to extract a coherent political theory. However, the sources do reveal that the sect parties associated democracy with representative government and insisted that the transition should begin with the formation of an assembly. *The Nation (Quốc gia),* the newspaper of the NRF, argued that an elected assembly was democratic because it expressed the popular will: "To speak of a national assembly is to speak of a democratic structure that includes representatives of the people, representatives who are elected through a process that accords with the will of the people and who have the responsibility for undertaking national affairs on behalf of the entire people."[24] *The Nation* expected Diệm to start the transition with elections for an assembly and proposed indirect elections to filter out communist candidates.[25] The SDP agreed that an assembly was important but worried that the preparation for an election could take months.[26] The party organ, *The Masses*

82   Chapter 3

(Quần chúng), proposed that the government convene a provisional assembly with appointed members so that the people could immediately benefit from representative institutions. The journal added that even an unelected assembly could temporarily serve as a symbol of democracy: "As an elected national assembly cannot be established swiftly under current conditions, then there should at least be a provisional national assembly to represent the form and principles of democracy."[27] The continual emphasis on a representative assembly suggests that the sect parties favored an empowered legislature and possibly even a parliamentary system in which the legislature enjoyed supremacy over the executive.

The removal of Bảo Đại was a key feature of the sectarian vision for the transition. The Cao Đài parties expected Diệm to immediately disavow the chief of state. But they grew frustrated as weeks passed and the premier took no action. In early July, Nhị Lang of the NRF and Hồ Hán Sơn of the ARV held a press conference demanding that Diệm clarify his position on Bảo Đại's status.[28] The Cao Đài leaders claimed that the RC ceased to recognize the incumbent government because it had been appointed by the chief of state.[29] The move provoked severe tensions within the RC and between the Cao Đài parties and the Diemists at large. The Diemist-controlled police raided the headquarters of the RC in mid-July and interrogated Nhị Lang for hours in early August.[30] Nguyễn Bảo Toàn privately agreed with the Cao Đài demands, but the SDP adopted a moderate public stance and suggested leaving the question of Bảo Đại's position to the future assembly.[31]

Meanwhile, Diệm and his advisers developed their own plans without consulting the sect parties. The premier defined democracy as an ethical and humanistic impulse rather than a specific institutional form.[32] His political thought drew from the personalist philosophy of Emmanuel Mounier, who believed that the basis of democracy should be the person, meaning a human being who exists in a web of social relations. Mounier defined democracy as the political framework that could best ensure the freedom of persons to actualize their potential and to fulfill their social obligations, and democratic leaders were spiritually superior individuals who tried to create such a framework.[33] Following the French thinker, Diệm associated democracy with social and personal morality. "Democracy is a spiritual state, a way of living that respects the human person, both within ourselves and in others," the premier philosophized in the fall of 1955 when he established the republic.[34] Diệm did believe in representative government, but he considered any political form to be the temporary means toward the ultimate ends. A report by the US embassy in Saigon explained that the Ngô family regarded basic features of democracy, such as free elections and a free press, to be tools. "As such, they are at times desirable and at other times unnecessary or even harmful," the report remarked drily.[35]

Some of Diệm's advisers unabashedly favored strongman rule rather than democracy. The premier's office produced a position paper that summer that was most likely authored by the palace insiders Nhu, Trần Chánh Thành, and Nguyễn Hữu Châu.[36] The paper contended that although the population clamored for democracy, Vietnam needed an undemocratic "strong state" (*chính quyền mạnh*) that could guide the country through present conditions. The authors insisted that only a strongman could simultaneously enjoy popular support and build a strong regime because Vietnamese people tended to rally around a leader rather than a party or a political theory. "In the East, in Vietnam, the populace has a practical way of thinking and will react to [a leader], will trust or disparage, will support or oppose [a leader], based on whether the individual is good or bad," the paper explained. The authors identified Diệm as the man of the moment: "Today, the masses no longer trust Mr. Bảo Đại and see only Mr. Ngô Đình Diệm as a worthy leader. There is no one else." The position paper concluded that the government should rally the people by "venerating" (*suy tôn*) Diệm. The premier's advisers believed that devotion to Diệm could bind citizens together better than any political system—a proposition that implicitly justified a cult of personality.[37]

Diệm decided in late July or August that the country needed a presidential system with a powerful, popularly elected head of government similar to that of the United States. Unfortunately few documents about his conception of presidentialism from this period remain, but sources suggest that he considered presidentialism to be more stable than a parliamentary government and more democratic than strongman rule. At the time, the primary models of democracy for Vietnamese anticommunists were French-style parliamentarism and American-style presidentialism, and Diệm's advisers nudged him toward the latter. The position paper quoted warned that a powerful legislature based on the French model was the "number one enemy of a strong state." The authors likely had in mind the French Fourth Republic with its revolving door prime ministership and feared such instability would trigger the collapse of the State of Vietnam (SVN). Instead, the paper favored a political system in which the executive was superior to the legislature. As the authors explained, "It is not yet possible to absolutely ensure that the prime minister's prestige will overwhelm the reputation of the national assembly." Until then, "power must be divided in such a way that the essential part remains in the hands of the government so that it can act with strength."[38] Lansdale also tried to persuade Diệm of the virtues of the American political system and spent long hours explaining how the separation of powers functioned in the United States.[39] The manifold arguments convinced the premier to embrace presidentialism.

The Diemists believed that the transition to presidentialism should start with an election for the chief executive rather than for an assembly. The position paper proposed that the government organize a plebiscite to depose Bảo Đại and to grant Diệm "full powers" to draft a constitution. The authors stressed that the premier should be the sole candidate in the regime's first national election to

84   Chapter 3

strengthen his legitimacy and that the assembly should not form until after the constitution had been written and promulgated.[40] The objective was to concentrate power in the presidency before establishing a legislature. Other cabinet ministers embraced the proposal and agreed that the premier should seek a popular mandate as the first step of the transition. The premier appears to have consented to the plan by the end of August.[41]

Significantly, the sect parties and the Diemists defined civil liberties narrowly and willingly accepted restrictions on freedom in order to block communism. Although the rallied sect elements certainly believed in basic freedoms, party organs defined civil liberties as the positive freedom to advocate for anticommunist nationalism rather than a negative freedom from external interference. In March 1955, the ARV's newspaper, *Vietnamese Politics (Việt chính)*, published a letter from a reader that likely reflected the party's position. The letter writer believed that freedom of speech only applied to certain ideas such as patriotism, democracy, and the "just nationalist cause" (*chính nghĩa quốc gia*), meaning anticommunist nationalism, but did not extend to promoting colonialism or communism.[42] In private, sect leaders brazenly accepted the violation of civil liberties. Nguyễn Bảo Toàn of the SDP even suggested that the government preemptively arrest all known communists and other subversives who might be elected to a national assembly.[43] The proposed measure, given the size of the communist party, would have constituted a massive violation of civil liberties.

Diệm and his followers espoused an even more restricted definition of liberty. The position paper dismissed freedom as a Western concept and considered only two types of liberty necessary for the Vietnamese people: the freedom of expression to allow the population to show loyalty to the government, and the freedom from the totalitarian system of surveillance and control allegedly practiced by communist regimes.[44] Diệm was similarly illiberal in conceptualizing freedom as the opportunity to fulfill one's obligation. When he promulgated the constitution in the fall of 1956, he admonished, "Every person must accept all aspects of his or her duty and must carry out that duty. That will create confidence and trust in society, which are the necessary conditions for democracy to develop and blossom."[45] In short, neither the sect parties nor the Diemists favored liberal democracy, but the latter camp was more authoritarian in advocating for the premier's personal leadership, the overconcentration of executive power, and severe limitations on civil liberties.

THE COMPETING ALLIES AND THE PLEBISCITE AGAINST BẢO ĐẠI

The premier and his associates decided that the key to winning the debate was to overpower the sect parties politically, and the Diemists poured their energy and funds into expanding the premier's faction. The National Revolutionary Movement and the Cần Lao party enjoyed explosive growth that summer, and the balance of power between the allies tipped decidedly in favor of the Diemists. Although figures for the Diemist parties were notoriously unreliable, American embassy officials estimated that the twin parties boasted a combined membership of hundreds of thousands by the early months of 1956.[46]

The parties owed their growth in part to the Denounce the Communists Campaign, launched in July under the leadership of Minister of Information Trần Chánh Thành. The name of the campaign was somewhat misleading in that its early phase emphasized recruitment into the Diemist parties and political indoctrination. Thành was the chair of the NRM and helped create a civil servants' league affiliated with the party.[47] All government employees were compelled to join and attend weekly study sessions extolling the premier and criticizing communism.[48] A parallel effort targeted the military, and officers found that the campaign's mandatory political training doubled as a recruitment drive into the Cần Lao.[49] Pressure to join the secret party was tremendous because the Cần Lao military committee reviewed military promotions, and a favorable assessment could fast track an officer's career.[50] The political study program would continue for the rest of Diệm's tenure and became the primary vehicle for teaching civil servants and soldiers the official line on government policies and current events.

The NRM and the Cần Lao performed complementary functions. The main task of the former was to display public support for the premier, to publicize the government's position on various issues, and, later, to help organize elections. Most notably, the NRM played a key role in creating a cult of personality around Diệm. On July 7, 1955, the party organized a massive demonstration to celebrate the first anniversary of Diệm's assumption of office. Some ten to fifteen thousand civil servants, northern émigrés, and children gathered in downtown Saigon bearing the premier's portrait, and a representative of the NRM proclaimed Diệm the president of the Vietnamese republic.[51] Similar demonstrations took place in Huế and Đà Nẵng.[52] Later that month, the party launched its official newspaper *National Revolution (Cách mạng quốc gia)* to serve as the unofficial mouthpiece of the regime.

In contrast, the shadowy Cần Lao party carried out secret surveillance and covert action. Partisans reported on local security conditions, and party members in the civil service and military monitored their peers for signs of disloyalty to the regime. Nhu's branch of the party created its own intelligence service innocuously named the Service for Political and Social Research (Sở Nghiên Cứu Chính Trị Xã Hội), known to the Americans by its French acronym, SEPES. The agency was under the direction of Trần Kim Tuyến, a northern Catholic and longtime supporter of the Ngô family, and received some funding and training from the Central Intelligence Agency (CIA). Active mostly in southern Vietnam,

86   Chapter 3

Tuyến's agency collected intelligence on other anticommunists, infiltrated rival organizations, and secretly transmitted Nhu's orders to state officials.[53]

Meanwhile, the sect parties found themselves at a disadvantage. Internal disagreements and military violence eroded the parties' political base, and leaders could not force civil servants and military officers to join the sect parties. The SDP faced the greatest difficulty. General Nguyễn Giác Ngộ and the party had split with other Hòa Hảo groups during the Battle of Saigon to rally to Diệm. The fissure deepened when fighting broke out between the VNA and dissident Hòa Hảo factions in the Mekong delta. In June, the national army stormed General Trần Văn Soái's headquarters in Cái Vồn and overran General Lê Quang Vinh's base upriver.[54] General Lâm Thành Nguyên agreed to rally to the government just days before the attack on Soái.[55] Not only did the fighting make political organizing difficult in the Hòa Hảo heartland, the sectarian population also resented the government's attacks and had little sympathy for a party that supported the president.

Political feuds similarly troubled the ARV.[56] The main branch of the Cao Đài faith was torn between the religious leader Phạm Công Tắc and General Nguyễn Thành Phương, the head of the ARV. The two men had taken opposing positions during the sect crisis, and popular support for the party declined because many adepts sided with the cleric. General Phương went on the offensive in early October 1955. He surrounded the Holy See, disarmed Tắc's Divine Guard, and arrested Tắc's associates.[57] The operation destroyed any possibility of reconciliation. Dignitaries protested Phương's actions and even some of his own soldiers deserted.[58] A few months later, two Cao Đài guerilla bands declared their loyalty to Tắc and established resistance zones in Tây Ninh province and the Plain of Reeds.[59] Compounding these myriad problems was a shortfall in funds. The government cut its subsidies to the rallied generals as more sectarian soldiers integrated into the VNA, and the parties had little choice but to curtail their operations.[60] By summer's end, the sect parties found themselves in a more precarious position than ever.

Superior strength enabled the premier to move forward with the Diemist plan for the constitutional transition, and the government staged a referendum on October 23, 1955, to depose Bảo Đại and to make Diệm the new chief of state. Although the plebiscite contradicted sectarian plans for the transition, the sect parties welcomed the removal of Bảo Đại and agreed to participate in the campaign. Their cooperation revealed an underlying similarity between them and their allies. The Diemists interfered in every step of the electoral process, the sect parties accepted the irregularities, and both camps engaged in an unfair election despite their professed respect for democracy.

The allies began working on the referendum as early as September. The Diemists organized a massive petition drive to create the impression of a popular demand for a plebiscite, and the sect parties obediently passed a motion requesting that Diệm become president and asking for a referendum to depose Bảo Đại.[61] The ARV, the Diemist parties, and a few other groups then formed a campaign committee, and the allies held rallies and canvassed voters throughout early October.[62] Additionally, the sect parties urged their members and the public at large to overthrow Bảo Đại and support Diệm in building a democracy.[63] By these actions, the sect parties demonstrated that they had few qualms about participating in a rigged election.

The government's campaign blatantly favored Diệm and reflected several tenets of Diemist politics, including the personalist conception of a democratic leader as a spiritually superior individual, the understanding of democracy as an ethical exercise, and the conviction that a leader could command loyalty better than an ideology could. Government propaganda cast the plebiscite as a moral choice between the debauched, perfidious Bảo Đại and the upstanding, democratic Diệm. The purest distillation of the theme can be found in the training materials used by the political study program for civil servants and soldiers. Study guides for government employees explained that the duty of every citizen was to vote for the worthiest leader. Bảo Đại was a lustful "nightclub emperor" who served foreign colonialism, whereas Diệm was "moral with a revolutionary spirit," and his government protected the people's interests, the study guide claimed.[64] Similarly, training materials for the military praised Diệm as the "nation's only savior" and argued that the entire population should "venerate" him as the new president.[65] The exhortation drew directly from the position paper written that summer. Even the ballot made it clear that choosing Diệm meant choosing democracy. The government asked citizens to vote affirmative or negative on the following proposition: "I depose (remove) Mr. Bảo Đại and recognize (accept) Mr. Ngô Đình Diệm to be the Chief of the State of Vietnam with the responsibility of organizing a democratic government." Accompanying the text was an unflattering picture of a stiff-lipped Bảo Đại in traditional garb and a photograph of a relaxed-looking Diệm in a modern suit standing among supporters.[66]

The plebiscite of October 23 was a landslide victory for the premier. The government pegged the turnout at almost 98 percent, and just over 98 percent of that number supported Diệm.[67] The vote count was obviously inflated given that the tallied ballots exceeded the total number of voters in some localities.[68] In fact, a report by the CIA in the mid-1960s considered the plebiscite to be the most dishonest election during Diệm's rule.[69] Yet the premier and his followers hailed the victory as a triumph for democracy. On October 26, Minister of the Interior (and former Minister of Justice) Bùi Văn Thinh announced the official results and declared, "The first brick has been solemnly laid to form the foundation of a democratic government."[70] Diệm then issued a provisional charter

88   Chapter 3

establishing the Republic of Vietnam (RVN) and making himself the first president.[71] His government would henceforth celebrate October 26 as a national holiday commemorating the founding of the republic.

The plebiscite had profound consequences for Vietnamese politics. The defamation campaign against Bảo Đại cemented his reputation as a debauched collaborator and ended his career as a figurehead of anticommunist nationalism. Meanwhile, the election elevated Diệm at the expense of all other anticommunists. The referendum purported to give him an exclusive mandate to oversee the constitutional transition, and the United States and other allies quickly recognized him as the new head of state.[72] The plebiscite also eroded the basis for the alliance between the Diemists and the sect parties. Opposition to Bảo Đại had been a cornerstone of the partnership, and his removal left the allies with less common ground. The final defeat of the Bình Xuyên that fall further weakened the relationship. The gang had entrenched itself in the Sát Jungle after the Battle of Saigon, and the national army crushed the Bình Xuyên in a month-long operation in September. Lê Văn Viễn and his closest associates escaped to France.[73] With these shared enemies defeated, Diệm had little use for his sectarian allies.

"TOO MANY SEEDS OF DISORDER": THE DIEMIST REJECTION OF PLURALISM

The removal of Bảo Đại opened the way for a constitution and inspired a fresh round of debate on the constitutional process. The allies agreed on the desirability of a constitution and a constituent assembly but clashed over who would draft the document and how to select the assembly. These issues touched off a related controversy over the most suitable party system for Vietnam. As before, the Diemists advocated for Diệm's personal leadership and the supremacy of executive power, and the sect parties wanted the president to share power with a representative assembly.

The SDP had argued that summer that an appointed constituent assembly chosen by the government and the various parties should draft the constitution. *The Masses* proposed that a special committee should determine the proportion of seats reserved for each party and that the parties should nominate deputies subject to the government's approval. "In that fashion, we can avoid dictatorialness [in the relationship] between the government and the organizations over the selection of deputies," *The Masses* explained regarding the proposal.[74] The plan was likely the brainchild of Nguyễn Bảo Toàn and aligned with the sectarian preference for an empowered assembly. *The Masses* further contended that a constituent assembly was the only body that could legitimately draft the constitution. Referring to the envisioned assembly, the newspaper declared, "Everyone acknowledges that the fate of a country cannot be determined by an individual or

Debate on Democracy 89

a group of people. The fate of a nation must be determined by the entire nation, but how can the entire nation participate in national affairs if not through a national assembly, which gathers representatives of all classes of people[?]"[75] Unfortunately I have not been able to locate any records of a Cao Đài plan for a constituent assembly. (The proposal for indirect elections discussed earlier did not specify that the assembly would have constituent powers.)

In contrast, the Diemists anticipated that the president would lead the constitutional process with little participation from other groups, though Diemist plans would continue to evolve for several months. The provisional charter of October 26 specified that a commission would write the constitution and submit the draft to an assembly for approval and that elections for the assembly would take place before the end of the year.[76] The charter did not explain how the commission was to be constituted, but Diệm had every intention of packing the body with his supporters and thereby controlling the outcome. Moreover, the charter limited the power of the assembly to mere ratification. Rival parties would have little influence even if they won seats in the chamber.

In late November, Diệm announced an eleven-member constitutional commission that effectively served as window dressing for palace insiders Nhu, Trần Chánh Thành, and Nguyễn Hữu Châu to write the document. Nhu had apparently penned a draft that fall with some help from Thành and Châu, and Diệm named the latter pair to the commission. The commission likely adopted Nhu's constitution as a preliminary draft, and Nhu covertly exercised influence through his protégés.[77] Countervailing voices to check the dominance of the Diemists were scarce. The president did not give any seats on the commission to the sect parties or rival anticommunist groups, and deliberations were closed to the public. Even the Americans found themselves stymied in their attempts to shape the constitution. Lansdale had arranged for the Filipino legal scholar Juan Orendain to come to Saigon in August 1955 to advise Diệm, and the president presumably consulted with Orendain on Nhu's draft. But the influence of the legal scholar waned after the commission began revisions, and an alternative draft composed by Orendain never reached the commission.[78] The body eventually produced a full draft by mid-February, though the government never publicized the document.[79]

The possibility of convening a national assembly in the near future fueled a related disagreement on party systems. The sect parties championed a pluralistic multiparty assembly. The SDP's *The Masses* claimed that the varied interests of the Vietnamese people led them to form many parties, and no one party could represent the entire population.[80] Therefore, a genuinely representative assembly would include diverse parties. The newspaper contended, "Only a national assembly, where the political parties meet, can realize the cooperation of all political forces in the country because a national assembly is an institution that

90   Chapter 3

represents the supreme interests of the nation."[81] The argument reflected the anticommunists' long-standing conception of national unity as the incorporation of differences.

The Diemist position was more complicated. The president and his inner circle thought that the government could not tolerate any internal opposition due to the communist threat, and the Diemists favored a temporary phase of single-party rule followed by a transition to a two-party system.[82] "Our country has too many seeds of disorder. To my mind, there should only be one National Revolutionary Movement and one single political party, the Cần Lao," Diệm told a close confidante.[83] Along somewhat similar lines, American embassy officials found that Nhu and Châu, the minister of state at the presidency, considered opposition to be meaningless because genuine patriots could not possibly disagree about the main tasks the government faced.[84] But the president and his followers publicly disavowed single-party rule because most anticommunists associated it with communism. When a reporter asked Minister of Information Trần Chánh Thành at a press conference whether plans had been made to combine all parties, Thành denied it: "On principle, that [single-party] system is not compatible with my approach because, as you know, single-party regimes only exist in communist countries."[85]

The logic of single-party rule required the dissolution of all groups that might oppose the Diemists, and the first target was the Revolutionary Council. The central Vietnamese branch of the council disbanded under the orders of either Thành or Ngô Đình Cẩn shortly after the plebiscite. Diệm then urged the RC's national chair, Nguyễn Bảo Toàn, to dissolve the entire organization.[86] Toàn stalled for weeks before publicly denouncing the unauthorized actions of the central regional branch and declaring that the council had yet to make a decision on dissolution.[87]

Yet the Diemists did aim to form a two-party system of sorts. Diệm indicated to the Americans as early as mid-October that he preferred a two-party system like that of the United States over a French-style multiparty system.[88] Following Diệm's lead, *National Revolution* rebutted the earlier argument by *The Masses* to warn against a multiparty system. The mouthpiece of the NRM admonished, "We do not want the future national assembly to turn into an arena with too many parties that are in opposition, that will tear each other apart, and that will exterminate each other."[89] The newspaper followed up with an editorial claiming that a two-party system was best for a country like Vietnam that was newly independent and threatened by communism.[90] The Diemists apparently envisioned a party system consisting of themselves and an extremely loyal opposition. A report by the US embassy explained that the Ngô brothers believed a loyal opposition should concur with the government's main objectives and disagree only on the ways to achieve them and that oppositionists should never publicly criticize the regime.[91] Such toothless opposition amounted to single-party rule parading as a two-party system, but the Diemists believed that their version of a two-party system could reduce factionalism without obliterating differences.

PHAN QUANG ĐÁN AND THE PROMISE OF MILITANT DEMOCRACY

Diemist control of the constitutional process distressed the sect parties. They watched from the sidelines as the commission worked in secret and grew anxious when the government repeatedly delayed the elections for the assembly. The growing frustration of the sect parties made them receptive to the arguments of the northern émigré politician Phan Quang Đán (figure 3). Đán moved the discourse in an unexpected direction. He declared that civil liberties and pluralism were essential for Vietnam and organized a political opposition to challenge the Diemists. The debate revealed that the anticommunists adopted a range of positions on the question of democracy and authoritarianism: the Diemists advocated for a highly authoritarian hybrid regime, the sect parties preferred a hybrid regime with a greater liberty and pluralism, and Đán favored a robust democracy with only minor restrictions on freedom.

Although he would go on to become the foremost oppositionist under Diệm's rule, Đán was a still minor activist in the fall of 1955. The middle-age doctor from north-central Vietnam was known more for his work in famine relief in 1944 and 1945 than for his revolutionary record. He had joined the Vietnamese Nationalist Party during his college days, fled to southern China to escape Việt Minh violence, and broke with his party in 1948 to serve in the incipient administration that would become the State of Vietnam. The French granted the SVN too little independence to satisfy Đán, however, and the doctor went abroad to establish the Republican Party (Đảng Cộng Hòa) to advocate for full independence, democracy, and republicanism.[92] Đán's party distinguished itself from other anticommunists in stressing the importance of liberty. The party's ideology proceeded from the belief that freedom of thought was the source of human civilization and the basis for all other freedoms. The doctor favored strong legal protections for civil liberties, representative government at the local and national levels, broad participation in public affairs, and an independent judiciary.[93] Despite these bold ideas, Đán's party consisted of only two tiny branches in France and Thailand. He eventually relocated to the Philippines, where he received a visit from Nguyễn Bảo Toàn in July 1955. The two men had collaborated in the late 1940s, and Toàn probably tried to recruit Đán into the RC.[94] The meeting facilitated the doctor's return to domestic politics in early fall, and he found a ready audience among the sect parties.

Figure 3. Phan Quang Đán (courtesy of Phan Quang Tuệ)

Đán brought clear rhetoric and fresh ideas to the debate and rarely resorted to the sloganeering that plagued Vietnamese political discourse. More liberal than the sects, Đán appeared to favor what is known as a militant democracy. A militant democracy is similar to a liberal democracy except that the former minimally restricts freedom in order to protect itself from extremist groups seeking to subvert democracy.[95] The concept was associated with the Federal Republic of Germany (West Germany) and other postwar democracies in Europe that sought to block the rise of communism and fascism through special legislation. Đán never used the term, but like that of other militant democrats, his vision combined pluralism and expansive civil liberties with specific, targeted restrictions.

The doctor argued that representative government would be meaningless without civil liberties and admonished Diệm for failing to ensure the freedom of Vietnamese citizens. "How can there be free elections in South Vietnam when essential democratic freedoms have not been promulgated, essential freedoms that allow Vietnamese nationalists to organize into legal political parties, to present their programs, and to defend their convictions?" Đán demanded in an updated version of his party's program issued in August 1955.[96] His complaint referred to regulations that predated Diệm's tenure regarding political parties. The law required that all parties receive legal recognition from the Ministry of the Interior before engaging in political activities. Under Diệm, the ministry ignored the applications of rival parties, and most groups remained in a legal gray zone in which they were neither prohibited nor permitted to operate openly. Only the Diemist parties, the sect parties, and the minor, pro-Diệm parties were considered legal.[97] Đán was especially concerned about freedom of speech and complained that the government controlled the press and censored all publications.[98] At the time, the Ministry of Information instructed newspapers on what they should report, and government censors deleted phrases, lines, or entire articles before a journal went to press.

Đán differed from many activists in that he worried more about the dangers of too little freedom than about excessive freedom. In an interview with the ARV's newspaper *Epoch (Thời đại),* he insisted that expanding liberty would strengthen support for the anticommunist struggle and implied that limiting freedom could hinder the cause. Greater liberty "will give the people a reason to oppose communism because if we do not have freedom, how are we different from the communists?" he asked rhetorically.[99] True to the principles of militant democracy, Đán believed that liberty should be restricted only in the case of specific, dangerous groups. The doctor conceded in an interview with *National Revolution,* "I also agree with virtually all of my nationalist comrades that there must be [measures to] prevent subversion from the communists, colonialists, and feudalists, but other than that, I think that the time has come to promulgate democratic freedoms so that the people of the nation can positively contribute to the project of nation-building in this new Vietnamese republic."[100] "Communists, colonialists, and feudalists" were epithets used by the sect parties and the Diemists to refer to national enemies, namely, the communists, the remaining French presence, and Bảo Đại. Đán did not explain the degree to which he thought freedom should be curtailed, but his minimizing of the problem suggests that his position was far more liberal than the sect parties' narrow understanding of civil liberties. The doctor agreed with the sect parties' embrace of pluralism and stressed that political diversity produced better decision-making. In a statement he sent to multiple newspapers in November, Đán explained that in a pluralistic political system, "the national people will hear the peal of many bells, will see many different aspects [of a problem], and will have the sufficient conditions to clear-sightedly determine how to resolve important national issues in a suitable manner."[101] He specifically championed the existence of a legal opposition. He told *Epoch* that democracies must have a legal, constructive opposition and considered the absence of one to be tantamount to communism or fascism.[102]

EXPERIMENTING WITH OPPOSITION POLITICS AND SINGLE-PARTY RULE

Đán put his words into practice and set to work organizing a political opposition. He worked with various parties that fall to form a political study group, as mentioned at the start of chapter 1, and the group issued a statement on December 18,

94   Chapter 3

1955, proposing an alternative constitutional process. The activists suggested that the government and other anticommunist elements form a committee. The committee would organize the elections for a constituent assembly, and the assembly rather than Diệm's commission would draft the constitution. Đán's group issued a list of minimum demands, including promulgating civil liberties, ceasing all censorship, and issuing press regulations that specifically blocked communist propaganda. Citizens should be free to engage in all political activities that were noncommunist, and all parties should have access to the public media during the elections, including the Saigon radio station.[103] The plan aimed to give the Diemists and their rivals equal involvement in the organization of the elections and to create a level playing field for candidates of all parties. Đán was clearly the main author of the statement, for it directly lifted many phrases from his previous writings.[104] Signatories included representatives of the ARV, the southern Đại Việt party, and the Vietnamese Nationalist Party, but the SDP and the NRF were absent. No record exists of Diệm's ever responding to the letter.

The oppositionists' growing assertiveness convinced Diệm and Nhu to implement a modified version of single-party rule. To preserve the appearance of multiparty politics, the Ngô brothers allowed the minor, pro-Diệm parties to persist. But Diệm and Nhu stepped up the pressure on the RC and the sect parties to dissolve. Sectarian politicians refused to comply. Nguyễn Bảo Toàn, the chair of the RC and the leader of the SDP, made clear that he would not dissolve either the council or his party. Stymied, the Ngô brothers went behind Toàn's back and arranged for the Diemist members of the RC to pass a motion disbanding the council in January 1956.[105] Toàn and the Cao Đài leaders struck back with a press conference a few days later. Toàn contended that one of the council's original objectives was to form a national assembly and declared that the organization would not dissolve until this goal was realized. He also criticized the constitutional commission for not including representatives of the leading parties.[106]

Toàn's response prompted the Diemists to escalate their tactics. First they sent the army and the police to seize the headquarters of the RC, which paralyzed the council's operations.[107] Then they tried to undermine the sect parties from within. Toàn's SDP was affiliated with General Nguyễn Giác Ngộ, and the president secretly compelled the general to remove Toàn from the party.[108] Toàn fled to Cambodia to avoid arrest.[109] The Diemists applied the same strategy to the NRF, which was now affiliated with General Văn Thành Cao. General Cao had succeeded General Trình Minh Thế as the commander of the guerilla army after Thế's death in the Battle of Saigon. When the NRF's Nhị Lang steadfastly resisted disbanding the party, Diệm persuaded General Cao to dissolve the party over Nhị Lang's objections. Cao's decision provoked a mass defection among his soldiers. Some 2,500 troops from his army and another five hundred from General Phương's withdrew into the maquis in Tây Ninh province—possibly with Phương's tacit approval.[110] The defecting officers decried the forced dissolution and Diemist nepotism. "The policy of family rule has eliminated all sincerely patriotic elements in order to gather political power into the hands of a few trusted followers of yours and Ngô Đình Nhu's," the defectors charged in a letter to the president.[111] The accusation of family rule (*gia đình trị*) would haunt the Ngô clan for Diệm's entire tenure. The ARV succumbed to Diemist pressure as well. The available evidence suggests that the government tried to convince party leader Hồ Hán Sơn to defect, and General Nguyễn Thành Phương executed Sơn for betrayal.[112] Around the same time, the Ministry of Information forced all sectarian newspapers out of business.[113]

Diệm's closest foreign adviser, Edward Lansdale, watched the growing repression with horror. Lansdale pleaded with the president that all anticommunists should have a chance to participate in political life. The tactics of the Cần Lao party would drive the other parties underground and trigger violent conflicts between anticommunists similar to the deadly struggles of the 1940s, the operative predicted. In actuality, the internecine conflict had begun a year earlier with the Battle of Saigon and the rebellions in central Vietnam. The president was no more amenable to Lansdale's counsel than to Toàn's or Đán's, especially given that the official American policy supported the creation of Diệm's political party. Lansdale's influence on Diệm waned, and the operative left Vietnam at the end of 1956. His independent CIA station dissolved after his departure.[114]

The attack on rival parties paralleled other efforts at political and military consolidation. After the plebiscite, the Denounce the Communists Campaign entered a more aggressive phase that specifically targeted the communists.[115] Government agents organized mass rallies in the countryside, pressured villagers to identify underground communists, and arrested numerous suspects.[116] The number of detainees swelled into the thousands and rose even higher as the campaign continued. Wide-ranging estimates suggest between one thousand and five thousand executions and between twenty-five thousand and 190,000 arrests from 1954 to the end of the decade.[117] The government also renewed its efforts to crush the Hòa Hảo dissidents. The national army, now renamed the Army of the Republic of Vietnam (ARVN), attacked General Trần Văn Soái's forces in the Plain of Reeds in January 1956. Soái rallied to the government a few weeks later and lived the remainder of his life in quiet retirement.[118] In Saigon, the shuttering of the sect newspapers reflected a larger drive to tighten the reins on the press. The Ministry of Information granted the Veterans' Association a monopoly on the distribution of newspapers in January. The Diemist police chief, Nguyễn Ngọc Lễ, was the head of the group, and the monopoly effectively allowed the police to block newspapers from reaching readers.[119] The following month, Diệm replaced the existing system of line-item censorship with a draconian regime of fines and imprisonment. The new ordinance made it illegal to publish or

96   Chapter 3

distribute "distorted" (*xuyên tạc*) news or commentary that was advantageous to the communists.[120] The trend toward greater repression would give special urgency to the coming debate on civil liberties and judicial independence.

THE SECT PARTIES' LAST STAND AND THE CONSTITUENT ELECTIONS OF 1956

Diệm finally unveiled his plans for the elections in the last week of January. He scheduled election day for March 4, 1956, and promulgated two ordinances establishing the procedures for the event. Altering earlier plans, the laws declared that the president would submit a draft of the constitution to the National Assembly, the latter would approve or propose revisions, and the president would promulgate the constitution if a majority of the body agreed. The assembly would have 123 seats with separate constituencies for émigrés and certain ethnic minorities. The election would employ a single-member voting system based on a simple majority, meaning each electoral district would have one deputy (*dân biểu*), and the candidate with the most votes would win. The most unusual feature of the laws was the mandate on uniform campaigning. Candidates were not allowed to use their own funds or to campaign independently. Instead, the government would provide all campaign expenses, and a committee in each district would allocate the funds equally to the candidates. The committee would also organize rallies for the candidates to appear together, print the same volume of materials for every office seeker, and determine a uniform size and format for the materials. All campaigning was to take place within an official two-week period. These detailed rules ostensibly gave rich and poor candidates equal opportunities for electoral success, but the government could also seize on minor violations of the regulations to disqualify candidates.[121] The Diemists and many journals referred to the future assembly as a constituent assembly (*quốc hội lập hiến*), though the laws did not describe the body as such. The electoral ordinances served as the model for all future electoral regulations in Diệm's republic.

The president's opponents immediately attacked the ordinances. Nhị Lang sent an open letter to Diệm on behalf of the rump RC, which now consisted mostly of the Cao Đài parties. Phan Quang Đán likely helped draft the document, given that it clearly reflected his ideas. The RC lamented that the ordinances failed to provide for civil liberties, insisted on proportional representation rather than a single-member voting system, and complained about the limited power of the assembly in the constitutional process. Nhị Lang and his colleagues further argued that the ordinances gave excessive power to the president. "The President of the Republic has been given both constituent and constituted power," the letter deplored.[122] Constituent power is the power of the people to establish a government, and constituted power is that of the government to rule based on the people's delegated authority. The RC implied that it was wrong for Diệm to both write the constitution and govern based on it. The group threatened to boycott the elections if Diệm did not revise the ordinances.[123] But behind the bold posturing, the opposition that Đán sought to create was on the verge of collapse. The SDP was in disarray after Nguyễn Bảo Toàn's abrupt departure, and the Vietnamese Nationalist Party and the Đại Việt party had withdrawn from Đán's study group. The withdrawals might have been attributable to the doctor's polarizing personality. Throughout Đán's career, his admirers praised his courage and integrity, but his detractors derided him as an arrogant opportunist, and his many efforts at coalition-building yielded only weak, fleeting alliances.

Diệm realized that the Cao Đài parties formed the core of the opposition and hatched a strategy to neutralize his rivals. At the time, the ARVN had already taken over most military posts in the Tây Ninh autonomous zone, but the area was still home to multiple factions opposed to the president, including the religious hierarchy under Phạm Công Tắc, the Cao Đài political parties, General Nguyễn Thành Phương's army, and the defectors from General Phương's and General Văn Thành Cao's armies. On February 15, Diệm ordered General Cao to lead the ARVN in taking over all of Phương's remaining posts, and the latter watched helplessly as his military authority melted away. General Cao even seized the Holy See. Phạm Công Tắc hastily escaped to Cambodia to avoid capture.[124] The government forced the remaining dignitaries to sign an agreement promising to abstain from politics and ceding all administrative functions to the provincial government.[125] The invasion of Tây Ninh dramatically exacerbated tensions between Cao Đài leaders, as Diệm undoubtedly predicted. Generals Cao and Phương were especially fierce rivals, and they pushed Nhị Lang of NRF to choose sides. The terrified Nhị Lang fled to Cambodia to avoid being killed by either Cao or Phương.[126] Meanwhile, the government suppressed the ARV by pressuring adherents in Tây Ninh and elsewhere to renounce their membership.[127] The wave of repression even extended to Phan Quang Đán. The police detained him in February, and the government news agency falsely accused him of engaging in secret contact with the communists.[128] The successive attacks weakened the sect parties so severely that they would play no further role in the constitutional transition.

The constituent elections took place in the wake of the attack on the opposition. The boycott by the rival parties meant that meaningful choice for voters was minimal. Only the Diemist and the minor, pro-Diệm parties participated in the elections, and the most prominent candidates were members of the president's inner circle. The Cần Lao party fielded Nhu and Assistant Minister of Defense Trần Trung Dung, and the NRM put forth Minister of Information Trần Chánh Thành and Nguyễn Hữu Châu, the presidential minister. Trần Văn Lắm, the southern regional delegate, was the leading candidate for the Citizens' Rally,

98   Chapter 3

and the health minister represented the Movement to Preserve Freedom. Numerous aspirants ran as independents, most notably Madame Nhu.[129] The exact circumstances of her candidacy remain unclear, though she chose an émigré constituency in Saigon and most likely drew on the contacts she made during the demonstrations against the Bình Xuyên in the fall of 1954.[130] The Ngô brothers' decision to have candidates run under different labels suggests that Diệm and Nhu wanted to avoid the appearance of single-party rule. Yet partisan affiliation had little meaning because voters found the parties indistinguishable, and many candidates switched tickets or disguised their true affiliation.[131] Deliberate manipulation of the electoral process narrowed the field. Local authorities disqualified or removed undesirable candidates from the ballot, and the Diemists arranged for Trần Chánh Thành and Trần Trung Dung to run unopposed.[132] Most ominous, two candidates went missing during the campaign period, and rumor claimed that they had been arrested.[133]

The elections of March 4, 1956, were a resounding success for the Diemists. Government-backed candidates won seventy-four of the assembly's seats, and the palace insiders and other prominent candidates all enjoyed wide margins of victory.[134] The Diemist majority grew even larger after the body convened, and dozens of deputies switched their affiliation or declared one for the first time. The four main parties subsequently came to account for almost ninety deputies. With this overwhelming majority, Diệm and his partisans were poised to impose their uniquely illiberal vision of democracy on the Republic of Vietnam. The president was now so confident of his control over the constitutional process that he allowed the assembly to draft the document and announced that he would provide only some guiding precepts, contrary to the electoral laws.[135]

A MORE PERFECT DEMOCRACY

The last phase of the debate focused on the content of the constitution. Diệm and his followers wanted the document to lay the foundation for a new type of democracy based on personalism. The president's faction also insisted on incorporating features typical of authoritarian regimes, including the overconcentration of power in the executive and explicit limitations on civil liberties. A handful of deputies and foreign advisers protested. The constitution, they argued, should affirm democratic principles such as the separation of powers, judicial independence, protections for civil liberties, and the legal rights of arrested persons. But the Diemists ignored the critics and pushed through a constitution that invoked democratic and personalist concepts while violating the former and providing few assurances of the latter.

On April 17, 1956, Diệm sent a long memorandum to the constituent assembly proclaiming personalism (*nhân vị*) to be the official ideology of the regime.

The message clearly took inspiration from Mounier's ideas. The French philosopher argued that capitalism corrupted democracy because it concentrated economic power in the hands of wealthy elites and enabled them to control political institutions. Consequently, a rich minority enjoyed political freedom but the economically oppressed masses were too impoverished to find political liberty meaningful.[136] Along the same lines, Diệm claimed, "From the eighteenth century and during the nineteenth century, many constitutions established political systems that were later called 'political democracy,' in which 'individualism' and 'liberty' were hailed as the key to liberating the person and bringing happiness to mankind." But the president considered Western liberal democracy to be the god that failed. He contended, "When applied in reality, that political system provided liberty to a number of citizens, but it [democracy] also decreased the government's ability to serve the common good and left the government unable to address social inequalities."[137] Diệm argued that personalism was a more perfect form of government that preserved the virtues and corrected the shortcomings of liberal democracy. Personalist-inspired constitutions provided for the common good by reconciling individual freedom with social obligations and championed positive economic and social rights in addition to negative political freedoms, he explained. The president instructed the deputies to give the RVN a "spiritualist foundation" (*căn bản duy linh*) and to incorporate three fundamental principles of personalism into the constitution: the absolute worth of the person, the duty of the state to ensure the person's basic rights, and a humanistic conception of democracy as a tool for the development of the person.[138] The memorandum ended with a brief reminder to respect the separation of powers, judicial independence, and unspecified democratic rights (*quyền tự do dân chủ*).[139] In presenting personalism as a more perfect form of democracy, the president implied that his envisioned political system would be an innovation on the anticommunists' republican project.

After receiving the memorandum, the Diemist deputies secretly directed the drafting of the constitution. First, the assembly nominated a committee to write the document. The committee chair Trần Chánh Thành and several other members had been part of the constitutional commission.[140] Thành and his colleagues quietly adopted the old draft written by the defunct commission as a basis for their new draft, though they always insisted that the committee wrote its version de novo.[141] Few records of the committee's internal discussions remain, unfortunately. Then, Thành and the committee presented the new draft to the entire assembly, and the latter debated the document in plenary sessions. Once again, the Diemists discreetly guided the discussion. Nhu skipped the plenary debates and relayed instructions to Thành over the phone during breaks, and Thành and his committee acted as the unofficial arbiter of whether proposals from the floor would be accepted. The debate was mostly timid and dull. The absence of the

100   Chapter 3

recently suppressed opposition meant little adversarial rhetoric. Few Diemist deputies openly criticized the draft, and virtually all of them voted to endorse the committee's position even when they privately disagreed. In fact, the assembly never overruled Thành and his colleagues. Flashes of substantive debate erupted from time to time thanks to a few brave deputies who repeatedly challenged the committee, but the Diemists silenced these politicians with threats and accusations.[142] Thành's covert manipulation enabled the assembly to approve a revised draft after only three weeks of plenary deliberations, and the revised version preserved many features of the original document by the old commission. Public participation in the constitutional debate was virtually nil, in part because the deputies did not have time to return to their districts to consult local constituents.

The central issue throughout the drafting process was the principle of executive supremacy. The old version written by the defunct commission had proposed a presidential system in which the executive could interfere in the legislature. That draft had allowed the president to attend and speak during legislative meetings and to dissolve the assembly in the case of serious, repeated conflicts between the executive and legislature.[143] Such provisions seriously violated the separation of powers. One of the very few checks on executive power included in the old draft was a measure allowing the assembly to override a presidential veto of a bill with a two-thirds vote.[144] Thành's committee amended these provisions slightly to state that the president could not dissolve the assembly until a year after it first convened; it also removed the clause about presidential attendance during legislative deliberations.[145] Even with these changes, however, the committee's new draft provoked consternation on the assembly floor. Many Diemist deputies vehemently objected in private, and the reaction was so strong that Diệm agreed to a rare compromise. Thành subsequently allowed the assembly to revise the article to state that the government would hold a national referendum to resolve conflicts between the executive and the legislature.[146] But in other ways, the assembly strengthened executive supremacy. The deputies increased the threshold to override a presidential veto from two-thirds to three-quarters.[147] Equally important, Thành's committee added an article allowing the president to issue a budget if the assembly failed to vote on one. Nguyễn Văn Cẩn, an independent deputy from Gia Định province, protested that only the legislature should have budgetary powers, but Thành would brook no substantial alterations.[148]

Judicial independence and the rights of arrested persons proved another area of controversy. Diệm was wary of an independent judiciary because he believed that he had to be able to act by decree to meet the communist threat. Lansdale had tried to convince the president to respect judicial independence, and the Filipino scholar Orendain worked directly with Thành's committee on the issue, but neither were successful.[149] The original version by the defunct commission had established a judicial high council to oversee the promotion and discipline of judges and had made the president the chair of the council.[150] By giving the president influence over the magistrates' careers, the old draft had left open the possibility that the head of state could pressure a judge into issuing a desired verdict. The original version had also allowed nonjudicial "competent authorities" (Fr. *l'autorité compétente,* Viet. *cơ quan có thẩm quyền*) to issue warrants of arrest, though arrested citizens enjoyed the presumption of innocence and could petition for a writ of habeas corpus.[151] Thành's committee modified the old draft, but not by much. He and his colleagues inserted a clause nominally recognizing the principle of judicial independence, preserved the president's leadership of the council, and deleted all references to habeas corpus and the presumption of innocence.[152]

These provisions caused intense debate during the plenary meetings. Many deputies had served as judges and protested that the president should not serve on the council at all.[153] Several argued that only the judiciary should issue warrants. A deputy of the MPF from Bến Tre province (later renamed Kiến Hòa province) insisted that detained persons should receive a preliminary hearing before a magistrate within twenty-fours of an arrest. Nguyễn Văn Cẩn demanded that the constitution recognize the presumption of innocence and include the provision of habeas corpus. The rights of arrested persons was an especially pressing issue because the government had arrested large numbers of suspects in the denunciation campaign, and riots erupted at Saigon's largest prison in mid-May over indefinite detentions. But a deputy of the NRM from Thừa Thiên province retorted that the judiciary should authorize the executive to issue warrants during times of turbulence. Thành's committee resolved the matter by inserting a note in the official transcript of the deliberations that required nonjudicial authorities to notify the courts within twenty-four hours of issuing a warrant.[154]

Civil liberties and labor rights were also fraught topics. The draft of the old commission had provided for the freedom of expression and association.[155] Trần Chánh Thành and his cowriters expanded the article to state that citizens could exercise the freedom of thought, expression, assembly, and association within the limits of the law. Several deputies wanted to add the freedom of press and to remove any mention of legal limitations. Thành's committee responded with a new article on press freedom: "Every citizen has the right to freedom of press, aimed at creating correct public opinion, which the state has the responsibility to defend from all actions that distort the truth." The committee did not explain what constituted a correct opinion and further undercut press freedom with a note in the transcript. The note defined the freedom of press to mean the absence of censorship and explicitly allowed future legislation to regulate publication and

102   Chapter 3

distribution. The move enabled the government to continue its existing system of indirect censorship based on publication licenses, fines, and controlled distribution.[156] Thành's committee added an article on labor rights, and the deputies spent almost an entire day debating whether civil servants had the right to strike. The committee brusquely ended the discussion with a note in the transcript prohibiting strikes by civil servants, military personnel, and workers employed in defense and security.[157] Thành and his colleagues also composed two new articles curtailing civil liberties. One made all speech and actions aimed at propagating or establishing communism contrary to the constitution, and the other stripped constitutional rights from any citizen who used their rights to destroy democracy, freedom, independence, national unity, or the republican form of government. The assembly voted to accept both provisions.[158]

The commission's original version had included several articles that were inspired by personalism. Thành and his colleagues adopted many of these, and the assembly passed the articles with relatively little debate. "All people are born equal in personal dignity, rights, and obligations and must treat each other in the spirit of mutual aid and affection," declared the committee's draft, reflecting the personalist belief in the absolute worth of the person, the equality of all people, and communitarianism. A new clause of the same article proclaimed, "The state guarantees to all people equal opportunity and necessary conditions for the enjoyment of rights and the fulfillment of duties."[159] The statement drew from the definition of democracy as the creation of conditions that enabled the fulfillment of obligations. Another article made it every citizen's duty to develop their own humanity and contribute to the development of others' humanity, which turned the personalist drive to actualize one's potential into a political obligation.[160] As for the positive economic rights, Thành's committee assured citizens that they had the right and duty to work.[161] The new draft did not elaborate on these abstract declarations and attached no consequences for violations of the personalist provisions. Last, the assembly approved measures that preserved the authority of the incumbent government. The committee's draft allowed the constituent assembly to stay on as the regime's first legislature and the current president to remain in office. The official legislative and presidential terms would commence on the promulgation of the constitution.[162] The deputies transmitted their revised draft to the president in early July.[163]

GIVING WITH ONE HAND AND TAKING WITH THE OTHER: THE CONSTITUTIONAL CRITICS

The draft remained in Diệm's hands the remainder of the summer while the assembly was in recess. During this interval, the independent deputy Nguyễn Văn Cẩn and a few foreign advisers urged the president to bring the constitution in line with democratic principles. Nguyễn Văn Cẩn was an independent Catholic

Debate on Democracy   103

intellectual from the Red River delta. He believed that his religion was incompatible with communism and accused Vietnamese communists of persecuting the Catholics. The deputy had won the election as a government-backed candidate and had supported Diệm based on their shared interest in Catholic political and economic thought. But the Diemist manipulation of the plenary debates dismayed Nguyễn Văn Cẩn, and he vocally criticized the draft on the floor of the assembly.[164]

Beginning in mid-August, the deputy published an incisive critique of the constitution in *Democracy (Dân chủ),* one of more independent newspapers still in circulation.[165] Writing under a pseudonym, he invoked Diệm's memorandum of April 17 as well as personalist and democratic principles to argue that the draft failed to live up to the president's ideals. The rhetorical strategy was an attempt to avoid offending Diệm. The president had called for a clear separation of powers, but Nguyễn Văn Cẩn contended that the measures allowing the president to issue a budget and requiring an unrealistically high threshold of a three-quarters majority to override a presidential veto amounted to executive encroachment.[166] "It appears that the proposed constitution is meant to create favorable conditions for the legislature to become dependent on the executive, a dependency that can turn democracy into dictatorship," the deputy warned.[167] Neither was he satisfied with the draft's treatment of judicial independence, and he complained that letting nonjudicial authorities issue warrants opened the way for other branches of the government to interfere in the judiciary. "With such a constitutional provision, will the person be respected in accordance with the personalist spirit?" he demanded.[168]

Nguyễn Văn Cẩn pointed out that many articles simultaneously granted and limited freedom, a contradiction he described as giving with one hand and taking with the other *(tay này đưa cho tay kia lấy lại).*[169] He complained that the document recognized the freedom of speech yet narrowed its scope by subjecting publication and distribution to legal restrictions. The deputy declared that greater press freedom was essential for the personalist fulfillment of human potential and for distinguishing democracy from communism: "In a communist regime, the freedom of press is stripped away; in a personalist democracy, that freedom must be given back to the citizens so that they can develop all of their abilities."[170] Nguyễn Văn Cẩn averred that the unspecified limitations on the freedom of assembly and association and the ban on strikes by civil servants contradicted the "spiritualist foundation" that Diệm favored. The deputy cited biblical passages, the Catholic theologian Thomas Aquinas, papal encyclicals, and papal speeches to prove that Christian spiritualism supported the freedom of assembly and association.[171] The deputy concluded that the proposed constitution needed significant revisions before the document could be considered truly democratic.[172] His argument also implied that the draft was not genuinely personalist.

Foreign advisers echoed many of Nguyễn Văn Cẩn's complaints. The American political scientist J. A. C. Grant came to Vietnam at Diệm's invitation to

104   Chapter 3

privately advise the president on the judiciary and the constitution, and the professor submitted notes and revisions to Diệm in September. Grant urged the government to protect the autonomy of judges by removing the president from the judicial council and by appointing judges to long preliminary terms followed by lifetime appointments. When Diệm demurred that the government was not ready to set up a permanent system of courts, the political scientist suggested removing much of the section on the judiciary while protecting judicial independence to the greatest extent possible. Grant agreed with Nguyễn Văn Cẩn and other dissenting deputies that only the courts should have the authority to issue warrants. Grant added a number of rights for arrested persons, including a preliminary hearing before a magistrate shortly after an arrest (meant to function like a writ of habeas corpus), a speedy public trial, the right to be informed of charges, the right to confront accusers and to call witnesses, and prohibitions against double jeopardy. The political scientist proved less demanding than Nguyễn Văn Cẩn in other respects. Grant preserved the vaguely worded limitations on freedom of assembly and association and kept several provisions ensuring executive supremacy. Interestingly, the professor departed from the constituent assembly the most over the prohibition against communist speech and action. The deputies had unanimously passed the measure. Grant, however, found it imprecise and reworded the provision to place all words and deeds aimed at overthrowing the government outside constitutional protection, regardless of ideology. Last, he derided the personalist-inspired articles as "useless platitudes" and deleted them altogether.[173]

But Grant and other foreign advisers exercised little influence on the final document. The United States declined to take a strong stand on constitutional issues, and neither the embassy nor the regular CIA station in Saigon had any instructions to intervene. The American intelligence agent Rufus Philipps later recalled that the United States viewed the constitution as a way to regularize Diệm's power rather than as a foundation for a fully democratic government.[174]

The president sent a revised draft back to the constituent assembly in mid-October 1956 with changes that made the constitution even more illiberal. Several revisions reinforced executive supremacy legally and symbolically. Diệm reinserted the clause allowing the president to attend and to speak during legislative deliberations. He also added the line, "The president leads the people of the nation." The president followed Grant's advice to strike many articles on the judiciary but ignored virtually all of the professor's suggestions on the rights of arrested persons. The president placed even severer restrictions on free speech than before. "This right [freedom of speech] cannot be used to make false accusations, to slander others, to violate public morals, or to incite rebellion against or the overthrow of the republican government," Diệm's draft declared.[175] The revisions reignited some earlier debates, but the deputies made only minor alterations to the newest draft.[176] The assembly returned the document to Diệm on October 23 and the constitution was ready for promulgation.[177]

The constitutional debate unfolded against the backdrop of the government's final assault on the sectarian opposition. The first victim was the Social Democratic Party. The SDP had gone underground after Nguyễn Bảo Toàn's departure and suffered mass arrests at the hands of security agents.[178] The government decided to remake it into a showcase party. During the elections in March, the authorities permitted some obscure party members loyal to Diệm to win seats in the National Assembly and recognized the deputies as the party's official leaders.[179] The move deprived the SDP's original leaders of the legal authorization to participate in politics. The next victim was the rump Revolutionary Council. The group was already weak after the earlier repression, and the police arrested yet another one of its leaders in June.[180] The organization collapsed the following month.[181] The Association for the Restoration of Vietnam limped along a little longer. Operatives from the Cần Lao intelligence agency infiltrated and usurped the leadership of the ARV in November, and the Ministry of the Interior immediately recognized the new leaders. The usurpers forced General Phương and the original officers out of the party.[182] The showcase SDP and ARV would henceforth remain loyal followers of the Diemist faction.

Meanwhile, the military went after the dissident sect groups still in the maquis. In mid-April 1956, the civil guards captured General Lê Quang Vinh, the only Hòa Hảo general still engaged in armed resistance, and the government executed him that summer. In May and June, the army crushed the forces of the Cao Đài defectors from General Văn Thành Cao's army in Tây Ninh province. The twin defeats marked the end of serious armed resistance by the sects.[183] Of the small, weak bands that remained at large, most eventually surrendered, some established resistance zones along the Cambodian border or found asylum in Cambodia, and still others joined the communists.[184] The last remnants of the French Expeditionary Corps departed around the same time.

Diệm promulgated the constitution on the first anniversary of the founding of the republic on October 26, 1956.[185] It was a triumphant moment for the president, and the government celebrated with firecrackers, airshows, a torchlight parade, and traditional lion dances.[186] The constituent assembly converted into a legislative assembly and divided itself into a majority and a minority bloc as a first step toward the Diemists' desired two-party system.[187] The president and his followers must have felt satisfied with their success as they looked back on the previous two years. The Diemists had steered the constitutional transition toward their peculiar version of independence and democracy over the protests of their many rivals. Yet the victory came at the price of national unity. Diệm's consolidation of power pushed most of his allies into the opposition and deepened the schism between the anticommunists in the RVN.

CHAPTER FOUR

Diversity and Fragmentation, 1956–1959

On the eve of the legislative elections of 1959, the High Court of First Instance in Saigon tried a string of lawsuits filed by candidates vying for seats in the National Assembly. Virtually every case dealt with violations of the electoral laws. One suit targeted Nguyễn Trân, the leading candidate to represent the capitol's downtown district. In a field of eight contenders, half accused Trân of printing handbills in the wrong size, plastering his posters on top of those of other candidates, and using his own loudspeakers during the campaign despite laws to the contrary.[1] Another set of suits emerged from a district bordering Saigon, where at least seventeen office seekers competed for the same seat. The candidate favored by the government sued two of his opponents for printing handbills in the wrong color, and the representative of yet another candidate charged a different competitor with campaigning ahead of the legally permitted campaign period.[2] The most sensational case was brought by an incumbent against two challengers in a district west of downtown. The incumbent Ngô Sách Vinh accused Phan Quang Đán of bribing and threatening voters and denounced Hoàng Cơ Thụy as an accomplice in the recent assault of a famous soccer player. The defendants countersued Vinh for violating the electoral laws, though the precise allegations remain unclear. In the end, the court convicted all three men and slapped them with suspended fines of several thousand piasters.[3] Had so many candidates actually broken the law?

The lawsuits reflected two defining features of Vietnamese politics in the late 1950s. The multitude of candidates involved in the trials illustrated the bewildering diversity of anticommunist nationalism, and the bitter legal battles dramatized the fragmentation that divided different politicians and groups. The diversity and fragmentation partly explain the rancor between the candidates and their

106

Diversity and Fragmentation 107

determination to bring legal charges against one another. It was an open secret that many of the lawsuits were politically motivated. The electoral laws regulated minute aspects of the campaign, including the size and color of campaign materials and strict prohibitions on the use of personal equipment. Any candidate found guilty of violating the rules was barred from taking office, even though the very specificity of the regulations made conformity difficult. Taking advantage of the situation, unscrupulous office seekers tried to eliminate their opponents by suing other candidates on petty, trumped up infractions.

As the trials showed, although diversity and fragmentation had long shaped Vietnamese politics, both tendencies intensified in the aftermath of Diệm's consolidation of power. The president had sidelined his rivals and refused to form any institutional framework for cooperation, such as a coalition government or a multiparty legislature; meanwhile, the various parties and leaders had no forum for exchanging ideas or reconciling differences. The anticommunists still subscribed to the ideals of independence, unity, and democracy, but they interpreted the shared vision differently and proposed competing programs to achieve it. The result was a wide range of ideas but also deepening divisions. The main fault line remained the schism between the Diemists and the oppositionists. The former insisted on monopolizing power and had no interest in incorporating rivals into the government. The latter continually criticized the Diemists and suffered frequent repression. In addition, minor fault lines created internal divisions within both camps. The oppositionists were too divided to mount a coordinated challenge to Diệm, and the president's faction lost partisans, allies, and its early idealism.

The centrifugal tendencies of the late 1950s were an echo of the past in some ways. The schism between the Diemist faction and the opposition recalled the earlier split between the communists and anticommunists during the Anti-French Resistance. Just as the anticommunists preserved their diversity despite the communist attempt to impose single-party rule, so the oppositionists maintained their differences in the face of the Diemist determination to enforce consensus. The plight of the oppositionists also resembled that of all revolutionaries under French colonialism in that Diệm's rivals often could not engage openly in politics. As mentioned, oppositionists in the Republic of Vietnam (RVN) operated in a legal gray zone because the government neither prohibited nor authorized rival parties. The arrangement allowed the authorities to tolerate or suppress any oppositionist at will.

In other ways, Vietnamese politics before the turn of the decade directly reflected contemporary concerns. Many leaders criticized Diệm's authoritarianism and expressed distress over the continued partition of the country. The Geneva Accords mandated that the two Vietnamese governments should start consultations for elections in July 1955 and hold reunification elections the following

108   Chapter 4

year, but Diệm rebuffed all attempts by the Democratic Republic of Vietnam (DRV) to initiate consultations. He declared that the RVN was not bound by an agreement that the government had never signed and complained that Hanoi could not be trusted to administer democratic elections—a charge that was equally true of his own administration.[4]

The president's consolidation of power transformed the geography of opposition politics. Anticommunist resistance to Diệm had been strong in the provinces until the government suppressed the sectarian zones in the south and the resistance areas in central Vietnam. The repression forced many leaders to flee to Saigon where they could more easily hide from security agents. Other politicians wanted to engage in public opposition and could more freely do so in the capital than in the surrounding countryside. The southern metropolis had a high concentration of foreign observers, and Diệm permitted its residents more liberty than elsewhere in the RVN. Consequently, Saigon emerged as the epicenter of opposition politics within Vietnam. Other politicians chose to escape overseas and could criticize the president with impunity. Most congregated in Paris and Phnom Penh and turned those cities into international hotbeds of activism against the president.

Four main organizations dominated anticommunist politics in the late 1950s. The first was the Đại Việt Nationalist Party, specifically, its southern and central branches. The party continued the earlier struggle for a national union government and demanded a second, more democratic constitutional transition. The activists established an international branch in Paris, tried to influence public opinion in the West, and secretly agitated against the government in Vietnam. The second was a faith-based peace organization founded by the exiled Cao Đài leader Phạm Công Tắc and headquartered in Phnom Penh. Tắc championed democratization in both the RVN and the DRV and a neutral foreign policy in the Cold War. The third was led by Phan Quang Đán and other Saigon-based critics of the constitutional transition. These politicians were the successors of the Revolutionary Council in that they engaged in public opposition. The last and most powerful group was the Diemist faction. The president and his supporters argued that genuine democracy started with economic reforms and postponed political liberalization indefinitely.

The study of multiple opposition groups significantly revises the scholarly understanding of anticommunist politics in the middle years of Diệm's tenure. Most accounts have reduced the conflict between the government and the opposition to two episodes: the shuttering of the newspaper *Contemporary Discourse (Thời luận)* and the unexpected victory of opposition candidates in the legislative elections of 1959.[5] These events conformed to Western conceptions of politics in that both were secular, public, and centered on elections and the media. This narrow focus, though, ignores religious groups, clandestine activism, and the exile community, all of which were integral to Vietnamese politics. By including a wider range of groups, the following analysis more accurately captures the breadth of ideas and practices among anticommunists. More important, emphasizing the diversity of the different groups necessitates a reassessment of the opposition. At the time, commentators argued that the fragmentation of the opposition inhibited effective cooperation.[6] Although true, such claims failed to appreciate that the diversity of ideas enriched the political discourse. A serious examination of the various programs and strategies reveals dynamism and creativity as much as fragmentation and discord. Ultimately, heterogeneity was a strength as well as a weakness for the opposition and for anticommunist nationalism as a whole. Any regime would have struggled to work effectively with such disparate groups, but the oppositionists had much to offer a government capable of channeling their energy.

THE ĐẠI VIỆT OPPOSITION AND THE PURSUIT OF NATIONAL UNION

The opposition of the Đại Việt party began early in Diệm's tenure, and party leaders continued to interpret unity to mean a national union government and democracy to mean a representative, multiparty political system. The party's political methods drew on those used during the late colonial period. Đại Việt oppositionists organized an underground network in Vietnam and an overt organization in Paris. The strategy replicated that of revolutionary groups in the 1940s that operated secretly in the country and openly in southern China. The Đại Việt party also experimented with new tactics targeting Western public opinion, but the effort yielded meager results. Taken together, the party's politics demonstrated the persistence of old ideas and methods. The Đại Việt opposition included the southern and central regional wings of the party but not the northern branch.

Nguyễn Tôn Hoàn (figure 4), the chief of the southern Đại Việt, left Vietnam during the disputes over the composition of the cabinet in fall 1954. Hoàn favored a government that incorporated all anticommunist parties and decided that the most effective strategy was to persuade the United States and France to pressure Diệm into forming such a government. Hoàn's foreign approach reflected his lifelong tendency to look outward. He fled to southern China in 1946 as a young activist to avoid Việt Minh violence, then returned to Vietnam to serve in the cabinet of the SVN before turning *attentiste*. In the early 1950s, Hoàn came to believe that the United States was his country's most important patron and maintained close contact with American embassy officers.[7] After leaving Diệm's Vietnam, the Đại Việt leader spent the next two years fruitlessly pleading his case in Washington and Paris. He tried to convince Western leaders that the key

Figure 4. Nguyễn Tôn Hoàn (photograph by David Holden, Camera Press London)

to defeating communism was for Diệm to establish a national union government and thereby inspire broad popular support.[8] "Were President Diem to accept the support and co-operation of all loyal Vietnamese[,] the resurgent moral force that would follow would more than match the violations and the infiltrations of the Viet Minh," Hoàn declared in a letter to Walter Robertson, the US assistant secretary of state. American assistance could not make up for the total absence of domestic popular support, Hoàn added.[9] His partisans in France went even further in their internal newsletter to lament that Diệm had become utterly dependent on Washington.[10] The source of his funds was a mystery during this early period, but he and his partisans later opened a small Vietnamese restaurant in Paris to finance their political activities.[11]

In 1956, in response to the constitutional transition, Hoàn began attacking Diệm's authoritarianism and launched a campaign to turn American public opinion against the Vietnamese president. The objective was to persuade US citizens to put pressure on their government, which in turn would force Diệm to liberalize the RVN. The plan was unrealistic given that Hoàn lacked the resources to influence the US media: he and his followers could do little more than write letters to American newspapers and magazines. The exiled leader correctly observed that Americans had a favorable perception of the Vietnamese president due to positive press coverage.[12] In a letter to the *Washington Post and Times Herald* in September 1956, Hoàn complained that reporters intentionally published flattering articles to bolster Diệm's popularity in the United States and to strengthen his position in Vietnam, pointing out that such gentle treatment inadvertently enabled authoritarianism. "It is this very immunity from the pressure of American public opinion that frees South Vietnam's dictator from the necessity of improvement or concessions," Hoàn asserted.[13] Hoàn had few partisans in the United States and apparently relied exclusively on one operative to wage this campaign of public relations. Huỳnh Sanh Thông was a Vietnamese-language instructor for the State Department (and later a renowned professor of Vietnamese literature at Yale University). Thông had attended college in the United States on scholarship and likely joined Hoàn's wing of the party during the latter's visit to Washington.[14] Thông tried to reach the American public through a steady stream of letters to newspapers and politicians. He wrote a missive to the *Washington Post and Times Herald* in January 1956 accusing Diệm of persecuting other anticommunists.[15] In February 1957, Thông proposed to Senator Russell Long of Louisiana that the US government invite opposition leaders to America so that they could share their experiences and views with the outside world.[16] The language teacher sent similar letters to Senator John F. Kennedy of Massachusetts and Eisenhower's former special representative, J. Lawton Collins.[17] The State Department showed no interest in Thông's proposal.[18]

A SECOND CONSTITUTIONAL TRANSITION?

In Paris, Hoàn struggled to form an opposition in exile. The French capital was home to many Vietnamese leaders who opposed Diệm, including the Bình Xuyên chief Lê Văn Viễn, dissident general Nguyễn Văn Hinh, former premiers of the State of Vietnam, and various Bảo Đại loyalists. Hoàn eventually beat out the others by allying with the American far right activist Hilaire du Berrier (real name, Harold Berrier). Berrier was one of the most colorful foreigners to become involved in Vietnamese affairs. A journalist and an international soldier of fortune, his politics was a peculiar mixture of monarchism, anticommunism, and extreme conservatism, and he made it his personal mission to remove Diệm.[19] Berrier seems to have intimated to the Parisian exiles that he had come to France on behalf of the US government to select a successor to the Vietnamese president.[20] Hoàn probably calculated that a partnership with any American would bolster his position among the exiles, and it is doubtful that he fell for Berrier's ruse for very long.

With Berrier's support, Hoàn established the Movement to Safeguard the Nation (Fr. Mouvement de Sauvegarde Nationale, Viet. Phong Trào Bảo Quốc, or

112 Chapter 4

MSN) in the spring of 1957 as a coalition of Diệm's Paris-based anticommunist opponents.[21] The MSN called for the overthrow of Diệm and declared that Vietnam should undergo a second, more legitimate constitutional transition. The objective was to establish a genuine democracy and to restore harmony among all anticommunists. First, Diệm's government would be replaced by a national union government, a provisional legislature, and a provisional high council made up of well-known anticommunists. The government would consult the legislature on all major issues and receive advice from the council. Then, after a transitional period of no more than two years, elections would be held for a constituent assembly to draft a new constitution. The program attempted to turn back the clock on the constitutional transition and revived older ideas from Diệm's first year in office, such as a multiparty advisory council. Hoàn seemed to ignore the fact that uniting all anticommunists would necessarily mean including the Diemist faction. The program also reflected concerns raised by the constitutional debate, and the MSN promised to abolish all laws restricting civil liberties, to free political prisoners, and to establish an independent judiciary.[22] Although the proposal hinged on the removal of Diệm, the MSN did not explain how it planned to achieve this difficult objective, an omission that rendered the program an exercise in wishful thinking. Nevertheless, the coalition was the most stable opposition group in the Parisian community of anticommunist exiles and remained active until the end of the decade.

While Hoàn was overseas, the central and southern branches of the Đại Việt party went underground in Vietnam. The suppression of the Đại Việt rebellions in the winter and spring of 1955 had pushed both branches into clandestinity, and Hà Thúc Ký, who led the party's central branch, went into hiding in Saigon. Ký collaborated with Hoàn's deputy Jean Phan Thông Thảo to reorganize the party. They tried to incite popular discontent against Diệm and funded their operations through varied enterprises including a rubber plantation, a film distributor, and illegal currency trading.[23] The activists established an underground radio station in Saigon, and Ký read daily broadcasts denouncing Diệm's policies and condemning the treatment of the opposition.[24] The station operated somewhat fitfully until shutting down in 1956.[25] The Đại Việt set up a different radio station the following year in Cambodia that claimed affiliation with the MSN and lambasted Diệm's policies in Vietnamese, English, and Khmer.[26] The influence of the radio propaganda must have been limited given the inconsistent character of the broadcasts and the sometimes weak signal.[27] In addition, the Đại Việt issued booklets denouncing Diệm's corruption and cult of personality and circulated an internal bulletin that reprinted articles critical of the president by Berrier and other Western journalists.[28]

Although largely uninfluential, underground activism attracted the attention of Diệm's government, and frequent repression punctuated the Đại Việt experience throughout the latter half of the 1950s. In the spring of 1956, police agents discovered the illegal currency trading and broke up the party's financial and propaganda apparatus. The government deported Jean Phan Thông Thảo to France because he was a French citizen; most of the other suspects went to prison.[29] In an unrelated trial in October 1957, the Military Court in Huế convicted more than forty Đại Việt cadres for their involvement in the failed rebellion in Quảng Trị province years earlier.[30] Hà Thúc Ký was convicted in absentia and began serving his sentence after his arrest a year later.[31] In 1958, the Military Court in Nha Trang tried more than fifty defendants for participating in the rebellion in Phú Yên province, including several relatives of Trương Tử Anh, the deceased founder of the Đại Việt party. The court's decision to convict Anh's siblings cast the government as the oppressor of one of the country's oldest nationalist parties.[32] The underground activism appeared to have ceased by 1960.

NONALIGNMENT AND THE CAO ĐÀI PATH TO PEACE

In contrast to the Western-oriented approach of the Đại Việt, the Cao Đài religious leader Phạm Công Tắc (figure 5) engaged with international currents beyond the Western world. When Diệm's troops occupied the autonomous zone in Tây Ninh in February 1956, the cleric fled westward into Cambodia and re-settled in its capital city of Phnom Penh. Life in exile greatly increased Tắc's exposure to the nonaligned movement, that is, the international movement led by decolonizing countries in Asia and Africa that advocated for a neutral foreign policy in the Cold War. Tắc arrived in Cambodia just as that nation was on the cusp of embracing neutralism, a movement in which he discovered what he believed to be the solution to Vietnam's most pressing problems.

The cleric considered the partition to be the greatest crisis facing his homeland. He worried that Saigon and Hanoi might go to war and blamed the division on the Cold War rather than the long-standing conflict between Vietnamese communists and anticommunists. Such reasoning led him to espouse the concepts of peaceful coexistence and nonalignment, especially as articulated by Indian Prime Minister Jawaharlal Nehru, a leader of the nonaligned movement. At the Colombo Conference in Ceylon in May 1954, Nehru praised the recent pact signed between India and China known as the Five Principles of Peaceful Coexistence. Peaceful coexistence meant that countries with different political and economic systems should refrain from intervening in each other's domestic affairs. Nehru argued that all states could avoid war by adopting this principle. At the Bandung conference in Indonesia a year later, the Indian statesman prophesized that the Cold War would lead to global warfare and warned that integrating into either the Soviet- or the American-led bloc would

114   Chapter 4

Figure 5. Phạm Công Tắc (from Savani, *Visage et images du Sud Viet-Nam*; courtesy of Cornell University Library)

erode a country's national identity. Nehru counseled newly independent countries like his own to contribute to world peace by refusing to align with either superpower.[33]

It does not appear that Tắc ever met Nehru, but the religious leader was deeply inspired by the ideas of the Indian nationalist. Creatively adapting concepts from Nehru's speech, Tắc redefined the shared ideals of independence, unity, and democracy. The Cao Đài spiritual leader understood Vietnamese independence to mean freedom from the influence of the superpowers. He shifted the discussion away from cooperation and unity (*đoàn kết*) to the territorial unification (*thống nhất*) of North and South Vietnam, and he expanded the meaning of democracy to include the democratization of the DRV as well as the RVN. Above all, Tắc believed that Vietnam should spearhead a global peace movement by ending the partition and adopting neutralism. The cleric was not the only Vietnamese politician who advocated nonalignment at the time but was by far the most prominent anticommunist to do so, and his activism foreshadowed the peace movement that emerged in the RVN in the mid-1960s.[34]

Drawing on Nehru's argument, Tắc warned that the division of Vietnam into a communist zone and an American-led zone threatened peace and independence. The partition would provoke a civil war and turn Vietnam into a permanent colony, the cleric predicted. In a set of identical letters to Diệm and Hồ Chí Minh in March 1956, Tắc wrote in his characteristically rustic prose, "If that great catastrophe [the partition] continues and causes fratricidal warfare, then it will sap the energy of the national liberation revolution and [national liberation] will turn into an illusion." The cleric elaborated, "Because when the revolutionary movement is exhausted, the yoke of dependency will be placed around the necks of our people, and that will be even more harmful than French colonialism."[35] Tắc condemned both Vietnamese governments for their authoritarianism and pushed for democratic reforms. In another set of identical letters, he exhorted Diệm and Hồ to respect the freedom of press in their respective regions and to permit the unrestricted circulation of information throughout the country.[36] The similar entreaties showed that Tắc remained opposed to the DRV even as he embraced neutralism.

About a month after his arrival in Cambodia, he issued a program called the Policy of Peaceful Coexistence (Chánh Sách Hòa Bình Chung Sống) to unite, democratize, and neutralize Vietnam. The plan included two distinct stages and combined the principles of the nonaligned movement with aspects of the unification process mandated by the Geneva Accords. In the first stage, neutral leaders from both halves of Vietnam would form a committee to delineate broad national interests. Tắc did not explain what he meant by neutral (*trung lập*), though he appears to have had in mind leaders that were not aligned with either the United States or the communist countries. Then, Vietnam would form a federal government but maintain two politically autonomous regions. This arrangement of "one government, two systems" was an adaptation of the principle of peaceful coexistence between different states. In the second stage, a campaign would inculcate the ideals of freedom and democracy among the Vietnamese people, and both Vietnamese governments would introduce democratic institutions and respect human rights. Afterward, the people would vote for a national assembly in an election supervised by the United Nations, and the assembly would establish a central government for the entire country. Tắc did not offer a timeline for the implementation of his program.[37]

Nonalignment was a central component of the proposal. The cleric declared that Vietnam should form ties with nonaligned countries such as India and Burma but avoid entanglements with the United States and the Soviet Union, which could drag Vietnam into an international war.[38] Interestingly, the cleric presented his proposal as a fulfillment of the Cao Đài religious mission. Religious leaders had long argued that the Cao Đài faith harmonized the world's major religions and that the divine deliberately chose Vietnam as the location for

116   Chapter 4

the final revelation. Similarly, Tắc argued that peaceful coexistence would reconcile the opposing ideologies of the Cold War and that Vietnam and the Cao Đài religion should lead other countries to peace.[39] "I propose the doctrine of peaceful coexistence for Vietnam so that foreign nations will be moved. Because they will understand that this method [peaceful coexistence] is the only path for the Cao Đài religion," he explained to his disciples in February 1958. Tắc predicted that all neutralist countries would soon follow the path the Cao Đài had charted. They would realize that peaceful coexistence was the only way to survive the Cold War and would join together into what he called a "third force bloc between the Russian and American blocs to protect peace for the world."[40] Although Diệm's refusal to have any relations with Hanoi doomed the proposal, Tắc's prediction of war would prove prescient.

IN THE FOOTSTEPS OF YAN HUI

The cleric was the leading oppositionist in Phnom Penh throughout the latter half of the 1950s. Although he faced competition from other exiled oppositionists in Cambodia, his spiritual authority easily elevated him above his rivals, such as the Cao Đài politician Nhị Lang and military officers affiliated with General Nguyễn Thành Phương and the late General Trình Minh Thế. Even though he lived abroad, Tắc still exercised administrative and spiritual authority over the Holy See, and most adepts of the Tây Ninh-based branch remained loyal to him rather than other Cao Đài leaders. The cleric's political methods continued the sectarian mobilization that the Tây Ninh branch had practiced during the Resistance. Tắc used religious appeals to convert followers to his program, and his organization recruited partisans through existing Cao Đài networks. Despite this purely sectarian membership, his peace group boasted greater geographical breadth and organizational strength than any opposition group at the time.

The cleric's activism had three main elements. First, he lobbied Vietnamese and foreign governments belonging to both camps of the Cold War to accept his program. Tắc sent the Policy of Peaceful Coexistence to the RVN, DRV, United Nations, and Four Powers that had presided over the Geneva Conference, that is, the United States, France, Britain, and the Soviet Union.[41] Nothing indicates that any government ever responded to Tắc's overtures.

Second, the cleric urged Cao Đài adepts to adopt his program and join his peace organization as an extension of their faith. His "sacred letters" (*thánh thư*) to his followers in Vietnam described the peace project in explicitly religious terms. Confucianism was one of the main religions included in the syncretic Cao Đài faith, and Tắc instructed his followers to serve peace in emulation of Confucius' favorite disciple, Yan Hui (Viet. Nhan Hồi).[42] According to Tắc's adaptation of a Confucian parable, Confucius asked his students what they would

Diversity and Fragmentation   117

do if war broke out, and Yan Hui replied that he would stand between the front lines with a white flag and try to reconcile the warring sides.[43] The parable placed Tắc's project within an imagined tradition of antiwar activism.

Tắc established the Committee for Peaceful Coexistence (Ban Vận Động Hòa Bình Chung Sống, or CPC) to advocate for his program and mobilize adepts. A small entourage of dignitaries had accompanied the cleric into exile, and he ordered them to secretly return to Vietnam to organize the CPC.[44] The partisans recruited other dignitaries and adepts, formed a strong organization in Tây Ninh, and extended the network across southern and central Vietnam. It is unclear whether the Holy See participated in the project directly.

The CPC's greatest achievement was a surprise political demonstration. On February 8, 1957, the Holy See celebrated an annual holiday that attracted tens of thousands of believers. Cao Đài temples from far-flung provinces sent delegations to march in the procession, and the audience included government officials and foreign diplomats. Unique to that year's celebration, an American film crew came to shoot scenes for Joseph Mankiewicz's adaptation of Graham Greene's *Quiet American*. The CPC seized on the opportunity to publicly promote its cause.[45] On the day of the festivities, the partisans hung banners in front of the Holy See with messages in English and Vietnamese calling for Tắc's return from exile. During the parade, activists among the provincial and youth delegations chanted slogans promoting peaceful coexistence and inserted a special float at the head of the procession to illustrate the objective of the CPC. Splayed across the float was a banner with a Vietnamese idiom about cockfighting: "Roosters of the same household paint their faces and fight each another" (*Gà nhà bôi mặt đá nhau*).[46] The expression described disunity and conflict within a family or community. Two men dressed as identical roosters stood on the float, and when they began to fight, a dignitary in white religious garb rushed into the middle to break up the altercation. The skit applied the idiomatic expression to partitioned Vietnam and cast the Cao Đài religion as a peacemaker similar to Yan Hui. The CPC also distributed handbills showing a cleric separating a pair of fighting roosters. As soon as the festival ended, the government's crackdown began. The police arrested numerous dignitaries and adepts and effectively paralyzed the CPC.[47]

The third and most ambitious element of Tắc's activism was to organize a multifaith peace movement. He envisioned an association called the Congregation for Peace (Hòa Bình Giáo Hội) that would advocate for national reunification and pray for world peace. The congregation would include Vietnamese religious leaders representing a variety of faiths, and each leader would form an organization of his or her own followers similar to the CPC.[48] Despite his best efforts, Tắc was unable to convince anyone outside of his faith to join the movement. The cleric's plan for the Congregation for Peace was idealistic to the point

118   Chapter 4

of being quixotic. He instructed members of the congregation to emulate Yan Hui and physically prevent the outbreak of war. In May 1956, four Cao Đài adepts answered Tắc's call. They trekked to the seventeenth parallel to stake a flag featuring Yan Hui's name at the demilitarized zone, but the army arrested the band on suspicion of being communist agents.[49] Other adepts followed, and the government reportedly detained more than twenty persons engaged in similar missions by the fall of 1957.[50] Unfortunately for Tắc, Diệm regarded nonalignment and peaceful coexistence to be communist ruses and resolved to curb the cleric's influence.[51] In May 1957, the government installed a different, more pliable dignitary to replace Tắc as head of the Holy See, and the new leader cut off Tắc's authority.[52] The exiled cleric died in Phnom Penh two years later, and his already weakened peace organization withered without his leadership.

THE DEMOCRATIC BLOC AND THE UNFINISHED REVOLUTION

The clandestinity of the Đại Việt opposition and the concentration of the Cao Đài peace movement in Tây Ninh left Saigon an open field for a third opposition group, the Democratic Bloc (Khối Dân Chủ, or DB), led by Phan Quang Đán and other critics of the constitutional transition. The DB formed in the fall of 1956 around the time that Diệm promulgated the constitution, and the bloc went public the following spring. The DB made democracy its signature issue. Đán and his colleagues regarded the constitutional transition as an unfinished revolution and urged Diệm to carry out democratization. The distinguishing feature of the bloc was its innovative method of political activism. Đán and his colleagues advocated for public opposition rather than underground organizing and openly disseminated their ideas through the media. The strategy turned the DB into the most visible opposition group in the RVN. The weakness the bloc never overcame, however, was its tiny membership. Thus the DB was an inverse of the Cao Đài peace movement that boasted a large organized following but was unknown outside sectarian circles.

The DB was the brainchild of Đán and two other oppositionists, Nguyễn Văn Cẩn and Hoàng Cơ Thụy. Nguyễn Văn Cẩn was the independent deputy in the National Assembly who had famously criticized the constitution in the Saigon press. Hoàng Cơ Thụy was unknown relative to his collaborators. The middle-aged lawyer previously supported Diệm, first as an officer in a minor pro-Diệm party, then as a founding member of the Revolutionary Council, and later as a member of the constitutional commission.[53] But the increasing number of arrests and detentions troubled the idealistic Thụy, and the lawyer dedicated much of his professional practice to defending the regime's opponents.[54] Thụy decisively turned to opposition when he helped found the Democratic Bloc. Đán, Thụy, and

Nguyễn Văn Cẩn were all northern émigrés who did not belong to any of the major parties, and they tried in vain to convince other groups to join the bloc. The only significant recruit was Đán's associate Nghiêm Xuân Thiện. Like Đán, Thiện was a former member of the Vietnamese Nationalist Party who had broken away to join the provisional administration that would become the State of Vietnam. Thiện served as the governor of northern Vietnam and edited a newspaper in Hanoi in the late 1940s. He later relocated to Saigon and founded the newspaper *Contemporary Discourse.*[55]

Đán, Thụy, and Nguyễn Văn Cẩn introduced the Democratic Bloc to the public at a press conference held at Thụy's private residence on May 3, 1957, and the next issue of *Contemporary Discourse* published the DB's press release and manifesto. First, the bloc attacked Diệm for imposing single-party rule in violation of unity and democracy. The oppositionists argued that the government consisted of only one party because the various groups in the National Assembly were actually identical. "Because all of the government's organizations follow the same policies, the same doctrine of personalism, the same program, and they all express loyalty to the same leader, President Ngô Đình Diệm, we can consider them to be a single party—the only party—and conclude that the political system in the South is a single-party regime," the bloc explained in its press release.[56] The oppositionists contended that the true meaning of unity was voluntary cooperation between anticommunists who harbored substantive differences but had the same goals. As the official appeal of the DB contended,

> Unity in a democracy is not forcing all [elements] into a single bloc to support the government unconditionally but must mean voluntary cooperation between dissimilar partisans that are different in their program of action and their methods yet similar in their purpose: the opposition to communism, the construction of democracy, and the improvement of living standards.

The activists declared that the government was not yet a democracy because the regime lacked a legally recognized opposition.[57] The argument resembled those made by Đán during the constitutional transition.

Second, the bloc explained that it would contribute to the democratization of the RVN by forming a unified, aboveground opposition. The activists pointed out that the current opposition took the form of silent dissatisfaction or clandestine organizing, and these hidden oppositionists could turn violent or join the communists. The solution was for the DB to organize all dissatisfied elements into a single group that would engage in public, peaceful, and legal opposition.[58] The goal was presumably the establishment of a two-party system consisting of the Diemist faction and a unitary opposition party. The activists knew that the Ministry of the Interior never granted legal recognition to opposition parties, but

120   Chapter 4

Ðán breezily explained in response to a reporter's question that the DB was legal because the constitution guaranteed freedom of assembly and association.[59]

Third, the oppositionists sketched a program that called for complete democratization and put particular emphasis on civil liberties. The DB urged the government to fully grant citizens the freedom of speech, press, association, and assembly. Concerned about the rising number of detentions, the activists advocated for an independent judiciary, the release of all political prisoners, the right of habeas corpus, the prohibition of torture and warrantless detentions, and greater oversight of the security and police apparatus.[60] The government should start the process of democratization by repealing all laws that were undemocratic or unconstitutional, including those that forced political parties to seek legal authorization, allowed the government to detain anyone suspected of endangering national security, required newspapers to obtain a license for publication, and punished journals for publishing "distorted" commentary or news deemed advantageous to the communists. The bloc anticipated the usual complaint that too much freedom enabled communist subversion and insisted that the government should specifically outlaw communism rather than restrict civil liberties. [61] The DB did not clarify how democratic it wanted the government to be, but the last point reflected Ðán's embrace of militant democracy.

Diệm at first treated the bloc with surprising lenience. The police detained the three founders only a few hours after the press conference, and the Ministry of Information even permitted local newspapers to report on the group.[62] The most immediate challenge facing the DB actually came from within. A power struggle between Ðán, Thụy, and Nguyễn Văn Cẩn broke out after the press conference, with Ðán emerging as the undisputed leader of the bloc, and the other two abruptly leaving the organization.[63] Even more worrisome for the DB was that it barely attracted any new members despite its ambition to unite all oppositionists.

THE RISE AND FALL OF *CONTEMPORARY DISCOURSE*

Unable to recruit successfully, the bloc embarked on a different method of activism that played to Ðán's strengths. The doctor differed from most oppositionists in that he was more effective at channeling popular sentiments than organizing followers, and he decided to expand the influence of the DB by using the media to attract constituents. That is, Ðán acted like a politician who tried to persuade citizens that he and his group represented their interests rather than like a revolutionary leader who aimed to recruit committed partisans. The main vehicle for reaching potential constituents was Nghiêm Xuân Thiện's newspaper, and the two men remade *Contemporary Discourse* into the de facto organ of the bloc and a popular forum for criticizing the government. The result was

Diversity and Fragmentation   121

sensational. The journal won widespread sympathy from the reading public and became the best-selling newspaper in the RVN. The historian Jason Picard has described *Contemporary Discourse* as the regime's first national opposition newspaper for its broad appeal.[64] But the journal overshadowed the DB itself and only heightened the fame of Ðán and Thiện as individuals. In the end, Ðán would reap the most political benefit from the newspaper.

Contemporary Discourse steadily wooed readers throughout the summer of 1957 by adopting popular positions on a series of controversial issues. In June and July, Ðán penned articles attacking the harsh new nationality policy targeting the ethnic Chinese minority and chiding the regime for clearing the slums by the Saigon harbor.[65] Diệm wanted to prettify the capital in anticipation of the Colombo Conference scheduled for that fall, Ðán charged. Because the journal was the only one to take a strong stance on either issue, ethnic Chinese and slum dwellers bought up the newspaper in droves to express their approval, and *Contemporary Discourse* reportedly increased its circulation ninefold.[66] Bolstered by the success, Thiện published letters from readers airing grievances against the government, including merchants complaining about heavy fines imposed by the Ministry of Economy, soldiers demanding demobilization from the army, Cao Ðài clerics decrying the encroachment of temple property by local authorities, and policemen asking for a raise commensurate with their promotion.[67] The willingness of the newspaper to publicize such complaints further drove up sales. The newspaper was even popular outside Saigon, and copies of the individual issues sold for as much as fifty piasters apiece in the southern provinces despite attempts by security agents to suppress circulation.[68] Irritated by the success of the newspaper, the Diemists arranged for some of their partisans to slap *Contemporary Discourse* with frivolous lawsuits that fall, and the courts forced Nghiêm Xuân Thiện to pay damages and heavy fines.[69]

Greater fame and more repression followed, and both served to cement Phan Quang Ðán's fame as the leading oppositionist in the RVN. In late August, the Military Court in Saigon sentenced to death eight defendants who had been arrested in 1955 in connection to the Bình Xuyên, including some renowned southern intellectuals and politicians.[70] After Ðán launched a campaign protesting the sentencing in the pages of *Contemporary Discourse,* the Diemists sent mobs to ransack the newspaper's office and the private residences of both Thiện and Ðán.[71] The repression cast the two men and their journal as the flagbearers of press freedom. The final straw for Diệm was a series of incendiary articles attacking the government in late 1957 and 1958. The unknown author used the pseudonym XYZ, and admirers and enemies alike assumed that Ðán was the behind the series, even though he had reportedly ceased writing for the newspaper months prior.[72] An installment by XYZ in early March especially infuriated the Diemists. The unknown author claimed that thousands

122   Chapter 4

of communist agents were in South Vietnam, demanded to know how the government intended to remedy the situation, and lamented that the RVN was an autocracy ruled by Diệm and his brother Nhu.[73] The government invoked the very same ordinance that the DB criticized earlier and charged Thiện and Đán with the crime of publishing distorted news that was advantageous to the communists.[74] The court gave Thiện a suspended sentence of ten months, withdrew his newspaper license, and after an unsuccessful appeal, permanently closed *Contemporary Discourse*. Đán was acquitted because no evidence indicated his authorship.[75]

The closure of the newspaper revealed the inherent weakness of Đán's method of activism: the government could silence any publication and cut off his contact with constituents. The turbulent fortunes of *Contemporary Discourse* may have convinced him to find a different political path. A few weeks after his acquittal, he formally withdrew from the DB to focus on his original party, the Republican Party, which he now renamed the Freedom and Democracy Party (Đảng Dân Chủ Tự Do). The DB invited Hoàng Cơ Thụy back to serve as its general secretary, but the group floundered without Thiện's newspaper and Đán's talented leadership.[76] Nevertheless, the brilliant if truncated career of the DB had a lasting influence on Vietnamese politics. As the next chapter relates, many oppositionists followed the model of the bloc in pursuing legal, aboveground opposition rather than returning to the old clandestine methods. The difference was that later groups could not secure permission to publish their own newspapers and could only disseminate their views through open letters and press conferences.

A careful examination of the programs of the Đại Việt opposition, the Cao Đài peace organization, and the DB reveal potential for cooperation between the groups. They all claimed that Diệm's republic was undemocratic and urged different elements to work together toward common goals, whether as a multifaith initiative or a unified, secular opposition group. Yet the differences pushed the activists into competition instead. The DB wanted to democratize the existing political system, the Đại Việt opposition insisted on establishing a new republic, and the Cao Đài peace group envisioned integrating the RVN into a reunified Vietnam. Moreover, the oppositionists actively criticized each other. The neutralist Phạm Công Tắc felt that the other groups tilted too far toward the Americans and derided Đán and Nguyễn Tôn Hoàn as pawns of the United States.[77] Đán had similar suspicions about the foreign ties of the Movement to Safeguard the Nation. When the Diemist-influenced newspaper *Freedom (Tự do)* asked Đán for his thoughts on the Paris-based group, the doctor abandoned his characteristic restraint and responded with an air of exasperation, "In my opinion, the work pursued by that 'movement' is very bizarre. Why is there a foreigner involved?"[78] The reply was a reference to Berrier. Ultimately, the

Diversity and Fragmentation 123

disagreement on objectives and strategies inhibited the emergence of a unified, coordinated opposition against the Diemist faction.

BUILDING THE "SUBSTRUCTURE OF DEMOCRACY"

The president and his followers agreed with the opposition that the RVN needed to democratize and that anticommunists should unite behind the effort, but Diệm's conception of democracy and unity differed vastly from his rivals'. He continued to draw inspiration from Mounier's philosophy of personalism and defined democracy as a continuous effort to create the perfect framework for realizing human potential. For Diệm, this effort started with economic reforms and only later culminated in political liberalization. Much as before, the president described unity as the duty of the entire population to assist the government in carrying out democratization. Yet the postponement of liberalization tacitly justified authoritarianism in the short term, and the expectation of popular support implied that Diệm and his faction were entitled to unconditional obedience.

According to Mounier, one of the shortcomings of Western democracy was that it provided civil liberties but neglected "material liberty," that is, freedom from hunger and need. Mounier believed that people could not exercise political freedom if they were preoccupied with economic survival; thus the most pressing task was to ensure a minimum level of material well-being for the masses.[79] Applying Mounier's philosophy to Vietnam, Diệm worried that the majority of his compatriots was too poor to enjoy the fruits of a political democracy. The president argued that the constitutional transition should be followed by sweeping economic change, but political liberalization should be delayed until much later. "We cannot complete our revolutionary mission if we change the political system without changing the old economic system," he declared in a speech commemorating the third anniversary of his assumption of power in July 1957.[80] In a different address that October, he explained that his economic reforms would build the "substructure of democracy" (*hạ tầng cơ sở dân chủ*) and dismissed political liberalization as "achievements of a superficial character" (*thành tích có tánh cách hình thức*).[81] Diệm announced that his government would provide all peasants with housing and a parcel of land. "In the current stage of civilization, that small, basic piece of private property will be the guarantor of true personal freedom," he proclaimed.[82]

The president and his followers believed that they had to teach the people to be democratic and imagined a gradual process of government-directed liberalization in the distant future, though the Diemists never offered a specific date. The president explained in the October speech that the regime's community-oriented personalist approach would help teach citizens their rights and responsibilities.[83] Similarly, Huỳnh Văn Lang, the director of the RVN's foreign

124   Chapter 4

exchange office and a leader of the southern Cần Lao party, insisted that reforms had to be gradual because Vietnamese democracy remained immature, and the people had yet to understand their rights and obligations.[84] The Diemists even contended that the National Assembly was unprepared to take on the responsibility of a legislature in a liberal democracy. The president compared the assembly to a small child who had not yet learned to walk, and at least one government official predicted that the body would take at least ten years to reach maturity.[85] Yet maturity did not mean Western liberal democracy or any specific political form because personalists believed democracy to be an ever-evolving endeavor. When the American journalist Albert Colegrove asked Diệm about the latter's political vision, the president bluntly responded, "Personalism is contrary of any final political system."[86]

Diệm valued unity as much as his rivals, but he believed that unity required them to support his policies rather than indulge in opposition politics. The president asserted in a speech from July 1957 that that all citizens were duty-bound to contribute to his program and condemned any initiative outside of Diemist control as contrary to national interests. "If every person works separately according to his own ideas rather than pursuing a shared path and shared objective, then that solitude will result in failure and harm not just to the individual but also the nation," he contended.[87] He faulted the oppositionists for their factionalism and premature demands for liberalization. "Newly independent and underdeveloped countries will, in my opinion, find it to their advantage [to] get used progressively to [a] constructive democratic process instead of scattering their efforts among [an] infinite number [of] parties which leave to a Providence State [the] mission [of] conciling [the] inconcilable," Diệm told Colegrove.[88] In the eyes of the president, it was not he who blocked other anticommunist groups from participating in government but they who refused to accept their proper roles.

True to Diệm's personalist vision, the president's program prioritized the economic "substructure of democracy." In October 1956, the government began a land reform program in the Mekong delta that aimed to turn landless peasants into smallholders. The reforms reduced rent for tenant farmers to no more than 25 percent of the main crop, limited landownership to a hundred hectares, and made the expropriated land available for purchase by other peasants. Diệm touted that these measures advanced the goal of personalist democracy, but they actually worsened conditions for many intended beneficiaries. The problem was that the DRV had already carried out a generous program of land redistribution in southern Vietnam during the Resistance, and Diệm's more conservative reform led to the eviction of some peasants and forced others to purchase property that they thought was already theirs.

Diversity and Fragmentation   125

In April 1957, Diệm followed up with a large-scale project of population resettlement, known as the Land Development Program (Dinh Điền). The objective was to redistribute the population from the overcrowded lowlands to the sparsely populated Central Highlands. Diệm expected the program to contribute to the creation of a personalist democracy by providing for the settlers' material needs and by fostering community spirit. Two years later, the president inaugurated the even more ambitious Agroville Program (Khu Trù Mật). The program aimed to regroup the dispersed rural population of the Mekong delta into mid-sized settlements called agrovilles. Although motivated primarily by security concerns, Diệm expected that the agrovilles would improve the lives of rural people by bringing them together into communities and by providing access to government services and other economic benefits. But, like his land reform, the later programs alienated many peasants. Participation in the Land Development and Agroville Programs was supposed to be voluntary, but both involved coerced relocations and compulsory labor.[89]

Diệm and his followers resisted political reforms, however. The president still dominated the legislature; his partisans continued to control both the majority and minority blocs in the national assembly; and the deputies never openly criticized the regime during their deliberations.[90] In fact, the general secretary of the assembly, Nguyễn Phương Thiệp, believed that all differences should be resolved privately within committees because public opposition would damage the prestige of the government.[91] Deputy Hà Như Chi even went so far as to defend blind loyalty to Diệm. During the debate on the national budget in February 1957, Chi proclaimed that the majority bloc "approve[d] without reservation the enlightened political line of the man who directs the people—that is, the President of the Republic!"[92] Even the minority leader, Đỗ Mạnh Quát, believed that his bloc should limit itself to analyzing the enforceability and clarity of legislation and refrain from criticizing any proposed law.[93] It was precisely this unquestioned obedience to Diệm's leadership within the assembly that caused the Democratic Bloc to label the RVN a single-party state.

THE TRANSFORMATION OF THE DIEMIST FACTION

The economic reforms took place at a time of profound transition for the Diemists. The president's consolidation of power transformed his faction from a band of dedicated partisans to the dominant party. The number of partisans multiplied, and Diemist leaders enjoyed more political and economic power than ever. Yet the change brought its own difficulties. The expansion undermined the faction's early idealism, and the group's growing influence gave rise to nepotism and corruption. As a result, complaints of favoritism and financial

126   Chapter 4

malfeasance dogged leaders throughout Diệm's presidency. The Diemists also faced serious internal disagreements. Some partisans were forced out, others joined the opposition, and still others became dissenters within the faction. Perhaps most significantly, the Diemists clashed with the Catholic church, and the alliance between the president and émigré Catholics ruptured. These manifold changes contributed to the overall fragmentation of anticommunist nationalism.

The Diemists' political tactics enlarged the faction's membership at the cost of genuine political commitment. As mentioned, the Diemists compelled civil servants and military officers to join the Cần Lao party and the National Revolutionary Movement, and legions of apolitical individuals complied to safeguard their careers. The government also awarded economic concessions and contracts to Cần Lao partisans with the expectation that they would siphon a portion of the profits to fill the party's coffers.[94] The lure of investment opportunities convinced large numbers of businessmen to join Diemist organizations.[95] Even peasants became members to gain protection from government harassment.[96] The result was that both the Cần Lao and the NRM grew exponentially; estimates suggest that by 1959 the former counted as many as sixteen thousand members and the latter less than half a million.[97] But the expansion irrevocably altered the composition of these parties. Many former Diemists recalled that early partisans were idealistic nationalists attracted to personalism or Diệm's integrity but later members were opportunists.[98] The faction's economic power also provoked widespread resentment. The practice of granting economic privileges to political supporters was not new—the sects and other groups had enjoyed concessions under Bảo Đại—but the Diemists reserved the perks exclusively for themselves and took advantage of the privileges on much greater scale.

At the apex of Diệm's faction was his family, and he allowed the Ngô clan to become the unofficial ruling family of the regime. Each member carved out his or her own niche in the RVN, sometimes in competition with each other. The nepotism prompted the oppositionists to accuse Diệm of practicing "family rule" (gia đình trị). Nhu remained the most influential of Diệm's relatives. Nhu's wing of the Cần Lao party steadily expanded its power in the south, and the Cần Lao intelligence agency, run by Trần Kim Tuyến, played a key role in cracking down on the opposition and identifying communist infiltrators. It was likely Tuyến's agents who instigated the first lawsuits against *Contemporary Discourse* and organized the mob attacks. The agency expanded its operations to include a secret police force and operated underground prisons separate from the regular justice system. Although Nhu's followers multiplied in number, his branch faced considerable turnover and rivalry. The Spirit Group abandoned the Cần Lao party over Diệm's decision to fight the Bình Xuyên in the spring of 1955. Nhu's old ally, the labor chief Trần Quốc Bửu, grew disillusioned too. Bửu was a tireless

Diversity and Fragmentation   127

advocate of labor rights and insisted that his union should not have to seek government authorization to hold large meetings or to field candidates in elections. He also decried the sporadic arrests of labor organizers.[99] Relations between the Ngô brothers and the union was often tense, though Bửu stopped short of publicly breaking with the president probably to protect his members from harsher treatment.

Under Nhu's leadership, turnover was high even in the uppermost echelons of the Diemist faction, and several of his close collaborators fell out of favor in the late 1950s. Minister of Information Trần Chánh Thành lost the confidence of the Ngô clan for reasons that remain unclear and had to give up his chairmanship of the NRM in 1957. Three years later, Diệm downgraded the Ministry of Information to a directorate and appointed Thành to serve as the ambassador to Tunisia as a sort of golden exile.[100] Nhu's brother-in-law Nguyễn Hữu Châu, the former presidential minister and later interior minister, alienated the Ngô family by divorcing his wife, who was Madame Nhu's older sister. He then resigned and fled to France in 1958.[101]

Another source of tension was Nhu's arbitrariness and manipulative methods. He initially encouraged cliques to proliferate within his wing of the Cần Lao party, then abruptly reorganized the party into a single, centralized hierarchy in the spring of 1958 and forced some cliques to dissolve. Huỳnh Văn Lang led one of the disbanded cliques and later claimed that the dissolution prompted many of his partisans to leave the party altogether.[102] Around the same time, Diệm and Nhu decided to merge the NRM and the Citizens' Rally, the last minor pro-Diệm party still in operation. The move provoked dismay and resentment among the cadres of the Citizens' Rally.[103] Yet true to Nhu's penchant for encouraging a multiplicity of groups, he launched the Republican Youth (Thanh Niên Cộng Hòa) to compete against the NRM in 1960. The Republican Youth recruited Vietnamese between the ages of eighteen and thirty-five and provided them with limited military training. The group received funding and other support from the government, and pressure from the authorities ensured an artificially high membership of more than 1.5 million by 1961.[104]

Nhu's growing influence strengthened the position of his wife, and Madame Nhu made a name for herself as a legislator and self-appointed leader of Vietnamese women. In early 1959, she strong-armed the assembly into banning divorce, polygamy, and concubinage. Madame Nhu claimed that the legislation would protect the traditional family, but rumor had it that her real motive was to block Nguyễn Hữu Châu's divorce. The Ngô family was the only known supporters of the law, and there is no evidence of any Catholic lobbying for the legislation despite claims to the contrary.[105] The unofficial first lady of the RVN also devoted herself to organizing women. She took over the women's section of the civil servants' league in the late 1950s and reconstituted it as the Women's

128   Chapter 4

Solidarity Movement (Phong Trào Phụ Nữ Liên Đới) under her personal leader-ship. Members consisted mostly of women civil servants and the wives of prom-inent officials who were obligated to join.[106] These endeavors raised Madame Nhu's profile but did little to improve her reputation. Her acerbic tongue and ag-gressive style combined with the cultural discomfort with powerful women made her the most reviled member of the ruling family, and the Saigon gossip mill churned out salacious stories about her personal life and her and her hus-band's commercial activities.[107]

Outside Saigon, Ngô Đình Cẩn and Bishop Ngô Đình Thục were the most powerful members of the clan. Cẩn and his wing of the Cần Lao party continued to rule over central Vietnam and made inroads into the south. In 1957, Cẩn founded a secret police force that arrested both communists and anticommunists and sometimes held them in secret jails.[108] It was these agents rather than the regular police who arrested the underground Đại Việt leader Hà Thúc Ký in Sai-gon.[109] Bishop Thục's main role in the late 1950s was to train government em-ployees in the regime's official ideology. He established a training center in his diocese in Vĩnh Long to teach personalism to Catholic civil servants, then ex-panded the center to welcome non-Catholic employees at Diệm's request. Al-though Thục claimed that personalism was compatible with all major Asian religions, the instructors at his center were mostly Catholic priests, and their presence raised suspicions that the government favored Catholics.[110] More broadly, the rise of Diemist power combined with the Ngô family's tendency to rely on family and friends resulted in a disproportionate number of central Viet-namese Catholics in positions of power, and rumors circulated that promotion within the government and military required individuals to adhere to three C's: Catholicism, the Cần Lao party, and central Vietnamese heritage.[111] The many charges of corruption and nepotism chipped away at Diệm's reputation as a prin-cipled leader, especially in the eyes of his rivals.

PARTING OF WAYS: THE DIEMISTS AND THE CATHOLICS

Ironically, the Diemists lost considerable Catholic support despite the wide-spread perception of religious favoritism.[112] Observers have long assumed that Catholics unwaveringly supported Diệm and enjoyed special privileges under his rule, especially northern Catholics. But the Ngô family's relations with the church actually soured early on. The feud began in the fall of 1955 when the Vatican skipped over Bishop Thục and appointed a different bishop to the archdiocese of Saigon. The move may have annoyed Thục because the leader of the émigré church, Bishop Phạm Ngọc Chi, backed the Vatican's choice.[113] The conflict escalated a year later after the government issued an ordinance imposing state control over the curriculum of private schools, including seminaries and

Catholic schools. All bishops in the RVN save Bishop Thục signed a joint letter protesting the measure, but Diệm declined to respond.[114] Matters finally came to a head in February 1957 when a respected southern priest named Hồ Văn Vui gave a sermon at Notre Dame Cathedral in Saigon implying that the church was under persecution. The comment incensed Nhu, and the government put Father Vui on trial. The church had to transfer the priest to a different parish to defuse tensions.[115]

Many lay Catholics turned against Diệm during those years as well. The government wanted to relocate northern émigrés, most of whom were Catholic, from the temporary reception centers and shantytowns around Saigon to new settlements in the Mekong delta and the Central Highlands as part of the Land Development Program. Settlers who went to the delta, though, were outraged when the government failed to grant them their own land, and others refused to leave the capital. Émigré priests backed their flocks against Diệm.[116] Madame Nhu exacerbated the situation with a provocative speech in 1957, during which she accused émigrés of being lazy and stupid for clinging to their slums rather than moving to more fertile land. Madame Nhu warned her audience not to listen to "robbers in monk's robes" (*bọn cướp khoác áo thầy tu*), meaning émigré priests. Clerics and parishioners fumed with indignation, especially because she represented an émigré constituency in the assembly.[117]

A newspaper affair that same month triggered the final rupture. Diệm had recently survived an attempted assassination during his visit to the Central Highlands, and the journal *The Way of Life* (*Đường sống*) published an article obliquely acknowledging his falling popularity among northern Catholics.[118] The newspaper claimed that many émigré communities held special prayers for Diệm after the incident, chanting, "May Providence ever preserve the president's health, safety, and intelligence, in order to recover the trust of the early days."[119] The journal was edited by an émigré priest and widely considered the mouthpiece of Bishop Chi and northern church leaders. Diệm considered the article to be a slap in the face, and before the month was out, a court convicted the editor, withdrew his license, and sentenced him to eighteen months in prison.[120] The verdict decisively turned Bishop Chi and his followers against the Ngô clan.[121]

Yet despite the bad blood, émigré priests never organized an active, enduring opposition against Diệm, such as a Catholic equivalent to Phạm Công Tắc's faith-based peace organization. The absence of a northern Catholic opposition group contributed to the myth that Diệm enjoyed steadfast support from the émigrés. A better explanation for this absence is that the organizational strength of all northern groups declined after the partition. The mass migration seriously disrupted the structure and operations of every organization that came south, and the northern branches of the Đại Việt party and the Vietnamese Nationalist

130   Chapter 4

Party did not engage in much organized activism after the migration either. Instead, the most active oppositionists of northern heritage were political independents unaffiliated with any of the major émigré groups, such as Phan Quang Đán and Nguyễn Văn Cẩn.

A PROFUSION OF CANDIDATES

The rupture between Catholic émigrés and the president widened the growing schism between the Diemist faction and rival anticommunists at the same time that the latter camp was itself internally divided. These many fractures combined to fragment anticommunist nationalism by the end of decade, as exemplified in the legislative elections of August 30, 1959.

The government modeled the elections after the constituent elections three years earlier. The new electoral laws preserved the single-member voting system, the mandate on uniform campaigning, and the limited time frame for active campaigning. The results of any candidate convicted of violating electoral procedures or bribing or intimidating voters would be voided. The only major change was that the laws abolished the ethnic minority and émigré constituencies.[122]

Numerous oppositionists ran for office even though they fully expected the government to manipulate the electoral process.[123] Phan Quang Đán, Nguyễn Văn Cẩn, and Hoàng Cơ Thụy—that is, the original founders of the Democratic Bloc—all put forth their candidacies. Thụy was now the leader of the DB, and several members of its executive committee decided to test their electoral appeal. The northern Đại Việt chief Đặng Văn Sung decided to seek office as well, though the central and southern branches of the Đại Việt party remained underground. Nguyễn Bảo Toàn, the leader of the Hòa Hảo–affiliated Social Democratic Party, returned from exile and organized almost a dozen campaigns in the Hòa Hảo heartland, but the government forced the party to withdraw most of its candidates.[124] Several office seekers were former supporters of the president who had turned to opposition, the most significant of whom was Diệm's first agricultural minister, Phan Khắc Sửu.[125]

As before, the most formidable contenders were candidates favored by the regime, though they ran under diverse labels to give the impression of a multiparty system. Cẩn and Nhu oversaw the election for the Diemists and determined which partisans could run for office. Cẩn knew that the opposition was too weak to pose an electoral threat in central Vietnam and allowed his partisans to compete against each other without picking favorites. Nhu, though, feared that the oppositionists were serious challengers in the south and decided to maximize the chances of the government candidates by eliminating any competition between the Diemists. Nhu likely tasked the Cần Lao intelligence director, Trần

Kim Tuyến, with selecting a specific candidate for each district, and the southern branches of the Cần Lao party and the NRM pressured other Diemist contenders to withdraw. As in the elections of 1956, the leading government candidates were Nhu and Madame Nhu.[126]

At least three known Diemists deliberately flouted Nhu's orders and ran rogue campaigns. Such individuals are best characterized as dissenters rather than oppositionists. These figures remained in the president's faction and never publicly criticized the government, but they discreetly disagreed with the Ngô brothers and disobeyed party instructions. The dissenting candidate with the highest profile was Nguyễn Trân, a central Vietnamese Catholic who had supported Diệm since 1945.[127] Trân served as a province chief in central and southern Vietnam during Diệm's early years but lost his position after clashing with Nhu over the best policy to counter the communist insurgency.[128] The labor chief Trần Quốc Bửu had also turned to dissent and may have fielded some candidates to represent the interests of his union, though he did not run himself.[129] Unfortunately information about these campaigns is scant. The most elaborate and well-documented scheme was that of the former Cần Lao chief Huỳnh Văn Lang, who was still bitter about the arbitrary dissolution of his clique. Lang agreed with the Ngô clan that democracy should be restricted given the communist threat and Vietnam's underdeveloped economy, but he wanted to give the regime a slight nudge toward liberalization. Lang aimed to create an opposition bloc occupying a tenth of the seats in the assembly, and the bloc would share the regime's political ideology and economic program but differ from the president in tactics. He had no interest in cooperating with the oppositionists, whom he dismissed as opportunists. He recruited some twenty candidates and provided them with campaign funds and personnel, and the candidates secretly promised to form an opposition bloc in the future assembly. Lang later claimed that he received encouragement from the Central Intelligence Agency and financial assistance from American Ambassador Elbridge Durbrow, though no documents from the American side are available to back up these claims.[130]

The elections dramatically highlighted the fragmentation of anticommunist nationalism. Most oppositionists and dissenters preferred to run for constituencies in Saigon and its environs because government interference was lower given the foreign presence. But the candidates did not coordinate with each other, and the races in and around the capital featured crisscrossing conflicts: Diemist dissenters against government-backed Diemists, rival oppositionists against each other, dissenters against oppositionists, and all challengers against the government candidate. The presence of multiple challengers undoubtedly split the potential protest vote in some districts. Meanwhile, many races in the provinces had no oppositionist or dissenting candidate at all. Had the oppositionists and dissenters cooperated, they could have mounted a more systematic electoral

132   Chapter 4

challenge to government candidates across a wider area. Not only did the lack of coordination benefit the Diemists, it also illustrated the president's warning that solitary endeavors undermined effective action.

The Diemists employed the usual arsenal of tactics to manipulate the electoral process. The NRM worked with local authorities to promote government candidates, and the civil servants' league went house to house canvassing voters. Government-sponsored mobs disrupted the political meetings of the challengers, and the police intimidated and arrested disfavored candidates and their campaign workers. Secret agents even planted small bombs outside printing houses that dared to print campaign materials for office seekers not backed by the regime.[131] At one of Phan Quang Đán's rallies, strange men seized the microphone from Đán's assistant and physically assaulted constituents who cheered for the candidate.[132] A candidate supported by Huỳnh Văn Lang complained that local authorities circulated handbills falsely smearing her as a communist.[133] Many government candidates tried to get their challengers disqualified by suing the latter for violations of the electoral laws, and the courts often handed down convictions on flimsy evidence.[134] The irregularities continued unabated on election day. The government boosted weak government candidates by transporting troops to vote in the most contested districts of Saigon, and local authorities outside the capital seized ballot boxes and reported inflated vote counts.[135] It came as no surprise when government candidates swept the polls with 115 of the 123 assembly seats.[136]

What was shocking was that three challengers won races in Saigon in spite of the interference: the dissenter Nguyễn Trân in the first electoral district, Phan Quang Đán in the second, and Phan Khắc Sửu in the fourth. In fact, Đán sailed to victory with more votes than any candidate in Saigon. Of these races, only Đán's left a substantial documentary record. His victory was a case of political talent and genuine appeal triumphing over Diemist manipulation. According to a report by the prefect of Saigon, Đán astutely chose a district filled with constituents who were sympathetic to him and with an exceptionally weak government candidate. One major voting bloc in the area was made up of ethnic Chinese, who were hit hard by Diệm's nationality laws; these voters chose Đán because he had attacked those laws in the pages of *Contemporary Discourse*. Another bloc comprised working-class residents displaced from the Saigon harbor by the government's slum clearing in 1957. They hailed Đán as a champion of the poor because he had spoken out against the forced removal.[137] The doctor knew that voters remembered *Contemporary Discourse* fondly, and he specifically campaigned on issues advanced by the newspaper, such as opposition to slum clearing, higher salaries for policemen and lower level civil servants, and greater press freedom.[138] Đán was so popular that the troops brought in to vote for the government candidate were not enough to offset the droves who preferred the oppositionist.[139] The unexpected victories deeply embarrassed the government. Diệm grudgingly accepted Phan Khắc Sửu's election but rejected Đán and Nguyễn Trân on the grounds that the latter two had been convicted of violating electoral laws.[140] US Ambassador Durbrow tried to intervene on Đán's behalf, as did the British and French ambassadors, but the president huffily retorted that the law had to be respected.[141] Sửu became the lone oppositionist in the second national assembly.

The upset victories were a testament to the dynamism and strength of the president's critics. Diemist leaders and American officials habitually ridiculed the oppositionists for appealing exclusively to Westernized intellectuals. But the success of Trân, Đán, and Sửu made it clear that at least some politicians could convince ordinary constituents to bravely vote their conscience. More generally, the legislative elections of 1959 were a sobering time for the anticommunists. The Diemists found the electoral losses disconcerting; the oppositionists were outraged that the president refused to seat rival candidates; and activists of every persuasion recognized the deep fragmentation that separated them. Whatever their conception of unity, the election demonstrated very clearly that the anticommunists were far from achieving any sort of national union.

CHAPTER FIVE

Rupture or Reconciliation? 1960–1962

Major Phạm Văn Liễu was devastated by the attack on his former regimental headquarters at Trảng Sụp. The base was located in northern Tây Ninh province about a dozen kilometers from the Cao Đài Holy See. During his time as the commanding officer of the regiment, Liễu had worked tirelessly to reinforce the security of the base. He had ordered his men to build an earthen wall around the perimeter and to dig communication trenches within the camp. He had positioned loaded mortars at the center of the camp and had sent a battalion to block the base's vulnerable northern flank every night. But the army abruptly transferred him to a noncombat role near Saigon in the fall of 1959, and his successor at Trảng Sụp undid much of Liễu's work. The trenches were filled, the guns were locked up every evening, and the nightly patrols ceased. Liễu worried that his men were now unprepared for an ambush.

Then came the shocking news. In late January 1960, just days before the Lunar New Year, communist insurgents overran Trảng Sụp, seized hundreds of weapons, and killed or wounded more than sixty troops before withdrawing into the jungle. The attack horrified Liễu. He mourned the death of his former comrades and felt that defeat was a stain on his personal honor as well as that of the army. Even more than that, he feared what the incident portended. As he soon learned, the assault was part of a coordinated communist offensive targeting the upper Mekong delta and the provinces northwest of Saigon. The guerillas attacked numerous army posts and government offices, and the administration of the Republic of Vietnam (RVN) temporarily collapsed in some areas before the army retook the territory. The incident at Trảng Sụp was the first communist assault on a regiment-size unit of the regular army, and the offensive made clear

134

Rupture or Reconciliation?   135

that the insurgency that had been growing in the countryside for the last few years now posed a serious threat to the regime.

Liễu had spent almost his entire adult life fighting communism, first as a militant in the Đại Việt party, then as an officer of the Vietnamese National Army and the founder of the marine corps under Diệm, and finally as a regimental commander in the Army of the Republic of Vietnam at Trảng Sụp. But Liễu doubted that Diệm's government could defend the RVN against the communists. In eyes of the Đại Việt partisan, the Saigon-based republic gave lip service to democracy while alienating the population and sidelining competent military officers like himself. Would the RVN fall to the communists and all his years of fighting come to naught? Liễu eventually concluded that the successful defense of the republic required the removal of Diệm.[1]

Anticommunist nationalists throughout RVN shared Liễu's fears, though not necessarily his resolution to overthrow the president. From muffled conversations among dissidents to anxious handwringing in government offices, many Vietnamese agonized over what the future would bring. The attack on Trảng Sụp aroused widespread anxiety about the viability of the regime and reframed the way politicians discussed democracy and national unity. All anticommunists wanted to halt the growth of the communist movement and to strengthen the RVN, but the Diemists and the oppositionists disagreed on whether political liberalization would help or hinder the cause. Both sides also believed that it was imperative for them to unite against the common enemy, especially given the political fragmentation of the late 1950s. But the politicians clashed over the meaning of unity and struggled to develop a program that would be acceptable to all camps. The anticommunists dug in their heels at times and compromised at others, and the turbulence of the early 1960s revived fleeting hopes of reconciliation while ultimately deepening the schism.

The debate between the Diemists and the oppositionists featured two distinct phases, each sparked by a major military event. First, the defeat at Trảng Sụp convinced many oppositionists that the president's authoritarianism and policies contributed to the communist insurgency. A group of southern progressives publicly urged Diệm to liberalize the government and formed a new party to agitate for change. But the president retorted that premature democratization would lead to a communist takeover and refused to implement reforms. Second, an aborted coup in November 1960 by anticommunist military officers provoked a violent rupture between the president and his rivals. Some oppositionists endorsed the putsch, and Diệm ordered the mass arrests of his rivals after the coup failed. The rebellion sparked another round of debate. The president believed that the failure of the coup amounted to an affirmation of his rule; he continued to resist the calls for reform. In contrast, some Diemists and northern Đại Việt leaders interpreted

136   Chapter 5

the incident as an alarming symptom of disunity and rededicated themselves to bridging the divide. They pointed out that both camps had contributed to the discord and tried to overcome the division by proposing centrist programs of limited, gradual liberalization. In the end, the centrist proposals proved too moderate for the oppositionists and too extreme for Diệm, and neither side trusted the other. The failure of these efforts ended the last hope of healing the rupture within anticommunist nationalism.

The rising insurgency prompted the Americans to reconsider the issues of unity and democracy as well. They sympathized with the oppositionists' concerns and hewed a middle path similar to the anticommunists who favored compromise. But the deteriorating security in the late months of 1961 eventually pushed the United States to increase assistance to Diệm and to drop demands for political reform. The change amounted to an endorsement of the president's dictatorial rule.

THE COMMUNIST INSURGENCY AND THE CALL FOR LIBERALIZATION

The communist insurgency was in part a response to Diệm's policies. From 1955 onward, the anticommunist denunciation campaign and other security measures devastated the underground communist organization in South Vietnam. The government arrested thousands of operatives and subjected them to lengthy detention and indoctrination. The communists resolved to fight back, even flouting admonitions from the party leadership in Hanoi to limit the use of violence. Beginning around 1958, local communists assassinated village officials, ambushed military officers, and raided remote rubber plantations and lumber camps for equipment and supplies. The insurgency was especially strong in the lower Mekong delta, which had been a bastion of the Democratic Republic of Vietnam (DRV) during the Anti-French Resistance. The communists were also active on the Vietnamese-Cambodian border and in the swath of territory north of Saigon, that is, areas formerly under Cao Đài and Hòa Hảo influence, including Trảng Sụp.[2]

Diệm's response to the insurgency inadvertently increased peasant support for the communists. In the spring of 1959, he promulgated Law 10/59 to expedite the prosecution of accused communists. The law created special military tribunals to try suspects for undermining national security and made the crime punishable by death or life in prison. The problem was that the law reduced the time that suspects had to prepare their legal defense yet dramatically increased the severity of punishment, and the heightened stakes allowed unscrupulous officials to more easily extract bribes from the population.[3] Diệm launched the Agroville Program around the same time. As mentioned in chapter 4, the program encouraged the voluntary relocation of peasants into concentrated settlements and aimed to separate the rural population from the communists. But Diệm did not allocate enough funds and imposed an unrealistic timeline for the construction of the new settlements. Consequently, local authorities resorted to forcibly relocating rural people and compelling them to perform unpaid labor. Torn away from homes and fields and forced to toil in poor conditions, peasants experienced the program as a catastrophe.[4] Together, these measures sharply escalated the repression in the countryside and pushed the peasantry further into the arms of the insurgency.

The deteriorating security and especially the incident at Trảng Sụp alarmed the president's rivals. Some oppositionists blamed Diệm's policies and hoped to persuade the president to change his ways. Leading the charge was Phan Khắc Sửu, the only oppositionist in the assembly, and his friend and political partner Trần Văn Văn (figure 6). The pair were educated professionals from southern landowning families and longtime revolutionaries. Sửu was an agricultural engineer by training and had helped organize an underground nationalist party in the 1930s, for which the French sentenced him to eight years of hard labor. Sửu

Figure 6.   Trần Văn Văn (courtesy of Trần Văn Tòng)

138   Chapter 5

probably met Văn, a wealthy industrialist, when the two served together in the southern resistance forces. Both sided with the Hòa Hảo in its conflict with the Việt Minh, and Sửu became a founding member of the Social Democratic Party in 1947. Sửu and Văn joined Bảo Đại's first government and helped negotiate the rally of General Nguyễn Giác Ngộ, but the friends resigned soon after to protest the French refusal to grant full sovereignty to the State of Vietnam. [5] They subsequently gathered around them a loose-knit clique of progressive southern professionals and Việt Minh defectors in Saigon, and several members of the clique attended the Unity Congress of 1953.[6] The clique initially supported Diệm and served in his government, but Sửu either resigned or lost his post as agricultural minister in the fall of 1954. The clique tried to mediate a reconciliation between Diệm and the sects before the Battle of Saigon, then broke with the prime minister immediately afterward.[7] Sửu's candidacy in the legislative elections marked the group's turn to active opposition.

Sửu, Văn, and their friends met regularly in the fall of 1959 to discuss the problems facing the RVN. The clique secured a meeting with Nhu shortly before the Lunar New Year and followed up with another meeting after the attack on Trảng Sụp. They unburdened their concerns about the growing insecurity, the Agroville Program, and the absence of democracy but found Nhu's response disconcerting. The presidential adviser dismissed the significance of the attack, insisted that young people wanted to perform unpaid labor on the agrovilles, and argued that Vietnam's underdevelopment made broad democratic freedoms impossible.[8] Văn, Sửu, and their friends feared that the Ngô brothers simply failed to appreciate the seriousness of the situation. The clique decided to send a private letter directly to the president, and Văn recruited additional signatories to increase the impact of the missive. He targeted mostly older men who occupied prominent social positions or who had served in Bảo Đại's government and Diệm's earlier administrations. Văn also made a point of including oppositionists from different regions, religious faiths, and political parties. His clique headed the final list of signatories, followed by a diverse roster of oppositionists: Trần Văn Đỗ, Diệm's first foreign minister and the head of the defunct Spirit Group; Trần Văn Tuyên, an émigré lawyer who once served as information minister and a leader of the Vietnamese Nationalist Party; Phan Huy Quát, the northern Đại Việt chief and former defense minister; Lê Quang Luật, who used to advise Bishop Lê Hữu Từ and served briefly in Diệm's first cabinet; Trần Văn Lý and Tạ Chương Phùng, former province chiefs from central Vietnam who supported Diệm back in 1954; Lương Trọng Tường, a Hòa Hảo politician and the economic minister in Diệm's short-lived coalition cabinet; and Hồ Văn Vui, the southern priest whose sermon had angered the regime back in 1957. It was a remarkable achievement to convince such different oppositionists to sign the same letter. Some absences were notable. Not a single signatory represented any of the

Rupture or Reconciliation? 139

main Cao Đài factions, and Văn apparently excluded younger oppositionists like Phan Quang Đán, Hoàng Cơ Thụy, and Nguyễn Văn Cẩn.

On April 26, Văn and Sửu sent the letter to Diệm via messenger and requested a meeting to discuss the document. The letter thoroughly criticized Diệm's government but stopped short of asking the president to step down. First, the signatories decried the absence of democracy and pluralism. They accused Diệm of erecting a bogus democracy using communist techniques such as rigged elections and a rubber stamp legislature. Equally bad were the arbitrary arrests, restrictions on press freedom, and the elimination of parties and organizations outside the Diemist faction. The president's suppression of the sects, the letter charged, had opened the way for the communists to infiltrate the old Cao Đài and Hòa Hảo autonomous zones. Addressing the president directly, the signatories contended that only political liberalization could remedy these shortcomings and win popular support:

> The people are thirsting for freedom at this moment. Sir, you should loosen the government, expand democracy, promulgate minimum civil rights, and recognize the opposition so that the people can express themselves, so that resentment and hatred will be no more, so that the population of the South will see the value of genuine democratic freedom in comparison to the North. Only then will they make sacrifices to protect democratic freedom.[9]

These arguments echoed earlier calls for pluralism, civil liberties, and representative government.

Next, the letter attacked "family rule" and the domination of the Cần Lao over the administration and the military. The oppositionists chided Diệm for making political rather than meritocratic appointments and complained that such policies sowed division within the civil service and the military. The letter writers blamed the stagnant economy on Diemist corruption and speculation. They also urged the government to put an end to the forced labor in the Agroville Program and warned that the suffering inflicted by the program created an opening for the communists. Last, the oppositionists explained that their purpose was to provide Diệm with the unvarnished truth so that he could understand the harm caused by his policies and alter them before they provoked rebellion. In ringing words, the letter predicted a coming day, "when that truth explodes in unstoppable waves of hate and vengeance, coming from a nation that has suffered too much and that rises up to break the fetters that have chained them and to sweep away the rot, corruption, and injustice that has exploited and oppressed them."[10] Diệm's response was silence. The letter writers seethed with frustration.[11]

On April 30, Văn and Sửu released the letter to the public during a press conference held at the Caravelle Hotel in downtown Saigon. They apparently did not inform the other signatories, and only Trần Văn Đỗ attended. Addressing a

140   Chapter 5

room full of local and foreign journalists, Văn introduced himself as the spokesperson of a new opposition group and proceeded to distribute copies of the letter to the reporters.[12] The press conference transformed the document from a discreet critique to a fierce declaration of resistance. The event recalled the congresses of 1953 in that the signatories demanded many of the same reforms from Diệm that the anticommunists had tried to wring from Bảo Đại, such as political liberalization and an end to corruption. At least half of the signatories had participated in the earlier congresses. The implicit message was that Diệm had failed to fulfill—if not outright betrayed—the ideals that all of them had once shared. The president continued to ignore Văn's group, and local newspapers dared not publish the letter.[13] Only the international press covered the press conference and dubbed the document the Caravelle Manifesto (Tuyên Ngôn Caravelle).

Sửu and Văn invited the other signatories to form a new party called the Freedom and Progress Bloc (Khối Tự Do Tiến Bộ, or FPB) and informed the Ministry of the Interior of the group's existence, but the ministry did not grant legal recognition to the party.[14] The FPB issued a series of petitions that summer protesting arbitrary arrests and detentions, demanding greater freedom of press, and urging the government to abolish the Agroville Program.[15] But though the party was vocal in its critique of Diệm, the FPB never developed a positive program of its own.[16] Sửu and Văn did not release an official agenda to explain how democratic they thought the government should be or how quickly they wanted Diệm to liberalize. Later police interrogations revealed nothing more than that the activists planned to put forth a candidate in the upcoming presidential election, with some members favoring Sửu.[17] In all likelihood, the party never advanced beyond the early stage of planning. The absence of documentary evidence clarifying the FPB's end goal makes it more accurate to describe the party's objective as liberalization rather than the more definitive goal of democratization.

THE DANGER OF "PROFLIGATE FREEDOM" AND PREMATURE DEMOCRATIZATION

Diệm's views on liberalization could not be more different from those of the oppositionists. Whereas the Caravelle Manifesto argued that opening up the government would rally the people against communism, the president insisted that rapid liberalization was bound to turn the RVN communist. In fact, Diệm argued against democratization in his Lunar New Year address of 1960. The president asserted that the premature adoption of Western-style democracy in underdeveloped countries led to political deadlock, "profligate freedom" (*tự do phóng túng*), and social chaos, and it was this disorder that prompted countries to switch to a communist dictatorship, which he described as a "stringently collective regime" (*chế độ tập trung nghiêm khắc*). Diệm offered no examples as evidence but insisted that Vietnam had avoided such a pitfall by adopting personalism rather than liberal democracy.[18] In the eyes of the president, Văn and Sửu were obstructionists who unwittingly hastened a communist victory.

The Americans were equally unreceptive to the FPB. Trần Văn Văn reportedly tried to contact the embassy through an American businessman named Frank Gonder, but officials curtly informed Gonder that it was US policy to support Diệm.[19] American attitudes grew more hostile after the manifesto became public. Ambassador Durbrow thought the oppositionists wanted outright democracy and strongly objected to the proposition. The ambassador told foreign reporters that complete freedom for the press and opposition parties would enable communist infiltration and insisted that some government control was necessary.[20] Similarly, the embassy's political counselor, Joseph Mendenhall, definitively told foreign diplomats that the United States had no intention of pressuring Diệm for full democratization. Mendenhall recounted in a report to the State Department, "I noted that in our view it would not be advisable for Viet-Nam to adopt a completely democratic system at this time because of the advantage that would give to the communists to undermine the government."[21] Durbrow and Mendenhall correctly perceived the FPB to be more liberal than Diệm, though it is unknown whether the party was actually as democratic as the Americans thought.

Durbrow's hostility to the oppositionists did not translate into a wholehearted endorsement of Diệm, however. The ambassador's position on liberalization is best understood as a centrist one located between Diệm and the oppositionists. Durbrow shared the FPB's concerns about nepotism, the overconcentration of power in the presidency, the severe restrictions on freedom, corruption, and political favoritism in the military. He also wanted Diệm to alter many policies. But, unlike the FPB, Durbrow advocated minimal political reforms and sought to strengthen the president against both the oppositionists and the communists. With the backing of the State Department, Durbrow approached Diệm on October 14 with a string of proposals. First, the envoy urged the Vietnamese leader to demonstrate national unity by including one or two oppositionists in the cabinet. Diệm should also delegate more power to his ministers and appoint a full-time defense minister to make the administration more efficient. Diệm had served simultaneously as head of government and defense minister since 1954. Second, Durbrow argued that the National Assembly should be allowed to play a more active role in introducing bills and conducting public investigations of government agencies. Third, Diệm should appoint a committee that included representatives of the press and the opposition to draft a press code, and the press could regulate itself. Fourth, the ambassador lamented that the secretiveness of the Cần Lao party gave rise to suspicions of nepotism and urged Diệm to either

142   Chapter 5

make the party go public or dissolve it. Durbrow also delicately brought up the rumors surrounding Nhu, his wife, and Trần Kim Tuyến, the head of Cần Lao intelligence, and suggested that Diệm send the trio on missions outside the country.[22]

The American démarche was too superficial to satisfy the oppositionists but too far reaching to be acceptable to Diệm—a pattern that would characterize the US position on liberalization for the next year. The FPB would have welcomed the suggested reforms had the party been privy to the discussion, though the changes failed to get at the heart of the problem for the oppositionists. The activists wanted to dismantle the Diemist monopoly on power, not just force the Cần Lao out of clandestinity, and the inclusion of token oppositionists was meaningless if the president continued to suppress rival parties. Nor did expanding the institutional power of the assembly resolve the problem of rigged elections. Yet Diệm found Durbrow's prescriptions to be excessive. The president defended Nhu's contributions to the RVN and implied that the oppositionists did not merit appointments to the cabinet. The president even derided his critics for having no constructive program and denounced them for failing to contribute to the struggle for independence.[23] The comment was disingenuous at best and dishonest at worst. Diệm's own restrictions on freedom discouraged the publication of detailed political programs, and many oppositionists had actively fought the French and the communists during the Resistance while Diệm spent a relatively comfortable exile abroad.

COMPETING CONSPIRACIES AND THE COUP OF 1960

Although the oppositionists responded to the insurgency and the attack on Trảng Sụp with calls for liberalization, the same incident spurred some military leaders to try to overthrow Diệm's government in a coup d'état. Resentment had long festered in the military over the president's habit of promoting officers on the basis of political loyalty. Although the actual extent of the practice is unclear, the widespread perception of favoritism generated intense jealousies between Diemist officers and those outside the president's faction. The humiliating defeat at Trảng Sụp convinced some disaffected officers that the policy also threatened the very survival of the RVN. Soldiers lamented that the commanding officer at Trảng Sụp was an unqualified and inexperienced Cần Lao cadre who had obtained the position through political connections.[24] The subsequent growth of the insurgency intensified the soldiers' fears. The number of communist assassinations of government officials reached an all-time high in southern Vietnam in April 1960, and the communists gained territory as terrified officials retreated to fortified posts for safety. The insurgency grew stronger in the Central Highlands as well. The communists achieved yet another deadly milestone in October 1960 when they carried out their first battalion-size attack in Kontum province near the Laotian border.[25] How much longer could the regime resist the onslaught when military defense was in the hands of Diemist lackeys? the president's critics wondered.[26] Trảng Sụp undoubtedly launched whispered conversations and more than a few conspiracies within the military. The most consequential of these were two related plots in the army's Airborne Brigade.

The most developed plot was the brainchild of Lieutenant Colonels Vương Văn Đông and Nguyễn Triệu Hồng, paratrooper officers and brothers-in-law who were married to sisters. The military had transferred the pair to the officer training school located outside Saigon, a typical fate for officers under political suspicion. The disgruntled men began plotting in secret, then stepped up their efforts following the attack on Trảng Sụp. They envisioned a lightning coup carried out by a few combat units based near the capital, followed by the formation of a provisional government to replace Diệm's administration. Đông and Hồng tried unsuccessfully to recruit senior officers and oppositionists and eventually turned to Hồng's maternal uncle Hoàng Cơ Thụy for political advice.[27] Thụy was an active, if rather minor, figure in the opposition. He had assumed the leadership of the Democratic Bloc after the withdrawal of Phan Quang Đán and later helped organize the Democratic Alliance (Liên Minh Dân Chủ), a semi-secret coalition made up of the Democratic Bloc, elements of the Vietnamese Nationalist Party, and Nguyễn Bảo Toàn's branch of the Social Democratic Party.[28] Thụy joined his nephew's plot but agreed to have no advance knowledge of the military details. He also kept the conspiracy a secret from the Democratic Alliance, though he probably expected the group to participate in the provisional government if the coup succeeded.[29] Other oppositionists eventually caught wind of the plot. An officer involved in the conspiracy leaked it to a different branch of the Vietnamese Nationalist Party, which itself was in close touch with members of the Freedom and Progress Bloc and the northern Đại Việt party.[30]

Parallel to Vương Văn Đông and Nguyễn Triệu Hồng's conspiracy was a less advanced plot led by Senior Colonel Nguyễn Chánh Thi, commander of the Airborne Brigade. Thi was a favored protégé of Diệm but had grown frustrated with political favoritism in the military and nepotism in the government. Thi's followers included mostly junior airborne officers, though the inspiration for the plot may have come from Thi's friend and marine officer, Major Phạm Văn Liễu, the former regimental commander at Trảng Sụp. Similar to Đông and Hồng, Thi and his coconspirators apparently envisioned a quick attack against the Independence Palace by a small number of combat units.[31] The twin conspiracies intersected when a partisan of the first plot recruited Phạm Văn Liễu, but neither group appears to have been fully aware that the other was an autonomous entity.[32] The existence of multiple, connected conspiracies goes far to explain the later

144 Chapter 5

disagreements between Vương Văn Đông and Nguyễn Chánh Thi over the direction of their joint coup.

The coup began in Saigon during the predawn hours of November 11, 1960. Moving swiftly under cover of darkness, a contingent of paratroopers laid siege to the Independence Palace and engaged the Presidential Guard while another contingent captured the Joint General Staff Headquarters and several strategic locations in the capital. [33] Bad luck and a series of missteps undermined the coup from the start, however. First, Vương Văn Đông and Nguyễn Triệu Hồng ordered an assault on the palace, but a stray bullet killed Hồng early that morning, and a badly shaken Đông struggled to carry out the plot alone. The death also broke the already weak link between the airborne officers and Hoàng Cơ Thụy, and Đông subsequently neglected their political plans.[34] The loss created an opening for Nguyễn Chánh Thi to assert his leadership over the coup, and Đông and Thi spent much of the next day and a half working at cross purposes. Second, the leaders of the coup had not obtained the cooperation of regional and local commanders and had to cut off communications with the capital to prevent Diệm from summoning loyalist troops. The soldiers failed in this objective due to poor planning and the lack of technical expertise. Third, the paratroopers had orders to neutralize the airfield in nearby Biên Hòa province and the armored cavalry regiment stationed just northwest of Saigon to prevent a loyalist counterattack. But the rebel troops failed to capture the airfield and lost to the cavalry, and a loyalist regimental commander rushed to the Independence Palace with a cavalry detachment to aid the beleaguered Diệm. The paratroopers could not even obtain the much-needed tanks to attack the palace.[35]

The many mistakes gave the president and his supporters considerable room to maneuver. The paratroopers occupied the Saigon radio station but were unaware that Diệm remained in contact with the personnel there. The president arranged for Radio Saigon to broadcast a message summoning loyalist troops, and the recording played on repeat for more than an hour before the rebel forces put an end to it. The paratroopers seized the post office and forced the postal workers to cut all telephone and telegram lines, but the workers never revealed the backup communications system that remained in good working order. Trần Kim Tuyến, the director of the Cần Lao intelligence service, deftly took advantage of the oversight. Aided in secret by the director of the post office, Tuyến used the backup phone lines to instruct loyalist troops in the surrounding region to come to the rescue of the president, especially the Seventh Division in Biên Hòa province and the Fifth Division, then on operation southwest of the capital. Diệm also benefited from the able assistance of General Nguyễn Khánh, chief of staff of the army, who slipped into the Independence Palace and directed the defense of the building. Khánh had at his disposal not only the Presidential Guard but also two marine battalions that had broken away from the coup forces.[36]

Meanwhile, the leadership of the coup split over the question of negotiations. Nguyễn Chánh Thi remained confident that the paratroopers could capture the palace before the arrival of loyalist reinforcements, and he ordered the airborne units to aim their guns directly at the building.[37] Diệm and his entourage realized that they had to stall for time and therefore around midday sent the president's private secretary to open negotiations with Thi. The talks immediately reached an impasse: the colonel insisted on Diệm's resignation and the president flatly refused.[38] In contrast to Thi's assessment, the rapidly changing military situation convinced Vương Văn Đông that an armed overthrow was no longer feasible. He concluded that it was best to persuade Diệm to make political concessions before loyalist troops gained the strategic advantage.[39] The president and his subordinates exploited the rift by pursuing parallel negotiations with Đông, who then made Thi halt the assault on the palace.[40]

Đông was an amateur negotiator and easily fell prey to the president's manipulation. The young officer waffled over the course of the afternoon and evening, first pushing for Diệm's resignation, then asking for the formation of the national union government convened by Đông, Hoàng Cơ Thụy, and their coconspirators.[41] Diệm made concessions to buy time. The president agreed to dissolve the government, accept a titular role, and hand over power to a group of army generals, who would then form a provisional government. Radio Saigon aired a recorded message announcing the agreement that night, read aloud by General Lê Văn Ty, who was now chief of the Joint General Staff of the military.[42] Đông then demanded another broadcast in Diệm's voice confirming the transfer of power; the president stalled by wrangling with Đông over the wording of the message.[43]

The Americans adopted a position of strict neutrality in the contest between the Diemists and the paratroopers. Early that morning, the Vietnamese president asked Ambassador Durbrow to send a contingent of American marines to protect the Saigon airport and US citizens, but the envoy declined to take action. Later, Diệm's presidential minister, Nguyễn Đình Thuần, requested that Durbrow pressure Đông to adopt a more moderate position in the negotiations. The ambassador refused to get involved except to urge both sides to compromise and avoid bloodshed.[44]

"REVOLUTION AGAINST THE RULING DICTATORSHIP": WELCOMING THE COUP

The possibility of Diệm's ouster exhilarated the opposition. The first politician to publicly express support for the coup was Phan Quang Đán. He received an invitation from Nguyễn Chánh Thi on the afternoon of November 11 and eagerly agreed to handle propaganda for the coup leaders. Thi apparently had no

146   Chapter 5

previous acquaintance with Đán and likely chose the latter for his prominence as an oppositionist.[45] Đán held a press conference that evening at the Joint General Staff headquarters, then spent the night denouncing Diệm over the airwaves of Radio Saigon. In his broadcasts, the activist accused Diệm of undermining the anticommunist cause both internationally and domestically. Not only had the president misled the RVN's anticommunist allies abroad, Diệm's authoritarianism made the Vietnamese people lose faith in the Free World, Đán complained. The oppositionist urged the population to gather in front of the Independence Palace the following morning for a popular demonstration in favor of the coup forces.[46]

The turn of events even roused Nguyễn Tường Tam, a former leader of the Vietnamese Nationalist Party (VNP). Tam had served in the Chinese-sponsored coalition government in 1946 and had helped found the Nanjing Front the following year. He subsequently retired from politics and abstained from any activism in the RVN, except to advise a minor branch of the VNP. But he was so eager to see Diệm removed that Tam willingly dove back into politics. He and his comrades in the VNP released a handbill that depicted the overthrow of Diệm as part of a broad struggle against multiple oppressors.[47] "The entire people [must] unite to resist communism. The entire people [must] unite to rise up against dictatorship and resolutely eliminate the avaricious and fatuous feudalism of the Ngo family," the handbill urged. Tam's faction issued the appeal in the name of the National People's Solidarity Front (Mặt Trận Quốc Dân Đoàn Kết) and appended a list of eighteen respected anticommunists, including Tam and several signatories of the Caravelle Manifesto.[48] The roster implied that these men had joined the front and endorsed the handbill. In actuality, the front existed only on paper, and the authors of the handbill added many names without informing the individuals in question.[49] One of Tam's partisans later claimed that the group distributed more than thirty thousand copies across Saigon. That night, the faction began planning for the demonstration in front of the palace.[50]

The seeming success of the coup also inspired a little-known Catholic discussion group with ties to Bishop Lê Hữu Từ. Unfortunately, the identity of the individual members is not known. The activists styled themselves the Christian Democratic Front and drafted a handbill that blamed Diệm for the rise of the insurgency. "We, Democratic Christians, are very indignant to see this treacherous invasion by the Communists made possible and facilitated by the mean and greedy behavior of the Ngo ruling family this last six years," the handbill averred. "By our position in regard to the Nation, we proclaim it necessary to carry out a Revolution against the ruling dictatorship, to set up a real Democracy with Peace and Freedom," the activists added. The emphasis on religious identity suggests that the group aimed to rally Catholic support against Diệm and to counter the popular misperception that his coreligionists blindly supported him. The activists completed the handbill on the morning of November 12 but decided not to distribute it in light of the changing fortune of the coup. Nevertheless, the handbill was a testament to the continuing conflict between the Diemists and certain Catholic elements.[51] The government later accused Hoàng Cơ Thụy's Democratic Alliance and Trần Văn Văn and Phan Khắc Sửu's Freedom and Progress Bloc of preparing handbills too, but no copies of such handbills have survived.[52]

Around daybreak on November 12, Radio Saigon broadcast a message in Diệm's voice confirming General Ty's announcement the night before. The president explained that he would dissolve the present government and coordinate with the leaders of the coup to form a coalition government.[53] The message elated the oppositionists and some sectors of the population. Answering the call of Phan Quang Đán, some five thousand cheering civilians crowded in front of the Independence Palace carrying banners denouncing Diệm and the Ngô clan. It was arguably the largest independent demonstration to take place in Saigon since Diệm returned to Vietnam. When the crowd rushed toward the palace, the tanks and loyalist forces defending the building open fired on the unarmed demonstrators and the rally ended abruptly.[54]

The contest tipped decisively in favor of Diệm over the course of morning. Loyalist forces, which had arrived the previous afternoon and overnight, gradually dislodged the paratroopers from the area around the palace and forced the rebel forces to retreat northward. Expecting imminent defeat, the paratrooper officers drove straight to the airport, seized a plane, and flew to Cambodia to avoid arrest. They left behind Hoàng Cơ Thụy, who sought asylum at the home of a CIA contact; the agency secretly whisked him away to safety out of the country.[55] Only Phan Quang Đán remained in Saigon to await his fate. By that afternoon, few vestiges of the armed mutiny that had gripped the city for thirty-six tense hours remained.

The failed coup was a watershed in the history of Diệm's tenure. The incident ended a long period of relative stability in civil-military relations. The president had not faced the threat of armed overthrow by his own military since the Hinh crisis in 1955. Now the paratroopers' putsch offered a model for other disaffected officers, and successive coup attempts followed in the early 1960s. The rebellion also marked a turning point for the opposition. Most of Diệm's rivals had previously disavowed the use of violence, and none had participated in planning the coup except Hoàng Cơ Thụy. Yet numerous oppositionists endorsed the rebellion when it appeared to be on the brink of success. The enthusiastic acceptance of a violent overthrow reflected the oppositionists' growing conviction that Diệm was an obstacle in the anticommunist struggle. The common theme in the Phan Quang Đán's broadcast and the handbills was that the president rivaled the communists as a threat to the Vietnamese nation

148   Chapter 5

and had set back the war against the insurgency. Various anticommunists drew different lessons from the coup, and the incident ushered in another round of debate on democracy and national unity.

THE GREAT CRACKDOWN

Diệm interpreted the failure of the coup as a vindication of his rule. The president believed that the military and the population remained steadfastly loyal and that only a minority of officers rebelled. In a radio address on the evening of November 12, Diệm explained that the coup leaders duped soldiers into believing that the troops were on a mission to rescue him from a revolt by the Presidential Guard, which meant that soldiers who attacked the palace did so to defend the president rather than overthrow him.[56] Diệm repeated the same claim in private conversations with foreign diplomats and declared that the people, except for the demonstrators in front of the palace, still supported him.[57] Evidence is clear that some officers lied to the troops, but whether all participating soldiers were victims of the ploy, as the president seemed to believe, is not. In sum, Diệm believed that his people were content and that his policies were sound; therefore, there was no need to liberalize the government or cooperate with his rivals. Equally important, Diệm and his supporters felt that the oppositionists showed their true, treacherous colors when they endorsed the putsch. One of his officials told the political scientist John Donnell that the rebellion exposed the inherently violent tendencies of the opposition and attributed those tendencies to the groups' origins as revolutionary parties.[58] Accordingly, the Diemists focused their efforts on rallying the population and punishing the opposition.

During the putsch, a group of diehard Diemists formed an organization called the People's Committee Against Rebellion (Ủy Ban Nhân Dân Chống Phiến Loạn) to carry out liaison missions on behalf of the government. The committee subsequently shifted to propaganda and mobilization in an effort to unite the population behind the president.[59] The leader of the organization was Lieutenant Nguyễn Văn Châu, the director of the army's office for psychological warfare and the chair of the military wing of the Cần Lao party.[60] The committee distributed handbills throughout the capitol on November 12 urging the people to support Diệm and held a large rally in front of the National Assembly building the next morning.[61] The demonstration featured only Diemist groups, and the crowd passed a scripted resolution expressing loyalty to the president.[62] The committee subsequently renamed itself the People's Committee Against Rebels and Communists (Ủy Ban Nhân Dân Chống Phiến Cộng) with the aim of strengthening the people's revolutionary spirit in order to eliminate both enemies.[63] The organizers dissolved the group at the end of December and planned to replace it with a broader political front.[64]

Accompanying these mobilization efforts was a brutal crackdown on the opposition. The manhunt targeted politicians suspected of involvement in the rebellion as well as their family members and associates. The dragnet even swept up oppositionists with no known connection to the putsch. The American embassy estimated that more than eighty people were arrested and dozens more questioned, though these figures were likely incomplete.[65] Phan Khắc Sửu and Phan Quang Đán headed the list of wanted suspects and suffered exceptionally harsh punishment. Signs, posters, and banners demanding their execution appeared throughout Saigon just days after the aborted rebellion.[66] Once arrested, the men were held in a secret, subterranean prison under the Saigon zoo and subjected to solitary confinement, frequent beatings, electric shock, and other forms of torture.[67] The government apparently targeted the pair for their prestige as oppositionists rather than actual participation in the coup. Đán certainly played a very visible role, but Sửu was not even marginally involved.[68] Instead, the men were a threat to Diệm because they won seats in the assembly despite government rigging and could be formidable challengers in the upcoming presidential elections, as numerous observers noted at the time. Sửu later recounted that his jailers questioned him extensively about his plans regarding the elections but not the rebellion for which he had been arrested.[69]

The government targeted three additional groups: Nguyễn Tường Tam's faction of the Vietnamese Nationalist Party, Hoàng Cơ Thụy's Democratic Alliance, and the Freedom and Progress Bloc. Security agents systematically hunted down Tam's branch of the VNP, though Tam himself received surprisingly lenient treatment. He initially sought refuge at the embassy of the Republic of China (Taiwan) and was then allowed to return home.[70] The government went after the Democratic Alliance with equal zeal. Hoàng Cơ Thụy convened the alliance on November 11 to draft a list of names for a provisional government, and Diệm's agents pointed to the list as evidence of treason. Thụy's colleagues in the alliance bore the brunt of the repression, especially Nguyễn Bảo Toàn and his wing of the Social Democratic Party. Toàn went into hiding and evaded arrest for more than a year, but the Cần Lao intelligence agency eventually abducted and murdered him. Security agents also detained the party's theoretician Phan Bá Cẩm and less prominent members.[71]

The Freedom and Progress Bloc fell victim to the government's crackdown despite not participating in the aborted rebellion. The regime presumably targeted the FPB for its record of opposition and the inclusion of several members in the VNP's handbill. The police questioned the signatories of the Caravelle Manifesto and released most after a few days or a few months but kept three in detention for the long term.[72] The crackdown effectively destroyed the FPB as an organized political group. Other oppositionists unconnected to the paratroopers also found themselves suddenly under scrutiny, including Nguyễn Văn Cần, the

150   Chapter 5

outspoken critic of the constitution in the first National Assembly, and Nguyễn Trân, the Diemist dissenter elected to the assembly in 1959 but blocked from taking his seat.[73] In addition, the government arrested more than a dozen military officers. The Ministry of Justice waited almost three years, until July 1963, to bring the suspects to trial. The Special Military Court in Saigon convicted twenty suspects of violating national security, with Phan Khắc Sửu and Phan Quang Đán receiving the harshest sentences.[74] Nguyễn Tường Tam famously protested the trial, as described later.

The crackdown extended beyond actual suspects to all elements in the media, the military, and the population that dared express sympathy for the paratroopers. The National Revolutionary Movement and the Cần Lao intelligence service organized mobs to ransack the offices of Saigon newspapers that reported favorably on the coup or printed announcements issued by the rebellious officers.[75] The military demoted, transferred, discharged, and even detained officers for failing to take a clear stance during the incident or for showing tacit support.[76] The authorities did not spare ordinary civilians. The police questioned a driver who bought food for hungry paratroopers, and security agents detained the owner of a banana storage facility for the possession of a stray handbill put out by the opposition.[77] Such people posed no threat to the regime, and the decision of the government to investigate such harmless actions undoubtedly frightened the population.

"A VERY HIGH LEVEL OF CONSCIOUSNESS": THE PRESIDENTIAL ELECTIONS OF 1961

The government's handling of the presidential elections of 1961 reflected Diệm's decision to stay the course rather than implement reforms. The election was no more free than earlier ones, though the president did loosen restrictions slightly to make his candidacy more attractive. The government permitted opposition candidates to run against Diệm, but because his most outspoken critics were still in detention or had been warned to stay out of politics, the only candidates available to challenge the president were so weak that they enhanced his prestige by comparison.[78] Diệm also gave the media greater freedom to cover his challengers' campaigns, and newspapers reprinted the candidates' blunt criticism of the regime. The arrangement made it appear that only unattractive candidates found fault with the government. Yet even this timid and temporary liberalization made the elections unique. Disfavored candidates received greater media coverage than ever before, and the opposition campaigns publicly attacked Diệm's policies and accused him of authoritarianism.

The election, scheduled for April 9, followed the familiar regulations on uniform campaigning. All funds came from the national budget, campaigning was

Rupture or Reconciliation?   151

limited to an official period, and a central campaign committee ensured that all candidates enjoyed the same resources, facilities, and access to Radio Saigon.[79] The law tacitly favored Diệm by making no mention of political organizations or newspapers. The president benefited from a well-developed political machinery in the form of the National Revolutionary Movement, and the government had recently approved licenses for several friendly newspapers that could be trusted to endorse Diệm's candidacy. In contrast, the regime never granted legal recognition to rival parties and shut down opposition newspapers, which meant that the challengers had no political organization or official organ to promote their candidacies.[80]

The election featured three slates of candidates, known officially by their numbers. Slate 1 featured the incumbents Ngô Đình Diệm and his vice president Nguyễn Ngọc Thơ, and they campaigned on a program of personalist democracy. Once again, Diệm explained to citizens that he favored a prolonged period of economic and social reform followed by gradual liberalization. The president argued in a radio broadcast that underdeveloped countries needed to achieve certain economic prerequisites to enable the holistic development of the person, which he associated with democracy.[81] He further elaborated at a press conference that the people must accept severe discipline if the RVN was to quickly meet the prerequisites. "Therefore, the issue that must be considered is to determine the limits of this discipline, a discipline necessary for the rapid establishment of the economic conditions that will pave the way for the realization of democracy," he declared.[82] That is, Diệm conceived of the problem in terms of placing limitations on authoritarianism rather than expanding freedom. Asked by a reporter how he intended to realize democracy, the president cited his own speech to the National Assembly three years earlier about building the "substructure of democracy."[83] The president also refuted the accusation of family rule. He argued that his family members were educated and well qualified for their positions and insisted that there was no evidence that Madame Nhu had engaged in illicit economic activities.[84]

Two opposition slates bravely challenged Diệm, though they harbored no illusions about their chances for electoral success. Instead, the challengers used their campaigns as an opportunity to call for political reforms and borrowed from the existing critiques and proposals developed by other oppositionists. Slate 2 consisted of Nguyễn Đình Quát for president and retired Cao Đài General Nguyễn Thành Phương for vice president. The former was a wealthy industrialist and rubber planter with no political experience, and General Phương had lived in relative obscurity since 1956 and no longer commanded a popular sectarian following.[85] Nguyễn Đình Quát reportedly enjoyed the secret assistance of more experienced oppositionists.[86] His program called for establishing a multiparty coalition government, promulgating democratic freedoms, recognizing the

152   Chapter 5

political opposition, releasing anticommunist political prisoners, and establishing a democratically elected assembly that would exercise oversight on the executive and amend the constitution. He also promised, rather unrealistically, that the Vietnamese piaster would rise to equal value with the American dollar within six months of his election.[87]

Slate 3 featured Hồ Nhựt Tân for president and Nguyễn Thế Truyền for vice president. Hồ was an obscure septuagenarian who had retreated from nationalist activism after 1950 to practice traditional Eastern medicine. The slightly younger Nguyễn was a leftist radical with an impressive revolutionary record, though he had not been politically active in the RVN. He had been a protégé of the early nationalist Phan Châu Trinh and a comrade of the budding communist Hồ Chí Minh in Paris in the 1920s. Nguyễn became a founding member of the French Communist Party before resigning his membership in response to the split between Stalinism and Trotskyism.[88] He endured prison alongside the Cao Đài religious leader Phạm Công Tắc in the early 1940s and, on his release, refused to support either the DRV or Bảo Đại's government. After Diệm returned to Vietnam, Nguyễn tried to mediate between the regime and the sects during the sect crisis and pleaded with the Ngô family to grant capital clemency to nationalist dissidents, including men with ties to the Bình Xuyên and the Đại Việt rebels in Quảng Trị.[89] Slate 3 pointedly attacked the unfairness of the elections. Hồ Nhựt Tân's manifesto contended that the opposition candidates were at a disadvantage because the incumbents enjoyed undue influence over the press and the support of the Diemist groups.[90] Nguyễn Thế Truyền joined his running mate in the critique. A journalist from Reuters asked Nguyễn during a press conference whether the slate had any hope of winning the election. The candidate slyly replied, "If it's completely free and democratic, then there is hope of winning. If not . . . then alas!"[91] The reporter let out a hearty laugh.

Hồ Nhựt Tân's complaint correctly identified the inherent bias in the election. The Directorate of Information, the successor to the Ministry of Information, coordinated with friendly newspapers to wage a press campaign against slates 2 and 3. Unregulated by the electoral law, the newspapers lambasted the opposition slates, and reporters hurled a barrage of hostile questions at the candidates during press conferences. Hecklers shouted down Diệm's challengers at public gatherings and sometimes even threatened to physically attack the candidates. In contrast, reporters were polite and patient toward the president despite his tendency to monologue, and the public meetings for slate 1 were orderly and peaceful. The organizational strength of the slates was similarly skewed. The opposition slates had a tiny staff, and employees faced arrest and intimidation by the police.[92] Meanwhile, the National Revolutionary Movement and other Diemist groups promoted the president's candidacy throughout the RVN, often with the assistance of local authorities. Thus it came as no surprise that the incumbents won reelection with 89 percent of the vote and that slates 2 and 3 received

Rupture or Reconciliation? 153

only 4 and 7 percent of the vote, respectively.[93] Diệm triumphantly declared in his inaugural address that voters had endorsed his gradualist program of personalist democracy. "Slate 1 won by a very large majority with a program of austerity that requires discipline and sacrifice so that we can quickly advance economically and socially and defeat the communists in all arenas," he announced with apparent satisfaction. "With that, our people have demonstrated a very high level of consciousness [*dân trí*]."[94]

THE MODERATES' SEARCH FOR MIDDLE GROUND

Although Diệm interpreted the failed coup to be an affirmation of his legitimacy, some of his followers and rivals considered the incident a dire warning. They feared that opposition hostility to Diệm had reached the point of armed rebellion. Many also thought that the putsch was a sign of popular resentment and that the people might rise up against the president. Not only did such weaknesses threaten to tear the regime asunder, the communists could exploit them to topple the RVN. The perceived gravity of the situation prompted some leaders to revisit the perennial questions of unity and democracy: How could they unite against their shared enemy? How could they create a democracy capable of withstanding a dangerous threat? After much soul searching, a few moderate Diemists and oppositionists worked together to develop a centrist program of limited liberalization that both sides could find attractive. The aim was to reverse the tendency toward fragmentation and achieve national unity.

In early 1961, a small coterie of Cần Lao leaders in Saigon received permission from the Ngô brothers to launch a broad political front known as the Unity Committee (Ủy Ban Đại Đoàn Kết, or UC) to supersede the defunct People's Committee Against Rebels and Communists.[95] The leader of the new initiative was Lieutenant Nguyễn Văn Châu, the former general secretary of the old committee. Châu remained devoutly loyal to the president, but the lieutenant's experience with the defunct organization probably convinced him that dissatisfaction with the government was dangerously high. According to the fragmentary evidence, Châu and his Diemist colleagues established the UC as sort of safety valve to alleviate the growing pressure on the regime. The UC would prevent another coup by providing an outlet for popular discontent and by coopting the opposition.[96] The fledgling organization held two conferences that winter and declared that it would realize national unity by reconciling the diverse political tendencies in the RVN.[97] The official name of the group recalled the Unity Congress of 1953 and evoked a recent past when anticommunists still believed in the possibility of cooperation.

Perhaps unsurprisingly, Nguyễn Văn Châu and his associates had little luck attracting members outside the Diemist faction, and the only significant oppositionist to join the group was the northern Đại Việt leader Phan Huy Quát (figure 7). Quát had been the Americans' choice to replace Diệm on the eve of the Battle of Saigon. But since then, Quát had proven himself to be a moderate oppositionist. He stayed away from the more extreme activism of the southern and central Vietnamese branches of his party in the late 1950s. He signed the Caravelle Manifesto and joined the Freedom and Progress Bloc, but, unlike other oppositionists, he reportedly drafted a handbill against a military takeover of the government during the attempted coup. Diemist mobs ransacked his medical office during the subsequent crackdown, but Quát steadfastly believed that the anticommunists could still unite.[98] He reluctantly accepted Nguyễn Văn Châu's invitation to chair the UC and conscientiously undertook the difficult task of bringing together diverse groups.[99] That spring, Quát and other leaders of the committee met with numerous political, religious, professional, and labor organizations to solicit their views on the "present state of unity" (hiện trạng đoàn kết).[100] In June, the UC presented its findings at a national conference in Saigon that attracted hundreds of attendees.[101]

Quát and his colleagues explained that the various organizations all agreed on the necessity of unity but disagreed on the meaning of the concept and its

Figure 7. Phan Huy Quát (photograph by H&E, Camera Press London)

relationship to democracy. The leaders of the UC reduced the diverse views to two main positions. The majority position conceived of unity as the ability of the government to rally the support of the people for the anticommunist struggle. Advocates argued that the government needed the support of the people to defeat the communists and had to implement democracy to win this support. Only when ordinary Vietnamese realized that democracy was superior to communism would they rally to the regime.[102] "The aspiration for democracy has a special meaning in the current stage of the country, in particular: [democracy will allow] everyone to see clearly that the reason we oppose communism is because we have more freedom and more love," the leaders of the UC explained. According to the majority position, the government should restrict freedom only when absolutely necessary, and the political system needed to include an opposition to faithfully reflect the will of the people.[103] In contrast, the minority position conceived of unity as the duty of the population to assist the government in combating communism. The sole purpose of unity at the time was the anticommunist struggle, and democracy should be temporarily set aside because it could undermine unity and decrease the effectiveness of the struggle, proponents of the second position claimed. What Quát and his colleagues left out that was the disagreement broke down partly along political lines. The majority position reflected the views of most groups and the leadership of the UC, possibly even Nguyễn Văn Châu, but the minority consisted only of the Diemists.[104] The argument recalled the competing interpretations of unity that animated Diệm's early months in power.

FORGING A COMPROMISE?

At a follow-up conference in July, Quát and the other leaders of the UC announced that they had synthesized the contradictory positions into a four-point program and submitted it to the audience for a vote. The centrist program reflected the concerns of both the moderate oppositionists and the Diemist members of the UC. The first and last points of the program called for the legalization of anticommunist parties and the release of anticommunist political prisoners, respectively. These demands drew straight from the opposition's long-standing call for a pluralistic multiparty system. The remaining points reflected the desire of the Cần Lao members of the UC to create a safety valve for Diệm's government. The second point proposed the establishment of a public forum in which citizens could freely express their views on national affairs, and the third point entailed the creation of a political advisory council that would have the right to interpellate, criticize, and offer suggestions to the government.[105] These proposals created an outlet for non-Diemist elements to air their views and an instrument for the government to gauge public sentiments, but neither measure granted citizens

156   Chapter 5

any actual power. That is, the program did not call for free and fair elections in which the people could vote officials out of office. Nor did it call for lifting restrictions on the press. Taken together, the program was substantive but modest. The conference passed it nearly unanimously.[106]

Although the UC attracted significant political interest, mutual suspicions undermined the attempt at reconciliation between the Diemist faction and the opposition. Many oppositionists thought that the government was using the UC to smoke out critics, and rumors circulated that Quát avoided arrest during the crackdown by cutting a deal with Nhu to chair the organization.[107] That the government continued to jail so many anticommunists reinforced the distrust. Nor did the middle-of-the-road program satisfy many oppositionists, and most groups refused to offer the UC anything beyond nominal support.[108] Conversely, the highest Diemist leadership remained wary of its rivals. Nhu refused to let the UC develop organically and arranged for the Cần Lao intelligence agency to clear all of Quát's public statements in advance.[109] The presidential adviser also informed the leaders of the UC that the government would grant the group de facto approval but not formal permission, thus keeping the UC in a legal gray zone. Even with these precautions, Nhu still found the group too assertive. According to various reports, he either strongly objected to the four-point program or was noncommittal. Perhaps the greatest weakness of the UC was that it depended entirely on the goodwill of the regime. The government abruptly ordered Quát and his colleagues to cease holding any large conferences for the next six months, and the organization lapsed into inactivity by the fall of 1961.[110]

Another northern Đại Việt leader experimented with a similarly centrist project. Đặng Văn Sung was an even greater exemplar of moderation than Phan Huy Quát and was not known to have engaged in any opposition activism at all.[111] Quát and Sung acted in their capacity as individuals rather than party leaders and did not collaborate on either project, but their willingness to seek middle ground reflected the northern Đại Việt tendency toward political accommodation dating back to the early 1950s. In April 1961, Sung announced the establishment of the Front for Democratization (Mặt Trận Dân Chủ Hóa, or FD) in a series of open and private letters and held a press conference that attracted an audience of about a hundred.[112] No evidence suggests that the Diemists supported Sung, but the government did allow him to convene the meeting and even permitted the press to report on the event.[113]

For Sung, the paratroopers' attempted coup revealed the widening gulf between the Diemist faction and the opposition. He explained that the anticommunist parties originated as revolutionary organizations that aimed to overthrow French colonialism. These parties should have engaged in legal politics after the establishment of the RVN, but Diệm refused to grant them permission, so they reverted to clandestinely conspiring against the government. The result was an ever-growing rift. "A harmful cycle began: the opposition used secretive and undemocratic methods to overthrow the government, and the government also used similar methods to defend itself," Sung explained in the official declaration of the FD.[114] The logical solution was to create a legal, aboveground opposition to bring the anticommunists parties to the surface and thereby prevent future rebellions.[115] Sung also contended that the existing regime was democratic in form but authoritarian in practice, and the gap between words and deeds angered the population. A loyal opposition was necessary to channel popular grievances, he warned, or the population might turn to communism instead. The Đại Việt leader stressed that the FD would be a moderate opposition party that eschewed clandestine activism and would regard the government as an ally rather than an adversary.[116]

Perhaps the most original aspect of Sung's proposal was his suggestion that the government implement democracy through a transparent, gradual process lasting three decades. The FD program proposed that a special government agency define the appropriate limitations on democratic freedom for each stage of the process, especially the freedom of press and association. The FD would facilitate democratization and help the regime develop into a two-party system by uniting all opposition elements.[117] The proposal was reminiscent of older Đại Việt plans for gradual democratization from the early 1950s as well as the more recent call for a unified opposition by the Democratic Bloc. Within the context of the early 1960s, Sung's program represented a compromise between the Diemist faction and the opposition. He agreed with the Diemists that liberalization had to be gradual but also insisted that the government liberalize when conditions permitted and be transparent when it restricted liberty. He accepted the oppositionists' call for a legal opposition but rejected what he considered to be the hostile, extremist attitude of the likes of Phan Quang Đán and the Freedom and Progress Bloc. It remains unclear whether Sung hoped to form a full-fledged democracy as an end goal or something less liberal. The project received fairly positive press coverage but met stiff resistance from the Ngô brothers. Diệm suspected that the FD was a ploy to reestablish the Đại Việt party, Nhu privately rebuked Sung that the latter did not "play fair," and the government never granted the FD legal recognition.[118] The oppositionists also showed no particular enthusiasm for the FD, not least because few were willing to wait thirty years for democracy.

AMERICAN POLICY AT A CROSSROADS

The failed coup of 1960 revived the question of democracy and national unity for the Americans as well. The paratroopers' mutiny erupted shortly after John F. Kennedy won the presidential election in the United States, and the change of administration raised the possibility of a reorientation in American foreign

158   Chapter 5

policy. US policymakers and diplomats initially proposed a middle way between liberalization and authoritarianism but faced pushback from Diệm. Eventually, the growth of the insurgency convinced the United States to stop pushing for reform and instead step up aid for the Vietnamese president. The decision amounted to a tacit endorsement of authoritarianism, much to the consternation of the oppositionists.

In mid-December, the US State Department instructed Ambassador Durbrow to renew the démarche he had delivered in October. The department stressed that Durbrow should push for "genuine, if limited, liberalization" and not just changes to improve efficiency.[119] Accordingly, the ambassador repeated his earlier suggestions to grant the assembly more authority and to loosen the regulations on the press. Diệm's response was unchanged, however, and a disappointed Durbrow reported to Washington that the United States should find a replacement for Diệm if the situation in Vietnam continued to deteriorate.[120] Meanwhile, the Department of Defense pushed an alternative plan spearheaded by Edward Lansdale, the intelligence operative who had formerly advised Diệm. After a whirlwind trip to Vietnam in January 1961, Lansdale flatly contradicted Durbrow and insisted that Diệm was the only Vietnamese who had the necessary character and competence to serve as president of the RVN. The general urged Washington to express unequivocal support for Diệm so as to discourage future coup attempts. At the same time, Lansdale argued that the United States should bring about gradual political change. Washington should send operatives to Vietnam to unite the oppositionists into a single group and to help them develop an attractive platform. The objective was to rechannel oppositionist frustrations into legal politics, and the RVN could transition to a two-party state.[121] Lansdale's plan died a quiet death after he failed to secure the appointment to succeed Durbrow as the ambassador to the RVN.[122]

A new proposal known as the Counterinsurgency Plan superseded earlier discussions the following month. Reflecting the growing concern over the insurgency, the plan offered to dramatically increase American military aid and called for the reorganization of the Vietnamese army, but the assistance depended on Diệm's willingness to implement the reforms from Durbrow's démarche.[123] The negotiations between Durbrow and Diệm regarding the plan went nowhere, however. The Vietnamese president deflected, rejected, or ignored most of the ambassador's suggestions, and the plan was never implemented.[124]

The various American proposals constituted a middle-of-the-road approach similar to concurrent Vietnamese initiatives. Durbrow and Lansdale prioritized stabilizing Diệm's government over democratizing the RVN, much as the Diemist leaders of the Unity Committee did, though the ambassador did consider the possibility of removing the Vietnamese president. Lansdale called for consolidating the opposition and transitioning to a two-party system, just like the FD.

Yet American policymakers and Vietnamese politicians apparently did not coordinate their actions. Instead, both sides drew on ideas that had been circulating for years. More important was a key difference, in that the Americans did not believe that the Vietnamese could achieve democracy on their own. Lansdale assumed that American operatives could successfully unite the opposition and oversee a change in the party system, which implied that the task was easier for Americans like himself than for experienced Vietnamese politicians who had been struggling to achieve those objectives for years. Durbrow countered that the Vietnamese were simply not ready for democracy. Commenting on Lansdale's plan, the ambassador declared, "The Vietnamese people lack the necessary sophistication and understanding, as well as the necessary sense of political responsibility to make a two-party democratic system work at this time."[125]

Diệm did implement reforms in late 1960 and 1961, but he did not liberalize the government, contrary to the hopes of the Americans and the oppositionists. The first set of reforms fulfilled constitutional mandates he had postponed since 1956, including a constitutional court, a national economic council, and a high judicial council. The other set of reforms, implemented in late May 1961, reorganized the cabinet ostensibly to increase efficiency. Most of the existing ministries came under the purview of three superministries; remnants of the old Ministry of Information and other propaganda outfits combined to form a new portfolio; and several agencies from the overburdened president's office transferred to other ministries.[126] Although Diệm appointed some new faces to the cabinet, the changes reflected shifts in the composition of his inner circle rather than a broadening of the administration. Two new appointees were rising stars in the Diemist faction who had recently proved their loyalty in the People's Committee Against Rebels and Communists. Other Diemists lost their posts due to internal rivalries.[127] What did not change was the absence of oppositionists in the highest levels of the administration.

CHOOSING DICTATORSHIP

The deteriorating security in Vietnam eventually prompted the Americans to ease up their pressure for even minimum liberalization. In the fall of 1960, the communist leadership in Hanoi instructed its cadres in South Vietnam to establish a new political organization to lead the insurgency, and the National Liberation Front (NLF) officially formed in December. The NLF presented itself as a broad nationalist front similar to the Việt Minh of the 1940s and attracted a broad swath of population that was dissatisfied with Diệm's rule. The insurgency, with the NLF at the helm, made steady gains throughout 1961.[128] An especially spectacular attack came on September 17 and 18, 1961, when communist forces captured the capital of Phước Thành province, located only sixty kilometers from Saigon,

160   Chapter 5

and executed the province chief.[129] This was the first time that insurgents seized a provincial capital—yet another milestone that rivaled the attack on Trảng Sụp the previous year. The situation prompted Diệm to declare a state of emergency on October 15, and the National Assembly voted to grant him emergency powers, including the authority to suspend any law for the purpose of protecting security and public order. The move signaled to the Americans and the domestic opposition that Diệm intended to prioritize internal security above liberalization.[130] President Kennedy's top military adviser, General Maxwell Taylor, arrived in Saigon that same day for a fact-finding mission. Taylor's firsthand observation led him to recommend a massive expansion of American military aid, a sharp increase in the number of foreign advisers, and the introduction of US ground forces, all of which would depend on Diệm's willingness to carry out political, social, and administrative changes.

Yet the new American ambassador, Frederick Nolting, could not coax Diệm into accepting reforms any more than Durbrow could. Nolting soon walked back on the demands. In a stark reversal of American priorities, he urged Washington to push for efficiency rather than the "more nebulous concept of 'political reform.'"[131] The ambassador considered Vietnamese society to be unprepared for democracy, just as Durbrow had. In his memoir decades later, Nolting argued that Vietnam did not have the necessary institutions and structures for democracy. By way of example, he related an incident in 1962 during which the assembly voted against its own inclinations to approve legislation that Diệm had proposed. Nolting insisted that the incident "demonstrated how thoroughly Western the concept of democracy is, how alien it was to the culture of Vietnam, and how deeply authoritarian rule was ingrained in the Vietnamese people."[132] The ambassador apparently assumed that the Diemist assembly reflected Vietnamese society as a whole. American skepticism about Vietnamese readiness for democracy frustrated the oppositionists. Đặng Văn Sung dismissed such attitude as "nonsense." In an interview with the *Christian Science Monitor,* he said with apparent exasperation, "The communists do not say we cannot go Communist. If underdeveloped countries like ours can go Communist but cannot go democratic, then some day we'll go Communist."[133] American assumptions about Vietnamese political immaturity partly explain why the United States backed the dictatorial Diệm over his more liberal critics.

Kennedy did not send troops as General Taylor suggested but did approve a twofold increase in military assistance and an even more dramatic rise in the number advisers over the following year, all without any expectation of liberalization. Ambassador Nolting exemplified the shift in American policy in a speech he gave to the Saigon Rotary Club in mid-February 1962. Ignoring the issue of reform, the ambassador urged the oppositionists to cooperate with Diệm in the name of national unity:

Rupture or Reconciliation? 161

> What a tremendous transformation there would be in this country if those who criticize their Government should decide to work for it or work with it, and give their efforts to improving it from within rather than attacking it from without, especially at this time, when national unity is so important. . . . If this were done, the very problems which have caused the divisions would give way to constructive solutions.[134]

The comment struck the oppositionists as tone deaf. Diệm had rejected liberalization, rebuffed every effort at compromise and cooperation, and thrown their friends in jail.[135] The oppositionists understood that they were powerless to alter Diệm's policies, but many hoped that the Americans would pressure him to reform. Nolting disabused the activists of such illusions.

Another aborted coup followed on the heels of the ambassador's speech. On the morning of February 27, 1962, two of the finest pilots in the Republic of Vietnam Air Force flew their planes over the Independence Palace and pummeled it with napalm, bomb, and rocket and cannon fire.[136] The main targets were the residential quarters of Diệm, Nhu, and Madame Nhu.[137] The government's anti-aircraft defenses shot down the first pilot, Lieutenant Phạm Phú Quốc, and forced him to crash land on the Saigon River less than an hour later. He reportedly asked on emerging from the wreckage, "Did I kill that filthy character?" in apparent reference to Diệm.[138] The second pilot, Lieutenant Nguyễn Văn Cử, escaped by flying to Cambodia and successfully sought asylum there. Years later, Cử explained that the attack was partly a response to Nolting's speech. "I felt that the Americans had slammed the door on those of us who really wanted to fight against the Communists," Cử lamented.[139] An investigation by the RVN linked the bombardment to a small cell of the Vietnamese Nationalist Party led by Cử's father, and some observers believed that the pilots hoped to start a coup rather than merely assassinate the president. In the investigation that followed, police and security agents detained more than sixty people for questioning.[140] The government even searched the home of the unsuccessful presidential candidate Hồ Nhựt Tân and detained his former running mate Nguyễn Thế Truyền.[141] Diệm and his family escaped without any serious injuries, though the damage forced them to relocate their residence to Gia Long Palace a few blocks away.

Opposition activism ceased after the bombing of the Independence Palace. Phan Huy Quát gave up his attempt to revive the Unity Committee and glumly predicted that another coup would follow.[142] Đặng Văn Sung's Front for Democratization faded from memory, and no other opposition organization emerged to replace it. *New York Times* correspondent Homer Bigart speculated that the repression following the bombing attack must have frightened the oppositionists into silence.[143] Bigart probably misjudged the situation, in that the arrests paled relative to the crackdown that took place after the paratroopers' mutiny. Instead,

162   Chapter 5

it was probably despair that kept the activists quiet. Anticommunist nationalists had championed unity and democracy for nearly a decade and hoped to fulfill these aspirations under an independent anticommunist government. But Diệm exiled his rivals to the political wilderness and blocked all attempts to carry out their vision. Even the Americans had turned away from liberalization and toward dictatorship, many activists feared. What the opposition experienced under Diệm's rule was not just repression but the death of a dream.

CONCLUSION

The Revolution of 1963 and the Legacy of Diệm's Republic

In March 1957, the Catholic émigré newspaper *The Way of Life* published an editorial criticizing the seemingly self-defeating logic that some anticommunists used to justify the government's restrictions on civil liberties. The editorialist Minh Sơn lamented, "Often, we see a vicious circle that looks like this: We are disgusted with communism because they [the communists] do not permit freedom. But at other times, it's said that we must sacrifice our freedom to defeat communism, even freedoms that cannot be sacrificed." The editorialist dismissed such arguments and countered that civil liberties were the best weapon for defeating the enemy: "We must break out of that vicious circle. There is only one way to oppose dictatorship, and that is freedom."[1] Minh Sơn's defense of civil liberties was a reaction to the government's scrutiny of *The Way of Life*. The newspaper had attracted the ire of the regime for publishing a different editorial following the attempted assassination of Ngô Đình Diệm, as described in chapter 4. Minh Sơn knew that the regime had shut down other periodicals for similar offenses and must have wondered whether the Catholic newspaper would meet the same fate. The suspense did not last long. Within a week, a court convicted the newspaper's editor of publishing distorted news and ordered *The Way of Life* to immediately cease publication.[2]

Minh Sơn's critique and the government's suppression of the newspaper highlighted the inherent contradictions of anticommunist nationalism in the Republic of Vietnam (RVN). The anticommunists had inherited the republican nationalism of the colonial period and affirmed their faith in it when they championed the ideals of democracy, unity, and independence during the congresses of 1953. Diệm's rise to power the following year raised hopes of fulfilling

163

164   Conclusion

this vision, but the aspiration remained unrealized because the anticommunists disagreed on the interpretation of the shared vision and violated their ideals.

The very meaning of democracy was the subject of continual debate between the anticommunists in Diệm's republic. The Diemists defined it as an unending effort to create a more perfect political framework to ensure the fulfillment of human potential. Economic reforms, they argued, would build the "substructure of democracy" appropriate to Vietnam's current stage of development. Political liberalization, they suggested, could take place in the future. Yet Diệm never thought that conditions in South Vietnam permitted liberalization, and the personalist quest for democracy stalled indefinitely at the preliminary stage of economic reform. In contrast, his rivals insisted that democracy meant a pluralistic political system with a legally recognized opposition, greater civil liberties, and fair elections. Inspired by this conception of democracy, the oppositionists organized new parties, published editorials, and released manifestos but were powerless to implement institutional reforms. Significantly, anticommunists in both camps willingly violated democratic norms. They limited civil liberties to block communist subversion and interfered in elections for political gain. When the Diemists organized the fraudulent plebiscite against Bảo Đại in 1955, the sect parties turned a blind eye to the irregularities and actively contributed to the elections. The contradiction between principle and practice in the RVN's politics recalled a similar contradiction in the republicanism of the French colonial state, which advocated for democracy while honoring it in the breach.

The anticommunists also struggled to find common ground on the question of national unity. Diệm's faction urged the entire population to unite behind his leadership. The president pressured other groups to dissolve and join his faction and arrested rival anticommunists who refused. The oppositionists contended that unity meant broad coalitions of distinct groups. They maintained their own organizations in defiance of Diệm and called for a multiparty political system. But the oppositionists tried in vain to form an enduring alliance and could no more achieve their conception of unity than the Diemists could. Neither side was willing to compromise and agree on a centrist program. Their intransigence created an unbreachable schism that rendered national unity impossible. Seen as a whole, anticommunist nationalists simultaneously tolerated authoritarianism while encouraging democratic resistance and accepted the suppression of differences while nurturing political diversity.

THE REVOLUTION OF 1963 AND BEYOND

Although the anticommunists failed to implement their vision for the country, they did succeed in transforming Vietnamese political culture. They popularized the ideals of 1953 as well as the long-standing anxieties surrounding those ideals. The repeated appeals to democracy and unity spread the concepts beyond the revolutionaries of old, and the ideals became the standard that all political actors in the RVN used to criticize the government and defend their interests. But the anticommunists also warned that the communists might infiltrate democratic institutions, that liberal democracy was disorderly and inefficient, that an excessive number of parties undermined national unity, and that opposition activism could turn insurrectionary. Such sentiments gained widespread acceptance by the early 1960s, reinforced by fears of the rising insurgency. Thus the RVN's political culture came to reflect the internal tensions of anticommunist nationalism.

The clearest indication of the transformed political culture was that groups and individuals with no connection to anticommunist nationalism employed the rhetoric of democracy and national unity to advance their causes. A succession of new groups emerged in 1963 and filled the void left by the declining political opposition. These groups challenged Diệm's government by appealing to the old anticommunist ideals. Leading the charge was the politicized Buddhist movement that began organizing in May of that year. The movement originated in the religious revival of the 1920s to the 1940s, when clerics and lay leaders argued that Buddhism was part of Vietnam's national essence and aimed to restore the faith. In the early 1960s, Diệm's apparent favoritism toward Catholicism threatened the Buddhists' goal, and the Buddhists demanded that the government grant Buddhism legal parity with Catholicism. They appealed to the democratic ideals of freedom and equality as much as revivalist arguments about Vietnamese identity. The movement's manifestos and declarations invoked religious freedom (*tự do tín ngưỡng*) and religious equality (*bình đẳng tôn giáo*) and accused the government of religious discrimination (*kỳ thị tôn giáo*).[3] The Buddhists held special prayers, staged hunger strikes, and organized demonstrations to push for change. The single most famous act of their movement was the self-immolation of Thích Quảng Đức on June 11, an incident captured by Malcolm Browne's iconic photograph of the monk calmly seated in a lotus position as his body burned. Such incidents convinced people around the world that Diệm's government was repressive, but the president was unmoved. Instead, the regime's security apparatus broke up the protests, jailed religious activists, and even raided houses of worship.[4]

Buddhist activism helped radicalize Vietnamese students, who were even more determined to confront the authorities. These young people had come of age imbibing democratic principles from the mandatory civics education provided in secondary school, but even the slowest of pupils could see that the government ran roughshod over those very principles. Many belonged to religious youth groups and had participated in religious activism that summer. In mid-August, student strikes erupted at the University of Huế in solidarity with the Buddhists and to protest the dismissal of the rector, a Catholic priest widely considered sympathetic to the Buddhist movement.[5] Sympathy strikes quickly

166   Conclusion

spread to universities and trade schools in Saigon, and activism flared in secondary schools throughout the RVN in September.[6] Young people creatively combined the arguments of the Buddhists and the political opposition to criticize the regime. The students warned that Diệm's mistreatment of the Buddhists weakened national unity and that his violation of religious freedom and other democratic rights undermined the struggle against communism. More radical than the Buddhists, these activists called for the removal of Ngô family from the government.[7]

The only member of the established political opposition to play a significant role in the struggles of 1963 was Nguyễn Tường Tam, a famous novelist and former leader of the VNP who had been behind the antigovernment pamphlet during the coup of 1960. Tam had stayed out of politics after the incident and was shocked to receive a court summons three years later, in July 1963, for his alleged involvement in the coup. The old revolutionary was indignant. Rather than come to court, he took his own life to protest Diệm's government. Tam's suicide note denounced the president's authoritarianism and suppression of the opposition:

> Let history render judgment on my life. I will accept no other judge. The arrest and condemnation of the nationalist opposition is a grave crime and will cause the country to fall into the hands of the communists. I oppose it [the government's treatment of the opposition] and am committing suicide, just as Thích Quảng Đức committed self-immolation, as a warning to those who trample on all forms of freedom.[8]

These parting words were an eloquent swansong for the moribund political opposition and an inspiration to educated Vietnamese throughout the RVN. Tam was a beloved cultural icon whose novels were part of the educational curriculum; he instantly became a martyr for generations of Vietnamese who grew up reading his books.[9]

Numerous waves of protests convinced yet a third group to turn against Diệm. A small cabal of army generals feared that the unrest had eroded the president's domestic and foreign support and had rendered him unable to fight the communists effectively.[10] The conspirators secretly secured the loyalty of most regional military commanders and received tacit approval from the new American ambassador to take action. On November 1, 1963, the generals stormed the temporary presidential residence at Gia Long Palace and seized power in the name of the military. Diệm and Nhu sought refuge at a church in Chợlớn, then surrendered the next day on condition that they receive safe passage out of the country. Instead, the officers who took Diệm and Nhu into custody assassinated the pair. It was an ignominious end for the founder of the republic and his closest adviser.

The victorious generals hailed the so-called Revolution of November 1, 1963 (Cách Mạng 1-11-1963) as an uprising against dictatorship. They formed a provisional military government, known as the Revolutionary Military Council (Hội Đồng Quân Nhân Cách Mạng, or RMC), and immediately invoked the ideals of 1953 to bolster the legitimacy of the new regime. The manifesto of the RMC proclaimed, "The establishment of a dictatorship is not the military's intention because it realizes that democracy and freedom are the greatest weapons to defeat communism."[11] The military government promised to promote the "unity of the entire people" (*đoàn kết toàn dân*), to tolerate all parties that were not communist, to protect freedom of the press, and, in a nod to the Buddhist movement, to champion religious freedom and equality. But the RMC also embraced the more authoritarian instincts of anticommunist nationalism. Echoing Diemist admonitions on profligacy and discipline, the manifesto declared, "The army does not favor a profligate democracy at a time when the entire country is still engaged in a war for survival against communism. We must implement a form of democracy that is in a spirit of discipline [suitable] to a wartime country."[12] The RMC promised to hand power to an elected civilian government but provided no timetable for the transfer. In keeping with the RVN's contradictory political culture, the manifesto simultaneously promised and postponed democracy.

The factionalism of Diệm's republic persisted under Vietnam's new rulers, and the coup of 1963 inaugurated another cycle of contentious politics that further entrenched the existing schism between the Diemists and other anticommunists. The RMC released oppositionists from prison, welcomed exiles back from Cambodia and France, and accepted the return of Cao Đài and Hòa Hảo bands still in the maquis. Some former oppositionists even served in the military government. In the mid-1960s, Phan Khắc Sửu and Trần Văn Văn's clique and the Đại Việt party dominated the RVN's weak civilian cabinets and advisory councils. Meanwhile, Diemists felt persecuted by the regime. The RMC and its successor governments carried out a systematic project of "de-Diemification." The civil service dismissed or demoted Cần Lao partisans, and the Ministry of Justice prosecuted, imprisoned, and executed prominent associates of the deceased president. The courts sentenced Ngô Đình Cẩn to death in an act of retribution against the Diemist faction. Madame Nhu and Bishop Ngô Đình Thục were abroad when Diệm fell and never returned to Vietnam. The government's harsh treatment of the Diemists and embrace of their rivals made any reconciliation all but impossible.

The contradictions of anticommunist nationalism continued to shape the RVN even as the regime made great strides toward democracy in the late 1960s and early 1970s. In the years after the coup, the military generals refused to relinquish power and unintentionally provoked an even more strident student movement. Young radicals took to the streets to demand a return to a civilian government, and their activism eventually pushed the generals to carry out a

168   Conclusion

second constitutional transition in 1967. Compared with Diệm's rule, the legislature was more independent and the elections were more fair but not truly free. The authorities enforced a lighter system of censorship, and opposition newspapers could more openly criticize the government. The regime also tolerated the existence of multiple parties and a limited degree of public activism, and Buddhists, students, and older anticommunist groups all organized popular demonstrations. In sum, the RVN became a more democratic hybrid regime and was a far cry from Diệm's dictatorial republic.

The political culture of anticommunist nationalism ultimately outlasted the Saigon-based state. When the communists defeated the RVN in 1975 and imposed a new communist orthodoxy throughout South Vietnam, numerous citizens of the fallen republic fled to the West and formed communities in the United States, France, Australia, and other countries. Many exile communities used anticommunist nationalism as a basis for creating and maintaining a collective political identity. They called for the liberation of Vietnam from communism, the restoration of the RVN, and the reintroduction of democracy to their homeland. Perhaps unsurprisingly, the diaspora could not escape the political factionalism of the southern republic. Diemists, Buddhists, former student activists, and the old anticommunist parties fiercely contested each other's political legitimacy and their memory of the RVN. An especially controversial topic was the rule of Ngô Đình Diệm. Writing in overseas Vietnamese newspapers and memoirs, exiles of all stripes tied the fate of the fallen republic to Diệm or his downfall. Partisans of the late president praised him as an enlightened ruler and claimed that his death had left the republic vulnerable to a communist invasion. Diệm's critics, on the other hand, denounced him as tyrant and lamented that his authoritarianism had eroded the legitimacy of the Saigon-based government.[13] The passage of time has moderated the fierceness of such controversies. Still, anticommunist nationalism remains an important part of the political culture of the Vietnamese diaspora, and the anticommunists' ideas and endemic factionalism survive among overseas Vietnamese to this day.[14]

THE REPUBLIC OF VIETNAM IN THE BROADER PERSPECTIVE

The foregoing history makes clear that the communist-centered and American-centered narratives of the RVN once favored by researchers are simply no longer tenable. The southern republic was neither an aberration in Vietnam's struggle for independence nor an "invention" or "offspring" of US foreign policy.[15] This study eschews the old approaches in favor of analyzing the regime within the history of Vietnamese republicanism and anticommunist nationalism, a history that predated and outlasted American intervention.

A Vietnam-centered narrative has an additional advantage. In studying the RVN's politics on its own terms, this book provides an alternative approach to

Conclusion   169

earlier studies that evaluated Vietnamese governments based solely on Western norms. In the past, scholars assumed that Western democracies represented a universal standard of political progress. Researchers implicitly compared the RVN with liberal democracies in Europe and America, puzzled over its failure to conform to the accepted model, and concluded that the regime was a deviation from universal norms. But Western democracies suffered from their own contradictions and shortcomings, and their norms were far from universal given the existence of numerous nondemocratic regimes throughout the world.

Liberating the RVN from the Western paradigm makes comparative analysis with countries that were more like the Vietnamese republic possible. Regional comparisons are especially fruitful, and an examination of the RVN in relation to its geographical neighbors suggests that the regime was not unusual in being torn between the ideal of democracy and the temptation of authoritarianism. Even a cursory comparison reveals that this tension was common across Southeast Asia in the 1950s and 1960s. Just as Vietnamese nationalists had adopted republicanism from the French during the colonial period, activists throughout the region absorbed democratic ideas from various colonial powers. Much like the RVN, most countries gained independence following World War II, and leaders championed democracy as a political ideal. At the same time, however, many politicians expressed reservations regarding Western democracy and eventually formed hybrid regimes that combined strongman rule with representative politics.

Cambodia and Indonesia offer striking parallels to the southern republic. Cambodia and the RVN shared a heritage of French colonial republicanism, and the governments in both Phnom Penh and Saigon were briefly members of the French Union. During the decade following World War II, Cambodian leaders agitated for independence and created a multiparty constitutional democracy.[16] Yet they understood democracy in different ways, criticized its shortcomings, and debated the speed at which their country should democratize. Some associated democracy with civil liberties and equality; others believed it combined representative government with social and economic justice; still others complained that democratic governments protected the interests of only the bourgeoisie.[17] Cambodia differed from Vietnam in that the monarchy continued to enjoy popular prestige, and Sihanouk dominated politics even as his Vietnamese counterpart, Bảo Đại, fell from power. Despite this key difference, the politics of the Cambodian monarch was akin to that of the nonroyal Diệm. Like the Vietnamese leader, Sihanouk believed that the Cambodian people should directly participate in politics without the mediation of parties and politicians; he thus styled himself as a populist leader who transcended partisan differences.[18] In 1955, two years after independence, Sihanouk held a fraudulent plebiscite to legitimize his leadership and to eclipse the political parties.[19] Also like Diệm, Sihanouk favored a disguised form of single-party rule. He founded a nominally nonpartisan political movement and interfered in elections in favor of

170   Conclusion

the movement's candidates, which effectively excluded rival parties from political life.[20] Although Sihanouk claimed that his reforms made the government more democratic, he actually dismantled the fragile democratic system that other Cambodian politicians had so painstakingly built.[21]

Sukarno's Indonesia also exhibited a contradictory impulse toward both democracy and authoritarianism. A former Dutch colony, the archipelago nation drew inspiration from the constitutional democracy of the Netherlands, and virtually all Indonesian leaders and parties favored a government that ruled by consent and in which the people participated.[22] Unlike in Vietnam, the central debate in Indonesia hinged on whether the future government should be an Islamic state or a representative republic. After Indonesia achieved independence in 1949, politicians established a parliamentary government with multiple parties and organized popular elections for a constituent assembly. The profusion of bickering parties caused high turnover in the cabinet and a stalemate in the constituent assembly—precisely the situation that Diệm's advisers feared when they warned against parliamentarism. Sukarno had long expressed skepticism toward liberal democracy and vigorously attacked the fledgling political system. Similar to Diệm, he argued that Western liberal democracy was purely political and failed to deliver social justice and collective prosperity.[23] He also insisted that partisan competition was divisive, individualistic, and contrary to Indonesian culture and called for a uniquely Indonesian form of democracy based on the indigenous concept of mutual cooperation.[24] Sukarno declared martial law in 1957 and appointed a nonpartisan cabinet. In the years that followed, he dissolved the constituent assembly, appointed a new parliament, and banned several prominent parties. Even as he rejected constitutionalism and multiparty parliamentarism, Sukarno proudly celebrated the new political system as "guided democracy."

The many similarities between the RVN and neighboring countries suggest that they belonged to a pattern of postcolonial hybrid regimes that simultaneously embraced and rejected democracy. By the end of World War II, the concept of democracy had become a widely accepted political idiom synonymous with modernity and legitimacy. But in trying to implement democracy, leaders in newly independent countries found that it resolved some problems but not others. In hybrid regimes and democracies across the globe, politicians, parties, and activists debated which groups and individuals have a legitimate place in politics and how democratic a government should be given competing concerns about stability, efficiency, and security. Even long-standing democracies continue to wrestle with these issues well into the twenty-first century. Far from being an exception to the norm, the RVN was part of this larger debate and represented an earnest but imperfect attempt at solving the great political problems of the modern age.

Appendix: Ngô Đình Diệm's Cabinet, 1954–1955

A1 Government of July 7, 1954

Position[1]	Name	Political Affiliations and Familial Relationships
Prime Minister, Minister of the Interior, Minister of Defense	Ngô Đình Diệm	
Minister of State (no portfolio)	Trần Văn Chương	Nhu's father-in-law, Diemist
Minister of Foreign Affairs	Trần Văn Đỗ	Nhu's uncle-in-law, Spirit Group, Cần Lao, Diemist[2]
Minister of Economy and Finance	Trần Văn Của	
Minister of Labor and Youth	Nguyễn Tăng Nguyên	Spirit Group, Cần Lao, Diemist
Minister of Public Works	Trần Văn Bạch	Diệm's relative?[3]
Minister of Health and Society	Phạm Hữu Chương	
Minister of Agriculture	Phan Khắc Sửu	
Minister of Education	Nguyễn Dương Đôn	
Secretary of State at the Premier's Office	Trần Chánh Thành	Spirit Group, Cần Lao, Diemist
Secretary of Information	Lê Quang Luật	Minor Đại Việt party, northern Catholics, ties to Bishop Lê Hữu Từ and Diemist faction[4]

(Continued)

172 Appendix

A1 (*Continued*)

Position	Name	Political Affiliations and Familial Relationships
Secretary of State Charged with the Mission at the Premier's Office	Phạm Duy Khiêm	
Secretary of the Interior	Nguyễn Ngọc Thơ	
Secretary of Defense	Lê Ngọc Chấn	Vietnamese Nationalist Party[5]
Assistant Secretary of Defense	Hồ Thông Minh	Spirit Group, Diemist[6]
Secretary of Justice	Bùi Văn Thinh	
Secretary of Economy	Nguyễn Văn Thoại	Diệm's brother-in-law, Diemist[7]
Secretary of Finance	Trần Hữu Phương	Diemist[8]

Appendix   173

A2 Coalition Government of September 24, 1954

Position[9]	Name	Political Affiliations and Familial Relationships[10]
Prime Minister, Minister of the Interior, Minister of Defense	Ngô Đình Diệm	
Minister of State, member of National Defense Committee	Trần Văn Soái	Hòa Hảo
Minister of State, member of National Defense Committee	Nguyễn Thành Phương	Cao Đài
Minister of Foreign Affairs	Trần Văn Đỗ	Nhu's uncle-in-law, Spirit Group, Cần Lao, Diemist
Minister of Justice	Bùi Văn Thinh	Future leader of the Movement to Preserve Freedom[11]
Minister of Information and Psychological Warfare	Phạm Xuân Thái	Cao Đài
Minister of Finance	Trần Hữu Phương	Diemist
Minister of Economy	Lương Trọng Tường	Hòa Hảo
Minister of Agriculture	Nguyễn Công Hầu	Hòa Hảo
Minister of Public Works	Trần Văn Bạch	Diệm's relative?
Minister of Planning and Construction	Nguyễn Văn Thoại	Diệm's brother-in-law, Diemist
Minister of Health	Huỳnh Kim Hữu	Spirit Group, Diemist[12]
Minister of Education	Nguyễn Dương Đôn	
Minister of Society	Nguyễn Mạnh Bảo	Cao Đài
Minister of Labor and Youth	Nguyễn Tăng Nguyên	Spirit Group, Cần Lao, Diemist
Minister of Reform	Nguyễn Đức Thuần	
Assistant Minister of Defense	Hồ Thông Minh	Spirit Group, Diemist
Secretary of State at the Premier's Office, Charged with Administration	Trần Ngọc Liên	Cần Lao, Diemist[13]
Secretary of State at the Premier's Office	Phạm Duy Khiêm	
Secretary of State at the Premier's Office	Bùi Kiện Tín	Spirit Group, Diemist[14]
Secretary of the Interior	Huỳnh Văn Nhiệm	Hòa Hảo
Deputy Secretary of the Interior	Nguyễn Văn Cát	Cao Đài

174 Appendix

A3 Government of May 10, 1955

Position[15]	Name	Political Affiliation and Familial Relationships
Prime Minister, Minister of Defense	Ngô Đình Diệm	
Minister of the Interior	Bùi Văn Thinh	Movement to Preserve Freedom
Minister of Foreign Affairs	Vũ Văn Mẫu	Movement to Preserve Freedom[16]
Minister of Justice	Nguyễn Văn Sĩ	
Assistant Minister of Defense	Trần Trung Dung	Diệm's future nephew-in-law, Cần Lao, Diemist[17]
Minister of Information	Trần Chánh Thành	National Revolutionary Movement, Cần Lao, Diemist[18]
Minister of Economy and Finance	Trần Hữu Phương	Diemist
Minister of Public Works	Trần Văn Mẹo	
Minister of Agrarian and Land Reform	Nguyễn Văn Thời	
Minister of Education	Nguyễn Dương Đôn	
Minister of Society and Health	Vũ Quốc Thông	Movement to Preserve Freedom[19]
Minister of Labor	Huỳnh Hữu Nghĩa[20]	
Minister of Agriculture	Nguyễn Công Viên[21]	
Minister of State at the Premier's Office	Nguyễn Hữu Châu	Diemist, Madame Nhu's brother-in-law[22]

Notes

Introduction: Rethinking the Republic of Vietnam

1 Philipps, *Why Vietnam Matters*, 7–15, especially 15. For contemporary descriptions of the demonstrations, see "Cuộc biểu tình ở đô thành chống Nga và Trung Cộng," *Thần chung* 1641 (August 9, 1954): 1, 4; joint weeka 33, August 13, 1954, NARA-RG59-CDF 1950–1954, 751G.00W/8-1354.

2 "Struggle Weird in South Vietnam," *New York Times,* April 29, 1955, 3.

3 Shaplen, *Lost Revolution,* 131.

4 For an alternative interpretation of the RVN that places it within the historical trend of republicanism rather than anticommunism nationalism, see Nu-Anh Tran and Tuong Vu, introduction to *Building a Republican Nation.*

5 The notable exception was John Donnell, who used Vietnamese-language sources to explore both Ngô Đình Diệm's faction and the political opposition. See Donnell, "Personalism in Vietnam" and "Politics in South Vietnam." For more typical examples of the first wave of research, see Goodman, *Politics in War*; Joiner, *Politics of Massacre*; and Scigliano, *South Vietnam.*

6 Jeffrey Race was one of the few Vietnam scholars from the second wave to devote attention to the RVN. See Race, *War Comes.*

7 Marr, *Vietnamese Anticolonialism*; Marr, *Vietnamese Tradition*; Duiker, *Communist Road*; Huỳnh Kim Khánh, *Vietnamese Communism*; Lockhart, *Nation in Arms*; and Thayer, *War by Other Means.*

8 Alternatives to the communist-centered narrative include general histories that incorporate noncommunists and monographs specifically about noncommunists. For the former, see Duiker, *Rise of Nationalism*; and Tai, *Radicalism.* For a sampling of the latter, see Guillemot, *Dai Việt*; Keith, *Catholic Vietnam*; Tai, *Millenarianism*; Trần Mỹ Vân, "Japan and Vietnam's Caodaists"; Trần Mỹ Vân, "Beneath the Japanese Umbrella"; Vũ Ngự Chiêu, "Other Side"; and Werner, *Peasant Politics.* The main architect of the communist-centered narrative, David Marr, later broadened his research to include noncommunists. See Marr, *Vietnam 1945*; and Marr, *Vietnam: State, War, and Revolution.*

9 For variations of this portrayal, see Anderson, *Trapped by Success*; Carter, *Inventing Vietnam*; Herring, *America's Longest War*; Jacobs, *Cold War Mandarin*; Kolko, *Anatomy of a War*; Prados, *Vietnam*; and Young, *Vietnam Wars.* See also Kahin, *Intervention.*

176   Notes to Pages 4–18

10 The most important monographs from the fourth wave about the Ngô Đình Diệm period are Catton, *Diem's Final Failure*; Chapman, *Cauldron of Resistance*; Miller, *Misalliance*; and Stewart, *Vietnam's Lost Revolution*.

11 I thank the first anonymous reviewer for suggesting the term "'Vietnam studies' turn" to describe the change in scholarship about the southern half of Vietnam.

12 Reilly, "Sovereign States."

13 Sean Fear is an American diplomatic historian, but his approach to the politics of the RVN aligns with that of scholars of the fifth wave. See Fear, "Ambiguous Legacy"; Dror, *Making Two Vietnams*; Nguyen-Marshall, "Tools of Empire"; P. Nguyen, "Fighting"; P. Nguyen, "Les résidus de la guerre"; Picard, "'Renegades'"; Picard, "'Fertile Lands'"; Picard, "Fragmented Loyalties"; and Quinn-Judge, *Third Force*. See also Hansen, "Bắc Di Cư" and "Virgin Heads South."

14 Tan, "Swiddens"; Biggs, *Quagmire*; and Biggs, *Footprints*.

Chapter One: Birth of Anticommunist Nationalism, 1920s–1954

1 Vĩnh Sinh, introduction to *Phan Châu Trinh*, 37.

2 Phan Châu Trinh, "Monarchy and Democracy," 136–137.

3 Phan Châu Trinh, "Monarchy and Democracy," 139.

4 "Các chánh đãng [*sic*]: Cộng Hòa, Đại Việt, VN Phục Quốc Hội, VN Quốc Dân Đãng [*sic*] và Xã Hội hiệu triệu đồng bào," *Thời đại* 208 (December 19, 1955): 1, 4, especially 4. All translations are the author's unless otherwise stated.

5 "Các chánh đãng [*sic*]," 1.

6 Van Nguyen-Marshall has made this precise point. See Nguyen-Marshall, review of *Vietnam's Lost Revolution*, 14–15.

7 Young, *Vietnam Wars*, 42–47; Herring, *America's Longest War*, 16–68 passim; Prados, *Vietnam*, 22–42 passim; and Duiker, *Communist Road*, 143–144, 179–182.

8 T. Vu, *Vietnam's Communist Revolution*, 17, 32, 79, 92.

9 Bergère, *Sun Yat-sen*, 356–365; and Chang and Gordon, *All Under Heaven*, 96–103.

10 Bergère, *Sun Yat-sen*, 371–377, 288–289; and Chang and Gordon, *All Under Heaven*, 110.

11 Zinoman, *Vietnamese Colonial Republican*, 4–6.

12 Peycam, *Birth*, 35–37, 40–41.

13 Zinoman, *Vietnamese Colonial Republican*, 7–8.

14 Osborne, *French Presence*, 118–130 passim; and Peycam, *Birth*, 53–54.

15 Phan Bội Châu, "Letter from Abroad," 357.

16 Phan Bội Châu, "Letter from Abroad," 354–355.

17 For more on Phan Bội Châu's biography and career, see Vĩnh Sinh and Wickenden, introduction to *Overturned Chariot*.

18 For more on Phan Châu Trinh's biography and career, see Vĩnh Sinh, introduction to *Phan Châu Trinh*; and Goscha, *Vietnam*, 102–105.

19 Goscha, *Vietnam*, 124–130; and Peycam, *Birth*, 63–64.

20 Hoàng Văn Đào, *Việt Nam Quốc Dân Đảng*, 38–39; and Goscha, *Vietnam*, 135–137. For Sun Yat-sen's program, see Bergère, *Sun Yat-sen*, 378–381.

21 Tai, *Radicalism*, 184–185, 218; and Huỳnh Kim Khánh, *Vietnamese Communism*, 92–93.

22 Huỳnh Kim Khánh, *Vietnamese Communism*, 92–93; and Tai, *Radicalism*, 218–219.

23 Goscha, *Vietnam*, 137–143; and Quinn-Judge, *Ho Chi Minh*, 11–78 passim.

24 Reilly, "Origins," 28–32.

25 Reilly, "Origins," 51.

26 T. Vu, *Vietnam's Communist Revolution*, 49–50.

27 Huỳnh Kim Khánh, *Vietnamese Communism*, 128–129.

28 Zinoman, *Colonial Bastille*, 229–230; and Reilly, "Origins," 52–54.

29 Reilly, "Origins," 51–52.

Notes to Pages 19–23　　177

30　Reilly, "Origins," 43–48.

31　Reilly, "Origins," 50–51.

32　Interestingly, some of these figures sided with the Việt Minh and the communists after 1945 despite earlier criticism of communism. See Zinoman, *Vietnamese Colonial Republican*, 15–16, 31–84, 85–130; Zinoman, "Vietnamese Urban Intellectuals"; and M. Nguyen, "Self-Reliant Literary Group," 143–178, 208–212.

33　The Đai Việt party was established in 1938 but not formalized until the following year.

34　Guillemot, *Dai Viêt*, 35–64.

35　Guillemot, *Dai Viêt*, 119, 139–145.

36　Guillemot, *Dai Viêt*, 148–150.

37　"The Dai Viet Party," September 11, 1953, CREST, CIA-RDP80-00810A002300140009-2.

38　Guillemot, *Dai Viêt*, 145–147.

39　T. Vu, *Vietnam's Communist Revolution*, 78–84.

40　Huỳnh Kim Khánh, *Vietnamese Communism*, 264–266.

41　T. Vu, *Vietnam's Communist Revolution*, 94–95.

42　Goscha, *Vietnam*, 195.

43　Marr, *Vietnam 1945*, 252–254; and Worthing, *Occupation and Revolution*, 41–46.

44　Marr, *Vietnam: State, War, and Revolution*, 410.

45　Guillemot, *Dai Viêt*, 185–186.

46　Tai, *Radicalism*, 232–243.

47　Ngô Văn, *Viêt-Nam*, 183–184; and Sacks, "Marxism," 127–128.

48　Hémery, *Révolutionnaires vietnamiens*, 395–411.

49　Trần Mỹ Vân, *Vietnamese Royal Exile*, 142–143.

50　Reilly, "Origins," 139–141.

51　Nguyễn Thế Anh, "Formulation," 59.

52　For a fuller explanation of Cao Đài syncretism, see Hoskins, *Divine Eye*, 15–16.

53　Hoskins, *Divine Eye*, 15, 86; and Jammes, *Les oracles*, 126–130.

54　Goscha, *Vietnam*, 174. For other estimates of Cao Đài membership, see Werner, *Peasant Politics*, 38; Trần Mỹ Vân, "Vietnam's Caodaism," 12; and Savani, *Visage et images*, 73, 78.

55　For Phạm Công Tắc's ambition to study in Japan, see Trần Mỹ Vân, "Vietnam's Caodaism," 3–4. For Cao Đài support of Prince Cường Để, see Jammes, *Les oracles*, 209.

56　Trần Mỹ Vân, "Japan and Vietnam's Caodaists," 184.

57　Trần Mỹ Vân, "Japan and Vietnam's Caodaists," 184–185; and Trần Quang Vinh, *Hồi ký*, 212.

58　Tai, *Millenarianism*, 115–116.

59　Bourdeaux, "Approches statistiques," 285.

60　Tai, *Millenarianism*, 25.

61　Huỳnh Phú Sổ, *Cách tu hiền*, 7.

62　Tai, *Millenarianism*, 120–124; and Bourdeaux, "Approches statistiques," 283.

63　For a nuanced account of the kidnapping and Huỳnh Phú Sổ's relationship with Cường Để's party and the Japanese, see Bourdeaux, "Émergence et constitution," 204–227.

64　Tai, *Millenarianism*, 127; Werner, *Peasant Politics*, 39; Trần Mỹ Vân, "Beneath the Japanese Umbrella," 78; and Bourdeaux, "Émergence et constitution," 216.

65　For the expansion of the Đại Việt party beyond northern Vietnam, see Guillemot, *Dai Viêt*, 270.

66　Guillemot, *Dai Viêt*, 231–233.

67　Whether the Trotskyists joined the coalition is disputed in some quarters. See Reilly, "Sovereign States," 116; Bourdeaux, "Émergence et constitution," 286–287; Tai, *Millenarianism*, 137; and Ngô Văn, *Viêt-Nam*, 327–328. For the involvement of the Empire of Vietnam in the coalition, see Reilly, "Origins," 161–163.

68　Nguyễn Long Thành Nam, *Phật Giáo Hòa Hảo*, 336–338, 342–344; Trần Quang Vinh, *Hồi ký*, 363–369; and Bourdeaux, "Émergence et constitution," 286–287.

178   Notes to Pages 23–29

69 Marr, *Vietnam 1945,* 457; and Nguyễn Long Thành Nam, *Phật Giáo Hòa Hảo,* 347–349.

70 Marr, *Vietnam 1945,* 461.

71 For the origins of the Bình Xuyên, see K. Li, "Entrepreneurs of Disorder," chap. 1: 3–9; and "Partisan to Sovereign," 143–144.

72 Keith, *Catholic Vietnam.*

73 Keith, *Catholic Vietnam,* 216; and Marr, *Vietnam: State, War, and Revolution,* 430, 433–435.

74 Marr, *Vietnam 1945,* 434–435.

75 Marr suggests that the decree outlawing the Đại Việt party was a response to a coup plot whereas Guillemot contends that the communists simply wanted to eliminate powerful rivals. See Guillemot, *Dai Viêt,* 278–284; and Marr, *Vietnam: State, War, and Revolution,* 395–396, 406–408.

76 Bourdeaux, "Émergence et constitution," 300–301.

77 Marr, *Vietnam 1945,* 467–469; Nguyễn Long Thành Nam, *Phật Giáo Hòa Hảo,* 367–373; Bourdeaux, "Émergence et constitution," 293–301; Savani, *Visage et images,* 88–89; and Savani, *Notes sur la secte,* 26–27.

78 Marr, *Vietnam: State, War, and Revolution,* 408–410; McHale, *First Vietnam War,* 59–60; Ngô Văn, *Viêt-Nam,* 345, 358–360; Ngô Văn, *Crossfire,* 126–144 passim; and Lữ Sanh Hạnh, "Some Stages."

79 Goscha, *Vietnam,* 203–204, 206–207; Marr, *Vietnam: State, War, and Revolution,* 410–413, 417–420; Worthing, *Occupation and Revolution,* 104–11; and Duiker, *Communist Road,* 114–117.

80 Marr, *Vietnam: State, War, and Revolution,* 453–454.

81 Tonnesson, *Vietnam 1946,* 39–64. For more on policy of the Chinese Nationalists toward the occupation, see Worthing, *Occupation and Revolution.*

82 Goscha, *Vietnam,* 200–201, 212–215.

83 Guillemot, *Dai Viêt,* 332–354, 376–389, especially 354 and 381; and Marr, *Vietnam: State, War, and Revolution,* 413–414, 422–428.

84 The DRV was never technically a single-party state in that the communists allowed show-case parties such as the Democratic Party to operate, but there was no legally permitted, partisan political opposition after 1946. See Goscha, *Vietnam,* 234–235.

85 D. V., "Muốn thực hiện đoàn kết phải thực hành những kế hoạch gì?" *Việt Nam* 166 (May 5, 1946): 1, 2, citation on 2.

86 For a personal account of the attacks against the anticommunist parties by the Việt Minh, see Nguyễn Tường Bách, *Việt Nam,* 247–282.

87 Keith, *Catholic Vietnam,* 225–226; and Marr, *Vietnam: State, War, and Revolution,* 432–434.

88 Trần Thị Liên, "Les catholiques vietnamiens," 311–312.

89 Goscha, *Vietnam,* 203–204, 213; and Bourdeaux, "Émergence et constitution," 301–308.

90 Bourdeaux, "Émergence et constitution," 292; McHale, *First Vietnam War,* 86–87; Savani, *Notes sur le Caodaisme,* 167; and Trần Quang Vinh, *Hồi ký,* 11–29.

91 Trần Quang Vinh, *Hồi ký,* 39–43.

92 Trần Quang Vinh, *Hồi ký,* 42–50.

93 Goscha, "'Popular' Side," 342–343.

94 Phạm Công Tắc, *Lời thuyết đạo,* 97.

95 Savani, *Notes sur le Caodaisme,* 134–136.

96 Bourdeaux, "Émergence et constitution," 342, 345.

97 For differing accounts of the composition of Nguyễn Bình's coalition, see Bourdeaux, "Émergence et constitution," 324–325; K. Li, "Partisan to Sovereign," 148–149; and Reilly, "Origins," 180–182.

98 Bourdeaux, "Émergence et constitution," 327.

99 For the composition of the SDP, see Bordeaux, "Émergence et constitution," 329–330; and Nguyễn Long Thành Nam, *Phật Giáo Hòa Hảo,* 417.

Notes to Pages 29–35   179

100 Văn Lang, "Dân chủ," *QC* 5 (November 20, 1946): 1–2; Như Thúy, "Để hiểu thực trạng Miền Tây," part XVIII, *QC* 67 (June 25–26, 1955): 1, 4; and BCH Liên Tinh Dân Xã MTNV, "Chương trình của Đảng Việt Nam Dân Chủ Xã Hội." For more on the ideology of the Social Democratic Party, see Vương Kim, *Lập trường Dân Xã Đảng.*

101 Văn Lang, "Dân chủ," 2.

102 "Đoàn kết," *QC* 37 (December 28, 1946): 2.

103 Bourdeaux, "Émergence et constitution," 353, 367–369.

104 Nguyễn Long Thành Nam, *Phật Giáo Hòa Hảo,* 393.

105 Savani, *Notes sur les Binh Xuyen,* 78–79; McHale, *First Vietnam War,* 114; and Bourdeaux, "Émergence et constitution," 366–367.

106 Goscha, "'Popular' Side," 343; McHale, *First Vietnam War,* 116–120; and Bourdeaux, "Émergence et constitution," 368–379.

107 McHale, "Understanding," 112.

108 For a Hòa Hảo perspective on the alliance, see Nguyễn Long Thành Nam, *Phật Giáo Hòa Hảo,* 437–451.

109 For different accounts of the composition of the Nanjing front and its leadership, see "The Nationalist Front," May 22, 1947, CREST, CIA-RDP82–00457R000600190001–8; Nguyễn Long Thành Nam, *Phật Giáo Hòa Hảo,* 393–394; and Guillemot, *Dai Viêt,* 418.

110 Goscha, *Vietnam,* 238.

111 Goscha, *Vietnam,* 216–219.

112 Goscha, *Vietnam,* 240.

113 Guillemot, *Dai Viêt,* 421–424.

114 Reilly, "Origins," 218–219.

115 Goscha, *Vietnam,* 246–27; and Reilly, "Origins," 238.

116 Grant, "Viet Nam Constitution," 438; Reilly, "Origins," 241–242; and Weiner, "Government and Politics," 50.

117 Fall, "Representative Government"; Hammer, *Struggle for Indochina,* 289–290; and Reilly, "Origins," 250.

118 K. Li, "Partisan to Sovereign," 152–169.

119 Savani, *Notes sur les Binh Xuyen,* 119. For the alliance with France and Lê Văn Viễn's activities after the rally, see K. Li, "Partisan to Sovereign," 169–172.

120 Trần Thị Liên, "Catholiques vietnamiens," 326–342.

121 For the origins of the radicalization, see T. Vu, "It's Time."

122 X. Li, *Building Ho's Army,* 40–129; Caulkins, *China,* 35–58; Zhai, *China,* 10–64; Kraus, "Border Region"; and Chen Jian, "China."

123 X. Li, *Building Ho's Army,* 112–113, 130–135; Zhai, *China,* 34–35, 41; Ninh, *World Transformed,* 103–107; Hy Văn Lương, *Tradition,* 151–152; and McHale, "Freedom," 94–95.

124 For more on the land reform trials, see Holcombe, *Mass Mobilization,* 139–158.

125 The term *dinh tê* was apparently a corruption of *rentrer,* meaning "to return" in French. See Phạm Duy, *Hồi ký,* 3:324–325.

126 Goscha, *Vietnam,* 247–248. See also telegram 336, Hanoi to Secretary of State, December 1, 1952, NARA-RG59-CDF 1950–1954, 751G.11/12–152; Bùi Diễm, *Jaws of History,* 29, 65–70.

127 Biography of Trần Văn Hữu, January 18, 1955, NARA-RG59-CDF 1955–1959, 751G.00/1–1855; Hammer, *Struggle for Indochina,* 281–282; and McHale, *First Vietnam War,* 165–166.

128 "Significance of the Shake-Up in the Vietnamese Cabinet," July 7, 1952, CREST, CIA-RDP79T00937A000200010062–2.

129 Lancaster, *Emancipation,* 283; and Pham, *Two Hamlets,* 76–77.

130 For a broader analysis of the states-within-a-state that made up the State of Vietnam, see Reilly, "Sovereign States." For an analysis of the sectarian autonomous zones as parastates, see McHale, *First Vietnam War,* 244–245.

180   Notes to Pages 35–41

131 Jammes, *Les oracles,* 127–128; and Bourdeaux, "Émergence et constitution," 495–497, 501–506.

132 For more on Bình Xuyên enterprises, see K. Li, "Entrepreneurs of Disorder," chap. 3: 11–20.

133 Guillemot, *Dai Viêt,* 488–498.

134 Guillemot, *Dai Viêt,* 546–550.

135 Bourdeaux, "Émergence et constitution," 391, 445–446.

136 "Viet Nam Dan Chu Xa Hoi Dang ou Dan Xa," April 1954, SHAT, 10H 4203; and McHale, *First Vietnam War,* 241–244.

137 For Diệm's participation in the conference in Hong Kong, see Hammer, *Struggle for Indochina,* 215. For more on Diệm's career prior to 1950, see Miller, *Misalliance,* 24–36.

138 Ngô Đình Diệm, "Lời tuyên bố của chí sĩ Ngô Đình Diệm ngày 16 tháng 8 năm 1949," in *CĐCN,* 1:223–224.

139 Miller, *Misalliance,* 38–41; and Morgan, *Vietnam Lobby,* 2–14.

140 Catton, *Diem's Final Failure,* 38–44. For an alternative argument that personalism was a form of Marxist humanism rather a middle way between communism and capitalism, see D. Nguyen, *Unimagined Community.*

141 For the various groups that made up the early Diemist faction, see Huỳnh Văn Lang, *Ký ức,* 2:213; and Donnell, "Politics in South Vietnam," 93–97. For Diệm's early efforts at political organizing, see Trần Thị Liên, "Les catholiques vietnamiens," 355–422.

142 Donnell, "Politics in South Vietnam," 99–101; and "Cao-Lao Charter," 559–572.

143 For more on Thế's biography and career, see Blagov, *Honest Mistakes,* 1–2, 27–37.

144 Nhị Lang, *Phong trào kháng chiến,* 30.

145 Lancaster, *Emancipation,* 233–234; and "A Bomb Makes Shambles of Sunny Saigon Square," *Life* 32, no. 4 (January 28, 1952): 19.

146 Hammer, *Struggle for Indochina,* 272–273.

147 Reilly, "Origins," 266.

148 Buttinger, *Vietnam: A Dragon Embattled,* 2:780; and Guillemot, *Dai Viêt,* 535.

149 Telegram 177, Hanoi to Secretary of State, July 27, 1953, NARA-RG59-CDF 1950–1954, 751G.11/7-2753; telegram 59, Saigon to Secretary of State, July 27, 1953, 751G.11/7-2753; "Historique," in "Mouvement d'Union Nationale Pour la Paix," April 1954, SHAT, 10H 4203; and Reilly, "Origins," 267.

150 Chapman, *Cauldron of Resistance,* 55.

151 Guillemot, *Dai Viêt,* 535–536.

152 Pierre-Albin Martel, "Le congrès des nationalistes à Saigon sera-t-il le prélude à la rentrée des 'attentistes' dans la vie politique vietnamienn?" *Le monde,* September 6–7, 1953, 8.

153 The organizers included accommodationists like General Lê Văn Viễn of the Bình Xuyên and General Nguyễn Thành Phương of the Cao Đài as well as *attentistes* like Ngô Đình Nhu and the southern Đại Việt leader, Nguyễn Tôn Hoàn. For the organizers, see "Historique," in "Mouvement d'Union Nationale Pour la Paix." For the public declaration, see "Dân chúng và các phái đoàn hãy đoàn kết để [*sic*] hoàn thành nền độc lập nước nhà," *Tin điển* 128 (September 6, 1953): 1, 4.

154 For the groups and individuals that attended the meeting, see "Première réunion du Dai Doan Ket chez les Binh Xuyen," September 11, 1953, SHAT, 10H 4023.

155 Annex 1, "Première réunion du Dai Doan Ket chez les Binh Xuyen."

156 Hà Thúc Ký, *Sống còn,* 162–163; and Lancaster, *Emancipation,* 277.

157 "Première réunion du Dai Doan Ket chez les Binh Xuyen"; and "Historique," in "Mouvement d'Union Nationale Pour la Paix."

158 Phong Thủy, "Ý nghĩa và giá trị cuộc Đại hội đoàn kết ngày 6-9-53," *Xã hội* 8 (September 15, 1953): 2, 35, especially 35.

159 "Historique," in "Mouvement d'Union Nationale Pour la Paix"; and Hà Thúc Ký, *Sống còn,* 163–164.

Notes to Pages 41–47   181

160 Miller, *Misalliance*, 50.

161 For the composition of the National Congress, see "Thành phần đại biểu dự đại hội toàn quốc sẽ gồm có những ai?" *Thần chung* 1373 (September 12–13, 1953): 1, 4; and "Hội nghị toàn quốc sẽ gồm 211 nhân viên," *Thần chung* 1395 (October 8, 1953): 1, 4.

162 "Hội nghị TQ đã bế mạc," *Thần chung* 1404 (October 19, 1953): 1, 4.

163 "Historique," in "Mouvement d'Union Nationale Pour la Paix."

164 "The Military and Political Situation in Vietnam," February 8, 1954, CREST, CIA-RDP81-01036R000100120094-5.

165 "Historique," in "Mouvement d'Union Nationale Pour la Paix."

166 "Historique," in "Mouvement d'Union Nationale Pour la Paix."

167 "Lời tuyên bố của Đức Quốc trưởng nhân dịp khởi [*sic*] hành sang Pháp," *Thần chung* 1548 (April 12, 1954): 1.

168 Telegram 4103, Paris to Secretary of State, April 27, 1954, NARA-RG59-CDF 1950–1954, 751G.00/4-2754.

169 "French Deny Talk with Ho Chi Minh," *New York Times*, April 21, 1954, 3.

170 VTX, "Việt Nam không chịu ký hiệp ước," *Thần chung* 1562 (April 28, 1954): 1, 4. For the origins of the proposed partition, see Logevall, *Embers of War,* 521–524.

171 VTX, "Chống lại mưu toan chia xẻ [*sic*] VN ra làm nhiều khúc," *Thần chung* 1566 (May 3, 1954): 1, 4; "Dân chúng khắp nơi phản đối việc mưu toan chia xẻ [*sic*] VN," *Thần chung* 1570 (May 7, 1954): 1, 4; "Biểu tình phản đối khắp nơi," *Thần chung* 1571 (May 8–9, 1954): 1, 4; "Điện tín của [*sic*] Thủ [*sic*] hiến Trung Việt," *Thần chung* 1574 (May 12, 1954): 1; "Phản đối mưu mô chia rẽ VN," *Thần chung* 1576 (May 14, 1954): 1, 4; "Phản đối mưu mô chia rẽ VN," *Thần chung* 1578 (May 17, 1954): 1, 4; and "Dân chúng khắp các tỉnh Nam Việt phản đối mưu mô chia rẽ VN," *Thần chung* 1579 (May 18, 1954): 1, 4.

172 "Ngoại trưởng Nguyễn [*sic*] Quốc Định đã đưa ra kế hoạch của Việt Nam để [*sic*] vãn [*sic*] hồi hòa bình," *Thần chung* 1576 (May 14, 1954): 1, 4; and "Vietnam's Peace Terms and Statements at Geneva," *New York Times*, May 13, 1954, 4.

173 Bảo Đại, *Le dragon d'Annam,* 328. See also Buttinger, *Vietnam: A Dragon Embattled,* 2:835–836.

174 For more on Bảo Đại's decision, see telegram 4396, Paris to Secretary of State, April 9, 1955, NARA-RG59-CDF 1955–1959, 751G.00/4-955; Bảo Đại, *Le dragon d'Annam,* 328–329; Bùi Diễm, *Gọng kìm lịch sử,* 146n1; Miller, *Misalliance,* 53; Anderson, *Trapped by Success,* 52–55; and Trần Thị Liên, "Catholiques vietnamiens," 1039–1043. The United States considered several other prominent political figures other than Diệm to be pro-American. See Hoey to Stuart, May 10, 1954, 751G.00/5-1054. For Ngô Đình Luyện's friendship with Bảo Đại, see Nguyễn Hữu Duệ, *Nhớ lại những ngày,* 25–28.

175 McHale, *First Vietnam War,* 263, 263n4.

176 Trương Bảo Sơn, "Những kỷ niệm riêng," 75–76.

Chapter Two: Quest for National Unity, 1954–1955

1 Telegram 4881, Saigon to Secretary of State, April 28, 1955, NARA-RG59-CDF 1955–1959, 751G.00/4-2855; telegram MG 376-P DTG 291140Z, Chief of Military Assistance Advisory Group Indochina to Secretary of State, April 30, 1955, 751G.00/4-3055; Đoàn Thêm, *Hai mươi năm qua,* 171; Simpson, *Tiger,* 146–147; and Trần Văn Đôn, *Việt Nam,* 124.

2 Chapman, *Cauldron of Resistance,* 70–115; Currey, *Edward Lansdale,* 167–177; Herring, *America's Longest War,* 63–66; Kahin, *Intervention,* 82–84; Miller, *Misalliance,* 95–123; and Young, *Vietnam Wars,* 48–49.

3 Huỳnh Văn Lang, *Ký ức,* 2:211; and despatch 279, Saigon to Department of State, March 2, 1959, NARA-RG59-CDF 1955–1959, 751G.00/3-259.

4 Donnell, "Politics in South Vietnam," 95.

182   Notes to Pages 47–50

5 During Diệm's tenure, the union used the religious appellation in Western-language translations, but the Vietnamese name of the group did not include any reference to religion. For more on Trần Quốc Bửu, the founding of his union, and his association with Nhu, see memorandum of conversation between Trần Quốc Bửu, Mendenhall, and Barbier, February 9, 1961, NARA-RG84-CGR, box 54, folder 350 Internal Political Affairs Vietnam-GVN 1961; Wherle, *Between a River,* 33–41, 67–68, 91; and Chính Đạo, *Việt Nam niên biểu,* 520–521.

6 Buttinger, *Vietnam: A Dragon Embattled,* 2:1066n98. For other membership figures, see Donnell, "Politics in South Vietnam," 96; and Wherle, *Between a River,* 69.

7 Although sources on Ngô Đình Cẩn's early organizing are scant, the biographies of central Vietnamese politicians who served in the National Assembly during Diệm's rule provide clues about the composition of Cẩn's followers. Typically, only Cẩn's partisans could win elections in the central region, and many deputies from his area of influence were activists in Catholic nationalist organizations or Việt Minh defectors who joined the Diemist faction after escaping communist-controlled territory. For example, see the biographies of Bùi Tuân and Nguyễn Bá Tín in Nguyễn Văn Nam, *Niên giám Quốc Hội,* 153–155, 162. For an account of the early Cần Lao party in central Vietnam, see Đỗ Mậu, *Việt Nam,* 82–85.

8 Huỳnh Văn Lang, *Nhân chứng,* 2:213; and Nguyễn Văn Minh, *Dòng họ Ngô Đình,* 42.

9 Despatch 160, Saigon to Department of State, November 8, 1954, NARA-RG59-CDF 1950–1954, 751G.00/11-854. For Nguyễn Đôn Duyến's membership in Ngô Đình Cẩn's wing of the Diemist faction, see Đỗ Mậu, *Việt Nam,* 83.

10 For more on Trần Trung Dung's politics and the origins of the northern branch of the Cần Lao party, see "Tiểu sử ông Trần Trung Dung, ứng cử viên tại Ninh Thuận," *CMQG* 191 (March 1, 1956): 1, 4; Tam, *Vietnam's War,* 156–158, 175–176; and Huỳnh Văn Lang, *Nhân chứng,* 2:210, 213.

11 "Populations contrôlées par les sectes confessionnelles," undated; and "Populations contrôlées par les sectes au 1.10.54," October 1, 1954, both in TTLTQGII-PThTVNCH 14685.

12 For biographical information on Nguyễn Thành Phương, see "Tiểu sử các nhân vật ra ứng cử tổng thống và phó tổng thống Việt Nam Cộng Hòa," *TD* 1178 (March 5, 1961): 1, 4; and Biographic Information Division, "Nguyen Thanh Phuong," March 15, 1961, NARA-RG84-CGR, box 72, folder 350.3 Biographical Data General. For varying estimates of the size of the Cao Đài army in 1954, see "Probable Developments in South Vietnam, Laos, and Cambodia Through July 1956," November 23, 1954, CREST, CIA-RDP81-01036R000100120094-5; "The Political Situation Since Geneva," c. fall 1954, NARA-RG59-CDF 1955–1959, 751G.00/11-256; and Savani, *Notes sur le Caodaisme,* 214. For Phương's ascension to the leadership of the Cao Đài political party, see Savani, *Notes sur le Caodaisme,* 136–137.

13 Correspondence 49-S, Province Chief of Biên Hòa Province to Governor of Southern Vietnam, July 18, 1954, TTLTQGII-PThTVNCH 14606; and "Việt Nam Phục Quốc Hội nhóm Đại hội toàn quốc," *TC* 1157 (February 8, 1955): 1, 4.

14 Chapman, *Cauldron of Resistance,* 65.

15 "Policy of Trinh Minh The's National Resistance Front," November 20, 1951, CREST, CIA-RDP82-00457R009200470002-1; and "Manifesto of the Vietnamese Nationalist Resistants [*sic*] Front," enclosure 1 attached to enclosure 2, despatch 32, Saigon to Department of State, July 22, 1954, NARA-RG59-CDF 1950–1954, 751G.00/7-2254.

16 For varying estimates of the Hòa Hảo forces, see "Probable Developments"; "Political Situation Since Geneva"; and Savani, *Visage et images,* 96. For the locations of the autonomous zones, see Lê Văn Dương, *Quân Lực,* 433.

17 Savani, *Notes sur la secte,* 49–50.

18 Savani, *Notes sur la secte,* 29.

19 Tai, *Millenarianism,* 120.

20 Bordeaux, "Émergence et constitution," 450–451.

21 Tai, *Millenarianism,* 130.

22 Trần Thị Hoa, *Hồi ký,* 69–71.

Notes to Pages 50–56   183

23 For differing accounts of the transaction, see McCoy, Read, and Adams, *Politics of Heroin,* 117–118; K. Li, "Entrepreneurs of Disorder," chap. 3: 15–20.

24 For various estimates of the size of the Bình Xuyên, see "Probable Developments"; "Political Situation Since Geneva"; and Lê Văn Dương, *Quân Lực,* 410. For the subsidies that Lê Văn Viễn received, see Savani, *Notes sur les Binh Xuyen,* 145–146; telegram 2772, Saigon to Secretary of State, January 15, 1955, NARA-RG59-CDF 1955–1959, 751G.00/1-1555; and correspondence 154/VP/QP/M/BB, Minister of National Defense Hồ Thông Minh to Premier, January 17, 1955, TTLTQGII-PThT-VNCH 14685. Note that the last document and many others list an incorrect title for Hồ Thông Minh.

25 Savani, *Notes sur les Binh Xuyen,* 155–157.

26 Lê Văn Dương, *Quân Lực,* 411. Note the typographical error in the year of Lại Văn Sang's appointment. Sang was appointed in spring 1954 and dismissed in spring 1955.

27 Buttinger, *Vietnam: A Dragon Embattled,* 2:816–817; and Lansdale, *Midst of War,* 148–149.

28 Telegram 214, Saigon to Secretary of State, July 15, 1954, NARA-RG59-CDF 1950–1954, 751G.00/7-1654.

29 Hansen, "Virgin Heads South: Northern Catholic Refugees in South Vietnam," 116.

30 Trần Thị Liên, "Les catholiques vietnamiens," 843–851.

31 Trần Thị Liên, "Les catholiques vietnamiens," 719.

32 Trần Thị Liên, "Les catholiques vietnamiens," 1048.

33 Guillemot, *Dai Viêt,* 610.

34 Guillemot, *Dai Viêt,* 607–608.

35 For the zones of influence of the regional branches of the Đại Việt party, see Guillemot, *Dai Viêt,* 562.

36 Guillemot, *Dai Viêt,* 562.

37 Statler, *Replacing France,* 185.

38 "Probable Developments."

39 Phạm Văn Liễu, *Trả ta sông núi,* 1:297–298.

40 For an example of Heath's attitude toward Vietnamese nationalists, see "The Ambassador at Saigon (Heath) to the Department of State," October 17, 1953, *FRUS, 1952–1954,* vol. 13, *Indochina:* 828–830.

41 Ahern, *CIA and the House of Ngo,* 14–16; Currey, *Edward Lansdale,* 142–149; and Wherle, *Between a River,* 67.

42 Telegram 2358, Saigon to Secretary of State, May 12, 1954, NARA-RG59-CDF 1950–1954, 751G.00/5-1254; and telegram 2524, Saigon to Secretary of State, May 24, 1954, 751G.00/5-2454.

43 Telegram 4396, Paris to Secretary of State, April 9, 1955, NARA-RG59-CDF 1955–1959, 751G.00/4-955.

44 Bùi Diễm, *Gọng kìm lịch sử,* 142–143.

45 Telegram 1441, Saigon to Secretary of State, October 14, 1954, NARA-RG59-CDF 1950–1954, 751G.00/10-1454.

46 Telegram 3537, Saigon to Secretary of State, February 25, 1955, NARA-RG59-CDF 1955–1959, 751G.02/2-2355.

47 Ngô Đình Diệm, "Ngỏ lời cùng dân chúng Truồi (Huế) (2-7-1954)," in *CĐCN,* 1:71.

48 Ngô Đình Diệm, "Hiệu triệu quốc dân ngày thành lập chánh phủ (7-7-1954)," in *CĐCN,* 1:17–19, especially 18–19.

49 Ngô Đình Diệm, "Hiệu triệu quốc dân ngày thành lập chánh phủ," 19.

50 "Thiếu Tướng Lê Văn Viễn cho biết: 'Tôi có thể đảm bảo 50.000 đồng bào Bắc Việt tản cư cơm ăn, nhà ở,'" *Thần chung* 1638 (August 5, 1954): 1, 6.

51 Despatch 51, Saigon to Department of State, August 2, 1954, NARA-RG59-CDF 1950–1954, 751G.00/8-254; and VTX, "Đức Hộ Pháp Phạm Công Tắc kêu gọi giáo hữu cứu trợ đồng bào Bắc Việt tản cư," *Thần chung* 1651 (August 21–22, 1954): 1, 4, especially 4.

52 Enclosure to despatch 147, Paris to Department of State, July 20, 1954, NARA-RG59-CDF 1950–1954, 751G.00/7-2054; and Trần Thị Liên, "Les catholiques vietnamiens," 1053–1054.

184   Notes to Pages 56–59

53 Correspondence 136-PTT-DL/M, Premier to Minister of Information, July 29, 1954, TTLTQ-GII-PThTVNCH 29157; Ngô Đình Diệm, "Lời hiệu triệu của Thủ Tướng Ngô Đình Diệm về việc đồng bào Bắc Việt và miền Bắc Trung Việt di cư vào dùng [sic] tự do," TC 1000 (July 31, 1954): 1, 4; and "Thủ Tướng Ngô Đình Diệm ra Hanoi," Thần chung 2636 (August 3, 1954): 1.

54 Telegram 304, Saigon to Secretary of State, July 23, 1954, NARA-RG59-CDF 1950–1954, 751G.00/7-2354; telegram 342, Saigon to Secretary of State, July 27, 1954, 751G.00/7-2754; telegram 458, Saigon to Secretary of State, August 5, 1954, 751G.00/8-554; and Hansen, "Virgin Heads South: Northern Catholic Refugees in South Vietnam," 112–113, 163–168.

55 Lansdale, Midst of Wars, 224–227; Currey, Edward Lansdale, 158–159; Ahern, CIA and the House of Ngo, 39–40; and Hansen, "Bắc Di Cư."

56 Picard, "Fragmented Loyalties," 5–7.

57 Hansen, "Virgin Heads South: Northern Catholic Refugees in South Vietnam," 104.

58 Hansen, "Bắc Di Cư," 180, table 1.

59 For Cao Đài and Bình Xuyên contributions to the resettlement, see Văn Liêm, "Cô nhi viện Mặt Trận Quốc Gia Cứu Quốc," Tin diễn 36 (November 6–7, 1954): 3; VTX, "Hằng ngàn dân tị nạn đã kham khổ thế nào trước và sau trận đánh?" TC 1245 (May 27, 1955): 1, 4; joint weeka 46, November 14, 1954, NARA-RG59-CDF 1950–1954, 751G.00W/11-1454; enclosure 1, despatch 440, Saigon to Department of State, June 4, 1955, NARA-RG59-CDF 1955–1959, 751G.5/6-455; and Nhị Lang, Phong trào kháng chiến, 222–223.

60 P. Nguyen, "Les résidus de la guerre," 183–184, 214; and Scigliano, South Vietnam, 53–54.

61 Telegram 580, Saigon to Secretary of State, August 14, 1954, NARA-RG59-CDF 1950–1954, 751G.00/8-1454; and telegram 790, Saigon to Secretary of State, August 28, 1954, 751G.00/8-2854.

62 Chiến Đấu, "Hãy phát động cách mạng dân tộc!" Chiến đấu 262 (September 10, 1954): front cover.

63 "Tuyên bố của đức Hộ Pháp trước khi lên đường," Thần chung 1659 (August 31, 1954): 1, 4, especially 4.

64 Telegram 370, Saigon to Secretary of State, July 29, 1954, NARA-RG59-CDF 1950–1954, 751G.00/7-2954; and telegram 580, Saigon to Secretary of State, August 14, 1954, 751G.00/8-1454.

65 Telegram 4538, Paris to Secretary of State, May 26, 1954, NARA-RG59-CDF 1950–1954, 751G.00/5-2654.

66 Telegram 872, Saigon to Secretary of State, September 2, 1954, NARA-RG59-CDF 1950–1954, 751G.00/9-254.

67 For the composition of the group, see telegram 515, Saigon to Secretary of State, August 10, 1954, NARA-RG59-CDF 1950–1954, 751G.00/8-1054; Chapman, Cauldron of Resistance, 77 n75; and P. Nguyen, "Les résidus de la guerre," 274. For the negotiations, see telegram 517, Saigon to Secretary of State, August 10, 1954, 751G.00/8-1054; telegram 580, Saigon to Secretary of State, August 14, 1954, 751G.00/8-1454; telegram 601, Saigon to Secretary of State, August 16, 1954, 751G.00/8-1654; despatch 78, Saigon to Department of State, August 21, 1954, 751G.00/8-2154; and telegram 790, Saigon to Secretary of State, August 28, 1954, 751G.00/8-2854.

68 For the conspirator's plans, see telegram 794, Saigon to Secretary of State, August 29, 1954, NARA-RG59-CDF 1950–1954, 751G.00/8-2954; telegram 807, Saigon to Secretary of State, August 30, 1954, 751G.00/8-3054; and telegram 752, Saigon to Secretary of State, August 26, 1954, 751G.00/8-2654. The plotters never mentioned Lê Hữu Từ but did claim Catholic support, possibly in reference to southern Catholics under Jean Leroy. See the last document listed for claims of Catholic support.

69 Miller, Misalliance, 102.

70 Telegram 751, Saigon to Secretary of State, August 26, 1954, NARA-RG59-CDF 1950–1954, 751G.00/8-2654.

71 Telegram 796, Saigon to Secretary of State, August 29, 1954, NARA-RG59-CDF 1950–1954, 751G.00/8-2954.

Notes to Pages 59–61   185

72 Telegram 791, Saigon to Secretary of State, August 28, 1954, NARA-RG59-CDF 1950–1954, 751G.00/8-2854; and telegram 842, Saigon to Secretary of State, August 31, 1954, 751G.00/8-3154.

73 My understanding of Diệm's strategy for dealing with General Hinh and the sects relies on Miller, *Misalliance*, 100–118. For Hinh's plot with his officers, see telegram 933, Saigon to Secretary of State, September 9, 1954, NARA-RG59-CDF 1950–1954, 751G.00/9-954; Đỗ Mậu, *Việt Nam*, 120–122; and Trần Văn Đôn, *Việt Nam*, 117.

74 Telegram 923, Saigon to Secretary of State, September 8, 1954, NARA-RG59-CDF 1950–1954, 751G.00/9-854; and telegram 976, Saigon to Secretary of State, September 12, 1954, 751G.00/9-1254.

75 Telegram 933, Saigon to Secretary of State, September 9, 1954, NARA-RG59-CDF 1950–1954, 751G.00/9-954; and telegram 953, Saigon to Secretary of State, September 10, 1954, 751G.5/9-1054.

76 Telegram 971, Saigon to Secretary of State, September 11, 1954, NARA-RG59-CDF 1950–1954, 751G.13/9-1154; and telegram 992, Saigon to Secretary of State, September 13, 1954, 751G.13/9-1354.

77 Telegram 1043, Saigon to Secretary of State, September 16, 1954, NARA-RG59-CDF 1950–1954, 751G.13/9-1654; and telegram MC 481-45, Army Attaché Saigon to Secretary of State, September 18, 1954, 751G.13/9-1854.

78 "Hai cuộc hội họp báo chí ở thủ đô Saigon," *Chiến đấu* 264 (September 30, 1954): 6–7, 19, especially 6.

79 Telegram 118, Saigon to Secretary of State, September 19, 1954, NARA-RG59-CDF 1950–1954, 751G.00/9-1954; and telegram 1203, Saigon to Secretary of State, September 21, 1954, 751G.00/9-2154.

80 Telegram 1213, Saigon to Secretary of State, September 24, 1954, NARA-RG59-CDF 1950–1954, 751G.13/9-2454.

81 For more on Madame Nhu's family background, see Demery, *Dragon Lady*, 17–25, 33–35.

82 Demery, *Dragon Lady*, 88.

83 For an extended treatment of the demonstration, see Demery, *Dragon Lady*, 86–88. See also telegram 1150, Saigon to Secretary of State, September 21, 1954, NARA-RG59-CDF 1950–1954, 751G.13/9-2154; joint weeka 39, September 25, 1954, 751G.00W/9-2554; Cao Văn Luận, *Bên giòng lịch sử*, 246; Huỳnh Văn Lang, *Nhân chứng*, 1:365–366; and P. Nguyen, "Les résidus de la guerre," 97–99.

84 Nhu and the American CIA apparently convinced Diệm to broaden the administration, but it is unclear whether they specifically pushed him to give in to Phương and Soái's demands. See Ahern, *CIA and the House of Ngo*, 43–44.

85 Phan Thị Bình, "Thư số 19," 174; Nguyễn Lý Tưởng, "Thư số 16," 158; and Miller, *Misalliance*, 49.

86 Memorandum of conversation between Nguyễn Tôn Hoàn, Byrne, and Kattenburg, April 20, 1955, NARA-RG59-CDF 1955–1959, 751G.00/4-1055; and Phan Thị Bình, "Trà đàm với sinh viên," 233–234, 239.

87 Hoàn and his supporters later claimed that he broke with Diệm over the latter's handling of the sects, but the Diemists insisted that Hoàn left after not receiving his desired cabinet appointment. For recriminations between the former allies, see Buttinger, *Vietnam: A Dragon Embattled*, 2:868n48; and Ngô Đình Diệm to Buttinger, May 29, 1956, quoted in Buttinger, *Vietnam: The Unforgettable Tragedy*, 66–67. For a contemporary explanation of Hoàn's departure from Vietnam, see telegram 1885, Saigon to Secretary of State, November 18, 1954, NARA-RG59-CDF 1950–1954, 751G.00/11-1854.

88 VTX, "Mở rộng thêm nội các," *Tin điển* 7 (October 4, 1954): 1, 4.

89 Telegram 1286, Saigon to Secretary of State, October 1, 1954, NARA-RG59-CDF 1950–1954, 751G.00/10-154.

186   Notes to Pages 61–64

90 "Điện văn của Đức Quốc Trưởng Bảo Đại gởi cho Trung Tướng Ng. Văn Hinh và Thiếu Tướng Lê Văn Viễn," *Tin điển* 5 (October 5, 1954): 1, 4.

91 Telegram 1397, Saigon to Secretary of State, October 10, 1954, NARA-RG59-CDF 1950–1954, 751G.00/10-1054.

92 Telegram 1401, Saigon to Secretary of State, October 10, 1954, NARA-RG59-CDF 1950–1954, 751G.00/10-1054.

93 Telegram 1321, Saigon to Secretary of State, October 4, 1954, NARA-RG59-CDF 1950–1954, 751G.00/10-454; telegram 1330, Saigon to Secretary of State, October 5, 1954, 751G.00/10-554; telegram 1417, Saigon to Secretary of State, October 12, 1954, 751G.00/10-1254; telegram 1440, Saigon to Secretary of State, October 14, 1954, 751G.00/10-1054; telegram 1472, Saigon to Secretary of State, October 16, 1954, 751G.00/10-1654; and telegram 1493, Saigon to Secretary of State, October 19, 1954, 751G.00/10-1954.

94 "The Ambassador in France (Dillon) to the Department of State," October 4, 1954, *FRUS, 1952–1954*, vol. 13, *Indochina:* 2116; and telegram 1361, Saigon to Secretary of State, October 7, 1954, NARA-RG59-CDF 1950–1954, 751G.00/10-754.

95 "US Bids Vietnam Rally to Premier," *New York Times,* November 18, 1954, 3.

96 "President Eisenhower to the President of the Council of Ministers of Vietnam (Ngo Dinh Diem)," undated, *FRUS, 1952–1954*, vol. 13, *Indochina:* 2166–2167.

97 My interpretation of the mutinies is based on Miller, *Misalliance,* 106–107. However, I disagree with Miller that Ngô Đình Cẩn instigated and directed the rebellions. At least three memoirs by former participants have emphasized the role of provincial and local Diemist leaders rather than Cẩn, and Nguyễn Trần even claimed that Cẩn opposed the plan to form a resistance zone. See Đỗ Mậu, *Việt Nam,* 124–129; Nguyễn Trân, *Công và tội,* 111–122; and Huỳnh Văn Cao, *Lòng ái quốc,* 36–47.

98 Despatch 160, Saigon to Department of State, November 8, 1954, NARA-RG59-CDF 1950–1954, 751G.00/11-854.

99 Regional Delegate for Central Vietnam, monthly report for November and December 1954, January 1955, TTLTQGII-PThTVNCH 13; Nguyễn Trân, *Công và tội,* 118; and telegram 1965, Saigon to Secretary of State, NARA-RG59-CDF 1950–1954, November 24, 1954, 751G.00/11-2454.

100 Telegram 1642, Saigon to Secretary of State, October 29, 1954, NARA-RG59-CDF 1950–1954, 751G.02/10-2954; telegram 1908, Paris to Secretary of State, November 4, 1954, 751G.00/11-454; and telegram 1809, Saigon to Secretary of State, November 12, 1954, 751G.00/11-1254.

101 "'En tout état de cause je rejoindrai Saigon,' affirme le général Hinh," *Le monde,* November 24, 1954, 16; and telegram 2193, Paris to Secretary of State, November 23, 1954, NARA-RG59-CDF 1950–1954, 751G.00/11-2354.

102 Telegram 2290, Paris to Secretary of State, December 1, 1954, NARA-RG59-CDF 1950–1954, 751G.00/12-154.

103 Miller, *Misalliance,* 103.

104 Joint weeka 48, November 28, 1954, NARA-RG59-CDF 1950–1954, 751G.00W/11-2854; and telegram 3264, Saigon to Secretary of State, February 8, 1955, NARA-RG59-CDF 1955–1959, 752G.00/2-855.

105 Ngô Đình Diệm, "Tuyên bố trong dịp cải tổ nội các lần thứ nhất (24-9-1954)," in *CĐCN,* 1:22–24.

106 "Programme minimum proposé par la délégation Hoa Hao, Cao Dai," October 24, 1954, TTLTQGII-TĐBCHNP 1564.

107 Decree 974-QP, October 9, 1954; and decree 1026-QP, November 3, 1954, both in TTLTQ-GII-PThTVNCH 14685.

108 Anderson, *Trapped by Success,* 95–97.

109 Miller, *Misalliance,* 110.

110 "The Chargé in Vietnam (Kidder) to the Department of State," December 15, 1954, *FRUS, 1952–1954*, vol. 13, *Indochina:* 2376.

Notes to Pages 64–66   187

111 Đoàn Thêm, *Hai mươi năm qua,* 160.

112 Correspondence 1974-VP/QP/M/BB, Minister of National Defense Hồ Thông Minh to Premier, December 29, 1954; and correspondence 154/VP/QP/M/BB, Minister of National Defense Hồ Thông Minh to Premier, January 17, 1955, both in TTLTQGII-PThTVNCH 14685.

113 [Name redacted] to Ambassador, memorandum on "Vietnamese Government Confidential Funds," January 20, 1955, USDDO, CK2349538206.

114 General Nguyễn Thành Phương to Premier and Minister of National Defense, December 18, 1954, TTLTQGII-PThTVNCH 14685.

115 Diệm agreed to reduce the national army to one hundred thousand by the end of 1955. See telegram 2876, Saigon to Secretary of State, January 21, 1954, NARA-RG59-CDF 1955–1959, 751G.5MSP/1-2155.

116 Correspondence 1974-VP/QP/M/BB, Minister of National Defense Hồ Thông Minh to Premier, December 29, 1954.

117 The three thousand spots allocated to the Cao Đài would have constituted 3 percent of the reduced national army, but General Phương's demand for 10 percent would have equated to ten thousand troops. See telegram 3462, Saigon to Secretary of State, February 18, 1955, NARA-RG59-CDF 1955–1959, 751G.5/2-1855.

118 Correspondent no. 4124/CHT, General Nguyễn Giác Ngộ to Premier, December 30, 1954, TTLTQGII-PThTVNCH 14685.

119 Telegram 3381, Saigon to Secretary of State, February 14, 1955, NARA-RG59-CDF 1955–1959, 752G.00/2-1455.

120 Decree 1197-QP, December 31, 1954; and decree 1199-QP, December 31, 1954, both in TTLTQGII-PThTVNCH 14658.

121 Ahern, *CIA and the House of Ngo,* 67; and Miller, *Misalliance,* 112.

122 Telegram 2807, Saigon to Secretary of State, January 17, 1955, NARA-RG59-CDF 1955–1959, 751G.00/1-1755.

123 "Tướng Nguyễn Giác Ngộ tuyên bố hoàn toàn ủng hộ chánh phủ Ngô Đình Diệm," *TC* 1171 (February 24, 1955): 1, 4; and joint weeka 8, February 27, 1955, NARA-RG59-CDF 1950–1954, 751G.00W/2-2754.

124 The government had outlawed Lê Quang Vinh's branch of the Social Democratic Party earlier when he withdrew into the maquis, but the Ministry of the Interior recognized the wing of the party that was affiliated with Nguyễn Giác Ngộ in February 1955. See Vương Kim, *Đức Huỳnh Giáo Chủ,* chap. 16.

125 Ngô Đình Diệm, "Hiệu triệu nhân dân Tây Ninh (31-1-1955)," in *CĐCN,* 1:94–96.

126 Nhị Lang, *Phong trào kháng chiến,* 215.

127 Despatch 588, Saigon to Department of State, June 21, 1954, NARA-RG59-CDF 1950–1954, 751G.00/6-2154; despatch 32, Saigon to Department of State, July 22, 1954, 751G.00/7-2254; Ahern, *CIA and the House of Ngo,* 41–43, 67; and Miller, *Misalliance,* 113–114.

128 Ngô Đình Diệm, "Diễn từ đọc tại Tòa Thánh Tây Ninh (31-1-1955)," in *CĐCN,* 1:96–97, especially 97.

129 Ngô Đình Diệm, "Diễn từ đọc tại Tòa Thánh Tây Ninh," 97.

130 "Diễn văn của Thiếu Tướng Trình Minh Thế đọc trong buổi lễ tiếp nhận sự hợp tác củ Mặt Trận Quốc Gia Kháng Chiến Việt Nam với chánh phủ Ngô Đình Diệm, cử hành tại Saigon hôm 13 tháng 2 năm 1955," February 18, 1956, TTLTQGII-ĐICH 4334. This copy of the speech was not from the actual event but a verbatim rereading of the speech during the anniversary of the rally a year later.

131 "Việt Nam Phục Quốc Hội nhóm Đại hội toàn quốc," 4.

132 Nutt, *Regroupment,* 22–37. I thank Alec Holcombe for suggesting this source.

133 Despatch 260, Saigon to Department of State, February 16, 1955, NARA-RG59-CDF 1955–1959, 751G.5/2-1655; and Corley, "Viet-Nam Since Geneva," 540.

188 Notes to Pages 66–69

134 Telegram 2406, Saigon to Secretary of State, December 22, 1954, NARA-RG59-CDF 1950–1954, 751G.00/12-2254.

135 Telegram 3296, Saigon to Secretary of State, February 9, 1955, NARA-RG59-CDF 1955–1959, 752G.00/2-955.

136 Telegram 2777, Saigon to Secretary of State, January 15, 1955, NARA-RG59-CDF 1955–1959, 751G.00/1-1555; and Nguyễn Long Thành Nam, *Phật Giáo Hòa Hảo,* 534.

137 Telegram 3296, Saigon to Secretary of State, February 9, 1955, NARA-RG59-CDF 1955–1959, 752G.00/2-955; telegram 3319, Saigon to Secretary of State, February 10, 1955, 752G.00/2-1055; telegram 3381, Saigon to Secretary of State, February 14, 1955, 752G.00/2-1455; and telegram 3470, Saigon to Secretary of State, February 18, 1955, 751G.00/2-1855.

138 Telegram 3363, Saigon to Secretary of State, February 12, 1955, NARA-RG59-CDF 1955–1959, 752G.00/2-1255.

139 Telegram 3319, Saigon to Secretary of State, February 10, 1955, NARA-RG59-CDF 1955–1959, 752G.00/2-1055.

140 For the cooperation between the Đại Việt party, the VNP, and the Diemists, see Ngô Đình Diệm to Buttinger, May 29, 1956, quoted in Buttinger, *Vietnam: The Unforgettable Tragedy,* 67; Lê Nguyên Long, "Bất đắc dĩ"; Hà Thúc Ký, *Sống còn,* 163–164, 178–179; and Nguyễn Văn Minh, *Dòng họ Ngô Đình,* 53. For a French assessment of the political composition of the regional and provincial administrations, see despatch 160, Saigon to Department of State, November 8, 1954, NARA-RG59-CDF 1950–1954, 751G.00/11-854.

141 Despatch 160, Saigon to Department of State, November 8, 1954, NARA-RG59-CDF 1950–1954, 751G.00/11-854; Hà Thúc Ký, *Sống còn,* 180–181, 190–194; and Trần Văn Giàu, *Miền Nam,* 1:74.

142 Directorate of Police and Security Service for Central Vietnam, "Vấn đề Pháp trong vụ phiến loạn Ba Lòng, Quảng Trị," 1955; Directorate of Police and Security Service for Central Vietnam, "Tổng kết vụ Ba Lòng (Quảng Trị)," 1955, both in TTLTQGII-PThTVNCH 14702; joint weeka 9, Saigon to Secretary of State, March 5, 1955, NARA-RG59-CDF 1955–1959, 751G.00W/3-555; telegram 3987, Saigon to Secretary of State, March 19, 1955, 751G.00/3-1955; Lê Văn Dương, *Quân Lực,* 404; and Hà Thúc Ký, *Sống còn,* 198–199, 206–208.

143 Hà Thúc Ký, *Sống còn,* 209; and Phạm Văn Liễu, *Trả ta sông núi,* 1:332–333.

144 "Vụ án chánh trị lớn tại Tòa Án Quân Sự Nha Trang," *TD* 531 (October 9, 1958): 1, 4; correspondence 00366/DPG/NT/N, Mai Hữu Xuân, General Director of Army Security, to Assistant Minister of National Defense, January 10, 1956, TTLTQGII-ĐICH 4349; Trường Giang, "Phú Yên," 49; and Quang Minh, *Cách mạng Việt Nam,* 228–230.

145 Trần Văn Giàu, *Miền Nam,* 1:75; and despatch 11, Saigon to Department of State, July 8, 1955, NARA-RG59-CDF 1955–1959, 751G.00/7-855.

146 Lê Nguyên Long, "Bất đắc dĩ."

147 Despatch 351, Saigon to Department of State, April 27, 1955, NARA-RG59-CDF 1955–1959, 751G.00/4-2755; despatch 11, Saigon to Department of State, July 8, 1955, 751G.00/7-855; and Nguyễn Liệu, *Đời tôi,* 178–190.

148 At the time, Phạm Đình Nghị, province chief of Quảng Ngãi, claimed that he actively suppressed the party, but other accounts suggest that the Diemists sacked him as part of the crackdown. See Phạm Đình Nghị, Province Chief of Quảng Ngãi province, to Premier, August 2, 1955, TTLTQGII-PThTVNCH 29226; and Lê Nguyên Long, "Bất đắc dĩ."

149 Open letter from the Vietnamese Nationalist Party to Ngô Đình Diệm, May 9, 1955, TTLTQGII-PThTVNCH 30387.

150 Office of the Regional Delegate for Central Vietnam, monthly report for May 1955, June 30, 1955; summary of the monthly report of the Office of the Regional Delegate for Central Vietnam for June and July, 1955, undated, both in TTLTQGII-PThTVNCH 15; "Thành tích tổng quát đệ nhị chu niên của chánh phủ Cộng Hòa Việt Nam," Nghiên cứu và tài liệu column, *VTX* 1976 (July 29, 1956, full day edition): X-XVI, TTLTQGII-ĐICH 13; Trần Văn Giàu, *Miền Nam,* 1:75–76; and Guillemot, *Dai Việt,* 574.

Notes to Pages 69–73   189

151 "Vụ án chánh trị lớn tại Tòa Án Quân Sự Nha Trang," 1, 4; and correspondence 00366/DPG/ NT/N, Mai Hữu Xuân, General Director of Army Security, to Assistant Minister of National Defense, January 10, 1956, TTLTQGII-ĐICH 4349.

152 Phạm Đình Nghị, Province Chief of Quảng Ngãi province, to Premier, August 2, 1955.

153 Open letter from the Vietnamese Nationalist Party to Ngô Đình Diệm, May 9, 1955.

154 Telegram 3462, Saigon to Secretary of State, February 18, 1955, NARA-RG59-CDF 1955–1959, 751G.5/2-1855.

155 Enclosure 1, despatch 272, Saigon to Department of State, March 1, 1955, NARA-RG59-CDF 1955–1959, 751G.00/3-155. See also telegram 3470, Saigon to Secretary of State, February 18, 1955, 751G.00/2-1855.

156 Telegram 2562, Saigon to Secretary of State, January 4, 1955, 7 NARA-RG59-CDF 1955–1959, 751G.00/1-455; "Thiếu Tướng Lê Văn Viễn đề nghị đóng cửa nhà giải trí Đại Thế Giới," TC 1139 (January 10, 1955): 1, 4.

157 Miller, Misalliance, 114.

158 I have not been able to locate a full text of the Vietnamese original. Translation from telegram 3754, Saigon to Secretary of State, March 8, 1955, NARA-RG59-CDF 1955–1959, 751G.00/3-855.

159 "Cuộc điều đình giữa chánh phủ và các giáo phái đã chấm dứt hẳn chưa?" Đuốc Việt 17 (March 29, 1955): 1, 4, especially 1.

160 Telegram 3754, Saigon to Secretary of State, March 8, 1955, NARA-RG59-CDF 1955–1959, 751G.00/3-855.

161 Telegram 3770, Saigon to Secretary of State, March 8, 1954, NARA-RG59-CDF 1955–1959, 751G.00/3-855.

162 Buttinger stated that Phan Quang Đán joined the United Front, but I have no evidence to support that assertion. Also note that some intellectuals later denied that they were part of the group. For the composition of the front, see Buttinger, Vietnam: A Dragon Embattled, 2:868–869; and Nguyễn Long Thành Nam, Phật Giáo Hòa Hảo, 561. For a later denial, see Hồ Hữu Tường, "Le défi vietnamien," 301.

163 VTX, "Dư luận về bản tuyên ngôn của Mặt Trận Thống Nhứt Toàn Lực Quốc Gia: Lập trường của Thiếu Tướng Nguyễn Giác Ngộ," TC 1180 (March 7, 1955): 1; and telegram 3770, Saigon to Secretary of State, March 8, 1954, NARA-RG59-CDF 1955–1959, 751G.00/3-855.

164 "Thủ Tướng Phủ đính chánh các tin tức sai lầm về tình hình nội bộ Việt Nam," TC 1192 (21 March 1955): 1, 4.

165 "Lời tuyên bố của Chủ Tịch Đoàn Mặt Trận Thống Nhứt Toàn Lực Quốc Gia," March 21, 1955, TTLTQGII-PThTVNCH 29236.

166 Ngô Đình Diệm, "Bức thư gởi đại diện 'Mặt Trận Thống Nhất Toàn Lực Quốc Gia' (27–3–1955)," in CĐCN, 1:106–107.

167 In actuality, the Cao Đài ministers resigned a little later at the behest of Nguyễn Thành Phương rather than Phạm Công Tắc. See telegram 4231, Saigon to Secretary of State, March 30, 1955, NARA-RG59-CDF 1955–1959, 751G.00/3-3055; and Lê Văn Dương, Quân Lực, 414–416.

168 VTX, "Thiếu Tướng Trịnh Minh Thế giải thích về lập trường của ông," Đuốc Việt 17 (March 29, 1955): 1, 4.

169 Trình Minh Thế to Ngô Đình Diệm, March 9, 1955, TTLTQGII-ĐICH 21534.

170 For the negotiations and possible funds involved, see Ahern, CIA and the House of Ngo, 69–70. For the recognition of the party by the Ministry of the Interior, see decree 14-BNV/CT from Minister of the Interior, March 31, 1955, TTLTQGII-ĐICH 5972.

171 Telegram 4194, Saigon to Secretary of State, March 30, 1955, NARA-RG59-CDF 1955–1959, 751G.00/3-3055.

172 Telegram 4213, Saigon to Secretary of State, March 30, 1955, NARA-RG59-CDF 1955–1959, 751G.00/3-3055; and telegram MC952–55 300403Z, Army Attaché Saigon to Secretary of State, March 30, 1955, 751G.00/3-3055.

190 Notes to Pages 73–75

173 Telegram 4264, Saigon to Secretary of State, March 3, 11955, NARA-RG59-CDF 1955–1959, 751G.00/3-3155.

174 Some dispute the number of Cao Đài soldiers that Diệm agreed to integrate, though the most frequently mentioned figure is eight thousand. See telegram 4194, Saigon to Secretary of State, March 30, 1955, NARA-RG59-CDF 1955–1959, 751G.00/3-3055; telegram 4230, Saigon to Secretary of State, March 30, 1955, 751G.00/3-3055; and telegram 4250, Saigon to Secretary of State, March 30, 1955, 751G.00/3-3055.

175 Phạm Xuân Thái indicated to American embassy officials that the size of the subsidy was also a point of negotiation. See telegram 4231, Saigon to Secretary of State, March 30, 1955, NARA-RG59-CDF 1955–1959, 751G.00/3-3055; and Ahern, *CIA and the House of Ngo,* 69–70.

176 Memorandum of conversation between Ngô Đình Nhu, Trần Chánh Thành, Gatewood, Blaufarb, and McKesson, June 5, 1956, NARA-RG84-CGR, box 42, 350 Vietnam, 1956–1958.

177 Nguyễn Long Thành Nam, *Phật Giáo Hòa Hảo,* 567.

178 Telegram 3654, Paris to Secretary of State, NARA-RG59-CDF 1955–1959, 751G.00/3-155.

179 Telegram 4372, Saigon to Secretary of State, April 6, 1955, NARA-RG59-CDF 1955–1959, 751G.00/4-655.

180 Telegram 4666, Saigon to Secretary of State, April 20, 1955, NARA-RG59-CDF 1955–1959, 751G.00/4-2055.

181 Telegram 4396, Paris to Secretary of State, April 9, 1955, NARA-RG59-CDF 1955–1959, 751G.00/4-955; telegram 4576, Saigon to Secretary of State, April 21, 1955, 751G.00/4-2155; and memorandum of conversation between Nguyễn Đệ, Gibson, and Bane, April 21, 1955, 751G.00/4-2155.

182 Telegram 4643, Saigon to Secretary of State, April 25, 1955, NARA-RG59-CDF 1955–1959, 751G.00/4-2555.

183 Telegram 4263, Saigon to Secretary of State, March 31, 1955, NARA-RG59-CDF 1955–1959, 751G.00/3-3155.

184 "Telegram from the Secretary of State to Embassy in France," April 27, 1955, *FRUS, 1955–1957,* vol. 1, *Vietnam:* 297–298; Young to Robertson, April 30, 1955, NARA-RG59-CDF 1955–1959, 751G.00/4-3055; and Anderson, *Trapped by Success,* 108–110.

185 Telegram 4745, Saigon to Secretary of State, April 30, 1955, NARA-RG59-CDF 1955–1959, 751G.00/4-3055.

186 VTX, "Đại tá Nguyễn Ngọc Lễ được bổ nhiệm thay ông Lại Văn Sang giữ chức Tổng Giám Đốc Cảnh Sát và Công An Quốc Gia Việt Nam," *Thời đại* 8 (April 28, 1955): 1, 4.

187 For an example of a young officer determined to fight the Bình Xuyên, see Trần Văn Đôn, *Việt Nam,* 123. For the success of the national army in pushing the gang out of the capital, see joint weeka 18, May 8, 1955, NARA-RG59-CDF 1955–1959, 751G.00W/4-855.

188 "Lực lượng Bình Xuyên đã rút về Rừng Sát," *TC* 1228 (May 7, 1955): 1, 4.

189 Trần Ngọc Sơn, "Xung đột và hỏa hoạn thảm khóc chưa từng có!" *TC* 1223 (April 30, 1955): 1, 4; and "Tin thêm về vụ xung đột hôm chiều 28 tháng 4–1955," *Thời đại* 11 (May 3, 1955): 1, 4.

190 For various estimates of the dead, wounded, and displaced, see joint weeka 18, May 8, 1955, NARA-RG59-CDF 1955–1959, 751G.00W/4-855; and Lancaster, *Emancipation,* 389n43.

191 McCoy, Read, and Adams, *Politics of Heroin,* 119.

192 Joint weeka 18, May 8, 1955, NARA-RG59-CDF 1955–1959, 751G.00W/4-855.

193 Chapman, *Cauldron of Resistance,* 112.

194 Telegram 4831 from Secretary of State to Saigon, May 1, 1955, NARA-RG59-CDF 1955–1959, 751G.00/5-155.

195 Telegram 4263, Saigon to Secretary of State, March 31, 1955, NARA-RG59-CDF 1955–1959, 751G.00/3-3155.

196 Fall, *Two Viet-Nams,* 245–246; Buttinger, *Vietnam: A Dragon Embattled,* 2: 867–872; Spector, *Advice and Support,* 243–245; and Young, *Vietnam Wars,* 48.

Notes to Pages 76–80   191

Chapter Three: Debate on Democracy, 1955–1956

1 The description of the meeting relies on Nhị Lang, *Phong trào kháng chiến,* 282–283, 287–291; and Hoàng Cơ Thụy, *Việt sử khảo luận,* 5:2723–2727.

2 Telegram 4917, Saigon to Secretary of State, April 29, 1955, NARA-RG59-CDF 1955–1959, 751G.00/4-2955; telegram 4928, Saigon to Secretary of State, April 29, 1955, 751G.00/4-2955; and telegram 4743, Paris to Secretary of State, April 30, 1955, 751G.00/4-3055.

3 Telegram 4776, Saigon to Secretary of State, April 24, 1955, NARA-RG59-CDF 1955–1959, 751G.00/4-2455. For a list of the invited groups, see enclosure 1, despatch 381, Saigon to Department of State, May 16, 1955, 751G.00/5-1655.

4 Nhị Lang, *Phong trào kháng chiến,* 298–299; and Scigliano, *South Vietnam,* 23n35.

5 Buttinger, *Vietnam: A Dragon Embattled,* 2:865–889; Herring, *America's Longest War,* 63–68; Young, *Vietnam Wars,* 47–49; and Prados, *Vietnam,* 42–54.

6 Chapman, *Cauldron of Resistance,* 116–195; and Miller, *Misalliance,* 124–148.

7 "Ba bản quyết nghị lịch sử của Hội đồng Nhân dân Cách mạng," *QC* 21 (May 3, 1955): 1, 4.

8 Telegram MC 974-55, DTG 280918Z, Army Attaché Saigon to Secretary of State, April 28, 1955, NARA-RG59-CDF 1955–1959, 751G.00/4-2855.

9 "Ba bản quyết nghị," 4.

10 I shorten the name of the alliance from the People's Revolutionary Council to the Revolutionary Council (RC) to avoid the confusion with the common abbreviation for the People's Republic of China (PRC).

11 Although multiple attendees later claimed to be the first person to propose the overthrow of Bảo Đại at the conference, Nhị Lang's version is the most credible. He recounted that he and Hồ Hán Sơn initiated the effort and that Nguyễn Bảo Toàn immediately supported it. The motions closely resembled the political demands of the Cao Đài parties and could not have passed without the endorsement of the sectarian bloc. For the different claims, see telegram 5183, Saigon to Secretary of State, May 10, 1955, NARA-RG59-CDF 1955–1959, 751G.00/5-1055; *Quốc Hội Lập Hiến,* 21; Nhị Lang, *Phong trào kháng chiến,* 282–291; and Hoàng Cơ Thụy, *Việt sử khảo luận,* 5:2723–2724. For the composition of the permanent committee of the RC, see despatch 381, Saigon to Department of State, May 16, 1955, 751G.00/5-1655.

12 "South Vietnam," May 4, 1955, CREST, CIA-RDP79R00890A000500050019-7.

13 Như Thúy, "Để hiểu thực trạng Miền Tây," part XVIII, *QC* 67 (June 25–26, 1955): 1, 4, especially 1; Nguyễn Long Thành Nam, *Phật Giáo Hòa Hảo,* 392–394, 411, 417, 581; and Vương Kim, *Đức Huỳnh Giáo Chủ,* chap. 16.

14 Nhị Lang, *Phong trào kháng chiến,* 61–64; Nguyễn Tường Thiết, "Chuyến tàu trong đêm," 318–319; and "Tiểu sử chí sĩ Nhị Lang (1923–2005)."

15 Telegram 5119, Saigon to Secretary of State, May 7, 1955, NARA-RG59-CDF 1955–1959, 751G.00/5-755; Cao Văn Luận, *Bên giòng lịch sử,* 158; and Nhị Lang, *Phong trào kháng chiến,* 283–284.

16 Đỗ Mậu, *Việt Nam,* 148–150.

17 Huỳnh Văn Lang, *Nhân chứng,* 1:444.

18 For the founding, composition, and politics of the minor, pro-Diệm parties, see despatch 246, Saigon to Department of State, February 6, 1956, NARA-RG59-CDF 1955–1959, 751G.00/2-656; Hoàng Cơ Thụy, *Việt sử khảo luận,* 5:2719; Trương Vĩnh Lễ, *Vietnam,* 21; and Scigliano, *South Vietnam,* 79.

19 For the attempted coup, see telegram 4984, Saigon to Secretary of State, May 1, 1955, NARA-RG59-CDF 1955–1959, 751G.00/5-155; telegram 5019, Saigon to Secretary of State, May 3, 1955, 751G.00/5-355; Simpson, *Tiger,* 148–149; Nhị Lang, *Phong trào kháng chiến,* 304–316; and Trần Văn Đôn, *Việt Nam,* 124–131.

20 The mysterious circumstances surrounding General Thế's death sparked speculation that the French, the Bình Xuyên, or Ngô Đình Diệm had ordered Thế's assassination. For a survey of the

192 Notes to Pages 81–84

various theories, see Nhị Lang, *Phong trào kháng chiến,* 334–339; and Blagov, *Honest Mistakes,* 173–194.

21 "Tiểu sử ông Trần Chánh Thành," *CMQG* 189 (February 28, 1956): 1, 4; and Lansdale, *Midst of War,* 340.

22 "Ông Nguyễn Hữu Châu ứng cử viên tại quận I đô thành," *CMQG* 190 (February 29, 1956): 1, 4; and enclosure 1, despatch 323, Saigon to Department of State, April 30, 1957, NARA-RG59-CDF 1955–1959, 751G.521/4-3057.

23 Despatch 246, Saigon to Department of State, February 6, 1956, NARA-RG59-CDF 1955–1959, 751G.00/2-656.

24 Quốc Gia, "Quốc hội dân cử," Dưới mắt chúng tôi column, *QG* 67 (August 22, 1955): 1, 4, especially 1.

25 Quốc Gia, "Hảy [*sic*] tiến gấp tới quốc hội dân cử," Dưới mắt chúng tôi column, *QG* 5 (June 10, 1955): 1; and Quốc Gia, "Nên bầu cử quốc hội theo cách nào?" Dưới mắt chúng tôi column, *QG* 8 (June 14, 1955): 1.

26 Quần Chúng, "Để tiến đến quốc hội dân cử," Ý kiến quần chúng column, *QC* 99 (August 2, 1955): 1, 4.

27 Quần Chúng, "Cần phải có mặt của nhân dân!" Ý kiến quần chúng column, *QC* 100 (August 3, 1955): 1, 4, especially 1.

28 Telegram 66, Saigon to Secretary of State, July 6, 1955, NARA-RG59-CDF 1955–1959, 751G.00/7-655.

29 "Đảng Cộng hòa Việt Nam trước tình thế hiện tại," July 20, 1955, TTLTQGII-HĐQNCM 130.

30 Joint weeka 28, July 17, 1955, NARA-RG59-CDF 1955–1959, 751G.00W/7-1755; "Ông Nhị Lang Tổng Thư Ký Hội Đồng NDCM Quốc Gia Việt Nam đã bị công an bắt," *QG* 53 (August 5, 1955): 1, 4; "Ông Tổng Thư Ký Hội Đồng Nhân Dân Cách Mạng đã bị công an bắt giữ," *QG* 54 (August 6, 1955): 1, 4; "Ông Tổng Thơ Ký HĐNDCM bị bắt trong trường hợp nào?" *QG* 55 (August 8, 1955): 1, 4; and Nhị Lang, *Phong trào kháng chiến,* 304, 343–347.

31 Enclosure 2, despatch 13, Saigon to Department of State, July 13, 1955, NARA-RG59-CDF 1955–1959, 751G.00/7-1355; and Quần Chúng, "Quốc hội lâm thời là một vấn đề khẩn yếu," Ý kiến quần chúng column, *QC* 106 (August 10, 1955): 1, 4.

32 Miller, *Misalliance,* 137–140.

33 Mounier, *Personalist Manifesto,* 247–249; and Deweer, "Political Theory of Personalism," 116–117.

34 Ngô Đình Diệm, "Bản tuyên cáo của Quốc Trưởng Việt Nam thành lập chế độ cộng hòa (26–10–55)," in *CĐCN,* 2:16–18, especially 17.

35 Despatch 44, Saigon to Department of State, August 8, 1956, NARA-RG59-CDF 1955–1959, 751G.00/8-856.

36 I believe that Ngô Đình Nhu, Trần Chánh Thành, and Nguyễn Hữu Châu were the authors of the position paper because they were the most powerful men in the Diemist inner circle. The arguments in the paper also resembled the conversations that Nhu and Thành had with American embassy officers and the claims that Thành later made in the constituent assembly. For conversations with embassy officers, see telegram 244, Saigon to Secretary of State, July 16, 1955, NARA-RG59-CDF 1955–1959, 751G.00/7-1655; and telegram 494, Saigon to Secretary of State, July 29, 1955, 751G.00/7-2955.

37 "Vấn đề chính thể, hiến pháp, quốc hội," undated, TTLTQGII-PThTVNCH 3908.

38 "Vấn đề chính thể, hiến pháp, quốc hội."

39 Lansdale, *Midst of War,* 328–330.

40 "Vấn đề chính thể, hiến pháp, quốc hội."

41 Lansdale later claimed that he suggested the idea of the plebiscite to Diệm in late September 1955, but contemporary documents clearly indicate Diệm and his advisers had discussed and approved the idea much earlier. For Lansdale's account, see Lansdale, *Midst of Wars,* 331–333. For discussion by cabinet ministers and members of Diệm's circle, see telegram 6041, Saigon to

Secretary of State, June 29, 1955, NARA-RG59-CDF 1955–1959, 751G.00/6-2955; telegram 244, Saigon to Secretary of State, July 16, 1955, 751G.00/7-1655; telegram 494, Saigon to Secretary of State, July 29, 1955, 751G.00/7-2955; and despatch 57, from Saigon to Department of State, August 26, 1955, 751G.13/8-2655.

42 Trần Thành Chí, "Cần phải xác định lại thái độ kiểm duyệt với văn nghệ và báo chí phản [sic] bội," Việt chính 8 (May 27, 1955): 1, 4.

43 Enclosure 2, despatch 13, Saigon to Department of State, July 13, 1955, NARA-RG59-CDF 1955–1959, 751G.00/7-1355.

44 "Vấn đề chính thể, hiến pháp, quốc hội."

45 Ngô Đình Diệm, "Hiệu triệu quốc dân ngày lễ tuyên bố ban hành hiến pháp (26-10-1956)," in CĐCN, 3:11–14, especially 13. See also Miller, Misalliance, 139.

46 Despatch 246, Saigon to Department of State, February 6, 1956, NARA-RG59-CDF 1955–1959, 751G.00/2-656.

47 For the origins of the civil servants' league, see "Quyết nghị của Đại Hội Công Tư Chức Cứu Trợ Đồng Bào Tản Cư," Thần chung 1645 (August 14–15, 1954): 1, 4; "Tìm hiểu 'Liên Đoàn Công Chức Cách Mạng Quốc Gia,'" Nghiên cứu column, VTX 2633 (May 19, 1958, afternoon edition): C-I, TTLTQGII-ĐICH 16799; Đoàn Thêm, Hai mươi năm qua, 154; and Joiner, Politics of Massacre, 39–41.

48 Despatch 266, Saigon to Department of State, March 2, 1960, NARA-RG84-CGR, Box 64, Folder 560.1, Trade Unionism, Trade Union Movement-Vietnam.

49 Phạm Văn Liễu, Trả ta sông núi, 1:340.

50 Donnell, "Politics in South Vietnam," 235.

51 "100 ngàn người biểu tình kéo đến Dinh Độc Lập," QC 78 (July 8, 1955): 1, 4; and telegram 73, Saigon to Secretary of State, July 7, 1955, NARA-RG59-CDF 1955–1959, 751G.00/7-755.

52 Joint weeka 27, July 9, 1955, NARA-RG59-CDF 1955–1959, 751G.00W/7-955.

53 Nguyễn Thái, Is South Vietnam, 207–208; and Ahern, CIA and the House of Ngo, 117–118.

54 Correspondence 847-/PSCT-S, General Directorate of National Police and Security Service for Southern Vietnam to Director of National Police and Security Service for Southern Vietnam and Province Chief of Cần Thơ Province, June 6, 1955, TTLTQGII-ĐICH 4320; military dispatch 24, July 15, 1955, TTLTQGII-PThTVNCH 14671; "Tường thuật trận tấn công loạn quân Ba Cụt trên miền duyên hải Rạch Giá Hà Tiên," undated, TTLTQGII-ĐICH 14671; joint weeka 28, July 17, 1955, NARA-RG59-CDF 1955–1959, 751G.00W/7-1755; and joint weeka 29, July 23, 1955, 751G.00W/7-2355.

55 Joint weeka 22, June 5, 1955, NARA-RG59-CDF 1955–1959, 751G.00W/6-555.

56 My account of Cao Đài developments draws from a long, unpaginated intelligence report: Service for Political and Social Research, "Hoạt động Cao Đài," c. 1957, TTLTQGII-ĐICH 4908. The next several notes refer to specific sections of the report.

57 "Nguyên nhân cuộc thanh trừng nội bộ," in Service for Political and Social Research, "Hoạt động Cao Đài," c. 1957, TTLTQGII-ĐICH 4908; intelligence dispatch 3574/DPG/QC/51/P, "Hoạt động Quốc gia Cao Đài Tây Ninh," October 10, 1955, TTLTQGII-ĐICH 4324; and telegram 1650, Saigon to Secretary of State, October 13, 1955, NARA-RG59-CDF 1955–1959, 751G.00/10-1355.

58 "Phản ứng trong giới Cao Đài," in Service for Political and Social Research, "Hoạt động Cao Đài," c. 1957, TTLTQGII-ĐICH 4908; and intelligence report 3800/DPG/QC/CT/P, "Hoạt động quốc gia: Cao Đài Tây Ninh," November 10, 1955, TTLTQGII-ĐICH 4324.

59 The Service for Political and Social Research described two breakaway Cao Đài bands with ties to Phạm Công Tắc in 1955. After General Nguyễn Thành Phương fell from favor, the agency retroactively linked one of the groups to Phương, but this claim is suspect. For the ties with Tắc, see intelligence dispatch 3896/DPG/QQ/CT/P, "Hoạt động quốc gia: Cao Đài Tây Ninh," November 22, 1955; intelligence dispatch 4097/DPG/QC/CT/P/102/N, "Hoạt động quốc gia: Cao Đài Tây Ninh," December 19, 1955, both in TTLTQGII-ĐICH 4324; and correspondence 114/TT/TMBB/TTP from Special Staff, Office of the President, "Tổng quát tin tức góp nhặt trong tháng 11/1955," November 25, 1955, TTLTQGII-ĐICH 4029. For later claims about ties with Phương, see "Tổ chức Cao Đài Tự

194   Notes to Pages 86–89

Do" and "Chuẩn bị đối lập," in Service for Political and Social Research, "Hoạt động Cao Đài," c. 1957, TTLTQGII-ĐICH 4908.

60 Intelligence dispatch 3475/DPG/QC/51P, "Hoạt động quốc gia: Mặt trận Quốc gia Kháng chiến," September 29, 1955; intelligence dispatch 3592/DPG/CC/51P, "Hoạt động quốc gia: Việt Nam Phục Quốc Hội," October 12, 1955; and intelligence dispatch 3690/DPG/QC/51P, "Hoạt động quốc gia: Mặt trận Quốc gia Kháng chiến," October 22, 1955, all in TTLTQGII-ĐICH 4349.

61 *Chánh nghĩa đã thắng,* 45–59; and various petitions in TTLTQGII-ĐICH 18091.

62 "Phong trào nhân dân đòi truất phế Bảo Đại," *TD* 256 (October 5, 1955): 1, 4; and despatch 146, Saigon to Department of State, November 29, 1955, NARA-RG59-CDF 1955–1959, 751G.00/11-2955.

63 "Hiệu triệu của Mặt Trận Quốc Gia Kháng Chiến Việt Nam," *QG* 114 (October 15, 1955): 2; "Hiệu triệu của Đảng Dân Chủ Xã Hội Việt Nam," *Lửa sống* 86 (October 20, 1955): 2; and intelligence dispatch 3663/DPG/QC/71/P, "Hoạt động quốc gia: Việt Nam Phục Quốc Hội," October 19, 1955, TTLTQGII-ĐICH 4349.

64 "Tài liệu học tập về cuộc trưng cầu dân ý ngày 23-10-1955," c. October 1955, TTLTQGII-ĐICH 639.

65 Official document 40/SD3DC/5 of the Third Field Division, Fourth Military Region, National Army, on the preparation for the plebiscite, October 15, 1955, TTLTQGII-ĐICH 21132.

66 For a facsimile of the ballot, see *Lửa sống* 82 (October 15, 1955): 1.

67 *Chánh nghĩa đã thắng,* 71.

68 Ahern, *CIA and the House of Ngo,* 93–94. For more on the electoral irregularities, see telegram 1846, Saigon to Secretary of State, October 25, 1955, NARA-RG59-CDF 1955–1959, 751G.00/10-2555; and despatch 146, Saigon to Department of State, November 29, 1955, 751G.00/11-2955.

69 "A Review of Election Processes in South Vietnam," March 9, 1966, CREST, CIA-RDP79T00826A000400010040-7.

70 *Chánh nghĩa đã thắng,* 71.

71 "Hiến ước tạm thời của nước Việt Nam," *TC* 1376 (October 27, 1955): 1, 4.

72 Telegram CA-3369, Department of State to Amman and other embassies, October 28, 1955, NARA-RG59-CDF 1955–1959, 751G.02/10-2855.

73 Lê Văn Dương, *Quân Lực,* 423–426.

74 Quần Chúng, "Cần phải lập ngay quốc hội," Ý kiến quần chúng column, *QC* 101 (August 4, 1955): 1, 4, especially 4.

75 Quần Chúng, "Nhiệm vụ của quốc hội lâm thời," Ý kiến quần chúng column, *QC* 102 (August 5, 1955): 1, 4, especially 4.

76 "Hiến ước tạm thời của nước Việt Nam," 4.

77 Telegram 1468, Saigon to Secretary of State, September 28, 1955, NARA-RG59-CDF 1955–1959, 751G.00/9-2855; telegram 2065, Saigon to Secretary of State, November 11, 1955, 751G.03/11-1155; telegram 2338, Saigon to Secretary of State, December 4, 1955, 751G.00W/12-455; executive order 25-TTP determining the membership of the committee tasked with writing the draft of the constitution, November 28, 1955, TTLTQGII-ĐICH 762; and Huỳnh Văn Lang, *Nhân chứng,* 2:191.

78 Telegram 3164, Saigon to Secretary of State, February 4, 1956, NARA-RG59-CDF 1955–1959, 751G.03/2-456; Ahern, *CIA and the House of Ngo,* 104. For Orendain's draft, see despatch 250, Saigon to Department of State, February 6, 1956, 751G.03/2-656.

79 I have not been able to locate the Vietnamese-language draft, and the only available copy is an undated French-language version. That copy closely resembles a description of the completed draft by the American embassy in February 1956. For the French-language draft itself, see "Draft Constitution," 160–184. For the description, see telegram 3287, Saigon to Secretary of State, February 15, 1956, NARA-RG59-CDF 1955–1959, 751G.03/2-1556.

80 Quần Chúng, "Thế Nhân dân," Ý kiến quần chúng column, *QC* 108 (August 12, 1955): 1, 4, especially 1.

81 Quần Chúng, "Quốc hội lâm thời," 1.

82 Cao Văn Luận, *Bên giòng lịch sử,* 265.

83 Cao Văn Luận, *Bên giòng lịch sử,* 260.

84 Despatch 44, Saigon to Department of State, August 8, 1956.

85 "Ông Trần Chánh Thành Chủ Tịch PTCMQG tuyên bố về Quốc Hội: 'Chỉ có các nước CS mới có chế độ độc đảng mà thôi,'" *Ngôn luận* 299 (January 24, 1956): 1, 4, especially 4.

86 Hoàng Cơ Thụy told US embassy officials that the order came from Trần Chánh Thành, but the central Vietnamese branch of the RC undoubtedly answered to Ngô Đình Cẩn. See Hoàng Vinh, "Thông cáo của Hội Đồng Nhân Dân Cách Mạng Quốc Gia Trung Việt," *CMQG* 100 (November 9, 1955): 1, 4; and telegram 2814, Saigon to Secretary of State, January 13, 1956, NARA-RG59-CDF 1955–1959, 751G.00/1-1356.

87 Joint weeka 47, November 27, 1955, NARA-RG59-CDF 1955–1959, 751G.00W/11-3055.

88 Telegram 1672, Saigon to Secretary of State, October 14, 1955, NARA-RG59-CDF 1955–1959, 751G.00/10-1455.

89 Cách Mạng Quốc Gia, "Đảng phái trong nước Việt Nam dân chủ," Xây dựng column, *CMQG* 94 (November 2, 1955): 1, 4.

90 Telegram 2338, Saigon to Secretary of State, December 4, 1955, NARA-RG59-CDF 1955–1959, 751G.00W/12-455.

91 Telegram 2529, Saigon to Secretary of State, December 17, 1955, NARA-RG59-CDF 1955–1959, 751G.00/12-1755; and despatch 44, Saigon to Department of State, August 8, 1956.

92 Phan Quang Đán first joined a small party led by Nguyễn Tường Tam in the 1940s, and the party fused with the Vietnamese Nationalist Party. It appears that Đán remained close to Tam and other members of the VNP until about 1946 or 1947, when the party declined to support Bảo Đại. For Đán's relations with the VNP just before the Hong Kong conference, see Trương Bảo Sơn, "Những kỷ niệm riêng," 70. For more on Đán's biography and career before 1954, see "Lịch trình tranh đấu của Đảng Cộng Hòa," July 20, 1955, TTLTQGII-HĐQNCM 130; Trường Thanh, "Chúng tôi phỏng vấn bác sĩ [sic] Phan Huy Đán," *Thời đại* 121 (September 8, 1955): 1, 4; Thời Luận, "Để trả lời những sự vu khống về bác sĩ Phan Quang Đán," *TL* 418 (September 29–30, 1957): 1, 4; Trần Văn Ngay, "Đảng Dân Chủ Tự Do," 192; Scigliano, *South Vietnam,* 82–83; Fontaine, *Dawn of Free Vietnam,* 4–33; and Bảo Đại, *Le Dragon d'Annam,* 201.

93 Phan Quang Đán, *Volonté vietnamienne,* 9–11, 71–73.

94 Phan Quang Đán's Republican Party often claimed Nguyễn Bảo Toàn as an early member, but Toàn never publicly described himself as such after 1954. The two men may have met in southern China during the establishment of the Nanjing front. See "Đảng Cộng Hòa Việt Nam trước tình thế hiện tại," July 20, 1955, TTLTQGII-HĐQNCM 130; Phan Quang Đán, *Volonté vietnamienne,* 2nd ed., vii; telegram 1166, Paris to Secretary of State, September 13, 1955, NARA-RG59-CDF 1955–1959, 751G.00/9-1355; and Trần Văn Ngay, "Đảng Dân Chủ Tự Do," 192.

95 Capoccia, "Militant Democracy."

96 Phan Quang Đán, *Volonté vietnamienne,* 2nd ed., ix.

97 Despatch 146, Saigon to Department of State, September 27, 1961, NARA-RG59-CDF 1960–1963, 751K.00/9-2761; Scigliano, *South Vietnam,* 80; and Honey, "Problem of Democracy," 73–74.

98 Phan Quang Đán, *Volonté vietnamienne,* 2nd ed., ix.

99 Trường Thanh, "Chúng tôi phỏng vấn," 4.

100 Lê Công, "Cuộc phỏng vấn bác sĩ Phan Quang Đán," *CMQG* 112 (November 23, 1955): 1, 4, especially 4.

101 Phan Quang Đán, "Bác sĩ [sic] Phan Qu. Đán thanh minh về thái độ đối với chánh phủ," *QG* 145 (November 21, 1955): 1, 4, especially 4.

102 Trường Thanh, "Chúng tôi phỏng vấn," 4.

103 For the formation of the group, see joint weeka 47, November 27, 1955, NARA-RG59-CDF 1955–1959, 751G.00W/11-3055. For the group's statement, see "Các chánh đảng [sic]: Cộng Hòa, Đại

196   Notes to Pages 94–96

Việt, VN Phục Quốc Hội, VN Quốc Dân Đảng [*sic*] và Xã Hội hiệu triệu đồng bào," *Thời đại* 208 (December 19, 1955): 1, 4.

104 For the similarity to Phan Quang Đán's previous writings, compare the statement of December 18, 1955, with Đán's letter to Ngô Đình Diệm a month and a half earlier. See Phan Quang Đán to Ngô Đình Diệm, November 7, 1955, TTLTQGII-ĐICH 21296.

105 "Tuyên ngôn chung về việc giải tán Hội Đồng Nhân Dân Cách Mạng," *Ngôn luận* 288 (January 11, 1956): 1, 4; and telegram 2814, Saigon to Secretary of State, January 13, 1956, NARA-RG59-CDF 1955–1959, 751G.00/1-1356.

106 Telegram 2814, Saigon to Secretary of State, January 13, 1956, NARA-RG59-CDF 1955–1959, 751G.00/1-1356.

107 "Revolutionary Body's Headquarters Seized," *Times of India,* January 17, 1956, 1.

108 Nguyễn Ngọc Thơ to Ngô Đình Diệm, c. January 1956, TTLTQGII-HĐQNCM 129; and telegram 3126, Saigon to Secretary of State, February 1, 1956, NARA-RG59-CDF 1955–1959, 751G.00/2-156.

109 Nguyễn Bảo Toàn, "Thông cáo Đảng Dân Chủ Xã Hội Việt Nam," *QC* 248 (January 24, 1956): 1; and Vương Kim, *Đức Huỳnh Giáo Chủ,* chap. 16.

110 Despatch 229, Saigon to Department of State, January 23, 1956, NARA-RG59-CDF 1955–1959, 751G.00/1-2356; Nguyễn Tấn Mạnh, Nguyễn Văn Đờn, Trần Thế Nguyên, and Lê Phước An to Ngô Đình Diệm, December 30, 1955, TTLTQGII-ĐICH 4033; and Nhị Lang, *Phong trào kháng chiến,* 357–361.

111 Nguyễn Tấn Mạnh, Nguyễn Văn Đờn, Trần Thế Nguyên, and Lê Phước An to Ngô Đình Diệm, December 30, 1955.

112 Despatch 336, Saigon to Department of State, April 16, 1956, NARA-RG59-CDF 1955–1959, 751G.00/4-1656; and Nhị Lang, *Phong trào kháng chiến,* 284–286.

113 Telegram 3167, Saigon to Secretary of State, February 4, 1956, NARA-RG59-CDF 1955–1959, 751G.00W/2-456; and telegram 3447, Saigon to Secretary of State, February 26, 1956, 751G.00W/2-2656.

114 Lansdale, *Midst of War,* 341–345; Currey, *Edward Lansdale,* 182–183; and Ahern, *CIA and the House of Ngo,* 96–97, 108.

115 Office of the Regional Delegate for Southern Vietnam, summary of the general monthly report for October 1955, c. October 1955, TTLTQGII-PThTVNCH 17; and Thayer, *War by Other Means,* 49.

116 Scigliano, *South Vietnam,* 167; and Elliott, *Vietnamese War,* 101.

117 Kahin, *Intervention,* 96; Thayer, *War by Other Means,* 116–117, especially tables 6.2 and 6.3; and Duiker, *Communist Road,* 184.

118 Correspondence 540-LX/M, Nguyễn Kim Anh, Chief of Security Service and Deputy Chief of Police for Long Xuyên Province, to General Director of Police and Security Service for Southern Vietnam and Province Chief of Long Xuyên Province, February 19, 1956, TTLTQGII-ĐICH 4320; and Trần Văn Soái to Ngô Đình Diệm, January 1960, TTLTQGII-ĐICH 7185.

119 Telegram 2643, Saigon to Secretary of State, January 1, 1956, NARA-RG59-CDF 1955–1959, 751G.00W/12-3155.

120 "Từ nay, Cộng Hòa Việt Nam đã có luật lệ duy nhứt về báo chí: Thông tin hoặc bình luận xuyên tạc có lợi cho cộng sản hay phản quốc gia có thể bị phạt tới bạc triệu và bị án đến 5 năm tù," *TC* 1472 (February 23, 1956): 1, 4; and telegram 3447, Saigon to Secretary of State, February 26, 1956, NARA-RG59-CDF 1955–1959, 751G.00W/2-2656.

121 "Dụ số 8 ngày 23-1 dương lịch năm 1956 thiết lập Quốc Hội," *CMQG* 169 (January 28, 1956): 1, 4; "Dụ số 9 ngày 23-1-1956 ấn định thể thức thi hành Dụ số 8 ngày 23-1-56," *CMQG* 169 (January 28, 1956): 1, 4; "Dụ số 8 ngày 23-1 dương lịch năm 1956 thiết lập Quốc Hội," *CMQG* 170 (January 30, 1956): 1, 4; and despatch 253, Saigon to Department of State, February 7, 1956, NARA-RG59-CDF 1955–1959, 751G.00/2-756.

Notes to Pages 96–100   197

122 The only available version of this document is in French. See Nhị Lang to Ngô Đình Diệm, January 27, 1956, enclosure 2, despatch 245, Saigon to Department of State, February 2, 1956, NARA-RG59-CDF 1955–1959, 751G.00/2-256.

123 Telegram 3147, Saigon to Secretary of State, February 3, 1956, NARA-RG59-CDF 1955–1959, 751G.00/2-356.

124 Report on activities in the Tây Ninh Special Sector from January 21, 1956, to July 7, 1956, c. January 26, 1957, TTLTQGII-ĐICH 4171; despatch 261, Saigon to Department of State, February 9, 1956, NARA-RG59-CDF 1955–1959, 751G.00/2-956; and telegram 3376, Saigon to Secretary of State, February 20, 1956, 751G.00/2-2056.

125 "Thỏa Ước Bính Thân," TTLTQGII-ĐICH 16215.

126 Nhị Lang, *Phong trào kháng chiến,* 364–365.

127 Communiqué 105-TP/TUVP, Association for the Restoration of Vietnam to cadres of all ranks and the national executive committee, March 1, 1956, TTLTQGII-PThTVNCH 29520; and VTX, "1000 người gồm cán bộ và hội viên Việt Nam Phục Quốc Hội tại tỉnh Ninh Thuận tổ chức biểu tình," *Ngôn luận* 317 (February 21, 1956): 1.

128 Police interview of Phan Quang Đán, February 19, 1956, TTLTQGII-ĐICH 5969; telegram 3447, Saigon to Secretary of State, February 26, 1956, NARA-RG59-CDF 1955–1959, 751G.00W/2-2656; "Le Dr. Phan-Quang-Dan serait-il à la fois agent des rebelles et collaborateur des Vietcong?" *Vietnam Presse* 1833 (February 22, 1956, evening edition): IV–V, TTLTQGII-HĐQNCM 130; and Phan Quang Tuệ, "From the First to the Second Republic," 119.

129 For an incomplete list of candidates and their affiliation, see "Cuộc tuyển cử Quốc Hội," *CMQG* 180 (February 17, 1956): 2; "Ứng cử viên Trung Việt," *CMQG* 182 (February 20, 1956): 1, 4. For a general description of the candidates, see also despatch 332, Saigon to Department of State, April 9, 1956, NARA-RG59-CDF 1955–1959, 751G.00/4-956.

130 For Madame Nhu's own explanation of her candidacy, see Thanh Tao, "Chúng tôi phỏng vấn bà Ngô Đình Nhu ứng cử viên đơn vị di cư tỉnh Chợ Lớn," *CMQG* 191 (March 1, 1956): 1, 4; Robert Trumball, "First Lady of Vietnam," *New York Times Magazine* (November 18, 1962): 33, 70, 72, 74.

131 Despatch 332, Saigon to Department of State, April 9, 1956, NARA-RG59-CDF 1955–1959, 751G.00/4-956.

132 Telegram 3502, Saigon to Secretary of State, February 29, 1956, NARA-RG59-CDF 1955–1959, 751G.00/2-2956; and despatch 336, Saigon to Secretary of State, April 16, 1956, 751G.00/4-1656.

133 The missing candidates were most likely Hồ Ngọc Cứ and Lê Thành Tương, both of whom formerly belonged to the ARV. See telegram 3502, Saigon to Secretary of State, February 29, 1956, NARA-RG59-CDF 1955–1959, 751G.00/2-2956; and report on the March 20, 1956 congress of the Association for the Restoration of Vietnam, March 22, 1956, TTLTQGII-ĐICH 4349.

134 Robert Alden, "Diem Is Winner in Vietnam Vote," *New York Times,* March 6, 1956, 1, 2.

135 Ngô Đình Diệm, "Diễn văn của Tổng Thống trong buổi lễ khai mạc Quốc Hội Việt Nam ngày 15-3-1956," in *CĐCN,* 2:25–27.

136 Mounier, *Personalist Manifesto,* 186–187, 213, 243–244.

137 Ngô Đình Diệm, "Thông điệp của Tổng Thống gởi Quốc Hội ngày 17-4-56," in *CĐCN,* 2:29–33, especially 29.

138 Ngô Đình Diệm, "Thông điệp của Tổng Thống gởi Quốc Hội," 31.

139 Ngô Đình Diệm, "Thông điệp của Tổng Thống gởi Quốc Hội," 32.

140 The other members of the committee that had been part of the constitutional commission were Vũ Quốc Thông, Nguyễn Hữu Châu, and Nguyễn Phương Thiệp. For the composition of the committee, see despatch 44, Saigon to Department of State, August 8, 1956.

141 Weiner, "Government and Politics," 123n1.

142 Despatch 32, Saigon to Department of State, July 31, 1956, NARA-RG59-CDF 1955–1959, 751G.21/7-3156. For the threats against dissenting deputies, see telegram 4997, Saigon to Secretary of State, June 26, 1956, 751G.03/6-2656.

198 Notes to Pages 100–103

143 "Draft Constitution," 171.

144 "Draft Constitution," 177.

145 *CBVNCH* 2, no. 55 (November 28, 1956): 3054.

146 *CBVNCH* 2, no. 55 (November 28, 1956): 3130–3135; telegram 18, Saigon to Secretary of State, July 2, 1956, NARA-RG59-CDF 1955–1959, 751G.21/7-256; and despatch 32, Saigon to Department of State, July 31, 1956, 751G.21/7-3156.

147 *CBVNCH* 2, no. 55 (November 28, 1956): 3050, 3095; and telegram 4997, Saigon to Secretary of State, June 26, 1956, 7 NARA-RG59-CDF 1955–1959, 51G.03/6-2656.

148 *CBVNCH* 2, no. 55 (November 28, 1956): 3055, 3107–3108.

149 Phillips, *Why Vietnam Matters,* 87.

150 "Draft Constitution," 180–181.

151 "Draft Constitution," 162–163.

152 *CBVNCH* 2, no. 55 (November 28, 1956): 3059–3060.

153 *CBVNCH* 2, no. 55 (November 28, 1956): 3113–3114; and despatch 32, Saigon to Department of State, July 31, 1956.

154 *CBVNCH* 2, no. 55 (November 28, 1956): 3071–3072; and despatch 32, Saigon to Department of State, July 31, 1956. For the prison riots, see despatch 378, Saigon to Department of State, June 7, 1956, 751G.00/6-756.

155 "Draft Constitution," 164.

156 *CBVNCH* 2, no. 55 (November 28, 1956): 3074–3077, especially 3076; and despatch 32, Saigon to Department of State, July 31, 1956.

157 *CBVNCH* 2, no. 55 (November 28, 1956): 3082–3083; and despatch 32, Saigon to Department of State, July 31, 1956.

158 *CBVNCH* 2, no. 55 (November 28, 1956): 3070, 3088–3089; and despatch 32, Saigon to Department of State, July 31, 1956.

159 "Draft Constitution," 162; and *CBVNCH* 2, no. 55 (November 28, 1956): 3069.

160 "Draft Constitution," 166–167; and *CBVNCH* 2, no. 55 (November 28, 1956): 3069–3070.

161 This provision was the only one among the personalist-inspired articles to inspire significant debate. See "Draft Constitution," 165; *CBVNCH* 2, no. 55 (November 28, 1956): 3075–3076; and despatch 32, Saigon to Department of State, July 31, 1956.

162 *CBVNCH* 2, no. 55 (November 28, 1956): 3136–3137. For the origins of these articles, see "Draft Constitution," 184.

163 For an English translation of the assembly's draft, see despatch 6, Saigon to Department of State, July 10, 1956, NARA-RG59-CDF 1955–1959, 751G.03/7-1056.

164 For more on Nguyễn Văn Cẩn's biography, see *Quốc Hội Lập Hiến,* 47. For his role in the plenary debates, see despatch 32, Saigon to Department of State, July 31, 1956. For his status as a government-favored candidate during the elections, see despatch 332, Saigon to Department of State, April 9, 1956, 751G.00/4-956. For his views on communism, see Nguyễn Văn Cẩn, *Công giáo.*

165 I have relied on a published collection of Nguyễn Văn Cẩn's articles rather than the original version serialized in the newspaper. For the collection, see Nguyễn Văn Cẩn, *Phê bình.* For the characterization of the newspaper and English-language summaries of selected articles, see despatch 91, Saigon to Department of State, September 14, 1956, NARA-RG59-CDF 1955–1959, 751G.02/9-1456.

166 Nguyễn Văn Cẩn, *Phê bình,* 50–51, 58–59.

167 Nguyễn Văn Cẩn, *Phê bình,* 68.

168 Nguyễn Văn Cẩn, *Phê bình,* 12.

169 Nguyễn Văn Cẩn, *Phê bình,* 25.

170 Nguyễn Văn Cẩn, *Phê bình,* 27.

171 Nguyễn Văn Cẩn, *Phê bình,* 17–23, especially 18.

172 Nguyễn Văn Cẩn, *Phê bình,* 68.

Notes to Pages 104–106   199

173 Despatch 97, Saigon to Department of State, September 18, 1956, NARA-RG59-CDF 1955–1959, 751G.03/9-1856.

174 Phillips, *Why Vietnam Matters,* 87.

175 President to the Chair of the National Assembly, October 15, 1956, TTLTQGII-ĐICH 768.

176 *CBVNCH* 2, no. 58 (December 11, 1956).

177 Correspondence 2350-VPCT, Trần Văn Lắm, Chair of the National Assembly, to President, October 23, 1956, TTLTQGII-ĐICH 768.

178 Nguyễn Long Thành Nam, *Phật Giáo Hòa Hảo,* 411; and Vương Kim, *Đức Huỳnh Giáo Chủ,* chap. 16.

179 Donnell, "Politics in South Vietnam," 429–30; and Scigliano, *South Vietnam,* 79–80, 85.

180 Lê Văn Phiên to Ngô Đình Diệm, June 25, 1956, attached to memorandum from Deming to Kattenberg, September 4, 1956, NARA-RG59-CDF 1955–1959, 751G.00/9-456; and "Vì sao Linh mục Lê V. Phiên phải ra trước tòa án quân sự," *Dân chủ* 879 (March 11, 1957): 1, 4.

181 The RC tried to expand overseas but dissolved in July 1956. For the dissolution, see despatch 192, Paris to Department of State, July 17, 1956, NARA-RG59-CDF 1955–1959, 751G.00/7-2756; and telegram 435, Paris to Secretary of State, July 25, 1956, 751G.00/7-2556.

182 Phan Quang Đán, "Nhân mấy vụ án chính trị," *TL* 415 (September 1–2, 1957): 1, 4, especially 4; VTX, "VN Phục Quốc Hội đã bầu xong ban chấp hành mới," *Ngôn luận* 549 (November 20, 1956): 1; telegram 1704, Saigon to Secretary of State, November 22, 1956, NARA-RG59-CDF 1955–1959, 751G.00/11-2256; "Nguyên nhân sự chia rẽ nội bộ Việt Nam Phục Quốc Hội" and "Khai trừ Nguyễn Thành Phương," in Service for Political and Social Research, "Hoạt động Cao Đài," c. 1957, TTLTQGII-ĐICH 4908; and correspondence 032/BCH-TƯ, Nguyễn Thành Phương to the Prefect of Saigon, August 8, 1961, TTLTQGII-ĐICH 22427.

183 For more on Lê Quang Vinh's capture and execution, see despatch 368, Saigon to Department of State, May 23, 1956, NARA-RG59-CDF 1955–1959, 751G.00/5-2356; despatch 15, Saigon to Department of State, July 16, 1956, 751G.00/7-1656; Lê Văn Dương, *Quân Lực,* 456–457. For more on the operations against the Cao Đài defectors, see report on activities in the Tây Ninh Special Sector from January 21, 1956, to July 7, 1956, c. January 26, 1957, TTLTQGII-ĐICH 4171; and despatch 44, Saigon to Department of State, August 8, 1956, NARA-RG59-CDF 1955–1959, 751G.00/8-856.

184 Despatch 433, Saigon to Department of State, May 29, 1958, NARA-RG59-CDF 1955–1959, 751G.00/5-2958; Nhị Lang, *Phong trào kháng chiến,* 361–362; Nguyễn Long Thành Nam, *Phật Giáo Hòa Hảo,* 569; "Acceptance of Hoa Hao Offer to Join the Ranks of the Government," October 5, 1962, CREST, 242369. For differing views of communist influence on the armed sect elements, see Việt Hồng, "Vài nét đấu tranh," 43–44; Bùi Thị Thu Hà, "Đồng bào Phật Giáo Hòa Hảo," 93-98; Thayer, *War by Other Means,* 137–139; Turley, *Second Indochina War,* 25–26; and Chapman, *Cauldron of Resistance,* 189–191.

185 For the final constitution, see "Hiến pháp Việt Nam Cộng Hòa."

186 Thanh Thu, "Thủ đô Việt tưng bừng ăn Tết Cộng Hòa," *TC* 1683 (October 27, 1956): 1, 6; and Weiner, "Government and Politics," 135.

187 Telegram 1880, Saigon to Secretary of State, December 8, 1956, NARA-RG59-CDF 1955–1959, 751G.00/12-856; and telegram 1967, December 17, 1956, 751G.21/12-1756.

Chapter Four: Diversity and Fragmentation, 1956–1959

1 "Ô. Nguyễn Trân ứng cử viên quận 1 bị 4000 đồng vạ treo," *TC* 2547 (August 27, 1959): 1, 4.

2 "3 ứng cử viên ở Tân Bình đều bị Tòa Chung Thẩm phạt về tội vi phạm luật bầu cử," *TC* 2548 (August 28, 1959): 1.

3 "Ô. ô. Phan Qg. Đán, Hoàng Cơ Thụy bị mỗi người 8000$ vạ treo," *TC* 2549 (August 29, 1959): 1, 4, especially 4; and correspondence 1206-BTP/VP/M, Minister of Justice Nguyễn Văn Sĩ to President, September 8, 1959, TTLTQGII-ĐICH 1777.

200 Notes to Pages 108–112

4 Ngô Đình Diệm, "Lời tuyên bố truyền thanh của Thủ Tướng chánh phủ ngày 16-7-1955 về Hiệp Định Genève và vấn đề thống nhất đất nước," in *CĐCN*, 2:11–12; and *Tuyên cáo ngày 26-4-58*. See also various policy speeches in *Vấn đề thống nhất lãnh thổ*.

5 Fall, *Two Viet-Nams*, 258–259, 268–273; Anderson, *Trapped by Success*, 182–183; Moyar, *Triumph Forsaken*, 76; and Jacobs, *Cold War Mandarin*, 113–114. For rare accounts that offer a more expanded discussions of the opposition in the late 1950s, see Scigliano, *South Vietnam*, 81–85; and Donnell, "Politics in South Vietnam," 421–455 passim.

6 Scigliano, *South Vietnam*, 87.

7 Young to Robertson, June 19, 1956, NARA-RG59-CDF 1955–1959, 751G.00/6-1956; Paul Lewis, "Dr. Nguyen Ton Hoan, 84, Pro-Independence Vietnamese Official, Is Dead," *New York Times*, September 26, 2001, C14; Bảo Đại, *Le dragon d'Annam*, 257; and Phan Thị Bình, "Thư số 14," 145–146.

8 Memorandum of conversation between Nguyễn Tôn Hoàn, Byrne, and Kattenburg, April 20, 1955, NARA-RG59-CDF 1955–1959, 751G.00/4-1055. Note the discrepancy between the date of the document and the file number.

9 Nguyễn Tôn Hoàn to Robertson, June 5, 1956, NARA-RG59-CDF 1955–1959, 751G.00/6-556.

10 "Bức thư tâm huyết," no. 1 (September 1, 1956), TTLTQGII-ĐICH 4359.

11 Phan Thị Bình, "Thư số 22," 200–201.

12 For examples of positive American press coverage of Diệm, see "The Beleaguered Man," *Time Magazine* 65, no. 14 (April 4, 1955): 22–25; and Demaree Bess, "Bright Spot in Asia," *Saturday Evening Post* 229, no. 11 (September 15, 1956): 36, 127–128, 130. See also Jacobs, *Cold War Mandarin*, 101–103.

13 Nguyễn Tôn Hoàn, "Liberty in Vietnam," *Washington Post and Times Herald*, September 24, 1956, 16.

14 For more on Huỳnh Sanh Thông's life and career, see Division of Biographic Information, "Huynh Sanh Thong," March 4, 1957, NARA-RG59-FEV, Box 13, Folder GVN, Biographies T-Z; Huỳnh Sanh Thông, interview by Peter Zinoman; and "In Memoriam: Huynh Sanh Thong."

15 Huỳnh Sanh Thông, "Tyranny in Vietnam," *Washington Post and Times Herald*, January 25, 1956, 24.

16 Huỳnh Sanh Thông to Long, February 1, 1957, NARA-RG59-CDF 1955–1959, 751G.00/2-857.

17 Kocher to Robertson, February 13, 1957, NARA-RG59-CDF 1955–1959, 751G.00/2-857.

18 Hill to Long, February 21, 1957, NARA-RG59-CDF 1955–1959, 751G.00/2-857.

19 Berrier's opposition to Diệm may have stemmed from the journalist's former employment by the Ngô brothers in Geneva in 1955. For more on Berrier's life and career, see Lucier, "Hilaire du Berrier"; and Jasper, "Passing of a Patriot." For Berrier's connection to the American far right, see Caulfield, *General Walker*, 544. For Berrier's employment by the Ngô brothers, see Olson, *Mansfield and Vietnam*, 73–74.

20 Telegram 166, Department of State to Saigon, July 25, 1957, NARA-RG59-CDF 1955–1959, 751G.00/6-2657; and telegram 6638, Paris to Secretary of State, June 26, 1957, 751G.00/6-2657.

21 Phan Sĩ Cơ, "Từ Ba Lê, các nhân vật của chế độ cũ vận động lật đổ chính thể cộng hòa Việt Nam," *TD* 116 (June 4, 1957): 1, 2, 3, especially 1; and correspondence 51/57/M-PP from Republic of Vietnam Embassy, Paris, "Phúc trình về hoạt động của Nguyễn Tôn Hoàn," May 16, 1957, TTLTQGII-ĐICH 4903.

22 "Programme d'Action de Salut National," c. May 9, 1957; correspondence 51/57/M-PP from Republic of Vietnam Embassy, Paris, "Phúc trình về hoạt động của Nguyễn Tôn Hoàn," May 16, 1957, both in TTLTQGII-ĐICH 4903; and Phan Sĩ Cơ, "Từ Ba Lê," 2, 3.

23 "Vụ án Đại Việt xử ngày 26-9-59: Công tác tuyên truyền phá hoại và công tác kinh tài qui mô của Đảng Đại Việt tổ chức ra sao?" *TC* 2570 (September 23, 1959): 1, 4; "Vụ án Đại Việt: Việc thu lợi tức của ban kinh tài Đại Việt hằng mấy chục triệu tổ chức như thế nào?" *TC* 2571 (September 24, 1959): 1, 4; and correspondence no. 21633-/CSDB-M/VPĐB-DT, Director of Police for Southern

Notes to Pages 112–115   201

Vietnam to Bureau of Political Affairs, Regional Delegate for Southern Vietnam, August 29, 1956, TTLTQGII-ĐICH 4354.

24 Hà Thúc Ký, *Sống còn,* 209–214.

25 Correspondence 114/TT/TMBB/TTP from Special Staff, Office of the President, "Tổng quát tin tức góp nhặt trong tháng 11/1955," November 25, 1955, TTLTQGII-ĐICH 4029; telegram 3687, Saigon to Secretary of State, March 17, 1956, NARA-RG59-CDF 1955–1959, 751G.00W/3-1756; despatch 336, Saigon to Department of State, April 16, 1956, 751G.00/4-1656; and telegram 1245, Saigon to Secretary of State, October 13, 1956, 751.G00W/10-1356.

26 Correspondence 27708/PC.1/M, General Director of Police and Security Service for Southern Vietnam to Director of Cabinet, Office of the Advisor to the President, October 31, 1956; correspondence 16.537/TCSCA/TB/NC/M, General Director of Police and Security Service to the Minister of the Interior, November 28, 1957, both in TTLTQGII-ĐICH 5968; telegram 790, Secretary of State to Saigon, October 24, 1957; telegram 950, Saigon to Secretary of State, November 2, 1957, both in NARA-RG84-CGR, Box 43, Folder 350.2, Vietnam-Oppositionists, 1956–1958; and telegram 1105, Saigon to Secretary of State, November 24, 1957, NARA-RG59-CDF 1955–1959, 751G.00W/11-2457.

27 Telegram 3684, Saigon to Secretary of State, March 10, 1956, NARA-RG59-CDF 1955–1959, 751G.00W/3-1056; and telegram 1105, Saigon to Secretary of State, November 24, 1957, 751G.00W/11-2457.

28 "Hắc thơ," 1956, TTLTQGII-ĐICH 4129; General Director of National Police and Security Service to Minister of the Interior, May 22, 1958, TTLTQGII-ĐICH 5968; Đại Việt Nationalist Party to the people of the United States, "Miss Le My's letter and anti-Americanism in South Vietnam," March 15, 1958, VVA, John Donnell Collection, Box 6, Folder 7, 0720607005, accessed November 18, 2018, https://vva.vietnam.ttu.edu/repositories/2/digital_objects/91050; and memorandum of conversation between Nguyễn Tôn Hoàn, Quang Hinh, and Barbour, August 5, 1959, NARA-RG59-FEV, Box 13, Folder GVN, Biographies H-M.

29 Correspondence no. 21633-/CSDB-M/VPĐB-DT, Director of Police for Southern Vietnam to Bureau of Political Affairs, Regional Delegate for Southern Vietnam, August 29, 1956, TTLTQGII-ĐICH 4354; "Vụ án Đại Việt xử ngày 26-9-59: Công tác tuyên truyền phá hoại"; "Vụ án Đại Việt: Việc thu lợi tức"; "Bản án Đại Việt," *TC* 2574 (September 28, 1959): 1, 6; and telegram 1154, Saigon to Secretary of State, October 3, 1959, NARA-RG59-CDF 1955–1959, 751G.00W/10-359.

30 Despatch 10, Huế to Department of State, November 12, 1957, NARA-RG59-CDF 1955–1959, 751G.00/11-1257.

31 Hà Thúc Ký, *Sống còn,* 221–222.

32 "Vụ án chánh trị lớn tại Tòa Án Quân Sự Nha Trang," *TD* 531 (October 9, 1958): 1, 4; Vi Lang, "Kết liễu vụ án chính trị phá rối an ninh tại tỉnh Phú Yên," *TD* 531 (October 11, 1958): 1.

33 The concept of peaceful coexistence originated in Soviet foreign policy decades before the Bandung conference, but Phạm Công Tắc mistakenly believed that Nehru invented the idea. For Nehru's speeches, see Nehru, "Speech by Prime Minister Nehru," 66; and Nehru, *Jawaharlal Nehru's Speeches,* 253. For the Soviet origins and the later usage of the concept in the 1950s, see Lerner, "Historical Origins"; Fifield, "Five Principles"; and Nation, *Black Earth,* 208–209. For Tắc's assumption, see Phạm Công Tắc, "Thánh thư 12 ngày 08-04-1958 gởi HBCS và HBGH," in *Hòa Bình Chung Sống,* ed. Nguyễn Phúc Thành, 323–343, especially 327.

34 For more on Vietnamese peace efforts after 1965, see Quinn-Judge, *Third Force.*

35 Phạm Công Tắc, "Thơ gởi cụ Hồ Chí Minh và cụ Ngô Đình Diệm 28-3-1956," in *Tìm hiểu,* 43–44, especially 43.

36 Correspondence 40-HP/HN, Phạm Công Tắc to Ngô Đình Diệm and Hồ Chí Minh, April 28, 1956, TTLTQGII-ĐICH 4324.

37 Phạm Công Tắc, "Cương lĩnh của chính sách 26-3-1956," in *Tìm hiểu,* 21–24.

38 Phạm Công Tắc, "Cương lĩnh," 22.

202   Notes to Pages 116–118

39 Phạm Công Tắc, "Thánh Thư ngày 03-06-1957," in Nguyễn Phúc Thành, *Hòa Bình Chung Sống,* 208–213, especially 208.

40 Phạm Công Tắc, "Thánh Thư 10 ngày 22-02-1958," in Nguyễn Phúc Thành, *Hòa Bình Chung Sống,* 307–317, especially 313–314.

41 Correspondence 20/HP/HN, Phạm Công Tắc to Chair of the United Nations and Premiers of the Four Powers, March 26, 1956; Phạm Công Tắc to the United Nations, Four Powers, Democratic Republic of Vietnam, and Republic of Vietnam, "Chánh Sách Hòa Bình Chung Sống: Do dân, phục vụ dân, lập quyền dân," March 26, 1956, both in TTLTQGII-ĐICH 4324; despatch 379, Saigon to Department of State, June 8, 1956, NARA-RG59-CDF 1955–1959, 751G.00/6-856.

42 Note that Phạm Công Tắc referred to Yan Hui by the latter's courtesy name, Yan Yuan (Viet. Nhan Uyên, alternately Nhan Quyên and Nhan Huyên). See Phạm Công Tắc, "Thánh thư ngày 28-05-1956 giải thích về Hòa Bình Giáo Hội," in Nguyễn Phúc Thành, *Hòa Bình Chung Sống,* 110–112.

43 Phạm Công Tắc actually revised the Confucian parable substantially. For the version espoused by the Congregation for Peace, see "Ý nghĩa cây bạch kỳ Nhan Huyên," c. May 16, 1956, TTLTQGII-ĐICH 21656. For the original parable, see *K'ung Tzŭ Chia Yü,* 230–231. I thank Janet Hoskins, Jérémy Jammes, and Liam Kelley for their assistance identifying the parable and Peter Lavelle for finding the citations for the original version.

44 Report on activities in the Tây Ninh Special Sector from January 21, 1956, to July 7, 1956, c. January 26, 1957, TTLTQGII-ĐICH 4171; and Phạm Công Tắc, "Thánh thư ngày 01-04-1956 hướng dẫn các thành viên Ban Vận Động HBCS thể hiện dân mạnh (lập quyền dân)," in Nguyễn Phúc Thành, *Hòa Bình Chung Sống,* 86–89.

45 Internal histories produced by the Cao Đài faith claimed that Tắc's disciples in Phnom Penh organized the demonstration. See Nguyễn Phúc Thành, *Hòa Bình Chung Sống,* 183–187.

46 The reference to painted faces apparently alluded to the practice of smearing a substance on the faces of the gamecocks, either to prevent the animals from recognizing each other or to enhance the aesthetic presentation of the gamecocks.

47 For the surprise demonstration, see "Phúc trình v/v Hội thánh Cao Đài tổ chức Lễ Vía Đức Chí Tôn với mục đích hoan hô Hộ Pháp Phạm Công Tắc và ủng hộ đường lối chánh trị chống chính quyền hiện hữu của nhân vật này," February 8, 1957, TTLTQGII-ĐICH 4910; Hanley to Hackett, February 20, 1957, NARA-RG84-CGR, Box 43, Folder 350, Vietnam-Oppositionists, 1956–1958, 1957-02-20; and Tịnh Tâm, *Tiểu Sử,* chap. 2. For the crackdown, see correspondence 4151/PC.1/M, Director of Police and Security Service for Southern Vietnam to Director of Service for Internal Security and General Director of National Police and Security Service, January 12, 1958, TTLTQGII-ĐICH 5496.

48 "Tổ chức Hòa Bình Giáo Hội," in Service for Political and Social Research, "Hoạt động Cao Đài," c. 1957, TTLTQGII-ĐICH 4908; and Phạm Công Tắc, "Thánh thư ngày 28-05-1956," 110–112.

49 Correspondence 717-VP/TL, report by the General Staff of the Second Military Region to the President, May 16, 1956, TTLTQGII-ĐICH 21656. A later report by the army provides an entirely different account of the incident, but this report is suspect. See correspondence no. 01827/37/P.81, General Director of Security and National Defense, Army of the Republic of Vietnam, to President, Deputy Minister of National Defense, and Chief of General Staff of the Army of the Republic of Vietnam, July 16, 1956, TTLTQGII-ĐICH 21717. For a Cao Đài account of the incident, see "Trương cờ HBCS ở Bến Hải," in Nguyễn Phúc Thành, *Hòa Bình Chung Sống,* 561–580, especially 565–568.

50 Phạm Công Tắc, "Thánh Thư 01 ngày 22-11-1957 hủy bỏ việc đi vĩ tuyến 17 tụng kinh và từ đây ĐHP trực tiếp chỉ đạo," in Nguyễn Phúc Thành, *Hòa Bình Chung Sống,* 215–219, especially 216.

51 For an example of the RVN's position on peaceful coexistence, see Nha Chiến Tranh Tâm Lý, *Sống chung?*

52 "Trong một buổi lễ cực kỳ tôn nghiêm tại đền thánh Tâyninh tân giáo chủ Cao Đài đã làm lễ trình diện Đức Chí Tôn," *TD* 100 (16 May 1957): 1, 4; "Thượng Sanh Cao Hoài Sang thay thế

Phạm Công Tắc," in Service for Political and Social Research, "Hoạt động Cao Đài," c. 1957, TTLTQGII-ĐICH 4908; and Blagov, *Caodaism*, 109–110.

53 Enclosure 4, despatch 13, Saigon to Department of State, July 13, 1955, NARA-RG59-CDF 1955–1959, 751G.00/7-1355; telegram 2321, Saigon to Secretary of State, December 2, 1955, 751G.00/12-255; and Hoàng Cơ Thụy, *Việt sử khảo luận*, 5:2719.

54 For Hoàng Cơ Thụy's changing politics, see telegram 2763, Saigon to Secretary of State, January 10, 1956, NARA-RG59-CDF 1955–1959, 751G.00/1-1056. For his work as a defense lawyer, see "Luật sư Hoàng Cơ Thụy xin tòa án đình chỉ phán quyết chờ quan điểm của Viện Bảo Hiến," *Dân chủ* 880 (March 12, 1957): 1, 4; "Vụ Cha Hồ Văn Vui ra trước tòa tiểu hình," *TL* 390 (March 10–11, 1957) 1, 4; and "18 tháng tù và rút giấy phép báo," *Dân chủ* 890 (March 23, 1957): 1.

55 "Notice biographique de M. Nghiem Xuan Thien," TTLTQGII- PThTVNCH 3912; and enclosure 1, despatch 394, Saigon to Department of State, June 18, 1957, NARA-RG59-CDF 1955–1959, 751G.00/6-1857. Additionally, Nguyễn Thành Phương discreetly supported the Democratic Bloc but did not formally join it. See Biographic Information Division, "Nguyen Thanh Phuong," March 15, 1961, NARA-RG84-CGR, Box 72, Folder 350.3, Biographical Data General.

56 Khối Dân Chủ, "Lời tuyên bố với báo giới ngày 3-5-57 của Khối Dân Chủ," *TL* 400 (May 19–20, 1957): 1, 3, especially 3.

57 Phan Quang Đán, Liêu Quang Khình, Hoàng Cơ Thụy, Đinh Xuân Quảng, Lê Thị Ấn, Nghiêm Xuân Thiện, Nguyễn Văn Cần, Nguyễn Xuân Quang, "Kêu gọi của Khối Dân chủ," *TL* 399 (May 12–13, 1957): 4.

58 Phan Quang Đán, et al., "Kêu gọi của Khối Dân chủ"; and Khối Dân Chủ, "Lời tuyên bố," 3.

59 Despatch 394, Saigon to Department of State, June 18, 1957, NARA-RG59-CDF 1955–1959, 751G.00/6-1857.

60 Khối Dân Chủ, "Lời tuyên bố," especially 3.

61 Khối Dân Chủ, "Đối lập hợp pháp: Khối Dân Chủ đối lập có hợp pháp không?" *TL* 400 (May 19–20, 1957): 1, 4, especially 4.

62 Telegram 3347, Saigon to Secretary of State, May 4, 1957, NARA-RG59-CDF 1955–1959, 751G.00/5-457; and despatch 394, Saigon to Department of State, June 18, 1957, 751G.00/6-1857.

63 Hoàng Cơ Thụy and Nguyễn Văn Cần, "Tuyên bố của 2 ông Hoàng Cơ Thụy và Nguyễn Văn Cần về hoạt động của 'Phe đối lập' và ô. Phan Quang Đán," *TD* 120 (June 8, 1957): 1; "Phỏng vấn ô. Phan Q. Đán về đường lối của Khối Dân Chủ đối với 1 số vấn đề mới," *TD* 122 (June 11, 1957): 1, 2; "Phỏng vấn ô. Nguyễn Văn Cần về Khối Dân Chủ và một số vấn đề mới," *TD* 123 (June 12, 1957): 1, 2, especially 2; "Về việc hai ông Thụy và Cần," *TL* 405 (June 24–25, 1957): 2, 3, 4; and "Khối Dân chủ phân hóa," *TD* 379 (April 14, 1958): 1, 4.

64 My understanding of *Contemporary Discourse* draws heavily on Picard, "'Renegades.'"

65 Phan Quang Đán, "Từ vấn đề Hoa kiều bàn rộng ra," *TL* 405 (June 24–25, 1957): 1, 4; "Phản đối dời nhà Bến Chương Dương vì Hội Nghị Kế Hoạch Colombo," *TL* 406 (June 30–July 1, 1957): 1, 4; and "Quy chế ngoại kiều kiểm soát di trú," *TL* 407 (July 7–8, 1957): 1, 4.

66 Correspondence 10073/TCSCA/TBNC/M, General Director of National Police and Security Service to Minister at the Presidency, July 27, 1957, TTLTQGII-ĐICH 5969. For comparison, consider the racist and unsympathetic treatment of the Chinese minority in "Tuồng . . . Tàu," *Văn nghệ tiền phong* 51 (May 30, 1957): 10; and untitled cartoon, *Văn nghệ tiền phong* 54 (June 20, 1957): 3.

67 "Hậu quả biện pháp của Bộ Kinh tế thanh trừng những thương gia," *TL* 411 (August 4–5, 1957): 1, 4; "Nỗi thắc mắc của một số quân nhân," *TL* 414 (August 25–26, 1957): 1, 6; "Cho thăng trật mà không cho lương?" *TL* 414 (August 25–26, 1957): 6; and "Nguyện vọng của chức việc và đạo hữu Cao Đài," *TL* 416 (September 8–9, 1957): 1, 4.

68 Telegram 23, Saigon to Secretary of State, July 6, 1957, NARA-RG59-CDF 1955–1959, 751G.00W/7-657; and Linh Phương, "Kẻ nào đã hăm dọa người đọc báo Thời luận ở Mỹ Tho?" *TL* 424 (November 9–10, 1957): 1, 3.

69 Correspondence 581 BKT/VP/M, Minister of Economy to Minister of Justice, August 6, 1957, TTLTQGII-ĐICH 5563; Thời Luận, "Thời luận lại sắp ra Tòa Đại Hình về ba việc," *TL* 424

204   Notes to Pages 121–124

(November 9–10, 1957): 1, 4; "Phiên tòa xử báo Thời luận," *TD* 260 (November 19, 1957): 1, 4; and "Báo Thời luận thoát hiểm," *TD* 261 (November 20, 1957): 1, 4.

70 "Ủy viên chánh phủ xin kết 10 cái án tử hình," *TD* 188 (August 27, 1957): 1, 4; and despatch 82, Saigon to Department of State, September 6, 1957, NARA-RG59-CDF 1955–1959, 751G.00/9-657.

71 For a sampling of articles in the newspaper criticizing the sentencing, see Phan Quang Đán, "Nhân mấy vụ án chính trị," *TL* 415 (September 1–2, 1957): 1, 6, especially 6; Khối Dân Chủ, "Kiến nghị của Khối Dân Chủ xin ân xá cho các bị can trong vụ án Hồ H. Tường, Trần V. Ân," *TL* 416 (September 8–9, 1957): 1; and various letters to the editor in the same issue. For the demonstrations and mob attacks against the newspaper and its staff, see "Một số đảng viên Đảng Xã Hội và Việt Nam Phục Quốc đã kéo tới chất vấn ông Phan Quang Đán tại tư gia và phá tòa báo 'Thời luận,'" *VTX* 2380 (September 7, 1957, morning edition): Xa; "Về vụ đập phá hai báo 'Thời luận' và 'Tân dân' và những nhà in liên hệ," *VTX* 2381 (September 8, 1957, full day edition): IXa–IXb; "Công nhân bến tàu ở Khánh Hội biểu tình về vụ báo 'Thời luận' và 'Tân dân,'" *VTX* 2382 (September 9, 1957, afternoon edition): F-G, all in TTLTQGII-ĐICH 5563; Thời Luận, "Chính trị hay côn đồ?" *TL* 416 (September 8–9, 1957): 1, 4; "Cuộc tập hợp của trên 3000 công nhân tại bến Thương Khẩu," *TD* 200 (September 10, 1957): 1, 4; and correspondence 896-M, Police Chief of District 4 to General Director of the Prefectural Police, September 9, 1957, TTLTQGII-ĐICH 5969.

72 For the first article in the series, see XYZ, "Thư gởi ông đại biểu của tôi trong Quốc Hội," *TL* 431 (December 28–29, 1957): 1, 4. For claims that Đán had ceased writing for the newspaper, see correspondence 28891/PCl/M, General Director of Police and Security Service for Southern Vietnam to Director of Service for Internal Security and General Director of National Police and Security Service, November 12, 1957, TTLTQGII-ĐICH 5969; and Lý Thắng, "'Để cho hợp với tinh thần Hiến Pháp, xin tòa án hủy Dụ số 13 ấn định sự trừng phạt đối với báo chí vì hiện nay ta chưa có Viện Bảo Hiến,'" *TD* 354 (March 15, 1958): 1, 4, especially 1.

73 I have not been able to locate the original Vietnamese-language article. For a description of the article, see Tự Do, "Vụ án Thời luận 1–3–58," Lập trường column, *TD* 351 (March 12, 1958): 1, 4. For a translation of the original, see enclosure 1, despatch 320, Saigon to Department of State, March 16, 1958, NARA-RG84-CGR, Box 54, Folder 350, Internal Political Affairs Vietnam-GVN 1959.

74 TL, "Ông chủ nhiệm và bà quản lý báo Thời luận cùng bị ra tòa ngày 13–3–58 về số báo bị tịch thâu," *TD* 349 (March 10, 1958): 1, 4.

75 Correspondence 357-BTP/VP/M, Minister of Justice to President, March 13, 1958; and correspondence 1765-BTP/VP/M, Minister of Justice to President, December 26, 1958, in TTLTQGII-ĐICH 5563.

76 Phan Quang Đán, "Tại sao có đảng lại có khối?" *TD* 382 (April 17, 1958): 1, 4; "Ô. Phan Quang Đán đã lập xong ủy ban trung ương Đảng Dân Chủ đối lập," *TD* 392 (April 29, 1958): 1, 4.

77 Phạm Công Tắc, "Thánh thư 12 ngày 08-04-1958 gởi HBCS và HBGH," 326; and Phạm Công Tắc, "Thánh thư 15 ngày 19-05-1958 gởi HBCS và HBGH," in Nguyễn Phúc Thành, *Hòa Bình Chung Sống,* 388–406, especially 389.

78 "Phỏng vấn ô. Phan Q. Đán," 2.

79 Mounier, *Personalist Manifesto,* 72–73, 54–85, 190–191.

80 Ngô Đình Diệm, "Hiệu triệu quốc dân nhân dịp kỷ niệm ba năm chấp chánh (7-7-1957)," in *CĐCN,* 3:135–144, especially 139.

81 Ngô Đình Diệm, "Thông báo của Tổng Thống đọc trước Quốc Hội nhân dịp lễ khai mạc khóa họp thường lệ (7-10-1957)," in *CĐCN,* 4:9–26, especially 10. For an extended analysis of the Diemist conception of the substructure of democracy, see D. Nguyen, *Unimagined Community,* 77–82.

82 Ngô Đình Diệm, "Thông báo của Tổng Thống," 11.

83 Ngô Đình Diệm, "Thông báo của Tổng Thống," 11.

84 Huỳnh Văn Lang, *Ký ức,* 2:304.

85 Scigliano, "Electoral Process," 154.

Notes to Pages 124–127   205

86 Airgram G-19, Saigon to Secretary of State, July 31, 1959, NARA-RG59-CDF 1955–1959, 751G.5MSP/7-3159.

87 Ngô Đình Diệm, "Hiệu triệu quốc dân nhân dịp kỷ niệm ba năm chấp chánh (7-7-1957)," in *CĐCN,* 3:135–144, especially 143.

88 The unusual phrasing reflects the clipped language typical of reports by the US embassy. See airgram G-19, Saigon to Secretary of State, July 31, 1959, NARA-RG59-CDF 1955–1959, 751G.5MSP/7-3159.

89 For the land reform program, see Race, *War Comes,* 56–61; Catton, *Diem's Final Failure,* 51–56; and Miller, *Misalliance,* 171–177. For the Land Development and the Agroville Programs, see Catton, *Diem's Final Failure,* 56–71; and Miller, *Misalliance,* 177–184.

90 Telegram 263, Saigon to Secretary of State, July 28, 1958, 7 NARA-RG59-CDF 1955–1959, 51G.5MSP/7-2859; and Trương Vĩnh Lễ, *Vietnam,* 37.

91 Despatch 45, Saigon to Department of State, August 1, 1959, NARA-RG59-CDF 1955–1959, 751G.00/8-159.

92 Despatch 257, Saigon to Department of State, March 14, 1957, NARA-RG59-CDF 1955–1959, 751G.21/3-1457.

93 Despatch 24, Saigon to Department of State, July 18, 1959, NARA-RG59-CDF 1955–1959, 751G.00/7-1859.

94 Despatch 24, Huế to Department of State, June 13, 1958, NARA-RG59-CDF 1955–1959, 751G.00/6-1358; and despatch 279, Saigon to Department of State, March 2, 1959, 751G.00/3-259.

95 Despatch 40, Saigon to Department of State, July 30, 1959, NARA-RG59-CDF 1955–1959, 751G.00/7-3059.

96 Scigliano, *South Vietnam,* 77–78.

97 For estimates of Cần Lao membership, see despatch 279, Saigon to Department of State, March 2, 1959, NARA-RG59-CDF 1955–1959, 751G.00/3-259; and Donnell, "Politics in South Vietnam," 231–232. For estimates of the size of the NRM, see Donnell, "Politics in South Vietnam," 239–240; and Scigliano, *South Vietnam,* 77.

98 Nguyễn Văn Minh, *Dòng họ Ngô Đình,* 431; and Huỳnh Văn Lang, *Nhân chứng,* 1:534–535.

99 Tổng Liên Đoàn Lao Động Việt Nam, "Tổng Liên Đoàn Lao Động Việt Nam đòi hỏi 5 quyền tự do căn bản," *TD* 376 (April 10, 1958): 3; Wherle, *Between a River,* 70; and Nguyễn Văn Minh, *Dòng họ Ngô Đình,* 451–453.

100 For changes in Trần Chánh Thành's position, see telegram 3616, Saigon to Secretary of State, June 8, 1957, NARA-RG59-CDF 1955–1959, 751G.00W/6-857; and airgram G-204, Saigon to Secretary of State, November 7, 1960, NARA-RG59-CDF 1960–1963, 751K.00W/11-760. For various explanations of Trần Chánh Thành's fall from favor, despatch 279, Saigon to Department of State, March 2, 1959, NARA-RG59-CDF 1955–1959, 751G.00/3-259; and Nguyễn Thái, *Is South Vietnam,* 103n1.

101 Telegram 2007, Saigon to Secretary of State, March 30, 1958, NARA-RG59-CDF 1955–1959, 751G.13/5-3058; despatch 1005, Paris to Department of State, December 4, 1958, 751G.00/12-458; and despatch 1169, Paris to Department of State, December 31, 1958, 751G.00/12-3158.

102 Huỳnh Văn Lang, *Nhân chứng,* 2:258–266; and *Ký ức,* 2:267–278.

103 Letter 200, Canadian Delegation, International Commission for Supervision and Control, Hanoi, to Undersecretary of State for External Affairs, Ottawa, July 24, 1957, NARA-RG59-FEV, Box 1, Folder 321.5, ICC-1957; despatch 38, Saigon to Department of State, August 2, 1958, NARA-RG59-CDF 1955–1959, 751G.00/8-258; despatch 410, Saigon to Department of State, May 10, 1958, 751G.00/5-1058; and Trương Vĩnh Lễ, *Vietnam,* 33–34.

104 Donnell, "Politics in South Vietnam," 252–275.

105 The bill passed in the assembly in late 1958 and became law in 1959. For the bill and legislative debates, see despatch 250, Saigon to Department of State, January 11, 1958, NARA-RG59-CDF 1955–1959, 751G.21/1-1158; despatch 298, Saigon to Department of State, February 25, 1958, 751G.21/2-2558. For the support of the Ngô family, see Cao Văn Luận, *Bên giòng lịch sử,* 273–276. For gossip about Madame Nhu's motivations, see Demery, *Dragon Lady,* 102–103.

206 Notes to Pages 128–132

106 Donnell, "Politics in South Vietnam," 276–281.

107 Telegram 415, Saigon to Secretary of State, August 24, 1957, NARA-RG59-CDF 1955–1959, 751G.11/8-2457; despatch 279, Saigon to Department of State, March 2, 1959, 751G.00/3-259; and Demery, *Dragon Lady,* 103–104.

108 Nguyễn Văn Minh, *Dòng họ Ngô Đình,* 88–89.

109 Hà Thúc Ký, *Sống còn,* 221–222.

110 Despatch 263, Saigon to Department of State, January 20, 1958, NARA-RG59-CDF 1955–1959, 751G.11/1-2058; and despatch 213, Saigon to Department of State, December 22, 1958, 751G.07/12-2258.

111 Trần Văn Đôn, *Việt Nam,* 142; Phạm Văn Liễu, *Trả ta sông núi,* 1:349; and Race, *War Comes,* 19. For an alternate rendition, see Nguyễn Hiến Lê, *Hồi kí,* 2:121.

112 My understanding of relations between the government and Catholic émigrés relies heavily on Picard, "Fragmented Loyalties," 80–187. This and the next three paragraphs draws from despatch 333, Saigon to Department of State, May 9, 1957, NARA-RG84-CGR, Box 42, Folder 350, Vietnam, 1956–1958; and Lương Khải Minh and Cao Vị Hoàng, *Làm thế nào,* 1:137–149.

113 Picard, "Fragmented Loyalties," 109.

114 Despatch 333, Saigon to Department of State, May 9, 1957.

115 Telegram 2663, Saigon to Secretary of State, March 2, 1957, NARA-RG59-CDF 1955–1959, 751.G00W/3-257; "Vụ Cha Hồ Văn Vui ra trước tòa tiểu hình," *TL* 390 (March 10–11, 1957): 1, 4; and Lương Khải Minh and Cao Vị Hoàng, *Làm thế nào,* 1:147–148.

116 Picard, "Fragmented Loyalties," 87–99.

117 "Đọc bà nghị," *Đường sống* 153 (March 16–17, 1957): 1, 4.

118 I thank Kevin Grove for his advice on translating the name of the newspaper.

119 VT, "Bên lề cuộc mưu sát tại Ban Mê Thuột," Vì dân vì nước column, *Đường sống* 151 (March 2–3, 1957): 1, 4, especially 4.

120 For the politics of the newspaper and Diệm's reaction, see Picard, "Fertile Lands Await," 79–80; and Trương Vĩnh Lễ, *Vietnam,* 34. For the trial, see "Phiên Tòa Tiểu Hình ngày 22-3-57 xử báo Đường sống và Dân chủ," *TD* 55 (March 23, 1957): 1, 4.

121 Correspondence 187-A.5, "Báo cáo về luận điệu tuyên truyền của những nhóm Công Giáo bất mãn," March 27–28, 1957, TTLTQGII-ĐICH 22403.

122 *Bầu cử Quốc Hội Lập Pháp.*

123 The most complete list of candidates I have been able to locate was serially published from July 1 to July 7, 1959, in a Saigon newspaper. For the first in the series, see "Các đơn vị bầu cử Quốc Hội năm 1959," *TC* 2498 (July 1, 1959): 1, 4. For a list of candidates in Saigon, see "Danh sách 95 ứng cử viên dân biểu Quốc Hội khóa II tại 9 đơn vị đô thành Sàigòn niêm yết lần thứ nhứt ngày 3-8," *TC* 2527 (August 3, 1959): 1, 4.

124 Donnell, "Politics in South Vietnam," 430.

125 Like Phan Khắc Sửu, Nguyễn Tăng Nguyên and Tạ Chương Phùng were former supporters of Diệm back in 1954 who decided to run against government-backed candidates in the legislative elections of 1959.

126 Telegram 655, Saigon to Secretary of State, August 28, 1959, NARA-RG59-CDF 1955–1959, 751G.00/8-2859; and Nguyễn Thái, *Is South Vietnam,* 137–140.

127 Nguyễn Trân, *Công và tội,* 92.

128 Nguyễn Trân, *Công và tội,* 253–304 passim; and Huỳnh Văn Lang, *Ký ức,* 2:262–264.

129 Trần Quốc Bửu is known to have supported at least one candidate, Phạm Văn Thùng, who ran against Phan Quang Đán in the second legislative district of Saigon. See despatch 216, Saigon to Department of State, January 18, 1960, NARA-RG59-CDF 1955–1959, 751K.00/1-1860.

130 Huỳnh Văn Lang, *Nhân chứng,* 2:327–328, 350–353; and *Ký ức,* 2:299–306, 316–323.

131 Telegram 655, Saigon to Secretary of State, August 28, 1959, NARA-RG59-CDF 1955–1959, 751G.00/8-2859; correspondence 1975/PBC from Nguyễn Phú Hải, Prefect of Saigon, "Phúc trình về

Notes to Pages 132–140   207

cuộc đầu phiếu trong đơn vị II tại Saigon ngày 30/8/1959," September 24, 1959, TTLTQGII-ĐICH 1777; Scigliano, "Electoral Process," 151–152; and Race, *War Comes,* 89.

132 "Giải thích về vụ kiện vi phạm luật tuyển cử: Dân biểu Phan Quang Đán thân mến gởi đồng bào cử tri quận nhì," c. September 16, 1959, TTLTQGII-HĐQNCM 130.

133 Nguyễn Tuyết Mai, "Electioneering," 14.

134 Honey, "Problem of Democracy," 74–75.

135 Honey, "Problem of Democracy," 75; and Nguyễn Tuyết Mai, "Electioneering," 15–16.

136 Despatch 116, Saigon to Department of State, October 9, 1959, NARA-RG59-CDF 1955–1959, 751G.00/10-959.

137 "Tài liệu của Nha Cảnh Sát Đô Thành: Thử nghiên cứu những nguyên nhân nào đã làm cho ô. Phan Quang Đán đắc thăm trong cuộc bầu cử Quốc Hội khóa II," c. September 1959; and correspondence 1975/PBC from Nguyễn Phú Hải, Prefect of Saigon, "Phúc trình về cuộc đầu phiếu trong đơn vị II," in TTLTQGII-ĐICH 1777.

138 "Giải thích về vụ kiện vi phạm luật tuyển cử."

139 Correspondence 1975/PBC from Nguyễn Phú Hải, Prefect of Saigon, "Phúc trình về cuộc đầu phiếu trong Đơn vị II."

140 "Ô. Nguyễn Trân ứng cử viên quận 1", 4; and correspondence 1206-BTP/VP/M, Minister of Justice Nguyễn Văn Sĩ to President, September 8, 1959, TTLTQGII-ĐICH 1777.

141 Telegram 745, Saigon to Secretary of State, September 6, 1959, NARA-RG59-CDF 1955–1959, 751G.00/9-659.

Chapter Five: Rupture or Reconciliation? 1960–1962

1 For Phạm Văn Liễu's leadership at Tràng Sụp and his reaction to the attack, see Phạm Văn Liễu, *Trả ta sông núi,* 1:343–354. For the communist offensive, see despatch 17, Saigon to Department of State, July 12, 1960, NARA-RG59-CDF 1960–1963, 751K.5/7-1260; Ahern, *CIA and Rural Pacification,* 32–33; and Spector, *Advice and Support,* 338.

2 Despatch 377, Saigon to Department of State, April 24, 1958, NARA-RG59-CDF 1955–1959, 751G.00/4-2458; and despatch 71, Saigon to Department of State, August 21, 1959, 751G.00/8-2159.

3 Elliott, *Vietnamese War,* 103–105.

4 Elliott, *Vietnamese War,* 105–106; and Catton, *Diem's Final Failure,* 68–69.

5 For more on Phan Khắc Sửu's biography and career, see Nguyễn Văn Nam, *Niên giám Quốc Hội,* 145–146; Trần Văn Ân, "Tưởng nhớ," 75; and Nguyễn Long Thành Nam, *Phật Giáo Hòa Hảo,* 471. For more on Trần Văn Văn's biography and career, see Nelson, "Struggle to Build." For the two friends' acquaintance, see Ngô Quang Huy, *Nhớ bạn xưa,* 79–80.

6 Members of Trần Văn Văn and Phan Khắc Sửu's clique included Hồ Văn Nhựt, Nguyễn Lưu Viên, and Trần Văn Hương. For the attendance of Văn, Sửu, and Hương at the Unity Congress, see "Première réunion du Dai Doan Ket chez les Binh Xuyen," September 11, 1953, SHAT, 10H 4023.

7 Telegram 4485, Saigon to Secretary of State, April 12, 1955, NARA-RG59-CDF 1955–1959, 751G.00/4-1255; and Hồ Hữu Tường, "Le défi vietnamien," 300–301.

8 Donnell, "Politics in South Vietnam," 371–374.

9 "Tuyên Ngôn Caravelle."

10 "Tuyên Ngôn Caravelle."

11 Bùi Diễm, *Gọng kìm lịch sử,* 161.

12 Tillman Durdin, "Dictatorial Rule in Saigon Charged," *New York Times,* May 1, 1960, 1, 21.

13 Telegram 3185, Saigon to Secretary of State, May 12, 1960, NARA-RG59-CDF 1960–1963, 751K.00/5-1260; and telegram 3204, Saigon to Secretary of State, May 14, 1960, 751K.00W/5-1460.

14 Despatch 410, Saigon to Department of State, May 20, 1960, NARA-RG59-CDF 1960–1963, 751K.00/5-2060; airgram G-202, Saigon to Secretary of State, May 23, 1960, 751G.00/5-2360; and "Tờ tự khai của Trần Văn Văn," November 1960, TTLTQGII-HĐQNCM 101.

208   Notes to Pages 140–144

15 Despatch 461, Saigon to Department of State, June 24, 1960, NARA-RG59-CDF 1960–1963, 751K.00/6-2460; "Lời tự khai của Tạ Chương Phùng," November 13, 1960; and "Tờ tự khai của Trần Văn Văn," November 1960, both in TTLTQGII-HĐQNCM 101.

16 The only extant description of the aims of the Freedom and Progress Bloc came from American businessman Frank Gonder, but Gonder's claims were often contradictory and unreliable. For Gonder's account and the US embassy's assessment of Gonder, see telegram despatch 358, Saigon to Department of State, April 22, 1960, NARA-RG59-CDF 1960–1963, 751K.00/4-2260. For a scholarly account that takes Gonder's claims seriously, see Frankum, *Vietnam's Year of the Rat,* 51–52.

17 "Lời tự khai của Nguyễn Lưu Viên," November 1960; "Tờ tự khai của Trần Văn," November 1960; and "Tờ khai của bác sĩ Trần Văn Đỗ," November 14, 1960, in TTLTQGII-HĐQNCM 101.

18 Ngô Đình Diệm, "Thông điệp của Tổng Thống gởi quốc dân nhân dịp Tết Canh Tý 1960," in *CĐCN,* 6:27–29, especially 28.

19 Telegram 2671, Saigon to Secretary of State, March 16, 1960, NARA-RG59-CDF 1960–1963, 751K.00/3-1660; and despatch 358, Saigon to Department of State, April 22, 1960, 751K.00/4-2260.

20 Telegram 3092, Saigon to Secretary of State, May 2, 1960, NARA-RG59-CDF 1960–1963, 751K.00/5-260. Durbrow later suggested that the Americans contributed to the drafting of the Caravelle Manifesto, but I have found no evidence to support that claim. See oral history transcript, Elbridge Durbrow, interview 1 (I), by Ted Gittinger, June 3, 1981, Lyndon B. Johnson Library Oral Histories, Lyndon B. Johnson Presidential Library, https://www.discoverlbj.org/item/oh-dur-browe-19810603-1-86-21.

21 Despatch 450, Saigon to Department of State, June 17, 1960, NARA-RG59-CDF 1960–1963, 751K.00/6-1760.

22 Despatch 157, Saigon to Department of State, October 15, 1960, NARA-RG59-CDF 1960–1963, 751K.00/10-1560; and telegram 802, Saigon to Secretary of State, October 15, 1960, 751K.00/10-1560.

23 Telegram 866, Saigon to Secretary of State, October 20, 1960, NARA-RG59-CDF 1960–1963, 751K.00/10-2060; and despatch 175, Saigon to Department of State, October 29, 1960, 751K.00/10-2960.

24 Đỗ Mậu, *Việt Nam,* 397–405; and Trần Văn Đôn, *Việt Nam,* 149–150.

25 Despatch 37, Saigon to Department of State, July 25, 1960, NARA-RG59-CDF 1960–1963, 751K.00/7-2560; and Nguyễn Công Luận, *Nationalist,* 186–187.

26 Many former leaders of the coup of 1960 enumerated long lists of grievances in their memoirs, but documents from the time of the event emphasized political favoritism within the military as the main motivating factor behind the coup. For the later description of grievances, see Nguyễn Chánh Thi, *Việt Nam,* 33–68; Vương Văn Đông, *Binh biến 11-11-60,* 47–80; and Phạm Văn Liễu, *Trả ta sông núi,* 1:357–377.

27 Vương Văn Đông, *Binh biến 11-11-60,* 97–117; and Hoàng Cơ Thụy, *Việt sử khảo luận,* 5:2823.

28 Hoàng Cơ Thụy, *Việt sử khảo luận,* 5:2754, 2813; and Vương Kim, *Đức Huỳnh Giáo Chủ,* chap. 16.

29 Vương Văn Đông, *Binh biến 11-11-60,* 111–114.

30 Nguyễn Tường Bá (son of Nguyễn Tường Tam), interview with author, December 12, 2013; and Nguyễn Thành Vinh, "Mặt Trận Quốc Dân Đoàn Kết," 136–137.

31 Nguyễn Chánh Thi, *Việt Nam,* 42, 63–64, 103–104; Phạm Văn Liễu, *Trả ta sông núi,* 1:377–379; and Lương Khải Minh and Cao Vị Hoàng, *Làm thế nào,* 2:468.

32 Phạm Văn Liễu, *Trả ta sông núi,* 1:379–380; and Nguyễn Kiên Hùng, "Binh biến 11/11/60," 185.

33 Military Assistance Advisory Group, "After Action Report, Attempted Coup of 11-12 November 1960," November 21, 1960, NARA-RG84-CGR, Box 55, 350 Internal Political Affairs-Vietnam-November Coup 1960.

34 Vương Văn Đông, *Binh biến 11-11-60,* 135; and Hoàng Cơ Thụy, *Việt sử khảo lược,* 5:2823.

Notes to Pages 144–147   209

35 Military Assistance Advisory Group, "After Action Report"; Vương Văn Đông, *Binh biến 11-11-60*, 138; and Phạm Văn Liễu, *Trả ta sông núi*, 1:387–388.

36 Military Assistance Advisory Group, "After Action Report"; despatch 342, Saigon to Department of State, February 10, 1961, NARA-RG59-CDF 1960–1963, 751K.00/2-1061; Lương Đình Chi, "Phúc trình ti mĩ v/v chống bọn phản loạn do Nguyễn Chánh Thi và Vương Văn Đông cầm đầu rạng 11.11.1960 hồi 3 giờ," c. November 15, 1960, TTLTQGII-ĐICH 6531; Vương Văn Đông, *Binh biến 11-11-1960*, 133, 146; and Langguth, *Our Vietnam*, 108–111.

37 For different versions of Nguyễn Chánh Thi's reassertion of leadership, see Phạm Văn Liễu, *Trả ta sông núi*, 1:392–193; Vương Văn Đông, *Binh biến 11-11-60*, 138–139; and Nguyễn Chánh Thi, *Việt Nam: Một trời tâm sự*, 118–120.

38 Telegram 1012, Saigon to Secretary of State, November 11, 1960, NARA-RG59-CDF 1960–1963, 751K.00/11-1160; and telegrams CRTIC 9 and 10, Saigon to Secretary of State, November 11, 1960, 751K.00/11-1060.

39 Vương Văn Đông, *Binh biến 11-11-60*, 142–148.

40 Vương Văn Đông, *Binh biến 11-11-60*, 143–144; and Nguyễn Chánh Thi, *Việt Nam*, 130–131.

41 Telegram MAGTNPO 1429 111245Z, Chief of Military Assistance Advisory Group Saigon to Secretary of State, November 11, 1960, NARA-RG59-CDF 1960–1963, 751K.00/11-1060; telegram 1019, Saigon to Secretary of State, November 11, 1960, 751K.00/11-1160; telegram 1031, Saigon to Secretary of State, November 11, 1960, 751K.00/11-1160; and Vương Văn Đông, *Binh biến 11-11-60*, 150–151, 156.

42 Telegram MAGCH-CH 1403 111431Z, Chief of Military Assistance Advisory Group to Secretary of State, November 11, 1960, NARA-RG59-CDF 1960–1963, 751K.00/11-1160; despatch 342 and enclosure 1, Saigon to Department of State, February 10, 1961, 751K.00/2-1061, 751K.00/2-1061; and Vương Văn Đông, *Binh biến 11-11-60*, 156–158.

43 Vương Văn Đông, *Binh biến 11-11-60*, 158–159.

44 Telegram CX-154 110156Z, Office of US Army Attaché Saigon to Secretary of State, November 11, 1960, NARA-RG59-CDF 1960–1963, 751K.00/11-1160; and telegram 1019, Saigon to Secretary of State, November 11, 1960, 751K.00/11-1160.

45 Nguyễn Chánh Thi, *Việt Nam*, 136–138; and Fontaine, *Dawn of Free Vietnam*, 44.

46 "Les déclarations radiodiffusées," *Le journal d'Extrême-Orient* 3606 (November 12, 1960): 1; "Minute-By-Minute Account of the Coup," *Times of Viet Nam* 261 (November 12, 1960): 1–2, both in TTLTQGII-ĐICH 6537; telegram 1031, Saigon to Secretary of State, November 11, 1960, NARA-RG59-CDF 1960–1963, 751K.00/11-1160; telegram 1034, Saigon to Secretary of State, November 12, 1960, 751K.00/11-1260; and Lê Nguyên Phu, "Trích cáo trạng," 324.

47 Nguyễn Thành Vinh, "Mặt Trận Quốc Dân Đoàn Kết," 137–138.

48 I have not been able to locate the original Vietnamese handbill, but I did locate a Chinese-language translation of the handbill by the Taiwanese embassy and an English-language translation by the US embassy. I rely on the Chinese-language version because it appears to be a superior translation. I thank Peter Lavelle for locating and translating it into English. See "Handbill of the National People's Solidarity Front," c. November 1960, AS 11-01-06-01-02-010. For the English version, see enclosure 3, despatch 342, Saigon to Department of State, February 10, 1961, NARA-RG59-CDF 1960–1963, 751K.00/2-1061.

49 Nguyễn Tường Bá, interview with the author, December 12, 2013.

50 Nguyễn Thành Vinh, "Mặt Trận Quốc Dân Đoàn Kết," 137–138.

51 I have not been able to locate the original Vietnamese handbill and have relied on the English-language translation by the American embassy. Capitalization in the cited text follows the translation. See despatch 342 and enclosure 4, Saigon to Department of State, February 10, 1961, 7 NARA-RG59-CDF 1960–1963, 51K.00/2-1061; and despatch 146, Saigon to Department of State, September 27, 1961, 751K.00/9-2761.

52 Lê Nguyên Phu, "Trích cáo trạng," 315–316; and Trần Văn Thục, "Trích bản cáo trạng," 405–406, 408–409, 411.

210 Notes to Pages 147–149

53 Đinh Xuân Quảng, "Vụ mười một," 244–245; and telegram 1045, Saigon to Secretary of State, November 11, 1960, NARA-RG59-CDF 1960–1963, 751K.00/11-1160.

54 Military Assistance Advisory Group, "After Action Report"; Telegram CX-160 120330Z, Army Attaché Saigon to Secretary of State, November 12, 1960, NARA-RG59-CDF 1960–1963, 751K.00/11-1260; and despatch 342, Saigon to Department of State, February 10, 1961, 751K.00/2-1061.

55 Ahern, *CIA and the House of Ngo,* 142–143.

56 Ngô Đình Diệm, "Hiệu triệu của Tổng Thống Việt Nam Cộng Hòa (12-11-60)," in *CĐCN,* 7:31.

57 Telegram 1082, Saigon to Secretary of State, November 14, 1960, NARA-RG59-CDF 1960–1963, 751K.00/11-1560; and telegram 1120, Saigon to Secretary of State, November 23, 1960, 751K.11/1-2360. The latter document is misnumbered in the archives.

58 Donnell, "Politics in South Vietnam," 401–402.

59 Despatch 210, Saigon to Department of State, November 28, 1960, NARA-RG59-CDF 1960–1963, 751K.001/11-2860.

60 For Nguyễn Văn Châu's career and role in the Cần Lao party, see Nguyễn Vy Khanh, introduction to *Ngô Đình Diệm,* 7–10; and Đỗ Mậu, *Việt Nam,* 454.

61 Telegram 1054, Saigon to Secretary of State, November 12, 1960, NARA-RG59-CDF 1960–1963, 751K.00/11-1260. For the original Vietnamese handbill, see "Ủy Ban Nhân Dân Cách Mạng Chống Đảo Chánh," *Ngôn luận* 1768 (November 12–13, 1960): 1, in TTLTQGII-ĐICH 6537.

62 BBPV, "Một cuộc biểu tình cấp tốc mừng thủ đô giải phóng," *CMQG* 695 (November 13–14, 1960): 1, 4; "Cuộc biểu tình vĩ đại của các đoàn thể dân chúng thủ đô," *TC* 2921 (November 13, 1960): 1, 6; and "Kiến nghị của các đoàn thể nhân dân kính dâng Ngô Tổng Thống," *TC* 2921 (November 13, 1960): 1, 6.

63 "Một số báo chí a dua phản loạn," *CMQG* 698 (November 17, 1960): 1, 4; and despatch 210, Saigon to Department of State, November 28, 1960, NARA-RG59-CDF 1960–1963, 751K.00/11-2860.

64 Airgram G-346, Saigon to Department of State, February 16, 1961, NARA-RG59-CDF 1960–1963, 751K.001/2-1661.

65 This and the next two paragraphs rely heavily on the following documents: "Danh sách số bị can đề nghị đưa ra truy tố trước Tòa Án Quân Sự Đặc Biệt Saigon," undated; "Danh sách số bị can đề nghị trừng phạt bằng biện pháp hành chánh," undated; "Danh sách số bị can a tòng chạy theo phản loạn đã được Tổng Nha CSCA trả tự do sau một thời gian bị câu lưu," undated, all in TTLTQGII-HĐQNCM 100; and despatch 492, Saigon to Department of State, April 27, 1961, NARA-RG59-CDF 1960–1963, 751K.00/4-2761.

66 Telegram 1090, Saigon to Secretary of State, November 16, 1960, NARA-RG59-CDF 1960–1963, 751K.00/11-1660; despatch 210, Saigon to Department of State, November 28, 1960, 751K.001/11-2860; Đinh Xuân Quảng, "Vụ mười một," 245; and Trần Tương, "Tôi bị bắt," 147.

67 Phan Khắc Sửu, "Nhớ P-42"; Võ Hòa Khanh, "100 ngày ở P-42," 169–179; and Fontaine, *Dawn of Free Vietnam,* 46.

68 The government later accused Phan Khắc Sửu of convening the Freedom and Progress Bloc and helping to organize the National People's Solidarity Front during the coup, but I have found no evidence that Sửu expressed public support for the rebellious paratroopers or organized followers on their behalf. See Lê Nguyên Phu, "Trích cáo trạng," 322–323.

69 Phan Khắc Sửu, "Nhớ P-42," 155.

70 "Sơ kết về nội vụ Nguyễn Thành Vinh, giáo sư triết lý tư thục, kiêm hiệu trưởng tư thục Trung Học Thái Đức, đảng viên Quốc Dân Đảng," undated; "Sơ kết về nội vụ Trương Bảo Sơn, bí danh Bảo Sơn, giáo sư và viết văn, đảng viên Quốc Dân Đảng," undated, both in TTLTQGII-HĐQNCM 100; "Tờ khai của Nguyễn Tường Tam," November 19, 1960, TTLTQGII- TTLTQGII-HĐQNCM 101; and Nguyễn Thành Vinh, "Mặt Trận Quốc Dân Đoàn Kết," 139–140.

71 For Nguyễn Bảo Toàn's fate, see Nguyệt Đàm and Thần Phong, *Chín năm máu lửa,* 187–191, 325–327; and Warner, *Last Confucian,* 103. For a personal account of the arrest of a member of the Social Democratic Party, see Võ Hòa Khanh, "100 Ngày ở P-42," 158–164.

Notes to Pages 149–152   211

72 Donnell, "Politics in South Vietnam," 378–380.

73 For Nguyễn Văn Cẩn's fate after the failed coup of 1960, see correspondence 3569/Q5/M, Police Chief of District 3 to Director of Prefectural Police, December 15, 1960, TTLTQGII-ĐICH 6532; and memorandum of conversation between Nguyễn Văn Cẩn and Barbour, October 5, 1961, NARA-RG59-FEV, Box 7, Folder 14-A, Political Movements GVN 1961. For Nguyễn Trân's activities during the event and his subsequent treatment by security agents, see "Danh sách số nhân vật thuộc các nhóm đối lập có a tòng theo phản loạn, lợi dụng cuộc biến cố để hội họp, tiếp xúc thăm dò tình hình nhưng chưa có yếu tố buộc tội cụ thể," undated, TTLTQGII-HĐQNCM 100; and Nguyễn Trân, *Công và tội,* 329–330.

74 Airgram A-80, Saigon to Department of State, July 25, 1963, NARA-RG59-SNF 1963, Pol 29-1 S Viet.

75 Telegram 1076, Saigon to Secretary of State, November 14, 1960, NARA-RG59-CDF 1960–1963, 51K.00/11-1460; and correspondence 3296/Q5/M, Police Chief of District to the Director of Prefectural Police, November 16, 1960, TTLTQGII-ĐICH 6532.

76 "Tờ trình của bác sĩ Than gởi ông cố vấn về cuộc biến động vừa xảy ra hôm 11.11.1960," c. November 1960, TTLTQGII-HĐQNCM 100; Lương Khải Minh and Cao Vị Hoàng, *Làm thế nào,* 2:474–477; and Tôn Thất Đính, *Hai mươi năm,* 199.

77 Correspondence 11.071/TB/M, Director of Prefectural Police to General Director of National Police, November 18, 1960; and correspondence 3915/CSQI/TP/M, Nguyễn Quyền, Police Chief of District 1, to General Director of National Police, November 16, 1960, both in TTLTQGII-ĐICH 6532.

78 Donnell, "Politics in South Vietnam," 324.

79 "Luật 1/61 quy định thể thức bầu tổng thống và phó tổng thống VNCH," January 5, 1961, TTLTQGII-ĐICH 21282.

80 Despatch 417, Saigon to Department of State, March 21, 1961, NARA-RG59-CDF 1960–1963, 751K.00/3-2161; and Donnell, "Politics in South Vietnam," 325–326.

81 Ngô Đình Diệm, "Thông điệp truyền thanh ngày 15-3-1961," in *CĐCN: Tập đặc biệt,* 11–18, especially 15–16.

82 Ngô Đình Diệm, "Hội họp báo chí ngày 23-3-1963," in *CĐCN: Tập đặc biệt,* 19–37, especially 19.

83 Ngô Đình Diệm, "Hội họp báo chí ngày 23-3-1963," 36.

84 Ngô Đình Diệm, "Tiếp xúc với cử tri," in *CĐCN: Tập đặc biệt,* 67–75, especially 73–74.

85 For more background on candidates in slates 2 and 3, see "Tiểu sử các nhân vật ra ứng cử tổng thống và phó tổng thống Việt Nam Cộng Hòa," *TD* 1178 (March 5, 1961): 1, 4.

86 Despatch 429, Saigon to Department of State, March 29, 1961, NARA-RG59-CDF 1960–1963, 751K.00/3-2961.

87 "Hội báo của liên danh II Ng. Đình Quát-Ng. Thành Phương," *TD* 1189 (March 18, 1961): 1, 4; and "Cuộc họp báo đầu tiên của liên danh II ứng cử tổng thống và phó tổng thống," *VTX* 3663 (March 17, 1961, afternoon edition): H8-H10, in TTLTQGII-ĐICH 2538.

88 Goscha, *Vietnam,* 138–143; and Reilly, "Origins," 39.

89 "Tiểu sử và thành tích tranh đấu của ông Nguyễn Thế Truyền," attached to January 29, 1961, NARA-RG84-CGR, box 55, 350 Presidential Elections of 1961; and despatch 365, Saigon to Department of State, April 29, 1955, NARA-RG59-CDF 1955–1959, 751G.00/4-2955.

90 "Lời tuyên bố cùng đồng bào của ứng cử viên Hồ Nhựt Tân," *TD* 1192 (March 22, 1961): 1, 2, 4, especially 4.

91 "Tờ trình về cuộc họp báo của liên danh III Hồ Nhật Tân-Nguyễn Thế Truyền," March 21, 1961, TTLTQGII-ĐICH 2539.

92 For the hostile treatment of opposition candidates by the press and organized hecklers, see "Thái độ chống đối của cử tọa đã làm buổi nói chuyện của liên danh II hôm chủ nhật phải rút ngắn," *VTX* 3681 (4 April 1961, morning edition): H3; "Liên danh III lại thất bại khi ra mắt cử tri," *TD* 1204 (April 5, 1961): 1, 4, in TTLTQGII-ĐICH 2541; "Tờ trình về cuộc họp báo của liên danh

212 Notes to Pages 153–157

III Hồ Nhật Tân-Nguyễn Thế Truyền," March 21, 1961, TTLTQGII-ĐICH 2539; despatch 429, Saigon to Department of State, March 29, 1961, NARA-RG59-CDF 1960–1963, 751K.00/3-2961. For interference and police harassment of slates 2 and 3 as well as for the stark contrast between the treatment of opposition candidates and the incumbents, see despatch 509, Saigon to Department of State, May 8, 1961, 751K.00/5-861; despatch 20, Huế to Department of State, April 15, 1961, 751K.00/4-1561; and Donnell, "Politics in South Vietnam," 351–357. I have identified only one instance of a disorderly political meeting for slate 1. See Đoàn Hồng, "Buổi nói chuyện của liên danh I cũng gặp cảnh huyên náo đấm đá trước chợ Ng. Tri Phương," *Buổi sáng* (March 27, 1961), in TTLTQGII-ĐICH 2540.

93 Despatch 509, Saigon to Department of State, May 8, 1961, NARA-RG59-CDF 1960–1963, 751K.00/5-861.

94 Ngô Đình Diệm, "Lời tuyên bố của Ngô Tổng Thống ngày 11-4-1961," in *CĐCN: Tập đặc biệt,* 91–92, especially 91.

95 Airgram G-346, US Embassy Saigon to Department of State, February 16, 1961.

96 Airgram G-404, Saigon to Department of State, March 30, 1961, NARA-RG59-CDF 1960–1963, 751K.001/3-3061; Đỗ Mậu, *Việt Nam,* 454; and Scigliano, *South Vietnam,* 89–90.

97 Airgram G-346, Saigon to Department of State, February 16, 1961; and Donnell, "Politics in South Vietnam," 383–384.

98 Donnell, "Politics in South Vietnam," 378–379.

99 Airgram G-346, Saigon to Department of State, February 16, 1961.

100 Ủy Ban Tổ Chức Nghị Hội Đại Đoàn Kết, "Ủy Ban Tổ Chức Hội Nghị Đại Đoàn Kết kêu gọi đoàn thể và tư nhân," *TD* 1167 (February 21, 1961): 1, 4, especially 4.

101 Donnell, "Politics in South Vietnam," 388.

102 Donnell, "Politics in South Vietnam," 385.

103 "Thuyết trình của Ủy Ban Tổ Chức Nghị Hội Đoàn Kết," *TD* 1271 (June 22, 1961): 1, 4, especially 4.

104 "Cuộc hội báo của Tổ Chức Hội Nghị Đại Đoàn Kết," *TD* 1250 (May 28, 1961): 1, 5, 6; "Thuyết trình của Ủy Ban Tổ Chức Nghị Hội Đoàn Kết," 4; and Donnell, "Politics in South Vietnam," 385.

105 Văn Huyền, "Đại Hội Đoàn Kết tạm đạt được kết quả," *TD* 1281 (July 5, 1961): 1, 4; and Donnell, "Politics in South Vietnam," 391–393.

106 The near unanimous passage of the resolutions raises questions as to whether the vote was rigged, but unfortunately no sources shed light on the matter.

107 Donnell, "Politics in South Vietnam," 386.

108 Donnell, "Politics in South Vietnam," 395–396, 408–410.

109 Airgram G-507, Saigon to Secretary of State, June 13, 1961, NARA-RG59-CDF 1960–1963, 751K.00/6-1361.

110 Donnell, "Politics in South Vietnam," 399–400, 410–420; and Đỗ Mậu, *Việt Nam,* 455.

111 The only opposition activity that Đặng Văn Sung was known to undertake was his unsuccessful run for office during the legislative elections of 1959.

112 Đặng Văn Sung to the presidential and vice presidential candidates and to Vietnamese compatriots, April 4, 1961; Đặng Văn Sung to Ngô Đình Diệm, April 4, 1961; and Đặng Văn Sung to Ngô Đình Diệm, April 18, 1961, in TTLTQGII-ĐICH 2599. For the press conference, see "Cuộc hội báo của ông Đặng Văn Sung về dự định lập Mặt Trận Dân Chủ Hóa với lập trường đối lập ôn hòa," *TD* 1225 (April 28, 1961): 1–3.

113 Despatch 505, Saigon to Department of State, May 6, 1961, NARA-RG59-CDF 1960–1963, 751K.00/5-661.

114 "Cuộc hội báo của ông Đặng Văn Sung," 2.

115 Đặng Văn Sung to the presidential and vice presidential candidates and to Vietnamese compatriots, April 4, 1961.

Notes to Pages 157–161   213

116 "Cuộc hội báo của ông Đặng Văn Sung," 3. See also despatch 505, Saigon to Department of State, May 6, 1961.

117 "Cuộc hội báo của ông Đặng Văn Sung," 3.

118 Despatch 505, Saigon to Department of State, May 6, 1961.

119 Telegram 898, Secretary of State to Saigon, December 15, 1960, NARA-RG59-CDF 1960–1963, 751K.00/12-1560. See also despatch 264, Saigon to Department of State, December 27, 1960, 751K.00/12-2760.

120 Telegram 1231, Saigon to Secretary of State, December 29, 1960, NARA-RG59-CDF 1960–1963, 751K.00/12-2960.

121 Edward Lansdale, memorandum for Secretary of Defense and Deputy Secretary of Defense, January 17, 1961, NARA-RG59-CDF 1960–1963, 751K.00/1-1961.

122 Anderson, *Trapped by Success,* 196.

123 For a general overview of the Counterinsurgency Plan, see Miller, *Misalliance,* 224–227.

124 For an example of Diệm's response to Durbrow's suggestions, see "Telegram from the US Embassy in Vietnam to the Department of State," March 16, 1961, *FRUS, 1961–1963,* vol. 1, *Vietnam,* https://history.state.gov/historicaldocuments/frus1961-63v01/d20.

125 Telegram 1329, Saigon to Secretary of State, January 31, 1961, NARA-RG59-CDF 1960–1963, 751K.00/1-3161.

126 "Dự án quan trọng để cải tổ các cơ cấu của chính quyền," *VTX* 3625 (February 7, 1961, morning edition): H1-H5; and "Theo chương trình cải tổ, chính phủ Việt Nam Cộng Hòa sẽ gồm có 12 bộ," *VTX* 3625 (February 7, 1961, morning edition): H6–H7, both in TTLTQGII-ĐICH 2529.

127 Trương Công Cừu and Ngô Trọng Hiếu were new cabinet ministers who formerly belonged to the People's Committee Against Rebels and Communists. For commentary on the composition of the cabinet, see telegram 1817, Saigon to Secretary of State, May 30, 1961, NARA-RG59-CDF 1960–1963, 751K.13/5-3061. For internal rivalries within the Diemist faction, see Nguyễn Thái, *Is South Vietnam,* 103n1.

128 Despatch 83, Saigon to Department of State, August 22, 1961, NARA-RG59-CDF 1960–1963, 751K.5/8-2261.

129 Telegram 385, Saigon to Secretary of State, September 20, 1961, NARA-RG59-CDF 1960–1963, 751K.00/9-2061.

130 Telegram 676, Saigon to Secretary of State, November 18, 1961, NARA-RG59-CDF 1960–1963, 751K.00/11-1861.

131 "Telegram from the Embassy in Vietnam to the Department of State," November 25, 1961, *FRUS, 1961–1963,* vol. 1, *Vietnam,* https://history.state.gov/historicaldocuments/frus1961-63v01/d278.

132 Nolting, *Trust to Tragedy,* 60.

133 Takashi Oka, "Liberty Calls in Viet Nam," *Christian Science Monitor,* November 21, 1961, quoted in Donnell, "Politics in South Vietnam," 454–455.

134 Donnell, "Politics in South Vietnam," 417. For Nolting's version of events, see Nolting, *Trust to Tragedy,* 59–60.

135 For the reaction of the opposition to Nolting's speech, see Homer Bigart, "Leader of Opposition in Saigon Urges Reforms," *New York Times,* March 13, 1962, 6.

136 Despatch 384, Saigon to Department of State, March 21, 1962, NARA-RG59-CDF 1960–1963, 751K.00/3-2162.

137 Telegram 1100, Saigon to Secretary of State, February 27, 1962, NARA-RG59-CDF 1960–1963, 751K.00/2-2762.

138 "Durable Diem," *Time Magazine* 79, no. 10 (September 9, 1962): 31.

139 Karnow, *Vietnam,* 281.

140 Telegram 1126, Saigon to Secretary of State, 2 March 1962, NARA-RG59-CDF 1960–1963, 751K.00/3-262; telegram 1529, Saigon to Secretary of State, 28 May 1962, 751K.00/5-2862; Stanley

214   Notes to Pages 161–166

Millet, "Terror in Saigon," *Harper's* (September 1962): 31–39; Đỗ Mậu, *Việt Nam,* 468–471; and Phan Quang Tuệ, "From the First to Second Republic," 121.

141 Nguyễn Thế Truyền, *Pour la libération,* 4–12.

142 Donnell, "Politics in South Vietnam," 419–420.

143 Bigart, "Leader of Opposition," 6.

Conclusion

1 Minh Sơn, "Không nên sợ," Thời cuộc column, *Đường sống* 153 (March 16–17, 1957): 1, 4, especially 4.

2 "Đường sống ra trước pháp đình," *Đường sống* 154 (March 23–24, 1957): 1; and telegram 2966, Saigon to Secretary of State, March 30, 1957, NARA-RG59-CDF 1955–1959, 751G.00W/3-3057.

3 For references to religious equality and freedom, see "Bản tuyên ngôn của tăng, tín đồ Phật Giáo Việt Nam," May 10, 1963; "Bản Phụ đính 'Bản Tuyên ngôn' của Phật Giáo Việt Nam đã đọc trong cuộc hội họp của Phật tử tại Chùa Từ Đàm, Huế (ngày 10.5.1963)," May 23, 1963; "Lời nguyện tâm huyết của Thích Quảng Đức ngày mồng 8 tháng 4 nhuần năm Quý Mão," c. May 30, 1963; "Đại cương tình hình Phật Giáo Việt Nam trước và sau ngày Phật Đản 2507," May 30, 1963; and "Thông Bạch của Hòa thượng Hội chủ Tổng Hội Phật Giáo Việt Nam," June 17, 1963, in TTLTQGII-ĐICH 8526. For accusations of religious discrimination, see "Thư của Đoàn Thanh Niên Bảo Vệ Phật Giáo," undated; and "Thư của Đoàn Sinh Viên Phật Tử Huế gởi đồng bào toàn quốc," undated, in TTLTQGII-ĐICH 22483.

4 My account of the Buddhist crisis of 1963 relies heavily on Miller, "Religious Revival."

5 "Vụ biểu tình của sinh viên ngày 17 và 18–8–63 về việc Linh Mục Cao Văn Luận," August 1963, TTLTQGII-ĐICH 8524; special report 172/TTM/2/5/MM, by the Second Bureau, General Staff, Ministry of Defense, for August 19–20, 1963, TTLTQGII-ĐICH 8527; telegram 2, Huế to Secretary of State, August 18, 1963, NARA-RG59-SNF 1963, Pol 26 S Viet; telegram 3, Huế to Secretary of State, August 18, 1963, Pol 26 S Viet; telegram 266, Saigon to Secretary of State, August 20, 1963, Soc 14–1 S Viet; and Cao Văn Luận, *Bên giòng lịch sử,* 317–361.

6 For student strikes at trade schools and universities in Saigon, see special report 187/ TTM/2/5/M, by the Second Bureau, General Staff, Ministry of Defense, for August 23, 1963; special report 031/TM/QĐ3/2/3/TTS/M, by the Second Bureau, Staff of III Corps, for August 24, 1963; special report 188/TTM/2/5/M, by the Second Bureau, General Staff, Ministry of Defense, for August 24, 1963; special report 048/TM/QĐ3/2/3/TTS/M, by the Second Bureau, Staff of III Corps, for August 25, 1963, all in TTLTQGII-ĐICH 8527; telegram 317, Saigon to Secretary of State, August 24, 1963; and telegram 325, Saigon to Secretary of State, August 24, 1963, both in NARA-RG59-SNF 1963, Pol 25 S Viet. For student strikes at secondary schools, see special report 217/TTM/2/5/M, by the Second Bureau, General Staff, Ministry of Defense, for September 6–7, 1963; special report. 250/TTM/2/5/M, by the Second Bureau, General Staff, Ministry of Defense, for September 21, 1963, both in TTLTQGII-ĐICH 8527; "Âm mưu xúi giục sinh viên học sinh bãi khóa biểu tình," c. September 1963, TTLTQGII-ĐICH 8520; telegram 463, Saigon to Secretary of State, September 10, 1963, Pol 25 S Viet; airgram A-183, Saigon to Department of State, September 5, 1963, Pol 25 S Viet; telegram 756, Saigon to Secretary of State, October 21, 1963, Pol 25 S Viet; and airgram A-239, Saigon to Department of State, October 3, 1963, Pol 2 S Viet.

7 "Newsletter of the Free Students Front of Vietnam," enclosure 2, airgram A-183, Saigon to Department of State, September 5, 1963, NARA-RG59-SNF 1963, Pol 25 S Viet; "Declaration of the Student Steering Committee to Struggle for Freedom," enclosure 2, airgram A-198, Saigon to Department of State, September 12, 1963, Soc 14-1 S Viet; and airgram A-300, Saigon to Department of State, October 31, 1963, Pol 26 S Viet.

8 For a facsimile of the suicide note, see Nhất Linh, "Những di chúc của Nhất Linh," *Văn học* 41 (July 1, 1964): 32.

Notes to Pages 166–172   215

9 For more on the political significance of Nguyễn Tường Tam's suicide, see N. Tran, "'Let History Render Judgement.'"

10 Trần Văn Đôn, *Việt Nam,* 166–167.

11 "Tuyên cáo của Hội Đồng Quân Nhân Cách Mạng," *Văn hóa nguyệt san,* n.s., 87 (November 1963): unpaginated.

12 "Tuyên cáo của Hội Đồng Quân Nhân Cách Mạng." For similar phrasing by Diệm, see "Thông điệp của Tổng Thống gởi quốc dân nhân dịp Tết Canh Tý 1960," in *CĐCN,* 6:27–29.

13 For examples of the debate between diasporic authors on Diệm's rule, see Đỗ Mậu, *Việt Nam*; Nguyễn Văn Chức, *Việt Nam chính sử*; Cửu Long Lê Trọng Văn, *Những bí ẩn*; Nguyễn Văn Minh, *Dòng họ Ngô Đình*; and Vĩnh Phúc, *Những huyền thoại.*

14 A growing body of scholarship examines anticommunism in the Vietnamese diaspora. For a sampling of this research, see Bousquet, *Bamboo Hedge*; Vo-Dang, "Cultural Work"; and Y. Nguyen, "(Re)making."

15 For the origins of the phrase "America's offspring" and its persistence in the scholarship, see Kennedy, "America's Stake," 618; and Herring, "Our Offspring," chap. 2 in *America's Longest War.* For arguments that the RVN was an American fabrication or invention, see Carter, *Inventing Vietnam*; and Jacobs, *Cold War Mandarin,* 7.

16 Chandler, *History of Cambodia,* 211–230; and Keo, "Writing," 18–45.

17 Keo, "Writing," 19–22, 25–27.

18 Keo, "Writing," 45–47.

19 Chandler, *History of Cambodia,* 230; and Chandler, *Tragedy,* 76–77.

20 Chandler, *History of Cambodia,* 230–231; and Chandler, *Tragedy,* 79–84.

21 Keo, "Writing," 46–50.

22 Feith, *Decline,* 38–42.

23 Kahin, *Nationalism and Revolution,* 124–125.

24 Feith, *Decline,* 515–518; and Lev, *Transition,* 67–69.

Appendix

1 Both the government of July 7, 1954, and the coalition government of September 24, 1954, featured an upper tier of ministers (*tổng trưởng*) and a lower tier of secretaries (*bộ trưởng*). Diệm abandoned the two-tier system when he formed the government of May 10, 1955. For the composition of the first cabinet, see "Tân nội các Ngô Đình Diệm," *Thần chung* 1622 (July 7, 1954): 1.

2 Information on the political affiliation of Trần Văn Đỗ, Nguyễn Tăng Nguyên, and Trần Chánh Thành is derived from despatch 279, Saigon to Department of State, March 2, 1959, NARA-RG59-CDF 1955–1959, 751G.00/3-259; Donnell, "Politics in South Vietnam," 95–96; Lansdale, *Midst of War,* 340; and Chính Đạo, *Việt Nam niên biểu,* 369, 535–536.

3 The Pentagon Papers asserts that Trần Văn Bạch was related to Diệm, but I have been unable to verify that claim. See Pentagon Papers, Book 2: IV.A.5, Tab 2:14, Electronic Briefing Books, National Security Archives, accessed August 14, 2020, https://issuu.com/national_security_archive/docs/pentagon-papers-part-iv-a-5.

4 Guillemot, *Dai Viêt,* 72; Huỳnh Văn Lang, *Ký ức,* 2:213; Tam, *Vietnam's War,* 175–176; and Trần Thị Liên, "Les catholiques vietnamiens," 697.

5 Hoàng Văn Đào, *Việt Nam Quốc Dân Đảng,* 484.

6 "Thành phần tân chánh phủ," *Tin điển* 1 (September 27, 1954): 1.

7 Biographic Information Division, "Nguyen Van Thoai," June 20, 1960, NARA-RG59-FEV, box 13, folder GVN Biographies T-Z; and Cao Văn Luận, *Bên giòng lịch sử,* 190.

8 Cao Văn Luận, *Bên giòng lịch sử,* 190.

9 For the composition of the coalition government, see "Thành phần tân chánh phủ"; telegram 1226, Saigon to Secretary of State, September 25, 1954, NARA-RG59-CDF 1950–1954, 751G.00/9-2554.

216 Notes to Pages 172–173

10 For the coalition government of September 24, 1954, and the government of May 10, 1955, Diệm's administration released information on the political affiliation of some cabinet members but concealed or misrepresented that of others. The affiliations and relationships listed in this column and the corresponding column of table A3 reflects my own research while also taking into account the information provided by the government. For the information released by the coalition government of September 24, 1954, see "Thành phần tân chánh phủ."

11 Hoàng Cơ Thụy, *Việt sử khảo luận,* 5:2719.

12 Donnell, "Politics in South Vietnam," 95.

13 Despatch 160, Saigon to Department of State, November 8, 1954, NARA-RG59-CDF 1950–1954, 751G.00/11-854.

14 Donnell, "Politics in South Vietnam," 95.

15 For the composition of the cabinet and official titles, see "Thành phần tân nội các," *TC* 1232 (May 12, 1955): 1.

16 Hoàng Cơ Thụy, *Việt sử khảo luận,* 5:2719.

17 Despatch 279, Saigon to Department of State, March 2, 1959, NARA-RG59-CDF 1955–1959, 751G.00/3-259; Lansdale, *Midst of Wars,* 340; and Lâm Lễ Trinh, "Chín năm," 40.

18 "Thủ tướng Ngô Đình Diệm đã cải tổ chính phủ," *TC* 1232 (May 12, 1955): 1, 4, especially 4.

19 Hoàng Cơ Thụy, *Việt sử khảo luận,* 5:2719.

20 The government claimed that Huỳnh Hữu Nghĩa belonged to the National Resistance Front, but party leader Nhị Lang later insisted that the party had no role in choosing Nghĩa for the position. See Nhị Lang, *Phong trào kháng chiến,* 357.

21 The government claimed that Nguyễn Công Viên belonged to the Association for the Restoration of Vietnam, but I have found no evidence to support that assertion.

22 Demery, *Dragon Lady,* 103–104.

Bibliography

ARCHIVAL COLLECTIONS

Central Intelligence Agency Record Search Tool, https://www.cia.gov/library/readingroom/collection/crest-25-year-program-archive (CREST).

Institute of Modern History, Diplomatic Archives, Republic of China Ministry of Foreign Affairs Archives, Academia Sinica, Taipei, Taiwan (AS).

Lyndon B. Johnson Presidential Library Online Collection, https://www.discoverlbj.org.

National Archives Center II (Trung Tâm Lưu Trữ Quốc Gia II), Ho Chi Minh City, Vietnam:

—Office of the Regional Delegate for Southern Vietnam Collection (Phông Tòa Đại Biểu Chính Phủ tại Nam Phần, TTLTQGII-TĐBCHNP).

—Office of the Prime Minister of the Republic of Vietnam Collection (Phông Phủ Thủ Tướng Việt Nam Cộng Hòa, TTLTQGII- PThTVNCH).

—Office of the President of the Republic of Vietnam Collection, First Republic (Phông Phủ Tổng Thống Đệ Nhất Cộng Hòa, TTLTQGII-ĐICH).

—Revolutionary Military Council Collection (Phông Hội Đồng Quân Nhân Cách Mạng, TTLTQGII-HĐQNCM).

National Archives and Records Administration, College Park, MD.

—Record Group 59:

——Central Decimal Files (NARA-RG59-CDF).

——Subject-Numeric Files (NARA-RG59-SNF).

——Bureau of Far Eastern Affairs, Vietnam Subject Files, 1955–1962 (NARA-RG59-FEV).

—Record Group 84:

——Classified General Records, 1946–1963, Vietnam, Saigon Embassy (NARA-RG84-CGR).

National Security Archives, George Washington University, https://nsarchive.gwu.edu.

Service historique de l'Armée de terre, Château de Vincennes, Paris, France (SHAT).

United States Declassified Documents Online, Gale Primary Sources (USDDO).

Virtual Vietnam Archive, Vietnam Center and Sam Johnson Vietnam Archive, Texas Tech University (VVA).

218 Bibliography

HISTORICAL NEWSPAPERS AND JOURNALS

Cách mạng quốc gia (CMQG)
Chiến đấu
Dân chủ
Đuốc Việt
Đường sống
Harper's
Le monde
Life
Lửa sống
New York Times
New York Times Magazine
Ngôn luận
Quần chúng (QC)
Quốc gia (QG)
Saturday Evening Post
Thần chung
Thời đại
Thời luận (TL)
Tiếng chuông (TC)
Time Magazine
Times of India
Tin điển
Tự do (TD)
Văn hóa nguyệt san
Văn học
Văn nghệ tiền phong
Việt chính
Việt Nam
Việt Nam Thông Tấn Xã (VTX)
Washington Post and Times Herald
Xã hội

UNPUBLISHED AND INFORMALLY PUBLISHED MATERIALS

Bourdeaux, Pascal. "Émergence et constitution de la communauté du bouddhisme Hòa Hảo: Contribution à l'histoire sociale du delta du Mékong, 1935–1955." Phd diss., École pratique des hautes études, 2003.

Bùi Thị Thu Hà. "Đồng bào Phật Giáo Hòa Hảo An Giang trong cuộc Kháng Chiến Chống Mỹ Cứu Nước (1954–1975)." Phd diss., Trường Đại Học Sự Phạm Hà Nội, 2002.

"The Can-Lao Charter." In Donnell, "Politics in South Vietnam," appendix A, 555–576.

Donnell, John. "Politics in South Vietnam: Doctrines of Authority in Conflict." Phd diss., University of California, Berkeley, 1964.

"Draft Constitution Written by the Constitutional Commission Established by Presidential Decree No. 25, November 28, 1955." In Weiner, "Government and Politics," appendix B, 160–184.

Hansen, Peter. "The Virgin Heads South: Northern Catholic Refugees in South Vietnam, 1954–1964." PhD diss., Melbourne College of Divinity, 2008.

Hồ Hữu Tường. "Le défi vietnamien." Unpublished memoir, June 30, 1969. Typescript.

"In Memoriam: Huynh Sanh Thong." *YaleNews*, November 26, 2008. https://news.yale.edu/2008/11/26/memoriam-huynh-sanh-thong.

Keo, Siti. "Writing the Postcolonial City: Phnom Penh and Modernity during *Sangkum Reastr Niyum*, 1955–1970." PhD diss., University of California, Berkeley, 2019.

Li, Kevin. "Entrepreneurs of Disorder: Gangsters, Revolutionaries, and Collaborators During the Decolonization of Vietnam, 1945–1955." Unpublished manuscript, April 5, 2021.

Lữ Sanh Hạnh. "Some Stages of the Revolution in South Vietnam." Encyclopedia of Trotskyism Online, Marxists Internet Archive. Originally published in *Vietnam and Trotskyism*, edited by Simon Pirani ([Sydney?]: Communist League, 1987). Accessed July 23, 2020. https://www.marxists.org/history/etol/revhist/backiss/vol3/no2/hanh.html.

Nelson, Ryan. "The Struggle to Build a Viable, Modern Vietnamese State, 1945 to 1966: The Life and Death of Tran Van Van." Master's thesis, University of Wisconsin, Madison, 2013.

Nguyen, Martina. "The Self-Reliant Literary Group (Tự Lực Văn Đoàn): Colonial Modernism in Vietnam, 1932–1941." PhD diss., University of California, Berkeley, 2012.

Nguyen, Phi Van. "Les résidus de la guerre, la mobilisation des réfugiés du nord pour un Vietnam non-communiste, 1954–1965." Phd diss., Université de Québec à Montréal, 2015.

Picard, Jason. "Fragmented Loyalties: The Great Migration's Impact on South Vietnam, 1954–1963." PhD diss., University of California, Berkeley, 2014.

Reilly, Brett. "The Origins of the Vietnamese Civil War and the State of Vietnam." Phd diss., University of Wisconsin, Madison, 2018.

"Tiểu sử chí sĩ Nhị Lang (1923–2005)." Việt Nam Hải Ngoại Liên Minh Chống Cộng. Accessed July 18, 2017. http://www.vnfa.com/vietlien. Site discontinued.

Tinh Tâm. *Tiểu Sử Cải Trạng Nguyễn Ngọc Trân tự Minh Nhựt, 1926–2020*. Sydney: Centre for Studies in Caodaism, April 2020. http://www.daotam.info/booksv/NguyenNgocTran/tieusucaitrangnguyenngoctran/tieusucaitrangnguyenngoctran.htm#CH%C6%AF%C6%A0NG%20II.

Trần Mỹ Vân. "Vietnam's Caodaism, Independence, and Peace: The Life and Work of Pham Cong Tac, 1890–1959." PROSEA Research Paper no. 38. Academia Sinica, Taipei, 2000.

Trần Thị Liên Claire. "Les catholiques vietnamiens pendant la guerre d'indépendance, 1945–1954." Phd diss., Institut d'études politiques de Paris, 1996. Microfiche.

"Tuyên Ngôn Caravelle: Tự Do Tiến Bộ." April 28, 1960. Accessed March 7, 2019. http://www.tranvanba.org/new_website/documenttvv/tuyenngon_tudotienbo.pdf.

Weiner, Marjorie. "Government and Politics in South Vietnam, 1954–1956." Master's thesis, Cornell University, 1960.

Zinoman, Peter. "Vietnamese Urban Intellectuals and Anti-Communism in the 1930s." Paper presented at the Annual Conference of the Association of Asian Studies, Honolulu, March 20, 2011.

PUBLISHED COLLECTIONS OF GOVERNMENT DOCUMENTS

Công báo Việt Nam Cộng Hòa (CBVNCH). Vol. 2. Saigon: Nha Tổng Thư Ký Phủ Tổng Thống, 1956.

Ngô Đình Diệm. *Con đường chính nghĩa (CĐCN)*. 8 vols. Saigon: Sở Báo Chí Thông Tin, Phủ Thủ Tướng, 1955–1962.

———. *Con đường chính nghĩa: Tập đặc biệt gồm các thông điệp, lời tuyên bố và chương trình hoạt động của Ngô Tổng Thống trong cuộc bầu cử tổng thống và phó tổng thống ngày 9 tháng 9 năm 1961 (CĐCN: Tập đặc biệt)*. Saigon: Tổng Nha Thông Tin, 1961.

220   Bibliography

US Department of State. *Foreign Relations of the United States, 1952–1954 (FRUS, 1952–1954)*. Vol. 13. *Indochina*. Washington, DC: Government Printing Office, 1985.

———. *Foreign Relations of the United States, 1955–1957 (FRUS, 1955–1957)*. Vol 1. *Vietnam*. Washington, DC: U.S. Government Printing Office, 1985.

———. *Foreign Relations of the United States, 1961–1963 (FRUS, 1961–1963)*. Vol. 1. *Vietnam*. Washington, DC: Government Printing Office, 1988. https://history.state.gov/historical-documents/frus1961-63v01.

Vấn đề thống nhất lãnh thổ. [Saigon?], [1960?].

VIETNAMESE-LANGUAGE PUBLICATIONS

Bầu cử Quốc Hội Lập Pháp khóa II, 1959. Saigon: Bộ Thông Tin, 1959. In TTLTQGII-ĐICH 1756.

BCH Liên Tỉnh Dân Xã MTNV. "Chương trình của Đảng Việt Nam Dân Chủ Xã Hội." In *Sấm giảng thi văn giáo lý toàn bộ*, by Huỳnh Phú Sổ, 441–443. Saigon: Ban Phổ Thông Giáo Lý Trung Ương, 1966.

Bùi Diễm. *Gọng kìm lịch sử: Hồi ký chính trị*. Paris: Cơ sở xuất bản Phạm Quang Khải, 2000.

Cao Văn Luận. *Bên giòng lịch sử*. Saigon: Trí Dũng, 1972.

Chánh nghĩa đã thắng. [Saigon?], c. 1955.

Chính Đạo [Vũ Ngự Chiêu]. *Việt Nam niên biểu nhân vật chí*. Houston, TX: Văn Hóa, 1993.

Cửu Long Lê Trọng Văn. *Những bí ẩn lịch sử dưới chế độ Ngô Đình Diệm*. San Diego, CA: Mẹ Việt Nam, 1989.

Đinh Xuân Quảng. "Vụ mười một: Tù đày hữu ích cho cách mạng." In Trần Tương, *Biến cố II*, 242–251.

Đoàn Thêm. *Hai mươi năm qua: Việc từng ngày, 1945–1964*. 1966. Reprint, Los Alamitos, CA: Xuân Thu, c. 1986.

Đỗ Mậu. *Việt Nam máu lửa quê hương tôi*. Self-published, 1986.

Hà Thúc Ký. *Sống còn với dân tộc*. Phương Nghi, 2009.

"Hiến Pháp Việt Nam Cộng Hòa." In *Ánh sáng dân chủ*, by Nguyễn Phương, appendix 1, 147–174. Saigon: self-published, 1957.

Hoàng Cơ Thụy. *Việt sử khảo luận*. Vol. 5. Paris: Nam Á, 2002.

Hoàng Văn Đào. *Việt Nam Quốc Dân Đảng: Lịch sử tranh đấu cận đại, 1927–1954*. 2nd ed. Saigon: self-published, 1970.

Huỳnh Phú Sổ. *Cách tu hiền và sự ăn ở của một người bổn đạo*. Santa Fe Springs, CA: Văn Phòng Phật Giáo Hải Ngoại, 1980.

Huỳnh Văn Cao. *Lòng ái quốc*. [Saigon?]: Fatima, 1970.

Huỳnh Văn Lang. *Ký ức Huỳnh Văn Lang*. Vol. 2, *Thời kỳ Việt Nam độc lập*. Self-published, 2012.

———. *Nhân chứng một chế độ*. Vol. 1–2. Westminster, CA: Văn Nghệ, n.d.

Lâm Lễ Trinh. "Chín năm bên cạnh T. T. Ngô Đình Diệm: Mạn đàm với cựu Đổng Lý Quách Tòng Đức." *Diễn đàn giáo dân* 45 (August 2005): 39–42.

Lê Nguyên Long. "Bất đắc dĩ khơi lại đống tro tàn." *Khai phóng* 7 (1981). Accessed September 10, 2017. http://sachhiem.net/LICHSU/L/LeNguyenLong.php.

Lê Nguyên Phu. "Trích cáo trạng do Trung tá Ủy viên chính phủ Tòa Án Quân Sự Đặc Biệt lập ra." In Trần Tương, *Biến cố II*, 314–328.

Lê Văn Dương. *Quân Lực Việt Nam Cộng Hòa trong giai đoạn hình thành, 1946–1955*. Saigon: Bộ Tổng Tham Mưu, 1972.

Lương Khải Minh [Trần Kim Tuyến] and Cao Vị Hoàng. *Làm thế nào để giết một tổng thống.* Vol. 1–2. [Saigon?], 1970.

Ngô Quang Huy. *Nhớ bạn xưa.* Saigon: Khai Trí, 1971.

Nguyễn Chánh Thi. *Việt Nam: Một trời tâm sự.* Los Alamitos, CA: Anh Thư, 1987.

Nguyễn Hiến Lê. *Hồi kí.* Vol. 2. Westminster, CA: Văn Nghệ, 1990.

Nguyễn Hữu Duệ. *Nhớ lại những ngày ở cạnh Tổng Thống Ngô Đình Diệm.* San Diego, CA: self-published, 2003.

Nguyễn Kiên Hùng. "Binh biến 11/11/60." Interview by *Quốc Dân.* In *Nhìn lại biến cố 11/11/1960,* edited by Chính Đạo, 179–206. [Houston, TX?]: Văn Hóa, 1997.

Nguyễn Liệu. *Đời tôi.* Tiếng Quê Hương, 2008.

Nguyễn Long Thành Nam. *Phật Giáo Hòa Hảo trong dòng lịch sử dân tộc.* Santa Fe Springs, CA: Đuốc Từ Bi, 1991.

Nguyễn Lý Tưởng. "Thư số 16: Bộ trưởng thăm Miền Trung." In Trần Đỗ Cung, *Ông bà Nguyễn Tôn Hoàn,* 157–160.

Nguyễn Phúc Thành, ed. *Hòa Bình Chung Sống biên niên.* Sydney: Centre for Studies in Caodaism, 2015. Accessed June 9, 2021. http://www.daotam.info/booksv/pdf/Nguyen-PhucThanh/hoabinhchungsongbiennien.pdf.

Nguyễn Thành Vinh. "Mặt Trận Quốc Dân Đoàn Kết trong biến cố 11–11–1960." In Trần Tương, *Biến cố 11,* 133–145.

Nguyễn Trân. *Công và tội: Hồi ký lịch sử chính trị Miền Nam Việt Nam, 1945–1975.* Los Alamitos, CA: Xuân Thu, 1992.

Nguyễn Tường Bách. *Việt Nam một thế kỷ qua.* [Santa Ana?], CA: Thạch Ngữ, 1998.

Nguyễn Tường Thiết. "Chuyến tàu trong đêm." In Nhất Linh, et al., *Nhất Linh, người nghệ sĩ, người chiến sĩ,* 307–326.

Nguyễn Văn Cẩn. *Công giáo và cộng sản.* 2nd ed. [Saigon?], 1956.

———. *Phê bình dự án hiến pháp Việt Nam Cộng Hòa 1956.* Saigon: Nam Sơn, 1964.

Nguyễn Văn Chức. *Việt Nam chính sử.* San Jose, CA: Tiền Phong, 1989.

Nguyễn Văn Minh. *Dòng họ Ngô Đình: Ước mơ chưa đạt.* 4th ed. Garden Grove, CA, 2003.

Nguyễn Văn Nam. *Niên giám Quốc Hội Việt Nam: Quốc Hội Lập Pháp, pháp nhiệm khóa II.* Saigon: Phương Nam Văn Nghệ, 1959.

Nguyễn Vy Khanh. Introduction to *Ngô Đình Diệm, nỗ lực hòa bình dang dở,* by Nguyễn Văn Châu, 7–10. Translated by Nguyễn Vy Khanh. Los Alamitos, CA: Xuân Thu, 1989.

Nguyệt Đàm and Thần Phong. *Chín năm máu lửa dưới chế độ gia đình trị Ngô Đình Diệm.* [Saigon?]: self-published, 1964.

Nha Chiến Tranh Tâm Lý. *Sống chung?* Saigon: Bộ Quốc Phòng, 1955.

Nhất Linh, et al. *Nhất Linh, người nghệ sĩ, người chiến sĩ.* Westminster, CA: Thế Kỷ, 2004.

Nhị Lang. *Phong trào kháng chiến Trình Minh Thế.* Boulder, CO: Lion Press, 1985.

Phạm Công Tắc. *Lời thuyết đạo của Đức Hộ Pháp.* Vol. 1. New South Wales, Australia: Thánh Thất New South Wales, 2004. First published 1970 by Tòa Thánh Tây Ninh (Tây Ninh, Vietnam).

———. *Tìm hiểu Chánh Sách Hòa Bình Chung Sống.* Edited by Từ Vân. Sydney: Centre for Studies in Caodaism, 2013. Accessed June 9, 2021. http://www.daotam.info/booksv/pdf/pdf3/timhieuchanhsach-hoabinhchungsong.pdf.

Phạm Duy. *Hồi ký.* Vol. 3, *Thời cách mạng kháng chiến.* Midway City, CA: PDC Musical Productions, 1989.

Phạm Văn Liễu. *Trả ta sông núi.* Vol. 1. Houston, TX: Văn Hóa, 2002.

Phan Khắc Sửu. "Nhớ P-42." In Trần Tương, *Biến cố 11,* 155–157.

Phan Thị Bình. "Thư số 14: Hội nghị Hong Kong." In Trần Đỗ Cung, ed., *Ông bà Nguyễn Tôn Hoàn,* 145–152.

222 Bibliography

———. "Thư số 19: Lưu vong qua Pháp." In Trần Đỗ Cung, *Ông bà Nguyễn Tôn Hoàn*, 171–174.

———. "Thư số 22: Đi nghĩ hè ở Pháp." In Trần Đỗ Cung, *Ông bà Nguyễn Tôn Hoàn*, 199–208.

———. "Trà đàm với sinh viên Việt Canada và Bắc Mỹ." In Trần Đỗ Cung, *Ông bà Nguyễn Tôn Hoàn*, appendix 1, 233–241.

Quang Minh. *Cách mạng Việt Nam thời cận kim: Đại Việt Quốc Dân Đảng, 1938–1995.* Westminster, CA: Văn Nghệ, 2000.

Quốc Hội Lập Hiến. [Saigon?], 1956.

Tôn Thất Đính. *Hai mươi năm binh nghiệp.* San Jose, CA: Phụ Nữ Cali, 2013.

Trần Đỗ Cung, ed. *Ông bà Nguyễn Tôn Hoàn trong dòng sử Việt.* Santa Ana, CA: self-published, 2012.

Trần Quang Vinh. *Hồi ký Trần Quang Vinh và lịch sử Quân Đội Cao Đài.* Washington, DC: Thánh Thất Vùng Hoa Thịnh Đốn, 1997.

Trần Thị Hoa. *Hồi ký quân sử Nghĩa Quân Cách Mạng.* Derwood, MD: Giáo Hội Phật Giáo Hòa Hảo Hải Ngoại, 2002.

Trần Tương, ed. *Biến cố 11: Từ đảo chánh đến tù đày.* Saigon, 1971.

Trần Tương. "Tôi bị bắt." In Trần Tương, *Biến cố 11*, 146–153.

Trần Văn Ân. "Tưởng nhớ bạn Lương Trọng Tường." *Đuốc từ bi* 23 (November 1, 1986): 74–76.

Trần Văn Đôn. *Việt Nam nhân chứng.* Los Alamitos, CA: Xuân Thu, 1989.

Trần Văn Giàu. *Miền Nam giữ vững thành đồng.* Vol. 1. *1954–1960.* Hanoi: Nhà Xuất Bản Khoa Học, 1964.

Trần Văn Ngay. "Đảng Dân Chủ Tự Do và vụ án 11–11–1960." In Trần Tương, *Biến cố 11*, 191–197.

Trần Văn Thục. "Trích bản cáo trạng vụ án Caravelle." In Trần Tương, *Biến cố 11*, 404–415.

Trương Bảo Sơn. "Những kỷ niệm riêng về Nhất Linh Nguyễn Tường Tam." In Nhất Linh, et al., *Nhất Linh, người nghệ sĩ, người chiến sĩ*, 36–81.

Trường Giang. "Phú Yên, vùng địa linh nhân kiệt." *Thức tỉnh* 97–98 (Spring 1983): 47–52.

Tuyên cáo ngày 26-4-58 của chánh phủ Việt Nam Cộng Hòa về vấn đề thống nhất lãnh thổ. [Saigon?]: Bộ Thông Tin và Thanh Niên, 1958.

Việt Hồng. "Vài nét đấu tranh võ trang và lực lượng võ trang ở Nam Bộ trước cuộc Đồng Khởi 1959–1960." *Nghiên cứu lịch sử* 155 (March-April 1974): 39–55.

Vĩnh Phúc. *Những huyền thoại và sự thật về chế độ Ngô Đình Diệm.* London: Tam Vĩnh, 2006.

Võ Hòa Khanh. "100 ngày ở P-42." In Trần Tương, *Biến cố 11*, 158–183.

Vương Văn Đông. *Binh biến 11-11-60: Hồi ký.* Westminster, CA: Văn Nghệ, 2000.

Vương Kim [Phan Bá Cầm]. *Đức Huỳnh Giáo Chủ.* N.p.: VP Phật Giáo Hòa Hảo, 1997. Accessed May 6, 2020. https://www.hoahao.org/p74a2133/2/duc-huynh-giao-chu.

———. *Lập trường Dân Xã Đảng.* [Saigon?]: Dân Xã Tùng Thư, 1971.

WESTERN-LANGUAGE PUBLICATIONS

Ahern, Thomas, Jr. *The CIA and the House of Ngo.* Washington, DC: Center for the Study of Intelligence, 2000.

———. *CIA and Rural Pacification in South Vietnam.* Washington, DC: Center for the Study of Intelligence, 2001.

Anderson, David. *Trapped by Success: The Eisenhower Administration and Vietnam, 1953–61.* New York: Columbia University Press, 1991.

Bảo Đại. *Le dragon d'Annam*. Paris: Plon, 1980.

Bergère, Marie-Claire. *Sun Yat-sen*. Translated by Janet Lloyd. Stanford, CA: Stanford University Press, 1994.

Biggs, David. *Footprints of War: Militarized Landscapes in Vietnam*. Seattle: University of Washington Press, 2018.

———. *Quagmire: Nation-Building and Nature in the Mekong Delta*. Seattle: University of Washington Press, 2010.

Blagov, Sergei. *Caodaism: Vietnamese Traditionalism and Its Leap Into Modernity*. Huntington, NY: Nova Science Publishers, 2001.

———. *Honest Mistakes: The Life and Death of Trình Minh Thế, 1922–1955, South Vietnam's Alternative Leader*. Huntington, NY: Nova Science Publishers, 2001.

Bourdeaux, Pascal. "Approches statistiques de la communauté du bouddhisme Hòa Hảo, 1939–1954." In Goscha and de Tréglodé, *Naissance d'un état-parti*, 277–304.

Bousquet, Gisèle. *Behind the Bamboo Hedge: The Impact of Homeland Politics in the Parisian Vietnamese Community*. Ann Arbor: University of Michigan Press, 1991.

Bùi Diễm. *In the Jaws of History*. Boston, MA: Houghton Mifflin, 1987.

Buttinger, Joseph. *Vietnam: A Dragon Embattled*. Vol. 2, *Vietnam at War*. New York: Praeger, 1967.

———. *Vietnam: The Unforgettable Tragedy*. New York: Horizon Press, 1977.

Capoccia, Giovanni. "Militant Democracy: The Institutional Bases of Democratic Self-Preservation." *Annual Review of Law and Social Science* 9 (November 2013): 207–226.

Carter, James. *Inventing Vietnam: The United States and State Building, 1954–1968*. Cambridge: Cambridge University Press, 2008.

Catton, Philip. *Diem's Final Failure: Prelude to America's War in Vietnam*. Lawrence: University Press of Kansas, 2002.

Caulfield, Jeffrey. *General Walker and the Murder of President Kennedy: The Extensive New Evidence of a Radical-Right Conspiracy*. Moreland, OH: Moreland Press, 2015.

Caulkins, Laura. *China and the First Vietnam War, 1947–1954*. New York: Routledge, 2013.

Chandler, David. *A History of Cambodia*. 4th ed. Boulder, CO: Westview Press, 2008.

———. *The Tragedy of Cambodian History: Politics, War, and Revolution Since 1945*. New Haven, CT: Yale University Press, 1991.

Chang, Sidney, and Leonard Gordon. *All Under Heaven: Sun Yat-sen and His Revolutionary Thought*. Stanford, CA: Hoover Institution Press, 1991.

Chapman, Jessica. *Cauldron of Resistance: Ngo Dinh Diem, the United States, and 1950s Southern Vietnam*. Ithaca, NY: Cornell University Press, 2013.

Chen Jian. "China and the First Indo-China War, 1950–1954." *China Quarterly* 133 (March 1993): 85–110.

Corley, Francis, Jr. "Viet-Nam Since Geneva." *Thought* 33, no. 131 (1958): 515–568.

Currey, Cecil. *Edward Lansdale: The Unquiet American*. Washington, DC: Brassey's, 1998.

Demery, Monique. *Finding the Dragon Lady: The Mystery of Vietnam's Madame Nhu*. New York: Public Affairs, 2014.

Donnell, John. "Personalism in Vietnam." In *Problems of Freedom*, 29–58. Edited by Wesley Fishel. New York: Free Press of Glencoe, 1961.

Deweer, Dries. "The Political Theory of Personalism: Maritain and Mounier on Personhood and Citizenship." *International Journal of Philosophy and Theology* 74, no. 2 (2013): 108–126.

Dror, Olga. *Making Two Vietnams: War and Youth Identities, 1965–1975*. Cambridge: Cambridge University Press, 2018.

224 Bibliography

Duiker, William. *The Communist Road to Power in Vietnam.* 2nd ed. Boulder, CO: Westview, 1996.

———. *The Rise of Nationalism in Vietnam, 1900–1941.* Ithaca, NY: Cornell University Press, 1976.

Elliott, David. *The Vietnamese War: Revolution and Social Change in the Mekong Delta, 1930–1975.* Concise ed. Armonk, NY: ME Sharpe, 2007.

Fall, Bernard. "Representative Government in the State of Vietnam." *Far Eastern Review* 23, no. 8 (August 1954): 122–125.

———. *The Two Viet-Nams: A Political and Military Analysis.* 2nd rev. ed. New York: Praeger, 1967.

Fear, Sean. "The Ambiguous Legacy of Ngô Đình Diệm in South Vietnam's Second Republic, 1967–1975." *Journal of Vietnamese Studies* 11, no. 1 (winter 2016): 1–75.

Feith, Herbert. *The Decline of Constitutional Democracy in Indonesia.* Ithaca, NY: Cornell University Press, 1962.

Fifield, Russell. "The Five Principles of Peaceful Co-Existence." *American Journal of International Law* 52, no. 3 (July 1958): 504–510.

Fontaine, Ray. *The Dawn of Free Vietnam: A Biographical Sketch of Doctor Phan Quang Dan.* Brownsville, TX: Pan American Business Services, 1992.

Frankum, Ronald, Jr. *Vietnam's Year of the Rat: Elbridge Durbrow, Ngo Đình Diệm and the Turn in US Relations, 1959-1961.* Jefferson, NC: McFarland, 214.

Goodman, Allan. *Politics in War: The Bases of Political Community in South Vietnam.* Cambridge, MA: Harvard University Press, 1973.

Goscha, Christopher. "A 'Popular' Side of the Vietnamese Army: General Nguyễn Bình and the War in the South." In Goscha and de Tréglodé, *Naissance d'un état-parti*, 324–353.

———. *Vietnam: A New History.* New York: Basic Books, 2016.

Goscha, Christopher, and Benoit de Tréglodé, ed. *Naissance d'un état-parti: Le Viêt Nam depuis 1945.* Paris: Les Indes Savantes, 2004.

Grant, J. A. C. "The Viet Nam Constitution of 1956." *American Political Science Review* 52, no. 2 (June 1958): 437–462.

Guillemot, François. *Dai Viêt, indépendence et révolution au Viêt-Nam: L'échec de la troisième voie, 1938–1955.* Paris: Les Indes Savantes, 2012.

Hammer, Ellen. *The Struggle for Indochina, 1940–1955: Viet Nam and the French Experience.* Stanford, CA: Stanford University Press, 1955.

Hansen, Peter. "Bắc Di Cư: Catholic Refugees from the North of Vietnam and Their Role in the Southern Republic, 1954–1959." *Journal of Vietnamese Studies* 4, no. 3 (Fall 2009): 173–211.

———. "The Virgin Heads South: Northern Catholic Refugees and Their Clergy in South Vietnam, 1954–1964." In *Casting Faiths: Imperialism and the Transformation of Religion in East and Southeast Asia,* edited by Thomas Dubois, 129–151. New York: Palgrave, 2009.

Hémery, Daniel. *Révolutionnaires vietnamiens et pouvoir colonial en Indochine.* Paris: François Maspero, 1975.

Herring, George. *America's Longest War: The United States and Vietnam, 1950–1975.* 5th ed. New York: McGraw-Hill, 2014.

Holcombe, Alec. *Mass Mobilization in the Democratic Republic of Vietnam, 1945–1960.* Honolulu: University of Hawai'i Press, 2020.

Honey, P. J. "The Problem of Democracy in Vietnam." *World Today* 16, no. 2 (Feb 1960): 71–79.

Hoskins, Janet. *The Divine Eye and the Diaspora: Vietnamese Syncretism Becomes Transpacific Caodaism.* Honolulu: University of Hawai'i Press, 2015.

Bibliography   225

Huỳnh Kim Khánh. *Vietnamese Communism, 1925–1945*. Ithaca, NY: Cornell University Press, 1982.

Huỳnh Sanh Thông. Interview by Peter Zinoman. *Journal of Vietnamese Studies* 3, no. 1 (Winter 2008): 220–239.

Hy Văn Lương. *Tradition, Revolution, and Market Economy in a North Vietnamese Village, 1925–2006*. Honolulu: University of Hawai'i Press, 2010.

Jacobs, Seth. *Cold War Mandarin: Ngo Dinh Diem and the Origins of America's War in Vietnam, 1950–1963*. Lanham, MD: Rowman and Littlefield, 2006.

Jammes, Jérémy. *Les oracles du Cao Đài: Étude d'un movement religieux vietnamien et de ses réseaux*. Paris: Les Indes Savantes, 2014.

Jasper, William. "Passing of a Patriot," *New American* 18, no. 23 (November 18, 2002): 22–30.

Joiner, Charles. *The Politics of Massacre: Political Processes in South Vietnam*. Philadelphia, PA: Temple University Press, 1974.

Kahin, George. *Intervention: How America Became Involved in Vietnam*. New York: Anchor Books, 1987.

———. *Nationalism and Revolution in Indonesia*. Ithaca, NY: Cornell Southeast Asia Program, 2003.

Karnow, Stanley. *Vietnam: A History*. New York: Penguin Books, 1997.

Kolko, Gabriel. *Anatomy of a War: Vietnam, the United States, and the Modern Historical Experience*. New York: Pantheon Books, 1985.

Keith, Charles. *Catholic Vietnam: A Church from Empire to Nation*. Berkeley: University of California Press, 2012.

Kennedy, John F. "America's Stake in Vietnam: The Cornerstone of the Free World in Southeast Asia." *Vital Speeches of the Day* 22 (August 1, 1956): 617–619.

Kraus, Charles. "A Border Region 'Exuded with Militant Friendship': Provincial Narratives of China's Participation in the First Indochina War, 1949–1954." *Cold War History* 12, no. 3 (August 2012): 495–514.

K'ung Tzŭ Chia Yü: The School Sayings of Confucius. Translated by R. P. Kramers. Leiden: E. J. Brill, 1950.

Lancaster, Donald. *The Emancipation of French Indochina*. New York: Oxford University Press, 1961.

Langguth, A. J. *Our Vietnam: The War, 1954–1975*. New York: Simon and Schuster, 2000.

Lansdale, Edward. *In the Midst of War: An American's Mission to Southeast Asia*. New York: Fordham University Press, 1991.

Lev, Daniel. *The Transition to Guided Democracy: Indonesian Politics, 1957-1959*. Jakarta: Equinox Publishing, 2009.

Lockhart, Greg. *Nation in Arms: The Origins of the People's Army of Vietnam*. Sydney: Allen and Unwin, 1989.

Logevall, Fredrik. *Embers of War: The Fall of an Empire and the Making of America's Vietnam*. New York: Random House, 2012.

Lerner, Warren. "The Historical Origins of the Soviet Doctrine of Peaceful Coexistence." *Law and Contemporary Problems* 29, no. 4 (Fall 1964): 865–870.

Li, Kevin. "Partisan to Sovereign: The Making of the Bình Xuyên in Southern Vietnam, 1945–1948." *Journal of Vietnamese Studies* 11, no. 3–4 (Summer-Fall 2016): 140–187.

Li, Xiaobing. *Building Ho's Army: Chinese Military Assistance to North Vietnam*. Lexington: University of Kentucky Press, 2019.

Lucier, James. "Hilaire du Berrier: Spy from North Dakota." *Insight on the News* 15, no. 1 (1999): 21.

226   Bibliography

Marr, David. *Vietnam 1945: The Quest for Power*. Berkeley: University of California Press, 1995.

———. *Vietnam: State, War, and Revolution, 1945–1946*. Berkeley: University of California Press, 2013.

———. *Vietnamese Anticolonialism, 1885–1925*. Berkeley: University of California Press, 1971.

———. *Vietnamese Tradition on Trial, 1920–1945*. Berkeley: University of California Press, 1980.

McCoy, Alfred, Cathleen Read, and Leonard Adams II. *The Politics of Heroin in Southeast Asia*. New York: Harper and Row, 1972.

McHale, Shawn. *The First Vietnam War: Violence, Sovereignty, and the Fracture of the South, 1945-1956*. Cambridge: Cambridge University Press, 2021.

———. "Understanding the Fanatic Mind? The Việt Minh and Race Hatred in the First Indochina War, 1945–1954." *Journal of Vietnamese Studies* 4, no. 3 (Fall 2009): 98–138.

———. "Freedom, Violence, and the Struggle over the Public Arena in the Democratic Republic of Vietnam, 1945–1958." In Goscha and de Tréglodé, *Naissance d'un état-parti*, 81–99.

Miller, Edward. *Misalliance: Ngo Dinh Diem, the United States, and the Fate of South Vietnam*. Cambridge, MA: Harvard University Press, 2013.

———. "Religious Revival and the Politics of Nation Building: Reinterpreting the 1963 'Buddhist crisis' in South Vietnam." *Modern Asian Studies* 49, no. 6 (November 2015): 1903–1962.

Morgan, Joseph. *Vietnam Lobby: The American Friends of Vietnam, 1955–1975*. Chapel Hill: University of North Carolina Press, 1997.

Mounier, Emmanuel. *A Personalist Manifesto*. Translated by St. John's Abbey. New York: Longmans, Green, 1938.

Moyar, Mark. *Triumph Forsaken: The Vietnam War, 1954–1965*. Cambridge: Cambridge University Press, 2006.

Nation, R. Craig. *Black Earth, Red Star: A History of Soviet Security Policy, 1917–1991*. Ithaca, NY: Cornell University Press, 1992.

Nehru, Jawaharlal. *Jawaharlal Nehru's Speeches*. Vol. 3, *March 1953–August 1957*. 3rd ed. New Delhi: Ministry of Information and Broadcasting, Government of India, 1983.

———. "Speech by Prime Minister Nehru before the Political Committee of the Asian-African Conference, April 22, 1955." In *The Asian-African Conference*, edited by George Kahin, 64–72. Ithaca, NY: Cornell University Press, 1956.

Ngô Văn [Xuyết]. *Việt-Nam, 1920–1945: Révolution et contre-révolution sous la domination coloniale*. Paris: Nautilus, 2000.

———. *In the Crossfire: Adventures of a Vietnamese Revolutionary*. Translated by Hélène Fleury, Hilary Horrocks, Ken Knabb, and Naomi Sager. Edited by Knabb and Fleury. Oakland, CA: AK Press, 2010.

Nguyễn Công Luận. *Nationalist in the Viet Nam Wars: Memoirs of a Victim Turned Soldier*. Bloomington: Indiana University Press, 2012.

Nguyen, Duy. *The Unimagined Community: Imperialism and Culture in South Vietnam*. Manchester: Manchester University Press, 2020.

Nguyen, Phi Van. "Fighting the First Indochina War Again?: Catholic Refugees in South Vietnam, 1954–59." *Sojourn* 31, no. 1 (Mar 2016): 207–246.

Nguyễn Thái. *Is South Vietnam Viable?* Manila: Carmelo and Bauermann, 1962.

Nguyễn Thế Anh. "The Formulation of the National Discourse in 1940–45 Vietnam." *Journal of International and Area Studies* 9, no. 1 (June 2002): 57–75.

Nguyễn Thế Truyền. *Pour la libération de tous les détenus politiques nationalistes, pour la rénovation policière du Sud-Vietnam, pour la création du Secrétariat d'État à la guerre politique*. 2nd ed. [Saigon?], 1965.

Nguyễn Tuyết Mai. "Electioneering: Vietnamese Style." *Asian Survey* 2, no. 9 (November 1962): 11–18.

Nguyen, Y. "(Re)making the South Vietnamese Past in America." *Journal of Asian American Studies* 21, no. 1 (February 2018): 65–103.

Nguyen-Marshall, Van. "Tools of Empire? Vietnamese Catholics in South Vietnam." *Journal of the Canadian Historical Association* 20, no. 2 (2009): 138–159.

———. Review of *Vietnam's Lost Revolution*, by Geoffrey Stewart. *H-Diplo* 19, no. 45 (July 23, 2018): 14–15.

Ninh, Kim. *A World Transformed: The Politics of Culture in Revolutionary Vietnam, 1945–1965*. Ann Arbor: University of Michigan Press, 2002.

Nolting, Frederick. *From Trust to Tragedy: The Political Memoirs of Frederick Nolting*. New York: Praeger, 1988.

Nutt, Anita. *Regroupment, Withdrawals, and Transfers—Vietnam, 1954–1955*. Part 1. Santa Monica, CA: Rand Corporation, 1969.

Olson, Gregory. *Mansfield and Vietnam: A Study in Rhetorical Adaptation*. Lansing: Michigan State University Press, 1995.

Osborne, Milton. *The French Presence in Cochinchina and Cambodia: Rule and Response, 1859–1905*. Ithaca, NY: Cornell University Press, 1969.

Peycam, Philippe. *Birth of Vietnamese Political Journalism: Saigon 1916–1930*. New York: Columbia University Press, 2012.

Pham, David. *Two Hamlets in Nam Bo: Memoirs of Life in Vietnam through Japanese Occupation, the French and American Wars, and Communist Rule, 1940–1986*. Jefferson, NC: McFarland, 2000.

Phan Bội Châu. "A Letter from Abroad Written in Blood (1907)." In *Sources of Vietnamese Tradition*, 353–369. Edited by George Dutton, Jayne Werner, and John Whitmore. New York: Columbia University Press, 2012.

Phan Châu Trinh. "Monarchy and Democracy." In *Phan Châu Trinh and His Political Writings*, 125–139. Edited and translated by Vĩnh Sinh. Ithaca, NY: Cornell Southeast Asia Program, 2009.

Phan Quang Đán. *Volonté vietnamienne*. 1st ed. [Geneva?]: Thiết Thực, 1951.

———. *Volonté vietnamienne*. 2nd ed. Geneva: Imprimeries Populaires, 1955.

Phan Quang Tuệ. "From the First to the Second Republic: From Scylla to Charybdis." In *Voices from the Second Republic of South Vietnam, 1967–1975*, edited by K. W. Taylor, 117–126. Ithaca, NY: Cornell Southeast Asia Program, 2014.

Philipps, Rufus. *Why Vietnam Matters: An Eyewitness Account of Lessons Not Learned*. Annapolis, MD: Naval Institute Press, 2008.

Picard, Jason. "'Fertile Lands Await': The Promise and Pitfalls of Directed Resettlement, 1954–1958." *Journal of Vietnamese Studies* 11, no. 3-4 (Summer-Fall 2016): 58–102.

Picard, Jason. "'Renegades': The Story of South Vietnam's First National Opposition Newspaper, 1955–1958." *Journal of Vietnamese Studies* 10, no. 4 (Fall 2015): 1–29.

Prados, John. *Vietnam: History of an Unwinnable War*. Lawrence: University Press of Kansas, 2009.

Quinn-Judge, Sophie. *Ho Chi Minh: The Missing Years, 1919–1941*. Berkeley: University of California Press, 2003.

———. *The Third Force in the Vietnam War: The Elusive Search for Peace, 1954–75*. London: IB Tauris, 2017.

228   Bibliography

Race, Jeffrey. *War Comes to Long An: Revolutionary Conflict in a Vietnamese Province.* Berkeley: University of California Press, 1972.

Reilly, Brett. "The Sovereign States of Vietnam, 1945–1955." *Journal of Vietnamese Studies* 11, no. 3–4 (Summer-Fall 2016): 103–139.

Sacks, Milton I. "Marxism in Vietnam." In *Marxism in Southeast Asia*, ed. Frank Trager, 102–170. Stanford, CA: Stanford University Press, 1959.

Savani, A. M. *Notes sur les Binh Xuyen.* Saigon, 1954.

———. *Notes sur le Caodaisme.* Saigon, 1954.

———. *Notes sur la secte Phat Giao Hoa Hao.* Saigon, 1951.

———. *Visage et images du Sud Viet-Nam.* Saigon: Imprimerie Française d'Outre-mer, 1955.

Scigliano, Robert. "The Electoral Process in South Vietnam: Politics in an Underdeveloped State." *Midwest Journal of Political Science* 4, no. 2 (May 1960): 138–161.

———. *South Vietnam: Nation under Stress.* Boston, MA: Houghton Mifflin, 1963.

Shaplen, Robert. *The Lost Revolution: The US in Vietnam, 1946–1966.* Rev. ed. New York: Harper and Row, 1966.

Simpson, Howard. *Tiger in the Barbed Wire: An American in Vietnam, 1952–1991.* Washington, DC: Brassey's, 1992.

Spector, Ronald. *Advice and Support: The Early Years of the United States Army in Vietnam, 1941–1960.* Washington, DC: Center for Military History, 1983.

Statler, Kathryn. *Replacing France: The Origins of American Intervention in Vietnam.* Lexington: University Press of Kentucky, 2007.

Stewart, Geoffrey. *Vietnam's Lost Revolution: Ngô Đình Diệm's Failure to Build an Independent Nation, 1955–1963.* Cambridge: Cambridge University Press, 2017.

Tan, Stan B. H. "Swiddens, Resettlements, Sedentarizations, and Villages: State Formation among the Central Highlanders of Vietnam under the First Republic, 1955–1961." *Journal of Vietnamese Studies* 1, no. 1–2 (February/August 2006), 210–252.

Tai, Hue Tam Ho. *Millenarianism and Peasant Politics in Vietnam.* Cambridge, MA: Harvard University Press, 1983.

———. *Radicalism and the Origins of the Vietnamese Revolution.* Cambridge, MA: Harvard University Press, 1992.

Tam [Vũ Văn Cường]. *Vietnam's War, 1940–1975: The Causes of French and American Failures in Vietnam.* Lawrenceville, VA: Brunswick Publishing, 1983.

Thayer, Carlyle. *War by Other Means: National Liberation and Revolution in Viet-Nam, 1954–1960.* Sydney: Allen and Unwin, 1989.

Tonnesson, Stein. *Vietnam 1946: How the War Began.* Berkeley: University of California Press, 2010.

Trần Mỹ Vân. "Beneath the Japanese Umbrella: Vietnam's Hòa Hảo During and After the Pacific War." *Crossroads* 17, no. 1 (2003): 60–107.

———. "Japan and Vietnam's Caodaists: A Wartime Relationship, 1939–45." *Journal of Southeast Asian Studies* 27, no. 1 (March 1996): 179–193.

———. *A Vietnamese Royal Exile in Japan: Prince Cường Để, 1882–1951.* London: Routledge, 2005.

Tran, Nu-Anh. "'Let History Render Judgement on My Life': The Suicide of Nhất Linh (Nguyễn Tường Tam) and the Making of a Martyr in the Republic of Vietnam." *Journal of Vietnamese Studies* 15, no. 3 (2020): 79–118.

Tran, Nu-Anh and Tuong Vu. Introduction to *Building a Republican Nation in Postcolonial Vietnam, 1920–1963.* Edited by Nu-Anh Tran and Tuong Vu. Honolulu: University of Hawai'i Press, forthcoming.

Trương Vĩnh Lễ. *Vietnam, où est la verité?* Paris: Lauvauzelle, 1989.

Bibliography 229

Turley, William. *The Second Indochina War: A Short Political and Military History, 1954–1975*. Boulder, CO: Westview Press, 1986.

Vĩnh Sinh. Introduction to *Phan Châu Trinh and His Political Writings*, by Phan Châu Trinh, 1–55. Edited and translated by Vĩnh Sinh. Ithaca, NY: Cornell Southeast Asia Program, 2009.

Vĩnh Sinh and Nicholas Wickenden. Introduction to *Overturned Chariot: The Autobiography of Phan-Bội-Châu*, by Phan Bội Châu, 1–37. Translated by Vĩnh Sinh and Nicholas Wickenden. Honolulu: University of Hawai'i Press, 1999.

Vo-Dang, Thuy. "The Cultural Work of Anticommunism in the San Diego Vietnamese American Community." *Amerasia Journal* 32, no. 2 (2005): 65–86.

Vũ Ngự Chiêu. "The Other Side of the 1945 Vietnamese Revolution: The Empire of Viet-Nam (March-August 1945)." *Journal of Asian Studies* 45, no. 2 (February 1986): 293–328.

Vu, Tuong. " 'It's Time for the Indochinese Revolution to Show Its True Colours': The Radical Turn of Vietnamese Politics in 1948." *Journal of Southeast Asian Studies* 40, no. 3 (October 2009): 519–543.

———. *Vietnam's Communist Revolution: The Power and Limits of Ideology*. New York: Cambridge University Press, 2017.

Warner, Dennis. *Last Confucian*. New York: Macmillan, 1963.

Werner, Jayne. *Peasant Politics and Religious Sectarianism: Peasant and Priest in the Cao Dai in Vietnam*. New Haven, CT: Yale University Southeast Asian Studies, 1981.

Wherle, Edmund. *Between a River and a Mountain: The AFL-CIO and the Vietnam War*. Ann Arbor: University of Michigan Press, 2005.

Worthing, Peter. *Occupation and Revolution: China and the Vietnamese August Revolution of 1945*. Berkeley: Institute of East Asian Studies, University of California, 2001.

Young, Marilyn. *The Vietnam Wars, 1945–1990*. New York: Harper Perennial, 1991.

Zinoman, Peter. *The Colonial Bastille: A History of Imprisonment in Vietnam, 1862–1940*. Berkeley: University of California Press, 2001.

———. *Vietnamese Colonial Republican: The Political Vision of Vũ Trọng Phụng*. Berkeley: University of California Press, 2014.

Zhai, Qiang. *China and the Vietnam Wars, 1950–1975*. Chapel Hill: University of North Carolina Press, 2000.

Index

Page numbers in **bold** refer to figures and tables.

Agroville Program, 125, 136–137, 138, 139, 140

Anti-French Resistance (1945–1954), 5, 14, 25, 63, 107, 136

Army of the Republic of Vietnam (ARVN): assassination of Diệm and Nhu, 166–167; and attempted coup on Diệm (1960), 135, 142–148, 156–157, 208n26; invasion of Tây Ninh province, 97; political favoritism in, 139, 141, 142, 143, 208n26. *See also* Vietnamese National Army (VNA)

Association for the Restoration of Vietnam (ARV): conflict within, 86; establishment, 28; General Phương's leadership of, 48; government efforts to suppress, 95, 97, 105, 197n133; newspapers, 84, 93; in plan to overthrow Bảo Đại, 87; in the Revolutionary Council, 79, 80

attentisme, 36–39

August Revolution, 23–25

Ba Lòng Resistance Zone, 67

Bandung Conference (1955), 113, 201n33

Bảo Đại: and anticommunist nationalists, 30–31, 34, 140; appointment by Japanese, 23; attempt to replace Diệm with Phan Huy Quát, 73–74, 76; and Bình Xuyên, 50; and Catholic nationalists, 32; compared to Sihanouk, 169; concessions for sects and other groups, 126; failure to obtain autonomy for State of Vietnam, 34, 41, 138; and the French, 31, 34, 43; and Hinh crisis, 59–60, 61, 62; and Ngô Đình Diệm, 36, 42–44, 53, 59–60, 73; organization of National Congress, 41; plan to overthrow, 76, 77, 78, 82, 83, 84–88, 164; and the United States, 43; urged to establish a constitution, 40

Bình Xuyên: accommodationist stance, 34, 40, 51; in Battle of Saigon, 2, 45, 46, 74–75, 76, 78; control of security forces, 50–51, 73; death sentence for eight members of, 121; encouragement of southward migration, 56; excluded from coalition government of 1954, 60, 61; final defeat, 88; and Hòa Hảo Buddhists, 29, 74; inclusion in "the sects," 35; military power and vice operations, 48, 50, 70–71, 75; opposition to Movement for Unity and Peace coalition, 41; and United Front of Nationalist Forces, 71; and Việt Minh, 24, 32. *See also* Lê Văn Viễn (General)

Buddhism, 21, 165–166, 167. *See also* Hòa Hảo Buddhists

Bùi Chu diocese, 24, 27, 51, 56

Bùi Văn Thinh, 80, 87

Bửu Lộc (Prince), 42, 44

Cái Vồn, 50, 86

Cà Mau peninsula, 55, 66

231

232   Index

Cambodia: Đại Việt radio station in, 112; as a democracy, 169–170; in French Indochina, 14; in Indochinese Federation, 26, 31; Vietnamese dissidents in, 94, 97, 105, 108, 113, 116, 161

Cần Lao party: conflicts of interest, 70; Diệm on importance of, 90; Durbrow's assessment of, 141–142; and 1959 election, 131; in 1956 election, 97; establishment, 38–39; and the Hinh crisis, 61; intelligence and surveillance activities, 85–86, 105, 126, 149, 150, 156; Lansdale's assessment of, 95; and the military, 52, 139, 141, 142; military wing, 148; and Movement for Unity and Peace, 40–41; and National Revolutionary Movement, 80; Ngô Đình Cẩn's branch of, 47; and Unity Committee, 153, 155

Cần Thơ city, 24–25, 50

Cao Đài religious group: autonomous zone, 35, 62–63, 66, 75, 79, 97, 139; and Bảo Đại, 31, 36, 82; in coalition government of 1954, 60, 62; complaints in *Contemporary Discourse,* 121; and the constitutional process, 94, 96–97; Diệm's suppression of, 97, 105; encouragement of southward migration, 56; growth and fragmentation, 22, 23; as indigenous Vietnamese faith, 21; as member of Big Five, 34; in Movement for Unity and Peace, 41; and neutralist, nonaligned movement, 115–116, 117; political stances, 8, 28, 30; relations with Hòa Hảo Buddhists, 29; and Revolutionary Council, 191n11; source materials from, 10; split between Tắc and General Phương within, 86; Tây Ninh sect, 22, 25, 39, 48, 116; and Trần Văn Văn–Phan Khắc Sửu clique, 139; at the Unity Congress, 40. *See also* Cao Đài sect army; Phạm Công Tắc

Cao Đài sect army: affiliation with political parties, 75, **79**; integration into Vietnamese National Army, 63–66, 71–73, 187n117, 189n167; led by General Phương, 48, 70; led by General Thế, 65; rise of Hồ Hán Sơn within, 80; Việt Minh attempt to integrate, 27. *See also* Nguyễn Thành Phương (General); Trình Minh Thế (General)

Caravelle Manifesto, 138–140, 146, 149, 154, 208n20

Catholic Church, 21, 126, 128–129

Catholic nationalists: and Diemists, 39, 75, 126, 146–147, 182n7; in Diệm's government, 53,

128; and DRV, 24, 32; military arm of, 35, 51; newspaper, 163; northern group, 34–35, 40, 56; political favoritism toward, 128, 165; southward migration, 57

Central Highlands, 125, 129, 142

Central Intelligence Agency (CIA): activities under Lansdale, 52–53, 56, 64, 95; and coalition government of 1954, 185n84; and constitutional process, 104; and Huỳnh Văn Lang, 131; and Nhu's intelligence service, 85; report on Bảo Đại plebiscite, 87; shallow understanding of Vietnamese politics, 1–2. *See also* Lansdale, Edward Geary

China, 15, 18, 29, 33, 34, 113

Chinese Communist Party, 18, 33

Chinese ethnic minority, 121, 132

Chinese Nationalist Party, 17, 18, 20, 25, 26

Christian Democratic Front, 146–147

Citizens' Rally (CR), 80, 97, 127

Cold War, 33–34, 108, 113, 116. *See also* Soviet Union; United States

Collins, J. Lawton, 54, 61, 63, 73–74, 111

Colombo Conference (1954), 113, 121

Combat (Chiến đấu), 58

Comintern, 18, 19, 20

Committee for Peaceful Coexistence (CPC), 117

Confucianism, 21, 116–117, 202n43

Congregation for Peace, 117–118

Contemporary Discourse (Thời luận), 108, 119, 120–123, 126, 132

Cường Để (Prince), 16, 21, 22, 23, 28

Đại Việt Nationalist Party: accommodationist stance, 31, 35; central branch, 70, 108, 109, 112, 130; establishment, 19, 177n33; exclusion from coalition government of 1954, 60; exclusion from Diệm's governments, 53, 60; failure to capitalize on Japanese defeat, 23; fragmentation, 35, 51; in the Movement for Unity and Peace, 41, 67; northern branch, 34, 57, 75, 109, 129–130, 135–136, 143; opposition to Diệm after 1955, 75, 109–111; outlawed by Democratic Republic of Vietnam, 24, 178n75; and Phan Quang Đán's study group, 94, 97; in post-Diệm government, 167; secession from State of Vietnam, 46, **68**, 69; secret cells in the national army, 52; southern branch, 61, 70, 94, 108, 109, 112, 130; in the struggle for central Vietnam, 67–71; at Unity Congress, 40

Index   233

Đặng Văn Sung, **17,** 51, 130, 156, 160, 161, 212n111
democracy: and Christianity, 103; and civil liberties, 15, 38, 84, 123; as a contentious idea, 8, 81, 91, 164; gradual implementation of, 108, 123, 151, 157, 164; "guided," 170; "militant," 92–93; in nationalist revolutionary movement, 13–14, 164–165; and national unity, 119; and neutralism, 114; as opposed to communism, 29, 76–77; and opposition politics, 93–96; and personalism, 82, 87, 98–99, 103, 123, 125, 141; Phan Châu Trinh's admiration for, 12, 76; "profligate," 167; sect parties' notion of, 82, 91–93; as signature issue of Democratic Bloc, 118; Vietnamese readiness for, 8, 141, 159, 160; Western paradigm of, 169
Democracy (Dân chủ), 103
Democratic Alliance, 143, 147, 149
Democratic Bloc (DB), 118–120, 122, 125, 130, 143, 157, 203n55
Democratic Republic of Vietnam (DRV): in Anti-French Resistance, 25, 30, 32; Catholic support for, 24, 27; conflict with General Thế, 39; declaration of independence of, 5–6, 23; defections from and radicalization of, 32–34, 47; and the Geneva Accords, 55, 57, 108; incorporation of anticommunist and religious groups, 25; land redistribution program, 124; and lower Mekong delta, 136; Phạm Công Tắc's peace proposal and, 114–115, 116; prohibitions on political opposition, 178n84; scholarship on, 3; threat posed to State of Vietnam by, 42. *See also* Hồ Chí Minh
Denounce the Communists Campaign, 85, 95, 101, 136
Diemists: and attempted coup of 1960, 135–136, 148–150, 154; *attentiste* stance, 36–39, 51, 58, 65; composition, 38, 46–48; and constitutional process, 88–91, 96–102, 103; in Diệm's governments, 53, 60, 61, 171–174; election interference, 86, 96–98, 130–133; encouragement of mass migration south, 56; espousal of personalism, 2, 37–38, 47; expansion of membership, 85, 125–26; illiberal, authoritarian stance, 7, 77, 82–83, 84, 91, 98, 108; in Movement for Unity and Peace, 41; plebiscite to remove Bảo Đại, 84–88, 164; in the Revolutionary Council, 78–79, 80–81, 84–85; and Revolutionary

Military Council, 167; in struggle for central Vietnam, 67–71, 75; suppression of the sects, 94–96, 105; at the Unity Congress, 40; view on unity, 155. *See also* Ngô Đình Diệm
Điện Biên Phủ, 43, 56
Đỗ Mạnh Quát, 125
Donnell, John, 148, 175n5
Du Berrier, Hilaire, 111, 112, 122, 200n19
Dulles, John Foster, 74–75
Durbrow, Elbridge (Ambassador): attitude to oppositionists, 141–142; on the Caravelle Manifesto, 208n20; and coup attempt of 1960, 145; efforts to influence Diệm, 133, 158, 160; Huỳnh Văn Lang's claims about, 131; on Vietnamese readiness for democracy, 159

Eisenhower, Dwight D., 2, 61
Ély, Paul (General), 52, 73
Élysée Accords (1949), 31, 36, 40, 41
Epoch (Thời đại), **79**

France: alliance with Bình Xuyên, 32; conflict with General Thế, 39; devaluation of piaster, 39–40; and elections of 1959, 133; at the Geneva Conference, 42, 43, 116; military alliances with anticommunist groups, 28, 29–30, 35–36, 50; Nguyễn Tôn Hoàn's efforts to persuade, 109; opposition to Diệm, 59; Phạm Công Tắc's peace proposal and, 116; as political model for Vietnam, 15, 83, 90; Vietnamese exile community in, 19, 91, 108, 111, 112, 168; war with Democratic Republic of Vietnam, 25, 27, 30, 32
Freedom and Democracy Party, 122
Freedom and Progress Bloc (FPB): and American views on liberalization, 141, 142; and attempted coup on Diệm (1960), 143, 147; establishment and aims, 140, 208n16; and Front for Democratization, 157; Phan Huy Quát and, 154; Phan Khắc Sửu and, 210n68; target of government crackdown, 149. *See also* Phan Khắc Sửu; Trần Văn Văn
Freedom (Tự do), 122
French colonial regime: administrative division of Vietnam, 10, 14; crackdown on communists, 21; and Indochinese Federation, 26; and Japanese occupation, 19; reformers within, 6, 16, 41; revolutionary movement against, 5–6, 13–14, 21; stated republican principles, 15, 164; suppression of Cao Đài group, 22

234 Index

French Communist Party, 18, 152
French Expeditionary Corps (FEC): arrival in
Vietnam, 27; in Battle of Saigon, 78; in
command of Vietnamese National Army, 31,
66; in conflict with Democratic Republic of
Vietnam, 30; departure from Vietnam, 105;
General Ély's command of, 52; and the
Geneva Accords, 55, 57, 66; and the sect and
northern Catholic armies, 35, 50, 64
French Union, 26, 41
Front for Democratization (FD), 156–157, 161

Geneva Accords (1954): agreement on troop
movements, 66; and mass migration
southward, 55–57; opposed by Lê Quang
Vinh, 64; partition of Vietnam, 1, 8, 10; plans
for reunification under, 107–108, 115
Geneva Conference, 42–43, 116
Gonder, Frank, 141, 208n16
Grant, J. A. C., 103–104
Great Britain, 27, 34, 36, 42, 116, 133

Hà Như Chi, 125
Hà Thúc Ký, **17**, 51, 67, 112, 113, 128
Heath, Donald R. (Ambassador), 52, 58, 59, 61
Hòa Hảo Buddhists: autonomous zone, 35,
62–63, 79, 139; and the Battle of Saigon, 74;
in coalition government of 1954, 60, 62;
conflict with Việt Minh, 24–25, 28–30;
cooperation with Japanese, 22; criticism of,
attentistes, 58; General Soái faction of, 30,
35–36, 41, 49–50; as member of Big Five, 34;
military arm of, 27, 48–49, 63–66, 71, 75;
opposition to Diệm after 1955, 75;
participation in Bảo Đại's conference, 31;
political power in the south, 23; source
materials from, 10; Trần Văn Văn–Phan
Khắc Sửu clique and, 138; at the Unity
Congress, 40. *See also* Lê Quang Vinh
(General); Nguyễn Bảo Toàn; Nguyễn Giác
Ngộ (General); Trần Văn Soái (General)
Hoàng Cơ Thụy: and coup attempt on Diệm,
143, 144, 145, 147; and Democratic Bloc,
118–119, 120, 122; in elections of 1959, 106,
130; on the Revolutionary Council, 195n86;
and Trần Văn Văn–Phan Khắc Sửu clique,
139
Hồ Chí Minh: and Chinese Nationalists, 25;
declaration of independence of DRV, 23;
emergence as leading communist, **17**, 18; as
leader of Việt Minh, 20; and Nguyễn Thế

Truyền, 152; and People's Republic of China,
33; Phạm Công Tắc's letter to, 115. *See also*
Democratic Republic of Vietnam (DRV);
Việt Minh
Ho Chi Minh City. *See* Saigon
Hồ Hán Sơn, **79**, 80, 82, 95, 191n11
Hồ Ngọc Cứ, 197n133
Hồ Nhựt Tân, 152, 161
Hồ Thông Minh, 64, 73
Hồ Văn Nhựt, 207n6
Hồ Văn Vui, 129, 138
Huế, 47, 85, 113
Huỳnh Hữu Nghĩa, 216n20
Huỳnh Phú Sổ, **17**, 22, 24, 28–29, 48, 50. *See
also* Hòa Hảo Buddhists
Huỳnh Sanh Thông, 111
Huỳnh Văn Lang, 123–124, 127, 131, 132

Independence Palace: Bình Xuyên's shelling
of, 73; bombing of (1962), 161; conference
during Battle of Saigon in, 76; in coup
attempt against Diệm, 143, 144, 146, 147; in
Hinh crisis, 61; as Norodom Palace, 52, 60
Indochinese Communist Party (ICP), 18, 19, 20,
21, 23, 25, 26. *See also* Hồ Chí Minh
Indochinese Federation, 26, 31

Japan, 14–15, 19, 21, 22–23, 25, 27

Kennedy, John F., 111, 157, 160

Lại Văn Sang, 50–51, 73, 183n26
Lâm Thành Nguyên (General), **17, 49**, 50, 64,
71, **79**, 86. *See also* Hòa Hảo Buddhists
Land Development Program, 125, 129
Lansdale, Edward Geary: background, 52–53;
claim on Bảo Đại plebiscite, 192n41; efforts
to influence Diệm, 83, 89, 95, 100–101; plan
to unite oppositionists, 158–159; and
southward mass migration, 56. *See also*
Central Intelligence Agency (CIA)
Laos, 14, 26, 31
League for the Restoration of Vietnam, 21
Lê Hữu Từ (Bishop): call for abrogation of
Élysée Accords, 40; and Christian
Democratic Front, 146; control of
autonomous zone, 27, 39, 51; and Democratic
Republic of Vietnam, 24, 32; as a leading
revolutionary, **17**; and Ngô Đình Diệm, 56,
57; and proposed alternative coalitions, 53,
59. *See also* Catholic nationalists

Lê Quang Luật, 138

Lê Quang Vinh (General): area controlled by, **49**, 66; attacked by Vietnamese National Army, 86; execution, 105; as a leader of Hòa Hảo, **17**, 50, **79**; propaganda against Ngô Đình Cẩn, 70; protest against Geneva Accords, 64; and Social Democratic Party, 187n124; in United Front of Nationalist Forces, 71

Lê Thành Tương, 197n133

Lê Văn Ty (General), 73, 76, 145, 147

Lê Văn Viễn (General): accommodationist stance, 32, 40, 180n153; in alternative coalitions to Diệm's government, 53, 61; autonomous zone in western Saigon, 35, 50; control of security service, 50–51, 73; encouragement of southward migration, 56; exile in France, 88, 111; as leader of Bình Xuyên, **17**, 45; ordered to close Grand Monde casino, 71; in plot to remove Diệm, 58, 59–60; in United Front of Nationalist Forces, 71; and the Unity Congress, 180n153. *See also* Bình Xuyên

Lương Trọng Tường, 138

The Masses (Quần chúng), 29, **79**, 81–82, 88, 89–90

Mekong delta: and communist insurgency, 134, 136; and Democratic Republic of Vietnam, 24, 28, 136; General Soái's autonomous zone in, 50; Hòa Hảo Buddhists in, 22, 24, 28, 36, 66, 86; land reforms in, 124, 125, 129; plantation society of, 29, 60; support for Đại Việt party in, 51

Mendenhall, Joseph, 141

Minh Sơn, 163

Mounier, Emmanuel, 37, 82, 99, 123. *See also* personalism

Movement for Unity and Peace (MUP), 40–41, 48, 51, 53, 54, 60, 67

Movement to Preserve Freedom (MPF), 80, 98

Movement to Safeguard the Nation (MSN), 111–112, 122

Nanjing Front, 30–31, 79, 146, 195n94

National Alliance Army, 48

National Congress, 41

National Liberation Front (NLF), 3, 159–160

National People's Solidarity Front, 146, 210n68

National Police and Security Service, 50–51

National Resistance Front (NRF), 48, 79, 80, 81, 94, 216n20

National Revolutionary Movement (NRM): Diệm on significance of, 90; and Diệm's cult of personality, 85; and elections, 131, 132, 151, 152; as a front for Cần Lao, 80; membership, 126; merger with Citizens' Rally, 127; and post-coup attempt crackdown (1960), 150

National Revolution (Cách mạng quốc gia), 85, 90, 93

The Nation (Quốc gia), **79**, 81

Nehru, Jawaharlal, 113, 114–115, 201n33

neutralism, 113–116

Nghiêm Xuân Thiện, 119, 120–121

Ngô Đình Cẩn: branch of Cần Lao party, 47, 69, 128, 182n7; and elections of 1959, 130; establishment of National Revolutionary Movement, 80; and Hinh crisis, 186n97; as a leader in Diemist faction, **17**, 46; in Movement for Unity and Peace, 60, 67; and Revolutionary Council, 90, 195n86; rumors about, 70; secret police force, 128; sentenced to death, 167

Ngô Đình Diệm: accused of "family rule," 95, 126, 139, 141, 151; assassination attempt against, 129, 163; authoritarianism of, 78, 84, 123, 166; capture and assassination, 166; clash with General Hinh, 58–60; in coalition government of 1954, 60–63, 66, 185n84, 216n10; and constitutional process, 81–84, 89, 96–97, 98–102, 105; and *Contemporary Discourse*, 121–122; coup attempts against, 135, 142–148, 156–157, 161, 208n26; cult of personality around, 83, 85, 112, 125; denunciation of sect armies, 71–72; and elections, 151; encouragement of southward migration, 56; French opposition to, 59; legacy, 168; Phạm Công Tắc's letter to, 115; political emergence, 7, 36–39, 42–44; press freedom under, 95–96; push for military centralization, 63–66; reforms of 1960–1961, 159; relations with Bình Xuyên, 51; relations with Catholic nationalists, 51, 56, 128–129; in scholarship on Vietnam, 4, 9–10; suspicions about Front for Democratization, 157; treatment of Buddhists, 165–166; understanding of democracy, 82, 98–99, 140–141, 151; understanding of unity, 45–46, 53–55, 65; and United States, 8–9, 37, 59, 74–75; view of nonalignment, 118. *See also* Diemists

236 Index

Ngô Đình Luyện, **17,** 43, 53, 61

Ngô Đình Nhu: American concerns about, 142; assassination attempt against, 161; building of personality cult around Diệm, 83, 192n36; capture and assassination, 166; and coalition government of 1954, 185n84; and constitutional process, 89, 90, 94, 95, 99; and 1959 elections, 130–131; in 1956 elections, 97; espousal of personalism, 2, 37–38; and Front for Democratization, 157; intelligence activities under, 85–86; leadership of Cần Lao, 46–47, 80, 126–127; as a leading revolutionary, **17,** 42; meeting with Trần Văn Văn–Phan Khắc Sửu clique, 138; and Movement for Unity and Peace, 40, 51, 53, 54; and Unity Committee, 156; and the Unity Congress, 180n153. *See also* Nhu, Madame

Ngô Đình Thục (Bishop), **17,** 37, 128–129, 167

Ngô Sách Vinh, 106

Ngô Trọng Hiếu, 213n127

Nguyễn Bảo Toàn: abduction and murder, 149; call for arrest of communists, 84; in the Democratic Alliance, 143; and elections of 1959, 130; escape to Cambodia, 94, 97, 105; as a Hòa Hảo leader, **17;** in Nanjing Front, 30; and overthrow of Bảo Đại, 191n11; and Phan Quang Đán, 91, 195n94; and proposal for appointed constituent assembly, 88; in Revolutionary Council, 79–80, 82, 90, 94; and Social Democratic Party, 29, 65, 79, 94. *See also* Hòa Hảo Buddhists; Social Democratic Party (SDP)

Nguyễn Bình, 28, 32

Nguyễn Chánh Thi (Senior Colonel), 143–146

Nguyễn Công Viên, 216n21

Nguyễn Đình Quát, 151

Nguyễn Đình Thuần, 145

Nguyễn Đôn Duyến, 47

Nguyễn Giác Ngộ (General): area controlled by, **49,** 50; in Battle of Saigon, 74; defection to government, 65; as a Hòa Hảo leader, **17,** 50, **79;** paid by State of Vietnam and French military, 64; refusal to support United Front, 71; in the Revolutionary Council, 79; and Social Democratic Party, 75, 79, 94, 187n124; and Trần Văn Văn and Phan Khắc Sửu, 138. *See also* Hòa Hảo Buddhists; Social Democratic Party (SDP)

Nguyễn Hải Thần, 18, 20, 25, 30

Nguyễn Hữu Châu: background, 81; and candidate in 1956 elections, 97; and

constitutional process, 89, 197n140; and Ngô family, 127; and position paper on "strong state," 83, 192n36; view on political opposition, 90

Nguyễn Khánh (General), 144

Nguyễn Lưu Viên, 207n6

Nguyễn Ngọc Lễ, 95

Nguyễn Ngọc Thơ, 151

Nguyễn Phương Thiệp, 125, 197n140

Nguyễn Thái Học, 17, 18, 70

Nguyễn Thành Phương (General): area controlled by, **49;** and Association for the Restoration of Vietnam, 79, 95, 105; in the Battle of Saigon, 74; in coalition government of 1954, 60, 62, 185n84; defections from, 94, 97; and Democratic Bloc, 203n55; and Diệm, 58, 59, 70, 75; in elections of 1961, 151; and invasion of Tây Ninh province, 97; as a leader of Cao Đài army, **17,** 48, 65, **79;** opposition to Phan Huy Quát, 63–64; support for military and political centralization, 66, 187n117; as target of intelligence activities, 193n59; and United Front of Nationalist Forces, 71, 72–73, 189n167; and the Unity Congress, 180n153. *See also* Cao Đài sect army

Nguyễn Thế Truyền, 152, 161

Nguyễn Tôn Hoàn: break with Diệm, 60–61, 67, 185n87; as candidate for prime minister, 42; as a leader of Đại Việt party, **17,** 51; as oppositionist, 109–112; and United Front of Nationalist Forces, 71; and Unity Congress, 180n153. *See also* Đại Việt Nationalist Party

Nguyễn Trân, 106, 131, 132, 133, 150, 186n97

Nguyễn Triệu Hồng (Lieutenant Colonel), 143–145

Nguyễn Tường Tam: call for Diệm's overthrow, 146; as Hồ Chí Minh's foreign minister, 25–26; as a leader of the Vietnamese Nationalist Party, **17;** in the Nanjing front, 30; and Phan Quang Đán, 195n92; in post-coup attempt crackdown (1960), 149; suicide in protest, 150, 166. *See also* Vietnamese Nationalist Party (VNP)

Nguyễn Văn Cẩn: criticisms of constitutional process, 100, 101, 102–104; and Democratic Bloc, 118–119, 120; under government scrutiny, 149–150; lack of affiliation with major groups, 130; and Trần Văn Văn–Phan Khắc Sửu clique, 139

Nguyễn Văn Châu (Lieutenant), 148, 153, 154, 155

Nguyễn Văn Cử (Lieutenant), 161
Nguyễn Văn Hinh (General), 52, 57–60, 61–62, 69, 111
Nguyễn Văn Tâm, 34, 42, 52
Nguyễn Văn Vỹ (General), 76, 80
Nguyễn Văn Xuân (General), 59, 60, 61, 63
Nhất Linh. *See* Nguyễn Tường Tam
Nhị Lang: account of plan to overthrow Bảo Đại, 191n11; background, 80; escape to Cambodia, 97; as National Resistance Front leader, **79**, 94, 216n20; and Phạm Công Tắc, 116; in the Revolutionary Council, 80, 82, 96
Nhu, Madame: American concerns about, 142; as candidate in 1956 elections, 98; Diệm's defense of, 151; exile, 167; rally in support of Diệm, 60; as sister-in-law of Nguyễn Hữu Châu, 81; speech on émigrés, 129; targeted in bombing attack (1962), 161; and Women's Solidarity Movement, 125–126. *See also* Ngô Đình Nhu
Ninh Thuận province, 51, 61
Nolting, Frederick (Ambassador), 160–161
nonaligned movement, 113–114, 115–116
North Vietnam, 10

Operation Liberation, 69
Operation Liberty, 66
Orendain, Juan, 89, 100

Paris, 8, 108, 109, 111
People's Committee Against Rebels and Communists, 148, 153, 159, 213n127
People's Revolutionary Council. *See* Revolutionary Council (RC)
personalism: American reactions to, 2; as basis of Diệm's ideology, 37–38, 98; and democracy, 82, 87, 98–99, 103, 123, 125, 141; early Diemists' adherence to, 47, 126; theory of leadership, 87; training center for instruction in, 128
Phạm Công Tắc: adaptation of Confucian parable, 116–117, 202n43; in alternative government coalitions, 53, 59; call for complete independence, 40; call for national union government, 58; criticism of Phan Quang Đán and Nguyễn Tôn Hoàn, 122; encouragement of southward migration, 56; escape to Cambodia, 97; espousal of neutralism, 8, 113–116, 201n33; fervently anticommunist stance, 28; as leader of Cao Đài, **17**, 48, 75; and Nguyễn Thế Truyền, 152;

Phnom Penh-based organization, 108, 116–118, 202n45; support for Cường Đế, 22; as target of intelligence activities, 193n59; and United Front of Nationalist Forces, 71, 72, 189n167. *See also* Cao Đài religious group
Phạm Đình Nghị, 188n148
Phạm Ngọc Chi (Bishop), **17**, 51, 57, 128, 129. *See also* Catholic nationalists
Phạm Phú Quốc (Lieutenant), 161
Phạm Văn Liễu (Major), 134–135, 143
Phạm Văn Thùng, 206n129
Phạm Xuân Thái, 59, 190n175
Phan Bá Cầm, 149
Phan Bội Châu, 15–16, 18
Phan Châu Trinh, 12–13, 16, 18, 76, 152
Phan Huy Quát, **17**, 42, 51, 63–64, 138, 153–156, 161
Phan Khắc Sửu: as agriculture minister, 130; clique, 137–140, 167, 207n6; in crackdown after coup attempt (1960), 149, 150, 210n68; Diệm's attitude toward, 141; in elections of 1959, 132, 133. *See also* Freedom and Progress Bloc (FPB)
Phan Khôi, 19
Phan Quang Đán: arrest and torture, 149, 150; background, 91, 195n92; as candidate in 1959 election, 106, 130, 132, 133, 206n129; and Democratic Bloc, 108, 118–120, 143; detention, 97; ideas on democracy, 92–93; lack of affiliation with émigré groups, 130; and letter protesting electoral ordinances, 96; political study group, 13, 93–94; and Republican Party, 91, 122, 195n94; support for coup attempt (1960), 145–146, 147; and Trần Văn Văn–Phan Khắc Sửu clique, 139
Phan Thông Thảo, Jean, 112, 113
Phát Diệm diocese, 24, 27, 51, 56
Philipps, Rufus, 1, 104
Phnom Penh, 8, 108, 113, 202n45
Policy of Peaceful Coexistence, 115, 116
Preliminary Convention (1946), 51–52

Quảng Nam province, 51, 67, 69, 70
Quảng Ngãi province, 24, 67, 69, 70, 188n148
Quảng Trị province, 51, 67, 113, 152
The Quiet American (Graham Greene), 39, 117

Radio Saigon, 144, 145, 146, 147, 151
Republican Party, 91, 122, 195n94. *See also* Phan Quang Đán
Republican Youth, 127

238 Index

Republic of Vietnam Air Force, 161
Republic of Vietnam (RVN): archival records on, 9–10; civil liberties and labor rights in, 101–102, 120, 163; communist insurgency in, 134–135, 136–137, 139, 159–160; distinguished from South Vietnam, 10; elections of 1956, 96–98; elections of 1959, 106–107, 108, 130–133; elections of 1961, 150–153; freedom of speech in, 104; judicial independence in, 100–101, 103; land reform program, 124–125, 129, 136–137, 138, 139, 140; legal status of opposition parties in, 92–93, 107, 119–120, 140, 151, 156–157; peace movement in, 114; Phạm Công Tắc's peace proposal and, 116; press freedom under, 95–96, 101–102, 115, 121–122, 140, 151; under the Revolutionary Military Council, 167–168; scholarship on, 3–5; as a single-party state, 125; "spiritualist foundation," 99. *See also* State of Vietnam (SVN)
Revolutionary Council (RC): as alliance between Diemists and sect parties, 78–81; Diemist attempt to disband, 90, 94, 105, 195n86; dissolution, 199n181; and Phan Quang Đán, 91, 96–97; and removal of Bảo Đại, 82; successors of, 108, 118
Revolutionary Military Council (RMC), 166–167
Revolutionary Personalist Labor Party. *See* Cần Lao party

Saigon: as center of opposition to Diệm, 8, 108; Chợlớn area, 45, 50, 74; clearance of slums in, 121, 132; prison riots in, 101; student protests in, 166; U.S. embassy in, 8, 10, 82, 85, 90–91, 192n36, 195n86
Saigon, Battle of: American reactions to, 2; Bình Xuyên in, 45–46, 78, 88; Diemists and, 45–46; French Expeditionary Corps in, 78; and Independence Palace conference, 76, 78; and Social Democratic Party, 86; Trần Văn Văn–Phan Khắc Sửu clique and, 138; as watershed event, 74–75, 95
Saigon Military Mission, 53, 95, 104
Sát Jungle, 32, 74, 88
Self-Reliant Literary Group, 19, 26
Service for Political and Social Research, 85–86, 193n59
Social Democratic Party (SDP): break with Trần Văn Soái, 36; and constitutional process, 81–82, 88, 94; and the Democratic

Alliance, 143; and fragmentation of Hòa Hảo, 49, 86; government defanging of, 105; in the Nanjing front, 30; Nguyễn Bảo Toàn's leadership of, 65, 94, 97; and Phan Khắc Sửu, 138; progressive platform, 29; ties to General Ngô, 79, 187n124. *See also* Nguyễn Bảo Toàn; Nguyễn Giác Ngộ (General)
Society (Xã hội), 40–41, 54
South Vietnam, 10, 55, 77, 136
Soviet Union: at the Geneva Conference, 42, 116; Hồ Chí Minh's visit to, 18; and the nonaligned movement, 113–114, 115; as origin of "peaceful coexistence" concept, 201n33; recognition of Democratic Republic of Vietnam, 34; Vietnamese nationalists' attitude to, 19
Spirit Group, 47, 53, 60, 64, 75, 126
Spirit (Tinh thần), 47
State of Vietnam (SVN): administrative division of country, 10; agreement with France on military, 66; constitutional process, 88–96; criticized for lacking democracy, 40; and devaluation of piaster, 39–40; elections of 1956, 96–98; establishment through Élysée Accords, 31, 33; French sponsorship of, 6, 13, 41; plebiscite to remove Bảo Đại, 84–88, 164; premiers of, 34, 44; refugees from DRV in, 33; renaming as Republic of Vietnam (RVN), 2, 14, 88; secession of Ba Lòng Resistance Zone from, 67; secession of Đại Việt and VNP from, 46; and the sect armies, 64, 86. *See also* Republic of Vietnam (RVN)
student movement, 165–166, 167–168
Sun Yat-sen, 15, 17, 19
Survival of the People doctrine, 19

Tạ Chương Phùng, 138
Tạ Thu Thâu, **17**, 24
Taylor, Maxwell D. (General), 160
Tây Ninh province: as birthplace of Cao Đài religion, 21, 80; Committee for Peaceful Coexistence in, 117; resistance zone in, 86, 94, 105; Tràng Sụp base in, 134
Thích Quảng Đức, 165, 166
Thierry d'Argenlieu, Georges, 31, 59
Trần Chánh Thành: background, 81; as candidate in 1956 election, 97, 98; and Cần Lao party, 85; and constitutional process, 89, 99–100, 101–102; loss of favor with Ngô family, 127; and position paper on "strong

state," 83, 192n36; and the Revolutionary Council, 195n86; on single-party states, 90

Trần Điền, 67

Trảng Sụp incident (1960), 134–135, 137, 138, 142–143, 160

Trần Kim Tuyến, 85, 130–131, 142, 144

Trần Lệ Xuân. *See* Nhu, Madame

Trần Quang Vinh, **17**, 22, 28

Trần Quốc Bửu, 47, 126–127, 131, 182n5, 206n129

Trần Trung Dung, 47–48, 97, 98

Trần Văn Bạch, 215n3

Trần Văn Chương, 53

Trần Văn Đỗ, 47, 53, 138, 139

Trần Văn Giàu, **17**, 23, 24, 25, 27–28

Trần Văn Hương, 207n6

Trần Văn Hữu, 34

Trần Văn Lắm, 80, 97

Trần Văn Lý, 138

Trần Văn Soái (General): alliance with the French, 30, 35–36; in alternative coalitions to Diệm's government, 53, 59, 60, 62, 66; clashes with Vietnamese National Army, 66, 86, 95; in coalition government of 1954, 60, 62, 66, 185n84; as a leader of Hòa Hảo Buddhists, **17**, 49–50, **79**; opposition to Movement for Unity and Peace, 41; in plot to remove Diệm, 58; and push for military centralization, 63–64; in United Front of Nationalist Forces, 71, 72. *See also* Hòa Hảo Buddhists

Trần Văn Tuyên, 138

Trần Văn Văn, 137–140, 141, 147, 167, 207n6

Trình Minh Thế (General): areas controlled by, **49**; *attentiste* stance, 39, 65; in Battle of Saigon, 74; death, 80, 94, 191n20; as a leader of Cao Đài army, **17**, **79**; and National Resistance Front, 48, 75, 79; splinter guerilla army of, 39, 48; succeeded by Văn Thành Cao, 94; support for Diệm's centralization push, 65–66; and United Front of Nationalist Forces, 71, 72; and the Unity Congress, 40. *See also* Cao Đài sect army

Trotskyists, 21, 23, 24–25, 177n67

Trương Bội Hoàng, 69

Trương Công Cừu, 213n127

Trương Tử An, 69

Trương Tử Anh, **17**, 19, 26, 69, 113

Trương Tửu, 19

United Front of Nationalist Forces, 71–74

United Kingdom, 27, 34, 36, 42, 116, 133

United Nations, 43, 115, 116

United States: alliance with Republic of Vietnam, 2, 4; and attempted coup on Diệm (1960), 145, 157–158; and attempt to replace Diệm with Phan Huy Quát, 73, 154; and constitutional process, 89, 90, 104; at the Geneva Conference, 42, 116; military aid to France and anticommunists, 34, 35, 52; in neutralist world view, 113–114, 115, 122; and oppositionist politicians, 109–111, 133, 160–161; Phạm Công Tắc's peace proposal and, 116; as political model for Vietnam, 83, 90; proposals to Diệm on liberalization, 141–142, 157–158; providing transportation to southward migrants, 56, 57; recognition of State of Vietnam, 34; support for Diệm, 37, 59, 88, 136, 158, 162; Vietnamese exile communities in, 168; view on Vietnam's readiness for democracy, 8–9, 141, 159, 160. *See also* Central Intelligence Agency (CIA)

Unity Committee (UC), 153–156, 158, 161

Unity Congress (1953), 40, 51, 54, 75, 138, 153

US State Department, 10, 74, 111, 141, 158

Văn Thành Cao (General), 94, 97, 105

Việt Minh: in August Revolution, 23–25; break with Hòa Hảo Buddhists, 28–30; conflict with anticommunists, 26, 41; defections from, 32–34, 57, 80, 81, 138, 182n7; establishment, 20; friction with northern Catholics, 27; murder of Ngô family members, 36; and National Liberation Front, 159; in regional coalition government, 25; war against Cao Đài, 28. *See also* Hồ Chí Minh

Vietnamese Confederation of Christian Laborers, 47

Vietnamese Independence League. *See* Việt Minh

Vietnamese Labor Party, 25, 33

Vietnamese National Army (VNA): in Battle of Saigon, 74, 76, 78; fighting against Hòa Hảo factions, 86; and the Geneva Accords, 55; integration of sect and other armies, 51, 63–66, 73, 86, 187n115, 190n174; proposal to make a voluntary force, 62; reliance on French Expeditionary Corps, 31, 42, 52; renamed Army of the Republic of Vietnam, 95; suppression of rebellions in Central Vietnam, 67, 69. *See also* Army of the Republic of Vietnam (ARVN)

240   Index

Vietnamese Nationalist Party (VNP): alliance with other anticommunist parties, 20–21, 30; and bombing of Independence Palace (1962), 161; and the constitutional process, 94, 97; in the Democratic Alliance, 143; and Democratic Republic of Vietnam, 24, 25–26; in Diệm's government, 53, 59; establishment, 17; exclusion from coalition government of 1954, 60, 61; fragmentation and decline, 51–52; and the Hinh crisis, 69; members and leadership, 91, 119, 146, 149, 195n92; opposition to Diệm after 1955, 75; participation in Bảo Đại's conference, 31; rift with communists, 18–19; secession from SVN and resistance zones, 46, **68,** 69, 70; secret cells within the military, 52; southward migration, 57, 129–130; strength in southern China, 23; at the Unity Congress, 40. *See also* Nguyễn Tường Tam

Vietnamese Politics (Việt chính), **79**

Vietnamese Revolutionary League (VRL), 20, 25–26, 30

Vietnam War (1954–1975), 2–3

Vương Văn Đông (Lieutenant Colonel), 143–145

Vũ Quốc Thông, 197n140

Vũ Trọng Phụng, 19

The Way of Life (Đường sống), 129, 163

Women's Solidarity Movement, 127–128

About the Author

Nu-Anh Tran is an assistant professor at the University of Connecticut with a joint appointment in the Department of History and the Asian and Asian American Studies Institute. Her research focuses on the political, intellectual, and cultural history of the Republic of Vietnam. She is coeditor with Tuong Vu of *Building a Republican Nation in Postcolonial Vietnam, 1920–1963* (forthcoming). Her work has also appeared in the *Journal of Vietnamese Studies.*

Studies of the Weatherhead East Asian Institute

Columbia University

Selected Titles

(Complete list at: https://weai.columbia.edu/content/publications/)

Recovering Histories: Life and Labor after Heroin in Reform-Era China, by Nicholas Bartlett. University of California Press, 2020.

A Third Way: The Origins of China's Current Economic Development Strategy, by Lawrence Chris Reardon. Harvard University Asia Center, 2020.

Disruptions of Daily Life: Japanese Literary Modernism in the World, by Arthur M. Mitchell. Cornell University Press, 2020.

Figures of the World: The Naturalist Novel and Transnational Form, by Christopher Laing Hill. Northwestern University Press, 2020.

Arbiters of Patriotism: Right-Wing Scholars in Imperial Japan, by John Person. University of Hawai'i Press, 2020.

The Chinese Revolution on the Tibetan Frontier, by Benno Weiner. Cornell University Press, 2020.

Making It Count: Statistics and Statecraft in the Early People's Republic of China, by Arunabh Ghosh. Princeton University Press, 2020.

Tea War: A History of Capitalism in China and India, by Andrew B. Liu. Yale University Press, 2020.

Revolution Goes East: Imperial Japan and Soviet Communism, by Tatiana Linkhoeva. Cornell University Press, 2020.

Vernacular Industrialism in China: Local Innovation and Translated Technologies in the Making of a Cosmetics Empire, 1900–1940, by Eugenia Lean. Columbia University Press, 2020.

Fighting for Virtue: Justice and Politics in Thailand, by Duncan McCargo. Cornell University Press, 2020.

Beyond the Steppe Frontier: A History of the Sino-Russian Border, by Sören Urbansky. Princeton University Press, 2020.

Pirates and Publishers: A Social History of Copyright in Modern China, by Fei-Hsien Wang. Princeton University Press, 2019.

The Typographic Imagination: Reading and Writing in Japan's Age of Modern Print Media, by Nathan Shockey. Columbia University Press, 2019.

Down and Out in Saigon: Stories of the Poor in a Colonial City, by Haydon Cherry. Yale University Press, 2019.

Beauty in the Age of Empire: Japan, Egypt, and the Global History of Aesthetic Education, by Raja Adal. Columbia University Press, 2019.

Mass Vaccination: Citizens' Bodies and State Power in Modern China, by Mary Augusta Brazelton. Cornell University Press, 2019.

Residual Futures: The Urban Ecologies of Literary and Visual Media of 1960s and 1970s Japan, by Franz Prichard. Columbia University Press, 2019.

The Making of Japanese Settler Colonialism: Malthusianism and Trans-Pacific Migration, 1868–1961, by Sidney Xu Lu. Cambridge University Press, 2019.

The Power of Print in Modern China: Intellectuals and Industrial Publishing from the end of Empire to Maoist State Socialism, by Robert Culp. Columbia University Press, 2019.

Beyond the Asylum: Mental Illness in French Colonial Vietnam, by Claire E. Edington. Cornell University Press, 2019.

Borderland Memories: Searching for Historical Identity in Post-Mao China, by Martin Fromm. Cambridge University Press, 2019.

Arc of Containment: Britain, the United States, and Anticommunism in Southeast Asia, by Wen-Qing Ngoei. Cornell University Press, 2019.

Sovereignty Experiments: Korean Migrants and the Building of Borders in Northeast Asia, 1860–1949, by Alyssa M. Park. Cornell University Press, 2019.

The Greater East Asia Co-Prosperity Sphere: When Total Empire Met Total War, by Jeremy A. Yellen. Cornell University Press, 2019.

Thought Crime: Ideology and State Power in Interwar Japan, by Max Ward. Duke University Press, 2019.

Statebuilding by Imposition: Resistance and Control in Colonial Taiwan and the Philippines, by Reo Matsuzaki. Cornell University Press, 2019.

Nation-Empire: Ideology and Rural Youth Mobilization in Japan and Its Colonies, by Sayaka Chatani. Cornell University Press, 2019.

Fixing Landscape: A Techno-Poetic History of China's Three Gorges, by Corey Byrnes. Columbia University Press, 2019.